The Colour of Empathy

A Veterinarian's Story

STUART PHILLIPS

Copyright © Stuart Phillips 2023

All rights reserved. No part of this publication may be reproduced, stored in a retrieval system, or transmitted in any form or by any means, mechanical, photocopying, recording or otherwise, without prior permission in writing of the author.

ISBN: 9798374583489 (paperback)

Preface

IN ALL HONESTY

There is a huge temptation to make this account a cosy, feel-good story of trials and ultimate victory, of deep sacrifice and selfless devotion and dedication. There are, however, far better authors with deeper convictions out there already.

The truth is that I grew up in a deeply unjust society and since I was not politically active, I did nothing about it. There were many instances in which I failed to give the professional service that clients expected, and more importantly, failed to do what was needed for the patient. I can remember each catastrophe with crystal, cringing clarity.

I have had to omit a number of incidents that would hurt people, while other incidents proved too graphic or too painful for general discussion. For the remaining chapters, I have tried to be as honest as my soul can bear, allowing for gentle self-aggrandisement in just enough measure to keep me interested in finishing the work.

Doubtless there are aspects which will alienate those of strong convictions, and it was tempting to portray the work as being based on pure motives and faultless conviction, but in the end we are all subject to not only our own foibles but those forced on us by society as well.

The over-arching aim has been honesty. I have no intention of trying to win you over with hyperbole. I hope you enjoy the result.

Chapter 1

A BEE MINUS IN BRAVERY

I worked had late into the evening treating a horse with colic, which made the call at three in the morning even less welcome. I am not the bravest with horses. I have no problem admitting my fear of big bulls, horses and hamsters. I have been hurt by all of them too many times not to be afraid.

The horse was the biggest gelding at the local riding club, and the only way I could ever vaccinate him was to give his diminutive rider the syringe; she would gallop around the paddock as she plunged the needle in, while I watched in awe.

Treating colic involved inserting a thick tube into his nose and down into his stomach in order to pour in litres of liquid paraffin. For some reason he seemed to object to it, and I ended up with half the greasy liquid running down my arm and into my sleeve. I also had to give him several injections into his jugular vein. The only way to manage it was to hold firmly to his head collar and go up with him every time he reared up, desperately hoping to be able to keep my feet out of the way when we landed again.

Fortunately, the horse's intestines slowly relaxed as the pain seeped away and it ended with him breaking wind so loudly, I feared the windows of the stable block would shatter. His dedicated young owner had kept him walking for hours, refusing to allow him to lie down and thrash about helplessly. I was desperately tired as I drove the long, winding road back home.

The early morning call was for a Great Dane, whose head had 'swelled up enormously and looked about to burst'. I felt immensely grateful that the patient, who belonged to Mrs Van Zyl, was not her other dog, a tiny Chihuahua, one of the whirling dervishes that seemed to have snapping teeth in every direction. I had long since decided that the little dogs had to be aggressive since they were always being stepped on. Not the placid Great Danes. They did the stepping on.

Thor greeted me with a ridiculously huge head, like a piebald pumpkin with plump Yorkshire pudding lips and tiny slits for eyes. He stuck his head in my face as if to say, 'Look what I did. I ate a bee and now look at my face. I did it all by myself. Clever me.'

We see a case like this every few months and although they are dramatic, I have never had one develop complications. A single injection of a steroid tends to result in a resolution over a few hours. I dutifully administered the drug.

Thor's owners, however, seemed to want something more to be done and he proceeded to move between the three of us, demanding we pat him continuously and thanking us with a huge slobbery kiss, they stood there expectantly.

My mind drifted back to the horse I had treated the previous evening. One of the drugs we routinely used was called 'Vetibenzamine', an antihistamine aimed at preventing the serious complications of colic. We normally injected it under the skin in dogs but in horses it was given intravenously.

The logic of a sleep-deprived brain and a strong desire to return to the warmth of my bed linked Thor's size and piebald colour in my mind with that of the horse. If I administered the drug via the bloodstream, it would have a much faster effect on Thor. I triumphantly collected the drug from the pharmacy, gave a cursory glance at the formulary to see what side effects could occur and then injected the correct dose into my patient's huge vein. His owners at last seemed satisfied.

I was returning the bottle to the pharmacy when the air was rent with a demonic howl, followed by a crash and a duet of screams. I froze and then dashed back to the consulting room.

Through the open door I could see the two owners squeezed in the corner, sharing identical expressions of terror. I blundered in and then dodged in desperation as Thor charged towards me, jaws agape and emitting a second howl, while a spray of faeces seemed to propel him from behind. I joined the cowering couple and would have buried myself behind them if their combined strength had not exceeded mine.

I noticed that Thor had charged headlong into the door and that he seemed unable to see. He was listening with aggressive intent and when Mrs Van Zyl made a little whimpering sound, he whirled and charged. The two of them screamed, while I gave a manly shriek and jumped onto the countertop. Thor plunged into a nearby cupboard, inches from the three of us. He seemed unaware of us as we tried desperately to muffle the knocking of our knees.

On impulse, I picked up a stainless-steel bowl and tossed it across the room. Thor plunged after it with a howl. He was clearly navigating solely by sound.

Lowering my feet to the ground and trying to nonchalantly retrieve my dignity, I tossed a pair of scissors into the passageway, eliciting another howl and a gigantic pounce towards the noise.

By throwing anything that came to hand in the right direction, I managed to get Thor to make a frenetic dash through the practice and into our largest walk-in cage in the dog ward. I closed the gate and then fell backwards in fright as the big dog lunged against it at the sound of the bolt shooting home.

None of us got any sleep that night. Cecil appeared through the back door, alerted by the banshee howling and he silently set about cleaning up the chaos and mess left behind.

The Van Zyls eventually left and once Thor was sleeping peacefully, I slipped home to shave and grab some breakfast. On my return, Cecil had not only returned the place to normality but was chuckling delightedly as he and the dog that was a third bigger than he romped around the hospital ward in mutual delight. For the umpteenth time I felt blessed to have the diminutive Xhosa man on our staff.

Catching site of me, he straightened up and coaxed his friend into the cage. Turning he smiled and indicated the still partially swollen features of our patient.

'*Inja inyoka*,' he said, holding cupped hands on either side of his own head to demonstrate the flared head and neck of a cobra.

'Yes,' I said, 'he does look like a snake. And he sounds like a dragon.'

The owners returned later to take their charge home, and to my embarrassment, they insisted on presenting me with a bottle of wine, shrugging off my protests that I had been the cause of the midnight adventure.

Cecil eyed the bottle longingly. I had long since learned of his prowess with the fruits of the grape, so I made sure it was well secluded in a secure cupboard.

Two days later Thor came back to show me that he had fully recovered, although his owners had twice caught him hunting bees under the Jakaranda tree.

The next day Cecil left for his weekend off work, and I passed him the wine as he was about to go, knowing it would probably be finished before he made it to the taxi rank in the next street. All of us ended up smiling, but none as broadly as the gigantic canine snuffling for bees in the undergrowth.

Chapter 2

CHILD OF AFRICA

The dusty red African soil gave birth to my existence and germinated many of my earliest memories. I was six years old before I was coerced into wearing a pair of shoes for at least part of the day.

In many ways it was an idyllic, if one-sided, childhood, overflowing with life, death and procreation in a world shared with fluffy yellow, day-old chicks that arrived in hundreds by rail in cardboard boxes and cuddly, long-haired Alsatian puppies from the three breeding mothers, tumbling over themselves and over children who ventured into their pens.

Doe-eyed Jersey cows walked the half mile up to the milking parlour twice daily, eager to find the scoop of meal tossed into half a 44-gallon drum, while one of the milkers, perched on a tiny three-legged stool, tucked his head into a flank and began to draw long spurts of warm, frothy milk into a stainless-steel bucket.

Paint and Chaka, the two old horses, brought up the rear of the small herd of cows, eager to sneak into the parlour to steal a mouthful of meal. The brick-walled barn running beside the milking shed housed a flock of several hundred young pullets, clustering in groups to share gossip or rushing in waves to pursue the next imaginary treasure at the far end of the barn.

Serried ranks of peach trees stood like silent sentries in an orchard encircling the house and barns on three sides; they were irrigated by means of an open trench, filling with fast-flowing water from a cement reservoir and delighting small feet that squelched in the mud. Tadpoles and dragonfly larvae rushed past as the flood filled the temporary earthen-walled dam around each tree until a spade-full of soil was dumped at the entrance to halt the inrushing water and divert it to the next tree in the line. Little boys kept the Sotho men on the farm company many summer afternoons as the black men kindly kept watch over them while they worked.

A flock of geese patrolled the grounds, rushing with outstretched necks and hissing at the unwary; shy goslings hid behind their mother's skirts as they uttered high pitched peeps, ever seeking reassurance from their fierce parents.

Huge piles of peaches and tomatoes grew in the heat of summer, too ripe to join the neat rows of wooden boxes housing the greener fruit ready for the trip to the market in the early hours of the night. Children were expected to assemble the fruit crates from flat-packed wooden components and short, one-inch nails, or to line them with the fluffy but deceptively harsh 'wood-wool' from large square bales.

My imagination held no inkling of the path I would follow, chasing a dream of working with the creatures that share our planet, through the sapping hours of endless study, the mind-numbingly boring but tragic military service, an eclectic collection of years as an agricultural vet in the tiny Xhosa state of the Ciskei Republic, a stint in a diagnostic laboratory and eventually taking wing to follow the swallows as they migrated northwards to settle on the opposite side of the world.

With five siblings and hundreds of animals to share my world, I never longed for a friend or playmate. I was spoiled for choice and although I loved each member of the family to varying degrees, my social development was not just stunted, it never really occurred to any great degree. Who needed society when the world was populated by fascinating, warm-blooded, living creatures that never knew the depths that humans could sink to? I would struggle socially later in life, but in my early years I revelled in a world of life in so many forms.

Mom ruled the farm while Dad managed a family chain of hardware stores and ran a Sunday school with numbers in the hundreds. In between, he built the family home and housing for the livestock. Work ruled our parents' lives, and they gave everything to providing their six children with an incredible start to life.

Chapter 3

RED HERRING DISEASE

Mom bred German Shepherds, big black-and-tan dogs with an unbreakable loyalty to their masters. From a very early age I was familiar with the soft, fluffy coats and almost cloying smell of a litter of little black bear-like bodies sharing their bed with me.

These big 'Alsatians' could number their ancestors among royalty. Nicky, the dark stud dog, was bought from a breeder who told of her experiences at the end of the Second World War, before she fled the poverty of post-war Germany as a young girl. She had been running errands for her mother, now single after her father had died in the conflict. Her bicycle was not by any means new, but it was functional.

A soldier stepped into the road, barring her way and forcing her to brake to a halt. The man grabbed the crossbar on the front of the bike and then she suddenly became aware of a commotion behind her. Glancing around, she could see a second soldier who had quietly crept up behind her, grimacing in pain as her dog sank its teeth into his wrist. Both men fled and the dog would have given chase but returned instantly to the side of its owner at her command.

As a family, we prized these loyal animals, and it was only many years later that I came to understand how the breed had been altered by indiscriminate breeding and most of them now have serious genetic problems with skeletal and digestive problems.

Every birthday I asked for a puppy, but with four adult dogs in the family it was understandable that I was given a rat instead. I have to admit that I was not the best owner of this poor rodent. He got his basic necessities for life but I never took him for a walk or taught him any tricks. We just failed to bond as expected.

Rosemary, the sister just two years older than me, bred toy Poms and in one litter she had the tiniest little runt that stole everyone's heart. It was inconceivable that he could be sold and at last I became the proud owner of a dog, even if he was smaller than my rat.

Christened Rex, I soon changed it to Rexp, because he had a silent pee, generally in my slippers. Rex was small enough to spend a good deal of his life under the settee, only venturing out to bite unwary ankles or jump into my lap.

One afternoon this little tyrant staggered out to the middle of the room and promptly brought up a huge amount of bloody material and then passed even more from the other end. The pile of blood-stained material seemed even larger than Rex himself. Mom and I raced to the vet as fast as possible.

Dr Carey seemed to question the fact that his patient was actually a dog, but he could find nothing wrong with the tiny ball of fluff. We came home with some supportive treatment and unsettled concern.

Back at home, I spotted an empty bag that had once held raspberry-flavoured jelly babies. On closer examination of the carpet, it became clear that this little carnivore had decided to change his diet and devoured almost his own weight in red gelatine delicacies. He was in no danger of dying. That was if I could get the red stain out of Mom's new carpet.

Whenever a second vet is asked to examine a patient, they have the benefit of the work done by their predecessor and can often ignore the tests they would normally have done. A friend who became a pathologist confided in me that he chose his career because he was always right. No-one came after him to contradict his diagnosis.

When Frisk, a little spaniel, arrived with a history of touring all the veterinary practices in the area, it was obvious that it would be pointless investigating the usual causes of vomiting.

Six other vets had run blood tests showing a multitude of small discrepancies but nothing diagnostic. Various attempts at treatment had all failed. The history from the owners was even more obscure: 'He brings up large pools of yellow bile. No food in it and no diarrhoea.'

All I could find was a very low-grade heart murmur, unlikely to be related to gastro-intestinal signs. I decided to keep him in for the day and watch him closely.

Frisk had a gentle cough and watching him closely, I realised that after each bout of coughing, he swallowed repeatedly. When he eventually brought up a large pool of yellow bile, I was fairly convinced that I knew what his problem was.

The yellow-stained liquid was full of froth. Frisk was drowning in his own body fluids. As his failing heart strained to clear all the blood from the capillaries in his lungs, the serum seeped out into the air spaces, collecting and building up until he coughed it from the lungs into the back of his throat.

The froth in his throat was then swallowed bit by bit. Once the stomach was filled with foam, it emptied itself the only way it knew how.

Frisk responded miraculously to a diuretic to drain off the extra fluid in his body and a life-long prescription of digitalis. The advances in safer, more effective cardiac drugs would be years too late for him, but his vomiting ceased overnight.

We had made a diagnosis that thrilled his owners, but the work done by the other consultants had been stairs which we had leapt over to take one more step towards the solution.

At least Frisk's owner's carpet was not stained with bright red raspberry, but the red herrings had been at work again, diverting the attention of the profession down fruitless streams.

Chapter 4

RED HERRING DISEASE

Junior School proved to be a daily trial that kept me away from the farm where I felt comfortable. My first day at school happened to also be my birthday, which seemed monumentally unfair.

Joan, our eldest sister, who'd had her maternal instincts roused by the arrival of five siblings, a new one every few years, took me along to the classroom and left me in the care of one of the most gifted teachers in the school, aptly named Mrs Goodchild. On that first day I cared nothing for her gifts or her name. She tried to put me at ease, and I responded by kicking her sharply on the ankle.

It was a day in which I learned a great deal. The prowess with which Mrs Goodchild could deliver a stinging blow to my posterior was one I would not forget for some time. Sadly, it was not the last time I experienced this rather archaic method of correction that was regularly dealt out by teachers in that era.

The school had two classes for each year: one for the Afrikaans children and one for the English-speaking kids. We were all white and immensely privileged but none of us realised it. There were many schools for the indigenous tribes, but they were of a very low standard. I realised when I went to work in the Republic of Ciskei, home of the Xhosa nation, that many promising young indigenous scholars were forced to leave the country to get a higher standard of education elsewhere in the world.

On the second day of school, I was incensed to have to go again. I had already spent a day at school, and it had not helped me. To once again be forced to leave the toys I had been given the day before was intolerable. On impulse, I ran into the huge forest of fruit trees and hid among the leafy branches. I planned to wait until the rest of the family had departed before I made my way home again. In the meantime, I feasted on the abundance of fruit on the heavily laden trees.

Sadly, I had not taken into consideration that Mom would still be at home even after the rest of the family had departed. She apprehended me as I tried to sneak through the back door and for the second day in a row, I experienced the pain of discipline. Mom spared her hand by using one of her slippers she wore while getting the family of six children and a husband fed and out of the house.

School settled down to a mundane daily chore that had to be endured until we could escape back home when Mom came to collect us in the old Volkswagen Combi Van.

The school had two sports fields which were jealously guarded by the two language groups, respectively. The English-speaking children played football on one field each break time, while the Afrikaans kids preferred rugby.

Every now and then we would pour out of the classrooms to find that one of the fields was unusable due to a long row of heavy irrigation pipes set up to pump thousands of gallons of water into the grass. The two groups were forced to all use the same field and the game played depended on the preference of the group that usually used that field.

The Afrikaans boys had little skill in football but managed to hold their own largely because of the huge crowd of little players, enthusiastically chasing the ball in a swarm of unskilled energy. The English kids, however, proved hopeless when it came to rugby and barely managed to last the thirty minutes of break-time while the Afrikaans horde racked up an impressive score.

In the second year, one of the boys found a nest of newly hatched chameleons. There were dozens of tiny little creatures, exact replicas of their parents and all at the mercy of several hundred schoolchildren. Each one ended up with a new owner and was plied with flies almost as large as they were, caught by the more agile children.

The hatchlings were carefully tended and lovingly confined to matchboxes, little tin maths sets, and other containers. Several boys found that these little reptiles could swim, and races were arranged across a little earthen dam scooped out under a tap in the playground.

Fortunately, one of the teachers found out about the chameleon nest and most of the little creatures were rounded up and released back into the wild. Once on a leaf, they seemed to disappear magically from sight within seconds and we never saw them again.

John Ngoma was of the Ndebele tribe, an offshoot of the Zulus. What he lacked in stature he more than made up for in intelligence and guile. When my parents moved onto portion 88 of the original thousand-acre farm owned by the previous farmer, John was found to be residing on the lower slope of land. He had an impressive complex of mud brick rooms built in a square around an open courtyard. The walls of the complex were gaily decorated with geometric patterns of oil enamel paint. The courtyard and surrounds were swept several times a day by the many women in the complex.

Anna, John's wife, was the matriarch of the farm and although she claimed not to be able to understand English, she ruled through her much smaller husband, together with her two sons and three daughters. John became the longest-serving member of staff until his death from old age while I was away at university. Anna had a large number of copper and bead-covered necklaces that stretched her neck length to almost twice that of her husband. Each year she seemed to add more rings at every special occasion and as a small boy, I remember wondering if her head would flop over if she ever took them off.

John proved to be a remarkably able man and his thriving vegetable garden and herd of cattle increased each year. Dad realised that a fair proportion of fertiliser and cattle concentrate disappeared from the farm, but John was never caught and both sides accepted it as a small price for harmony.

Dad had bought a hand-held plough that was pulled by two mules. John was the only man able to control the stubborn animals, and he did so with impressive ease. I spent an afternoon under his tutelage and learnt the commands he shouted at the mules. '*Hot-om*' to turn left and '*Har-om*' for right. I clearly did not have the correct pronunciation because the two just ignored my efforts. I strongly suspected it was the expert way in which John twitched the long reins that communicated his wishes to his charges.

The mules regularly broke out of their camp in the night and wandered over to distant farms. John would hunker down and examine the land in the early sun, checking for shadows of hoof-prints. He showed me how, but I could only just make out the individual prints, while John moved fluidly along the path taken by the escapees, reading the spoor effortlessly. He was usually gone all morning before returning with his chastened mules, and I strongly suspected that he was complicit in their escape in order to give himself a morning stroll as opposed to more strenuous work.

My elder sister, Rosemary, decided that I needed to be educated in the feeds that we provided to the cattle on the farm and made me taste the nutty 'germ-meal' and the powdery little flakes of bran. They were not unpleasant but also not the first snack choice for a young farmer. I had no idea of the evil intentions of this sister that I adored.

A small herd of Jersey cows gave a plentiful supply of rich, creamy milk. The cream was separated in a machine that required energetic turning of a handle. John and Anna's three daughters, Salomina, Joanna and Sophie, all spent several years working in the kitchens until leaving to raise families of their own. One of their chief tasks was to separate the cream from the milk, which was then delivered by Dad to local stores while the family, including all the Ndebele staff, shared the skim milk.

The Jersey bulls had a courage and tenacity that belied their size. Smaller than many other cattle breeds, they would fight to the death if left to do so. We were always afraid of these aggressive animals, but John had no choice but to care for them, a task he performed with amazing ability. They were kept in isolation until a cow needed their attention, and only John dared venture into the field they were occupying. He would toss a few scoops of concentrate into a square wooden box and then use a pitchfork to throw a load of hay or silage next to it. Water was provided in a 200 litre metal oil drum that had been cut in half lengthwise.

The bulls would come charging out to each new meal and John would skip away smartly, knowing that they would stop at the food and ignore him as he retired out of the field.

Every now and then a bull would break out of the field, normally because they had a keener ability to detect when a cow came into season than we did, and they did not want to wait until invited to attend the party.

On one Sunday afternoon, one of the bulls broke free and was charging about the farm, with John in hot pursuit. The thudding hooves and testosterone-laden snorts as he pounded around were intensely exciting for little children. There was a huge willow tree that grew near the milking shed, a favourite place to climb up thick, gnarled branches. Very soon the upper limits of the tree were occupied by four small souls, watching the rippling muscles and heaving chest as the bull charged past the tree several times and then came to a halt directly below us. Despite the height from which we observed the bull, it was obvious that should we venture down, this behemoth could dispatch us with hardly any effort at all.

John eventually managed to corral his wayward Romeo and we ran to the house, babbling with excitement, only to be met by a furious mother whose anxiety for her offspring had kindled an anger that burst into flames, resulting in a severe scolding when we appeared all unscathed.

Rosemary continued with my education by offering me a taste of a new component of the food kept for the cattle, and when I spat it out in disgust she laughed uncontrollably, pointing to the label that read 'Carcass meal'. I was very fortunate that she had spared me a taste from the drum that housed the chicken droppings. This nitrogen-rich ingredient was at that time widely used to feed the microbes in the large fermentation stomachs of the ruminants on the farm. Little boys would undoubtedly not profit from a dose of this food source.

John Ngoma had a unique attitude towards veterinary care and put great store by any cure that involved pain. As with many of his countrymen, he valued excruciating injections from his doctor and when he developed conjunctivitis, he smeared Vicks Menthol Vapo-rub into his eye. It took a few weeks for the angrily swollen eyelids to subside, but the cure worked admirably, and the infection had gone.

Mom had noticed that one of the farm cats had a badly infected wound on its head and with John's help, she managed to corner it in one of the sheds and set about treating it.

Not particularly friendly, the farm cats were working animals that made a brave attempt to keep the rat population in check. While John held the squirming feline, Mom first cleaned the wound with iodine and then produced a syringe filled with Tetracycline, an antibiotic that all farmers regarded as the solution to all ills. The solution burned fiercely when injected, but it was the only drug effective against many of the diseases that larger farm animals got.

While John manfully kept hold of the cat's scruff, Mom pushed the needle under its skin and pressed the plunger with some force. The cat let out a yowl of anguish and shot out of the restraining hands and up a sheer wall and onto the shed roof and then on to freedom.

John was suitably impressed with the reaction. 'Good muti,' he commented. 'Very good muti that.'

Chapter 5

MY ANIMALS AND OTHER FAMILY

Mom and Dad had both grown up in the suburbs of Johannesburg and were determined to give their children the chance to live in a more natural, rural environment. Mom had read a book about self-sufficiency in which the author had a large family, and everyone chipped in, making for a harmonious and productive family. She enthusiastically aimed to follow his example.

Twenty years later, she read his second book, in which he related how the constant work regime adversely impacted the character and development of many of his children, and she was able to heartily agree. Nevertheless, my parents will forever be the most giving and hardest-working people I have ever known. They aimed to provide as many wholesome gifts to their children as they could.

They were also completely human, and favourite memories are those of Dad throwing his hat on the ground and jumping on it in frustration, or of Mom breaking a china plate on Mark's head when she thought we had ignored her instructions not to tease my eldest sister and her boyfriend. My delight was instantly tripled as Joan's beau suffered in silence,

Mark broke in shock and burst into tears and Mom followed suit, completely aghast at what she had done, even if the plate had sported a long crack weeks before the incident. I had a thoroughly enjoyable day.

Dad was prevailed upon to buy two horses for us, and with no knowledge at all, he was soon the proud, if wary, owner of a 17-hand piebald gelding with a lovely nature, called Paint, and a bay with the name of Chaka, who had a serious heart murmur which the seller knew about but had kept quiet.

Rosemary later made it a triple when she purchased Skyga, who became the main reason for her existence. She had bought the foal from a riding school owner when everyone agreed that the sickly little animal would not last more than a week. No-one had considered the total commitment that a young girl could give to an ailing horse, sleeping beside her charge on the floor of the stable on cold highveld winter nights.

As a novice family, we had no idea that horses spook from any quick movement, from little pieces of paper blowing in the wind, or from no more than a quirk of imagination. We also had little experience in fastening the girth of a saddle when the horse expands its chest as you place it on its back.

As a result, I had the interesting experience of bouncing around between Paint's four legs, suspended by the stirrups of a saddle that had slipped around and was hanging from his midriff. I suffered no injury but riding never became my favourite activity.

Dad proved to be an innovative and capable entrepreneur as he worked to provide a roof over his growing family. Unable to afford a builder, he set about constructing his own house, starting with the manufacture of the bricks.

John Ngoma had built his complex with large mud blocks, but they required regular maintenance after each thunderstorm softened some of them and made the walls sag. Dad used his contacts from the hardware store and managed to purchase a brick-making machine, and John was given the task of digging out suitable soil and sifting it in a large rotary sieve the size and shape of a 44-gallon oil-drum.

Dad decided to use psychology to achieve productivity. John proved that he was the more adept at the science. In the first week, John increased his production from one hundred to eight hundred bricks per day. Dad promised him one cent for every brick over a thousand that he could produce in 24 hours. The response was fifteen hundred on day two, rising rapidly to five thousand a day. It took some time before Dad realised that he was paying more for his bricks than if he purchased them from a local brickyard and so production ceased, but not before John had bought another cow to add to his growing herd.

The men who offloaded the bricks, like their counterparts who delivered the large bags of animal feed, were men I admired immensely.

The Feed Lorries would arrive with loud growling and huffing engines and a protesting hiss of brakes. Each man wore a helmet made from the shiny Chrysler hubcaps padded on the inside with cloth. A grain sack was used to cover the neck and shoulders of each man, placed under the helmet and running down their back. A man stood next to the bed of the lorry and two men lowered the heavy, eighty-pound bags onto their heads to be carried away into the sheds. The strongest men took two at a time.

The Brick Delivery Trucks disgorged a dozen men, who had made palm protectors from the inner tubes of car tyres. The protector had a hole through which they threaded their wrist and then the hand was covered by a large flap extending from the ring of rubber around the wrist. Men on the top of the load of bricks would pick up a dozen loose bricks stacked in a loose row between their hands and throw them to the waiting men below, who caught them in mid-air, all still in one long row, by clamping their hands on either end of the outer bricks and pressing them all together. I was vastly impressed.

Dad would question the tradesmen who came into his hardware store about each step as he constructed the house, and frequently visited building sites to see how they did things. He also showed his ingenuity in other fields and constructed a large peach sorting table, with two belts that ran down the raised centre, starting close together and slowly diverging.

Peaches placed on the two parallel belts were supported until they reached the point at which they could drop through into the correct section of the table. Mom lined the hard wood with sponge rubber to prevent the peaches from bruising.

The men who milked the cows would stop at the peach sorting shed and invariably rest the soil-encrusted bottom rim of the stainless-steel milk buckets on the pristine sponge rubber of the table. Mom despaired of remonstrating them and finally drew a cartoon depicting a milker placing his bucket on the table and then, in the following square, being chased by a large lady with a rolling pin. John solemnly looked at the cartoon and then stated sagely, 'That man is silly to run – he is dead already.'

The crime continued sporadically but the humour of the situation allowed Mom to accept it ruefully, as she cleaned away the dirt every few weeks and replaced the sponge each year.

A *cum laude* graduate in Classics from the University of the Witwatersrand, Mom had taught at a senior school for two years and then spent the rest of her life raising first her children and then most of her grandchildren, while managing the farm at the same time. Occasionally she would remember her academic career ruefully and, in many ways, it influenced her more mundane tasks.

As a teenager, Joan asked Mom to sketch all thirty of the children in her class at school and Mom did so, having never seen most of them, including in the sketches their characters as described by Joan. The following day, each subject was invariably able to identify every child in the class except themselves. Many were taken aback by their depiction, but all were resoundingly reinforced by every other child in the class.

Oldest brother Fred was as tardy as I was in completing homework assignments and when he announced that he had to hand in some research he should have done into factories, Mom wrote an account of the manufacture of spotted paint for rocking horses and holes for macaroni.

I skipped school one day for a very minor excuse and when a sick note was demanded, I badgered my long-suffering parent until she wrote a harrowing tale of the near-death experience of her son who had contracted rabies after doing battle with a vicious predator that had threatened the whole family. Both the factory account and the fictitious sick note were duly accepted and filed without anyone reading them. Mom had warned both Fred and me that she was only prepared to pen a humorous account and if found out, we would have to face the music ourselves. As a result, I developed a cynical view of authority, which has not helped me in my career, even if it has given me numerous grin-inducing memories.

Dad also built a long rectangular swimming pool that was lined with a plastic liner. The liner lasted half a dozen years and then developed too many holes to be patched and the pool was left dry. A load of anthracite for the furnace heater was dumped in one end of the empty pool.

On a balmy summer evening a little prickly visitor crossed our lawn and was accosted by four large dogs. We rescued the little hedgehog and spent several days digging up earthworms for her or feeding her the long black millipedes, or *shongalolos,* that she crunched through as if eating dried sausage. Mrs Tiggywinkles was given a temporary home in the empty pool with the intention of letting her roam free after a few days. On day two, she disappeared, and it was assumed that she had managed to climb up the pile of anthracite and escape.

The following spring, we were delighted when Mrs Tiggywinkles once again appeared, together with half a dozen little prickly hoglets. She had presumably managed to find a gap to hide in under the black chunks and had given birth to her new family. She must have been expecting before the onset of her confinement. It was a delight to set the little family free in the long grass at the edge of the garden once they were large enough to follow their spikey parent into the undergrowth.

A bird park close to our farm was run by a very powerful character named James Parker. He was a fount of knowledge, and there seemed to be little that he did not know about birds and their care. I was enthralled by the splendour of his collection, particularly the free-roaming parrots and ground hornbills.

As a teenager, I begged my parents to allow me to refurbish an old brick building formerly used to raise young chicks until they were old enough to lay eggs. The building had no roof, but I wanted to cover it with bird netting and turn it into a very large aviary. As a birthday gift, I was given the derelict building and my first foray into construction began. John taught me how to thatch the central section while I covered the perimeter with very fine wire mesh, small enough to keep little finches in and vermin out. Soon the twenty-foot-square enclosure was humming with little wings as the brightly coloured birds went about their lives. A few years later a large hole appeared in the wire mesh, allowing several birds to escape. I arrived home to find them desperately trying to get back inside.

A family of Chinese Painted Quail roamed the floor, hiding in the islands of grasses and other plants. In one corner I made a fishpond with a waterfall and in another I had a similar structure, but it was dry and housed a family of guinea pigs, who had a network of tunnels under a small pile of slasto stone. Every six months or so, a new litter of tiny, spikey little patchwork piglets would emerge, to everyone's delight.

The quail also laid a clutch of eggs, and I was entranced to find a dozen little chicks the size of my thumbnail chasing after their mother on the aviary floor one afternoon. I had knocked out a half brick at ground level to allow rainwater to escape from the aviary, and to prevent birds from escaping, I had used cement to stick a section of bird netting with 1cm mesh over it. To my dismay, the little flock of baby quail ran through the mesh as if it did not exist. I rushed out of the aviary and around the brick wall to where the brick drain had been constructed. After half an hour I had rounded up all the errant chicks and transferred them to a small box, which was placed under a heating lamp.

The brick-walled aviary became my happy place and even though I had a lot of interaction with my siblings, I fulfilled my need for a purpose in life from the farm work and the constant upkeep of the inhabitants of the aviary. It would be years before I realised that I missed out on the socialisation that other teenagers experienced, and I found it very difficult to interact in society.

I desperately wanted to become a farmer but soon realised that to do so, I would have had to be born the son of a farmer, since it was not possible to buy a farm and make enough from it to pay off the mortgage.

Nico Tinbergen and other ethologists were just exploring the new science of animal behaviour in the era in which I completed high school. Fascinated by animals of all species, I set my heart on working with them for a career and applied to do a degree in zoology and genetics at the University of the Witwatersrand.

James Parker was brought to our attention after having been missing for a number of months, when his photo was on the front page of *The Star*, the most widely read newspaper in Johannesburg. His prowess in the avian field had led to him sending an accomplice in Namibia several homing pigeons. The accomplice pushed uncut diamonds into the crops of the unfortunate birds and then put a loose-fitting ring around the neck to prevent them regurgitating the stone.

Most of the birds reached the bird park after the long flight half the distance across Africa, but one of them succumbed to exhaustion and was found in the back garden of a homeowner only ten miles from the intended destination. The deception was obvious, and James made a much shorter trip to the prison on the other side of the city. The bird park never re-opened.

Chapter 6

CULTURE SHOCK

Several times a year, Mom and Dad would invite all the staff and their families on the farm into our house to watch a film that Dad hired from an agency and played on an ancient projector. At times there were over 40 people crowded into the lounge.

As the young Ndebele children entered the house, they would immediately sit on the low, comfortable settees, a move which invariably irritated Mom. She spent the next ten minutes shooing them off so that the adults could take a seat. The same scenario played out every time the staff was invited.

It was twenty years later, while doing a course in Zulu at University, that I came to understand our misconception. Ndebele children showed respect by always taking a lower position than their elders. Dashing for the settee was not selfish bad manners but an innate show of politeness. The different cultures in South Africa lived side by side but we never really understood each other.

When Elijah, a Xhosa from the Ciskei, began working at the veterinary clinic as a young man, he kept his head down and mumbled softly when spoken to. I found it impossible to communicate and repeatedly told him to talk up. By the end of the first month, he began to speak more clearly and was brave enough to look up every now and them.

After two months, he went home for a long weekend, but when he returned, his face sported a huge, dark swelling and once again he reverted to conversing with his shoes.

It was five years later, emboldened by our improved relationship, that he found it in himself to tell me what happened. In Xhosa culture, the uninitiated young men were never allowed to meet the gaze of the older men and they were expected to answer softly and respectfully. I had done him a distinct disservice by making him change his mannerisms, with the result that on his first trip home, he had spoken to his father as he spoke to me and received a severe beating for his pains.

After six months, Elijah asked if I would help him transport some corrugated zinc roofing to his house in Dimbaza. I agreed without much concern. I knew the chief of the village, an imposing man with a similarly impressive name of Baron Umlimbe. Disconcertingly, despite being of imposing stature, Baron had the highest falsetto voice I have ever heard from a man.

The following morning, Elijah appeared with a single sheet of zinc. He steadfastly insisted that this was all he needed to be transported and after shaking my head, I agreed and drove him plus his cargo the fifteen miles to his village.

The house consisted of two rooms made from mud brick. The roof had three sheets of zinc covering roughly a fifth of one room. Dozens of cardboard sheets, plywood and other structures covered the rest of the structure.

I was deeply humbled by the cheerful smiles and greetings from the family, who all rushed out to help remove the corrugated metal sheet from the roof of the van.

Elijah had worked for months to afford a single sheet of roofing for his family—a family that consisted of his parents and six siblings. Elijah was the eldest and the only one not at school. His father earned a state pension, which lasted only as long as it took him to get to the bottle store. His mother fed the family from the few chickens scratching around the house, a patch of stunted maize and weeds and plants that she collected from the area around the village.

Elijah's small salary was supporting eight people counting himself.

Chapter 7

PLAN B

John's skills with the mules became redundant when I was ten years old. They had grown too old to pull the heavy plough and Dad invested in a red Massey-Ferguson tractor.

We kids were never allowed to get on it, but Mom found a new interest in life, as did eldest brother Fred. Although they ploughed the fields using the tractor, sowing the seed was still done by hand. As the tractor crawled up the one side of the field, on the opposite side, a labourer walked slowly with a bucket of maize in one hand, the other hand dribbling the seeds into the last furrow ploughed on his side. It was a job I enjoyed, and all of us became quite adept at getting single seeds to fall in fairly regular intervals.

The tractor with its two-share plough would then cross over and start at the beginning of the seed-filled row again. One ploughshare turned earth into the last furrow, covering the seed, while the second share opened up a new furrow, ready to be seeded.

A massive, heavy disc harrow, with two dozen concave steel plates arranged in two rows, was used to turn over the top six inches of soil without disturbing the deeper layers. It was primarily used in the peach orchard to combat the weeds between the trees and Mom became very proficient in clearing the weeds without hitting and damaging the tree trunks as she weaved the heavy machine between the rows.

Fred had developed a keen interest in keeping bees and purchased several hives, which were placed among the peach trees. They thrived during the spring and summer when the peach blossoms were out but had to be moved to other sources of nectar in the colder months.

On one memorable day, Mom came running down from the orchard and frantically slammed the door behind her, immediately closing all the windows of the house. An angry black swarm of insects slammed against the glass panes and a few managed to find their way into the house.

She had knocked over one of the hives with the disc harrow and the inhabitants had poured out to protect their hard-won harvest of honey.

Fortunately, she had only suffered a few stings, but our small flock of geese had been grazing nearby and they were attacked by the vicious mob, three of them dying from multiple stings and probably shock as well.

Fred was forced to go and retrieve the tractor after dark when the small, winged soldiers were all clustered protectively around their queen. A few days later, he managed to set the hive back upright and then erected a low fence around it to prevent a repeat incident.

Harvesting the honey proved to be a challenge. With care, and the use of a smoker, the bees could be coaxed to evacuate one layer of the hive, which was lifted off and removed. The individual combs could then be taken out and the honey removed from the cells.

A hot uncapping knife would take off the seal from each cell and a little honey would ooze out, but most producers employed a comb spinner, or centrifuge which made the liquid spurt out of the cells as the combs were whirled about at great speed. Fred could not afford a spinner and had to make alternate plans.

All was peaceful in the house when it was suddenly filled with a dense black smoke that had a strangely sweet tinge to it. Those of us near enough rushed to the kitchen, where the oven was belching out great clouds of acrid bitterness.

Fred had decided to try and melt the wax of the combs, hoping that as they cooled, the wax and the honey would separate into different layers. His ingenuity fell short in the selection of a suitable vessel in which to heat the combs, since he chose a plastic container that had once been a cylindrical flour container. The plastic melted almost as quickly as the honeycomb did, and he was now faced with several inches of hot plastic-wax-honey on the floor of the oven and slowly oozing out into the kitchen.

Mom was forced to mute her anger as a result of her recent fiasco with the bees, but Fred endured years of ridicule, perpetuated by the fact that the plastic receptacle had melted down to a thick-walled dog-bowl, which we used to feed several canines over the years.

Although John no longer had the mules to look after, he had a wide and growing list of responsibilities. I enjoyed many hours chatting with him as he worked, milking the cows, feeding the livestock, picking the fruit. Winter was the time for pruning the peach trees and the men spent most of every day cutting off extra branches. In the bitter cold, they would heap up the bits they cut off and make a fire over which to warm aching fingers. It amazed me that the green, although dormant, wood burned readily once enough heat had been generated beneath it.

South Africa was the last country in the world to get television. The government let it be known that they were waiting until a perfect system was available, but I strongly suspect that it was a ploy to keep the general population ignorant of world opinion.

Vague reports of South African incursions into neighbouring countries were denied by the ruling party, until troops returning from the front spread the truth. Fred managed to hitch a lift back home when given leave from the army and arrived in the dead of night. Not wanting to wake the family, he expertly lifted a loose pane in a window and managed to unlock the door. Exhausted, he lay down on the sofa and fell asleep.

Unknown to him, three little bantam cockerels raised by Sharon, the youngest in the family, had decided to follow him into the house. At five in the morning, he was rudely awakened by all three of them, perched on the back of the sofa and spontaneously erupting in a loud crowing competition. They soon learned the danger posed by heavy army boots launched in their direction.

Fred described in detail how his military group had spent the past month near Luanda in Angola. The government continued to deny any presence in this neighbouring state.

The embargo on television came to a head when the first astronauts landed on the moon. We were the only country in the world that could not watch this momentous event on the box. The newspapers had a field day, with extra editions filled with images taken by the spacecraft and the men inside it.

With excitement I described the events to John, standing in the early dusk in front of the peach packing shed. Pointing up into the sky, I commented that there were two men walking on that moon right at this moment.

John looked at me sceptically but nodded politely.

'They are stupid to go tonight,' he commented. 'There is only a quarter of a moon, and they could easily have missed it.'

It was my turn to look at him in puzzlement, unsure whether he was pulling my leg. It didn't matter. It was not going to change our lives and besides, the learned engineers were not able to drive a team of mules, or milk six cows by hand, or use any of the multitude of plants in the veld that John had shown me had medicinal properties.

I bid him goodnight in Zulu, the few words of his language that I knew, and he hoisted a heavy sack of maize-meal onto his shoulders and picked up a wooden crate filled with vegetables to take home to his family. Dad made sure he supplemented each labourer's wages with basic provisions, since the nearest store was several hours' walk away.

Chapter 8

THANK YOU FOR THE MEMORIES

Sitting in a crowded restaurant, I suddenly found myself chuckling, causing people at nearby tables to shake their heads and roll their eyes at their companions, while making motions with their hands to indicate excessive alcohol intake. A favourite memory had burst like an unexpected bubble onto my conscious mind and was playing havoc with the muscles of my face. Thank you, Mark, for this recurring cause of uncontrollable grinning.

Mom at one stage was almost spherical in shape, after having 6 kids and coping with them, plus a farm with 37 Ndebele or Sotho occupants on the land. Needing an operation, she was told firmly to lose weight, which she did with amazing control, halving her weight within a year. At the end of this time, the family took their annual holiday and booked into a resort in the Drakensburg mountains called The Cavern.

Each morning, all those going on the daily organised hike would assemble in front of the hotel near the edge of a natural amphitheatre's rim that would give modern health and safety officials apoplexy. On this particular morning the entire family apart from Mark were standing among the crowd of hikers along one side of the cliff face. On the other side of the chasm were a number of other guests enjoying the view.

I noticed a rotund lady on the far side that I had twice mistaken for Mom in the past few days and commented on it. Mom was horrified. 'I never looked like that,' she protested. The rest of the party nodded at me but none of them were brave enough to support me. I need not have worried. The proof was about to be demonstrated.

As we watched, we suddenly realised that there was a second figure, creeping up behind the poor lady with obvious malice in his mind. With one voice the entire family shouted urgently, 'No, Mark. Don't do it. Mark. Stop.' He either never heard or chose not to.

Evil takes no heed of anything but its own nefarious end, and he continued to creep up behind his victim and then darted forward to grab her by the shoulders and pretend to push her over the cliff face. The shock on the poor lady's face as she stared into the abyss has been etched into my memory forever.

Gamely she gathered up her handbag and whirled around to defend herself from her would-be assailant. He saw the movement and ducked, with the result that he never got to see her face clearly. She had turned in a full circle when he once again grabbed her from behind and made urgent pushing motions towards the edge of the rock.

The only saving grace that day was that this elderly lady did not suffer from a weak heart, or it could have been manslaughter.

The look on Mark's face as he suddenly registered the entire family pounding round the narrow path towards him, tears of laughter streaming down their faces, with the sick realisation that the shoulders he held did not belong to his mother, who was leading the charge to detain him, was something I would pay good money to see again.

As a shy, introverted teenager, this was the only time I have ever lain face down on the ground in front of 70 people and pounded the ground with my fists in glee as tears streamed down my face.

Recovering from the debilitating effect of being rendered helpless with laughter, we all duly followed the son of the resort owner as he led the way to begin the long climb up to the amphitheatre, the five-kilometre semi-circle of rock cliffs that rose a thousand feet almost perpendicularly. Under a blazing sun, the hike took most of the day and required frequent stops to drink from the multiple small pristinely clear streams on the way.

Amazingly, Mom persevered until she was two thirds of the way, and Dad continued to the end and was one of the first to reach the top. Sitting next to a pool of water that had two little waterfalls cascading from its lip, he welcomed each hiker as they staggered to a stop and watched them drink thirstily from the pool nearest to them. As they paused in their fluid replenishment, Dad politely pointed out the baboon droppings in the water near the rock on which he perched.

He waited until the effects of shock had worn off before kindly explaining that the pool was in fact two separate bodies of water running parallel to each other and not mixing at all. The baboon-flavoured option cascaded harmlessly off to one side while the unpolluted, clean source of water took a different path, passing the new arrival who had just swallowed copious amounts of it.

Not for the first time I wondered how anyone could expect me to grow up to be a model citizen amid brothers with sadistic tendencies and a father with a sneaky sense of mischief.

Chapter 9

BUSH HILL

The Boskop Primary School was designated as 'Dual Medium' and had separate classes for the Afrikaans children and the English. The school emblem was three trees, or *Bosse*, on top of a hill, *Kopie*.

The Afrikaans kids had a fierce national pride and scorned their weaker counterparts. Our half of the school were taught in English and for the most part we all had English ancestors, but there were also a large number of Greek, German, Italian and other nationalities. The daughter of a Swiss couple who owned the convenience store across the road from the school took a shine to me and I happily accepted a free ice cream from her father, while Mark collected a small hoard of gifts from female admirers, earning our amazement and amusement in equal measures as he displayed his small collection without the smallest embarrassment.

Mr Van Der Hooven, the headmaster, was typically Afrikaans but had a depth of character that appealed to all. My first encounter with him was when families were asked to bring in supplies for the school fete. Each day of the week, we were asked to provide one item if we could. Many of them could earn a prize.

Mom packed a tray of eggs from the 1200 battery hens with the largest offerings at the front but six tiny little pullet eggs at the back. During school assembly, Joan was duly called out to collect the prize for the largest egg and then to my embarrassment, I was made to go up in front of everyone to collect five cents as a prize for the smallest eggs.

The teacher we all feared was the librarian, Mrs Vermaas, who ate little children for breakfast if they forgot to return a book by the due date. She had twin boys and for one Christmas, she presented them with expensive little toy cars, which they swapped with two little Sotho boys who had made ingenious cars with a stiff wire frame and wheels made from shoe-polish tins. The wire cars had working steering mechanisms, which the driver could manipulate by means of a long piece of wire reaching from the front wheels to a steering wheel a few feet above the vehicle, used to both push and steer the automobile.

Mrs Vermaas was incensed and angrily tried to catch the boys who had made off with the store-bought Dinky toys, while her sons secretly cherished their more useable home-made versions.

Kenneth Young bet me that he could pee out of the toilet window while standing on the floor of the toilets. He must have had an oversized bladder, as he projected a stream of liquid through the small aperture and onto the walkway outside. Neither of us had seen Mrs Vermaas in the corridor.

The angry tornado that erupted into the cloakroom abruptly caused the stream of urine to cease instantly. All of us suffered a few stinging blows from the towel Mrs Vermaas had grabbed from the railing, but we managed to escape from under the fury. Not so for Kenneth, who dashed into a cubicle and locked the door, refusing to come out or even identify himself for the next half hour, until his nemesis was forced to leave to deal with her next class of despised infants.

In 1969, it snowed heavily in the Transvaal. We had never experienced either the magic of the white stuff that blanketed the world, or the bitter cold that came with it.

Mr Van Der Hooven rushed home and returned with a top hat, which he paraded around the playing fields, good-naturedly dodging snowballs fired in his direction. The rest of us were spared from injury. We made huge balls of snow which rolled down the bank and across the netball courts. I never again encountered snow until fifteen years later, when we raced up from our home in the Eastern Cape to the white-covered Hogsback mountains.

The school had an annual play that had a level of professionalism way above its humble standing. To select the choir and the solo performers, each class was made to assemble in the hall and sing together, while teachers patrolled along the rows, pulling stars forward and pushing a few of us backwards, removing those with discordant, toneless voices and relegating us to a group who would not be asked onto the stage. After a brief feeling of affront, I accepted the inevitable, but there were several sniffles and downcast eyes among the group.

Such tiny incidents went a long way to creating or destroying fragile self-esteem in little people. If I have a little angel on one shoulder and a devil on the other, they are surely named Van Der Hooven and Vermaas.

Chapter 10

PICKIN NUTS

The big Bull terrier walked into the room with a typical rocking gait on legs that never seemed to bend. He stopped in front of me, and I bent over and hooked one hand under his harness and the other beneath his chest, lifting him onto the examination table.

I rubbed his massive head and lifted his lips to look at two rows of powerful teeth. There were several battle scars on his muzzle and higher up. He was clearly a fighter. A few gentle slaps on his chest were hardly registered by this warrior tank. I turned to ask the owner what was wrong, only to see a look of pure shock on his face.

'I can't believe you just did that,' he exclaimed.

'What?' I asked, puzzled.

'The last vet I took Malice to ended up in hospital,' he said in a voice close to a whisper.

I felt the hairs on my neck begin to rise. Cautiously I turned back to the table, face to face with the powerful, conical muzzle that was grinning at me. I suddenly knew how a mouse felt between the paws of a cat. Malice pulled back his lips in a smile and then lunged.

I have no idea how it is possible to move through a closed door without seeming to open it, but one second I was eye-to-eye with my vicious nemesis and the next I was on the other side of the door as he slammed into it.

I finished the consultation at arm's length and even then, he tried desperately to tear off his owner's arm and get to my throat.

I should have grown up with a real fear of dogs. Big dogs in particular. I suspect that our lives were so intertwined with the lives of hundreds of animals that the occasional brush with fear was more than moderated by the daily delight in the soft tan coat of the young Jersey calves and the fluffy yellow day-old chicks in their hundreds huddling under the bright glow of infra-red lights.

The three big, fear-inducing dogs belonged to our neighbours, the Shaws, and they regarded the top corner of our farm as part of their territory. Whenever we drove past, they would explode through the inadequate fence and chase the car out into the main road. They always won and regarded themselves as territorially dominant. I in turn made the mistake of regarding our fence as the legitimate boundary between the properties.

I was wearing a pair of white shorts on the day that I went to pick up the fallen nuts on our side of the fence from our neighbours' pecan tree. I wore them because I was just too lazy to change after coming home from athletics at school. The dogs spotted me riding my bike up the gravel path and launched their attack. Vaguely aware of the rushing forms, I hopped off the bike and held it between me and the dogs, mistakenly assuming they would respect our borders.

Neither the fence, nor the bike, nor the innocence of a ten-year old, was any deterrent to them as they rushed around and took a huge bite of my buttocks. Blood poured down the white material and streaked my bare legs.

I would like to say I beat them off bravely, but I suspect my screams of pain made them turn victoriously and rush back to the neighbours' house. I abandoned my bike and limped home as fast as I could.

It was painful, very painful, but I never pinned it on the dogs. They had inflicted the injury, but at the most it gave me a healthy respect for dogs and ever since then, I have acknowledged their ability to cause instant pain and injury if taken too lightly.

The Shaws were very apologetic when an angry mother and an embarrassed ten-year-old confronted them with a red-and-white rag that had once been my shorts and from then on, they kept the dogs confined behind a fence that enclosed their house and garage.

The portion of land owned by the Shaws that was closest to our farm was a paddock, grazed by two horses, while a couple of stables stood at an angle to the boundary, the closest corner of the building only a few feet from the fence.

A huge pecan tree grew in the horse's paddock, but a number of large branches stretched over the fence with as blatant a disregard for borders as that of the dogs. I did not mind the trespass by the tree, because it meant that as a very young kid, I could collect the nuts that fell on our land.

When the dog bite had healed, I returned to the scene, and this time I climbed into the low-hanging branches and began to pick the ripe nuts. Soon I had a large bag filled to the brim. My addictive nature that had always prevented me from eating just one square of chocolate and generally left me feeling ill from overload came into force, and I climbed higher into the tree to collect all I could.

I very quickly found myself in the higher reaches, above the stables. A tinge of guilt was rapidly squashed by reason: If I left the nuts, they would just fall to the ground and be ignored by the neighbours until they rotted. I was putting them to good use.

Suddenly I froze, as a man I recognised as the groom from next door arrived and walked straight to the stables. Holding my breath, I watched as he bypassed the doors at the front and made his way between the stables and the fence, out of sight of the house. After a few minutes I heard the unmistakeable splashing tinkle as he began to relieve himself against the wall.

Halfway through his ministrations, my foot slipped, and I dropped a nut in my efforts to catch myself. Below me the sound stopped, and the figure froze. Both of us stood immobile, frozen in mischief, aware of being observed but not willing to call out each other's misdemeanour.

After a minute, he finished his ablutions without looking up at all and then strolled out and down to the lower paddock. I took the chance to make my way down the tree, but as I jumped to the ground, I caught sight of him peering over the tall Napier grass that grew between the paddocks.

We both looked away and then each of us sauntered off without acknowledging the existence of each other. Hear no evil, see no evil—two out of three was not so bad.

Chapter 11

THE HALLS OF INJUSTICE

The move from being seniors in a very small junior school to the role of 'newbie' in a much larger and far more intimidating senior school was traumatic, to say the least.

The headmaster openly gave the seniors the right to inflict humiliating initiation ceremonies on the hapless newcomers half their size. A junior could be commanded to stand up and sing the school song in front of any number of jeering students, with the threat of a serious punishment if they were unable to do so. I watched in horror as friends received merciless bullying, but I managed to fade into the background and remain unnoticed by the older boys.

It was only when the next intake of juniors occurred that we became less of a target for the amusement of those students prone to take advantage of anyone with fewer defences than they had.

I have long been cursed with a sense of the ridiculous that at times makes me shake with suppressed mirth in repeated, stifled waves. Victor was similarly afflicted with an uncontrollable urge for mischief.

The school was built with two floors of classrooms in the form of a rectangle, with a concrete walkway running through an archway in one of the longer sides and crossing the central grassed area.

Victor and I were the first to arrive at the locked classroom of the history teacher, Mr John Hall, on the top floor on the side opposite the archway. Mr Hall was a young, progressive man who had female colleagues and schoolgirls avidly hanging on his every word.

Victor had a powerful little catapult, with thick elastic attached to the two arms. He was clearly looking for a target. As we watched, Mr Hall appeared, walking through the archway, and starting to cross the square. In his arms he carried a heavy pile of exercise books.

'Watch this,' said Victor as he loaded his weapon with a heavy metal staple meant to secure wire by being hammered into wood.

Yeah, right, I thought. The catapult would never shoot across the five hundred metres, let alone be accurate enough to score a hit.

Victor pulled back with considerable effort and then let go.

Across the square, Mr Hall suddenly threw the pile of books into the air. His yell of anguish floated across to us a second later.

My mouth opened in astonishment, but Victor dropped as if he was the one who had been shot.

'Don't say anything,' he whispered frantically as he ducked under the cover of the brick wall balustrade of the balcony and then gave an impressive demonstration of a grasshopper as he walked away, bent double with his knees higher than his head.

The wildly searching schoolmaster, clutching at his nether reaches, had spotted me across the distance, so it was useless to try and follow Victor. I allowed a few other students who arrived shortly afterwards to push in front of me and enter the classroom before following them and choosing the relative safety of a seat in the back corner. Victor walked in nonchalantly and sat as far away from me as he could.

Try as I might, I just could not completely discount the suppressed laughter that welled up each time Mr Hall rubbed his rear end. I turned the chuckles into coughs and sneezes, pulling out a pile of facial tissues to smother my would-be confession of mirth. John Hall seemed to suspect that I knew more than I was letting on and glowered in my direction a few times, but nothing further developed.

The following week we had to submit a model depicting ancient Egypt. This had been a dream task for me. Rejecting pyramids as not much of a challenge, I had made a working *shaduf*, the bucket on a suspended pole for scooping water out of the Nile. I used two thin branches cut from a tree to add authenticity. The river was made from blue-coloured gelatine on a paper mâché landscape. I was the only student to submit a model.

Angrily, Mr Hall locked my masterpiece in his metal cupboard and informed the class that they had a two-week extension.

On the final day, a bevy of pyramids, sphinxes and shadufs appeared. Mr Hall opened the cupboard to retrieve my offering, only to find that the gelatine had spawned a fantastic crop of blue fungi that grew from the model and covered almost everything in the interior of the metal enclosure.

I was both fascinated and embarrassed but felt a deep sense of injustice when I was awarded the average mark. I felt I should have been top of the class, being the only one to meet the first deadline.

Nevertheless, overall, I think I gained the most from the twin events. I doubt the schoolmaster even remembers any of it, whereas it has provided me with scores of chuckles over the years when little events trigger off memory.

As for Victor, he lost both his weapon and his dignity a few days later when Barney Marais, the most feared master in the school, caught him shooting the few streetlights in the road alongside the school that still worked. Victor was given the choice of several punishments, but Barney had judged the boy accurately and he discarded both options of having his parents called and the alternative of a detention, but instead bent over to have the master sting him on his rear with the catapult drawn back to its limit. Victor showed that his mimicry extended further than imitating a grasshopper as he did a remarkable impression of a kangaroo on hot coals.

Victor was not the only partner in crime who entertained me through the excruciating boredom of secondary school. Alfred and his younger brother waged a war of attrition against each other, each one trying to score points on the other without incurring the wrath of a stern stepfather.

In the days when smart phones were not even a concept in the minds of the future tech geeks, we devoured paper comics with picture stories of super-heroes. Many of these flimsy publications had adverts on the back cover for tricks and gags that young people could spend their pocket money on. Alfred had splashed out and bought a bag of 'itching powder'.

Having the means to cause considerable discomfort to his brother, he could not think of a way of deploying his weapon without serious repercussions. Finally, he had the brilliant idea of unrolling a toilet paper roll and sprinkling it liberally with the powder before carefully returning it, rolled up once more, to its holder.

Little brother seemed to have no need of the bathroom that afternoon, despite Alfred's numerous suggestions. Eventually he forgot about the trap he had so deviously laid, until that evening, he heard an anguished bellow, and his stepfather came mincing into the room, in clear discomfort but also eagerly seeking the cause of his agony.

The culprit was obvious when the father was faced with one son's look of bewilderment and a second one of horror. The intended victim was then treated to the joyful display of his older brother bent over the arm of a chair and walloped with a belt.

Alfred's painful gait became exaggerated at the applause and adulation from his peers when he related the tale the next day. The daring incident would relegate him to our hall of fame for the rest of his life. It still makes me eye any less than perfectly rolled loo paper with extreme suspicion to this day.

Chapter 12

Elephant River

I had no perception of being poor or deprived as a child. We had a plentiful supply of fruit, veg and meat from the farm, although we tended to eat what was in season and during the tomato season, many lunches consisted of Tomato Soup, which was liquidised tomatoes sweetened with spoonsful of sugar. Any eggs that were cracked could not be sold and Mom developed her own version of an omelette, which was a thin layer of scrambled egg in a pan, rolled up around a filling of choice, most commonly cheese and bacon—possibly my favourite dish to this day.

Milk was difficult to market but the Jersey cows produced the highest percentage of cream of all cows, and it found a ready demand in a range of shops that the farm supplied. We only got to try a small amount on the bottled peach slices that were available year-round.

One of Joan's early boyfriends aimed to impress her by drinking a pint of cream and bore the resultant wrath of Dad when he saw a day's income disappearing down the young man's throat.

It was a surprise when an organisation offering holiday camps for the underprivileged told a number of us at school about a trip, they had arranged to a privately owned, undeveloped game farm bordering the

Kruger National Park, separated from the main reserve by the Olifants River, a strongly flowing water course in the North-Eastern Transvaal. I rather hesitantly put my name down, along with a handful of others from the school.

Fred was not as hesitant when I told the family of my intended excursion and contacted the organisers to offer his services as a camp warden and was gladly taken on. Together we spent a week in the hot bushveld with very little infrastructure but an enchanting freedom.

Not everyone enjoyed the week, with one of the boys spending the entire time dressed only in his underpants as he sprayed himself with water and hardly emerged from the cool of his room in an attempt to keep cool. The younger boys suffered a great deal from the older bullies, a fate I escaped since I was generally in the company of my older bodyguard. Fred learned that one of the boys was the grandson of the farm owner and they became firm friends, despite a large age gap.

Returning home, we enthused about the trip until the whole family found themselves invited by the grandson to return the following year for a holiday of our own.

The untouched virgin bushveld was intoxicating. Huge Maroela trees, with heavy, smooth trunks, lined the swiftly flowing river and a herd of hippo grunted away in the largest pool just a hundred paces from the old house.

We walked freely through the area each day and one afternoon, as we crested the top of a gentle rise, a herd of giraffe spotted us and thundered past. I was shattered by the size of these animated construction cranes as their dinner- plate-size hoofs left deep impressions in the dry soil, and the area beneath their chest was high enough for us to have walked through unimpeded.

I loved the smooth, round rocks near the river, that seemed to mimic the hippo close by, but when I ventured onto them the dominant hippo uttered an angry roar and splashed rapidly towards me. He was no match for a frightened young boy who wore only a pair of shorts and tennis shoes.

The nights were filled with a cacophony of sound from the vocalists of the animal kingdom, making it difficult to sleep. In the early hours of the night, I became aware of a shadowy figure walking past me as I lay in the open on top of a sleeping bag. Her identity suddenly became apparent when Mom launched the rock she was carrying towards a clump of dense grass from which the piercing call of a frog had emanated for the past six hours. Frog shut up for five minutes before resuming his courtship call.

The two trips were relegated to a distant memory until we tried to visit the farm again ten years later, only to learn that it had been turned into a private game resort, reserved for those who could afford vast sums to enjoy luxury in the bushveld. We had no idea how precious the experiences were when we enjoyed the almost free trips before the world discovered our Eden.

Chapter 13

MEANDERING WATERS

'If we meet a white rhino, select a tree. If we meet a black rhino, or a rhino with a calf, go to a tree. If we meet a buffalo, climb a tree fast.'

The ranger spoke with a quiet sincerity.

A very good show for tourists, I thought. At fifteen, I did not buy it. Piet Van Rensburg and Douglas Mpuna, the two men in khaki, each carried an impressive rifle and made a show of the serious nature of their pep talk.

I doubted we would see any of the big five animals on our hike through the Umfolozi Game Reserve. It didn't matter; there were a whole catalogue of birds and insects and small animals that enriched the experience for me, to say nothing of the vibrant flora of the Natal bush.

On top of it all, I was with Mom and Dad, at a time in my life before teenage rebellion set in. I felt a huge love and respect for them. Rosemary was also with us, together with the Kings, the middle-aged couple who had organised the trip.

There are several interpretations of the word Umfolozi, none of which give justice to the rich diversity of life in this reserve through which the Imfolozi river creates sharp bends, but some will hold that the word describes the zigzag course of the water.

The rangers certainly knew their stuff and pointed out not only the plants and animals that we stumbled across but also the tracks of many animals who had tantalisingly crossed our sandy path before us.

Douglas was the first to notice the small patch of grey among the shadows of a dense patch of bush off to one side. He quickly pointed out the rhino to us all and then urged us to get to a lone Acacia tree twenty yards away.

The rhino emerged from the bush and then we noticed the calf in front of her. This was more serious. The rangers quietly became more insistent.

The two older women managed to pull themselves onto the lower branches of the inadequate tree but stopped when confronted by the long thorns of the smaller growth higher up. The rangers urged us all on.

The men managed to get part way up, but there clearly was no space for Rosemary or me. I shrugged it off but made sure I edged behind the tree, putting it between me and the pair of rhinos, who still seemed placid and innocuous. Teenage reticence and a fear of ridicule kept my feet on the ground.

The rhino mother decided she needed to do more than just snort and charged. I looked for a way out of danger, but there was no easy route. Errol King clambered up and somehow managed to climb over both women until he was in among the smaller branches, swaying about precariously. The rangers pushed Rosemary onto the lowest branch and quickly turned to face the danger.

A shot rang out, ear-bursting and heart-stopping. Both the rhino and I jumped several feet into the air, and the thundering express train turned away a little as she charged by, but her horn was swinging towards us as if to try and catch something or someone unawares.

The two grey shapes thundered loudly and heavily off into the bush, leaving the eight of us behind in various states of emotion.

The rangers breathed sighs of relief, but I noticed they both reloaded their weapons immediately. Neither had aimed at the rhino, both barrels being aimed skywards. The only casualties of the encounter were six racing hearts and a dozen wounds from strong, unforgiving thorns that had to be overcome before the tree dwellers could extricate themselves from the greenery.

I had not managed to get into the tree, but only because there was no space. Given another encounter, I probably would have made sure I was in front of the rest of the group, but this time I had the pleasure of having shown less fear than the rest of them. Bravery is very closely aligned to stupidity, a fact I was very aware of that day.

We never had any other close encounters with fear, although on the final day we tracked a leopard for just over a mile along a dry riverbed, hoping for a glimpse of the elusive, shy creature. I suspect it was watching us for a long time from its out-of-reach hiding place, but all we got to see were the imprints of huge paws in the soft, moist sand.

Chapter 14

SIZE DON'T MATTER

As a student, I spent a few weekends at a nearby veterinary hospital in Krugersdorp.

There were two partners, Drs Woudstra and Carey, who were well known in the area and had a good reputation. I desperately wanted to get involved but did not want to interfere.

Both partners would start their day with routine operations at 7:30 and then, when the first clients arrived at 8:30, one of them would leave to deal with the public. The second partner would finish the operations before joining the fray.

Clients were seen on a first come – first serve basis and the partners just took the next patient on the list.

If there were large animal calls, one of the partners would leave late morning to attend to the horse or cow that needed attention. On some occasions, both partners had farm calls. The evening consultations started at 4:00 pm and finished when the last client had been seen.

I watched as these men dealt with a wide range of species and an even broader range of conditions. Although Dr Carey had spent a few years in Canada doing a post-graduate course in dairy cattle, neither of them seemed fazed by anything.

On the second day, everything seemed to be going well, with all the staff going about their tasks in well-practiced harmony, when suddenly both vets rushed out of their consulting rooms and down the passageway, using their shoulders to block the progress of their colleague in a frantic scramble for front place.

Dr Woudstra managed to reach his goal before Carey did and slammed the door of the cloakroom behind him. Dr Carey's shoulders slumped, and he dejectedly turned around and retraced his steps to his room.

I watched curiously, wondering what had precipitated the frantic tussle to get to the loo. Ten minutes later, Dr Woudstra left the cloakroom and resumed his treatment of the line of clients patiently waiting for his attention.

Yvonne Dominee, one of the receptionists, noticed my curiosity but said nothing until the client in Dr Carey's room came back to the waiting room with a little box and a bottle of medicine. As mother and daughter paid and then left the room, Yvonne chuckled. Dr Carey called the last patient of the day into his room and then Yvonne turned to me and let me into the secret.

'Whenever a hamster comes in, there is a mad rush to get into the safety of the toilets. The first one in stays there until the other vet has seen the hamster.'

'Why?' I asked in innocence.

'Vicious little things, they are.' She smiled. 'Most owners are unable to hold them and if you try to examine them, you often end up getting bitten. Many vets and nurses will tell you of horror stories in which the hamster sinks its teeth into your hand, and in pain and desperation the hand is jerked away, sending the little guy flying through the air.'

I nodded. Sharon had two little furry beasts and most of us had a healthy respect for them, despite their size.

There was a fearsome growling emanating from Dr Carey's room and the client was shouting at her Rottweiler in a desperate attempt to control him. Dr Carey's soft voice coaxed the vicious dog into complying and a short while later, owner, patient and vet emerged triumphantly into the waiting room. I noticed that Dr Carey had no hesitation in dealing with the enormous, aggressive animal.

'Clients expect you to be wary of big dogs. They are less understanding when you are afraid of a little rodent,' he commented later. 'Give me a vicious dog any time. At least I get a little respect from the client.'

Chapter 15

WHITE WATER REEF

Attending the University of the Witwatersrand required a sudden change from being treated as a child to the harsh reality of adult academia. It was the antithesis to our school environment in many ways. I received a rude shock upon finding, a month into the academic year, that I was supposed to be attending weekly tutorials and laboratories as well as the lectures. None of this was spoon-fed to us; we had to find it out ourselves, unlike the pampering we had experienced in school.

A second shock was when we sat an exam in the first week, only to find that our syllabus at school had been sadly lacking. I asked a question of the invigilator and the reply I got was, 'If you have to ask that, then you don't belong here.'

Things gradually improved and I scraped through the first year. The second was more rewarding. As a member of the Biology Society, I joined a small group of enthusiasts who spent weekends helping repair fences at a private cheetah reserve. We were rewarded by being given the opportunity to sit in the enclosure with a family of these majestic cats.

The mother was facing in the opposite direction to her four nearly adult cubs, when a herd of cattle appeared over the hill. 'Watch this,' the warden whispered. 'She will communicate with them at a level we cannot pick up.'

Seconds later, all four cubs simultaneously turned as if choreographed to face the cattle. The mother had alerted them to the presence of potential prey. None of us had heard or detected any communication between mother and cubs.

One of our tasks in our second year was to prepare the skeleton of an animal as if for a museum. I was fortunate in that a taxidermist lived a few farms away, and he was only too obliging in providing the bones of a hyena. Wiring the skeleton together, I was struck with both the complexity and the precision with which it had been constructed. If two bones were joined by a wire connection that was only a few millimetres out of place, the result looked wrong. There was very little room for error.

My daily commute to the university involved getting a lift from Dad and my elder brother Fred into Johannesburg, a journey of just over an hour. They would drop me off near the university and in the evenings, I would walk down a few blocks to wait for them outside a marble clad building, home to a prominent firm of undertakers.

On the day after our skeletons were examined and marked by the zoology department, I found myself walking through the streets of Johannesburg with a dog showing extreme emaciation. Heads turned in surprise to see this cumbersome skeleton on its wooden base preceding me around corners of buildings.

There was even more overt amazement as I sat outside the undertakers with a full-sized canine skeleton as passing traffic staggered past in the stop-start rush hour while numerous fingers pointed towards me. After a while I moved a short distance away, to allow my companion to enjoy the spotlight while I remained a little less conspicuous. I half expected the staff at the undertakers to come out and ask me to move, but Dad arrived after half an hour, and we sped off home again.

My three-year degree was highlighted by only one major triumph that sticks in my mind, but the glory was short-lived.

During a Genetics exam, we were presented with four bacterial cultures, and we were informed that two of them had been infected by viruses, or 'bacteriophages', the viruses that inhabit bacteria. The examiner set us sixteen questions to answer, such as identification of the bacteria that were infected or the relationship between the different cultures of bacteria. A long list of available equipment was supplied as well.

The task was two-fold: For the first hour, we had to design a set of experiments to answer the questions asked and in the second hour, we would be given both the correct set of experiments and the equipment in order to carry them out.

We all set about writing out a list of procedures that would help us penetrate the secrets held by the micro-organisms before us and after a while, I had sixteen methods I proposed to follow. Looking around, I noticed that no-one else seemed to be close to finishing the first half of the exam. I began to worry that perhaps I had got it all wrong. Desperately I read through everything once more and then it occurred to me that perhaps the examiner had provided the long list of equipment to confuse us. I had naturally assumed all of it would need to be used.

Studying the task once more, I was able to design only four experiments that would give us all sixteen answers. I was the last one to hand in the finished plan and to collect the master plan as set out by the examiner.

My heart plummeted. The original sixteen experiments were listed neatly on the examiner's form, almost exactly as I had set them out before changing it all. I was clearly going to get no marks at all for my work. I felt a little resentful, as I could have handed in the first draft if I had not finished it so early.

Engrossed in the work at the laboratory bench and fume cupboard, I was startled to feel a tap on my shoulder and turned to see the stern face of our lecturer, a woman I admired immensely. I stiffened, waiting for the reprimand, when she lowered the paper in her hand and said, 'I just thought you would like to see this.' It was my exam paper and a large red 100% was drawn on the top, enclosed in a ring of ink.

I was jubilant and finished the practical half of the exam walking on air. It was a singular triumph that I would never again be able to replicate. My moment of glory was known to only a few people and yet it was the highlight of my time at Wits.

The common fruit fly, *Drosophila melanogaster,* was the cause of both my rapid descent from glory and the prompt I needed to drive me to apply for the course in Veterinary Science.

In a subsequent genetics exam, each student was presented with several little bottles containing fruit flies. Each bottle held a strain of fruit fly that was unique, having distinctive eye-colours or crumpled wings, differences that made it obvious to identify them apart. Since some of the traits were recessive, the fruit flies that had only one gene of that characteristic did not show any outward sign proving that they had it. The task was to crossbreed the flies to identify which flies carried which genes. The great breeding program began and most of the students rapidly managed to identify the carriers of four different genes, apart from one hapless chap who left one of his bottles open in error and his flock of subjects spent the next few days circling the laboratory until they found an open window.

My breeding experiments just did not make sense. Whereas everyone else had clear results, my flies produced offspring that should just not have existed. At the end of the two-week practical exam, I still had no clear results and as the rest of the class handed in their papers, I quickly fudged my answers and handed them in as well.

The lecturer apprehended me the next day to say how disappointed she was: 'I hoped you would be up to the task, so we gave you fruit flies that had multiple gene disorders. I expected you to realise it but instead you chose to falsify the results.'

I was mortified.

'The first rule in research,' she continued, 'is to report everything with precision, even if it does not agree with your expectations.'

Never again did I enjoy the extreme restraint required by those whose minds were able to hone in on the minutiae that furthered the boundaries of science. Research just did not fill any need in my psyche.

My second exposure to my arch-nemeses, the little flies that abounded in the peach orchard at home, was when as a final-year student, I was required to assist a Zoology candidate doing his doctoral thesis. I presented myself smartly at his office and was surprised to find the son of my father's childhood best friend. I was even more surprised to learn what we would be doing over the next eight months.

'These flies are indigenous,' he said, pointing to a small colony of tiny flies in a flask with agar. 'Whereas these flies…' he pointed to a second flask, 'have been flown in from England. Our task is to determine whether they can talk to each other or not.'

I would probably have swallowed the flies in my gaping mouth if any of them had escaped from their little bottles of agar. Surely, he could not be serious.

'It's very important,' he said defensively when he noticed my look of incredulity. 'We need to know if animals have different languages, dialects, or accents. This is likely to be the first in a long list of experiments in the next ten years.'

Over the next few months, as we played matchmaker to the little insects and observed their total inability to understand each other's courtship and the resultant lack of interbreeding, my decision not to pursue an academic career in Zoology consolidated in my mind. I had no desire to limit my exposure to the countless animals I loved in the way my doctoral mentor had. Doubtless, I could possibly have ended up looking after Siberian tigers, but it was equally possible that I would spend my career in a classroom. I decided to apply for a position at Onderstepoort, the Veterinary Faculty that was part of the University of Pretoria, a city an hour's drive away.

Chapter 16

THE LOWEST GATE

The only veterinary faculty in the Southern African continent was Onderstepoort, founded by Sir Arnold Theiler, who was a giant in the research and control of infectious diseases in His Majesty's Union of South Africa.

The original Institute had eventually fallen under the jurisdiction of the University of Pretoria, although most of the academia and students regarded the faculty as independent. A literal translation of the name possibly refers to a gate in the long fences erected to prevent livestock and game from spreading disease in the seventeenth century, before vaccination became possible.

I was fortunate enough to apply in the only year in which a double intake of students was admitted. Prior to this date, all applicants had to complete the first year in one of the other universities, but in 1979, they changed the system and admitted one hundred applicants into second year and a further hundred into first year. My younger brother Mark, as always, had a higher ability and was taken in without going elsewhere for the first year. I found myself in the unique situation of studying together with my younger sibling, a privilege I cherish to this day.

Among the students were seasoned farmer's sons and green town-bred individuals. The selectors had very little to use as criteria apart from an ability to score highly in exams, a fact that they were acutely aware of. In our first year, we were all put through a series of interviews to try and create a better system of selection. After months of work, the researchers came up with only one solid fact: Whereas the percentage of the general population that is left-handed is only eight percent, over 25 percent of vets are southpaws. The significance of this fact still eludes the academics.

Three of the young school graduates from the centre of Johannesburg arrived on the bus that took us each day between the Pretoria campus and the Veterinary Institute at Onderstepoort. As they walked around the grounds, the feeling that they should at least know a little about their future patients grew, even though lectures on actual animal diseases only started in the third year.

Together they leaned on the rails around a paddock in which a spritely young horse pranced excitedly as he watched a group of mares in the distance. The sex of the animals and the obvious machismo of the lone horse completely eluded the embryo vets as they ducked under the rails of the fence and approached the horse. Two of them patted the animal on the neck and then posed on either side of him for the third student to take a photo.

Without any warning, the equine subject leaned over and grabbed one of the luckless students with his teeth clenched on the tender skin of his neck and shook him violently. Fortunately, the animal's grip broke just before the skin tore, and the young man was sent flying, to land only a foot in front of the other two, who had taken off in a desperate sprint for safety. As they reached the far border of the paddock, they had to negotiate a large sign that someone had inconsiderately nailed to the post and rails.

The three tumbled through the fence and retreated even farther when their assailant charged and seemed about to leap over the puny barricade. Looking back, they were able to make out the large letters on the sign that read '*Pasop – Perd Byt*'. We would all become perfectly fluent in both

English and Afrikaans by the end of the six-year degree, in which the two languages shared equal prominence in lectures and tutorials, but most school leavers knew enough to translate the sign, which read 'Beware – Horse Bites'.

A breeding stallion, he was driven by instinct to fight other suitors as they reared and bit and kicked at each other. The three young men were fortunate in that he did not regard them as any serious opposition to his ruling as herd stallion. All three of them graduated and became very successful general practitioners treating domestic pets.

There were many chuckles on the bus back to the Pretoria campus that evening, as the three related their brush with death, generously allowing the rest of the class to enjoy their innocent ineptitude.

Over the heads of the other students, I noticed the demure figure of a late arrival, a young student from Zimbabwe who had completed one year at the University of Pietermaritzburg. Ruefully I watched as half a dozen more suitable males clamoured for her attention. None of them had a warning sign in front of them, and I doubted if any of them would bite, but from experience I knew that I could not possibly compete in the arena in which young couples sparred with each other.

Chapter 17

TWO BEE OR NOT TO BEE?

Living with other students at the Onderstepoort Vet Faculty was fertile ground for exposing people's eccentricities, and everyone had a few—apart from me, of course.

Anton was a powerfully built young man from Cape Town who came from German stock. He soon earned a reputation for spending long hours at the gym and even longer hours monopolising the bathroom each morning in his quest for masculine perfection.

The toxicology lecturer had briefly described a plant found only in Namibia that caused paralysis of the oesophagus in goats. *Vermeersiekte* was usually fatal, although some research had been done on using the human drug 'Nootropil' for treatment. Nootropil was formulated to help damaged nerves to heal.

Anton confided in me just before our exams that he had started to take the drug, and his concentration while studying had improved dramatically. It was a very unwise thing for an intelligent student to do. Unwise to confide in a fellow student, that is.

Breakfast for Anton consisted of natural yoghurt, sweetened liberally with honey. He produced the honey from his own beehives. I was fascinated by his tales, and the idea of having a whole army of little beings working to produce a valuable product was beguiling. Caring for the bees was a very demanding occupation but it seemed to me to be an idealistic symbiosis. When he offered to teach me the ropes, I was more than just a little keen.

As we surveyed a huge willow tree in which a wild swarm had made its home, Anton was careful to explain that the protective boiler suits, gumboots, gloves, hat and veil would keep us from being stung. Nevertheless, he added, it was important not to provoke them by rapid movements or by allowing them to smell our fear.

'Sweat and fear drive them crazy,' he said 'So does the pheromone each bee releases as they inject their sting. It encourages others to come and help.' I was beginning to have a suspicion that the B side did not always play fair.

I was also soon to come to know the sweet, almost perfumed scent that honeybees release when they have driven home their sharp little venom-laden stings.

We were togged up in fine style except for the veils, which we had pulled back in order to discuss our strategy. I was confident that we had not yet got close enough to raise the alarm. Anton had unfortunately chosen a swarm that was blessed with the ability to see into the future. They detected not only those who were scared but could detect those who were going to be scared.

I had not even entertained a harmful thought towards our quarry when a lone bee swooped down in a long dive, rising just at the end to land on my nose and, without a 'how-do-you-do,' stung me just on the end of it.

I was admiring the perfect flight of this little warrior when suddenly I felt first her six little legs attach themselves to my proboscis, and then it was set on fire.

I howled and beat the air futilely, completely forgetting the strict instructions to remain calm. The actions attracted a whole swarm of bees, forcing me to run for my life. Anton rocked back and forth in uncomplicated glee.

When I finally recovered and cautiously made my way back under the protection of the veil, I found that Anton had coaxed most of the swarm into the portable hive which we had brought along and was encouraging the last stragglers to climb up the side of the box with little puffs from his smoker.

I could see no bees on him, but I was obviously a magnet for their wrath, since clumps of them covered various patches on my protective clothing.

I soon learned that my armour was less than perfect. Each seam on clothing is subject to possible holes and with hundreds of little bodies earnestly searching for them, I soon learned where they were.

Despite being brand new, the boiler suit was soon penetrated by a few vindictive little beings in both armpits and, even more disastrously, in the seam joining the legs to the body. Even the gumboots proved less than perfect, as some of the bees that fell off me landed in the tops of the boots and with my frantic movements, they slowly worked their way down to strike terror into my very soul. It was a very eventful and painful afternoon. Anton enjoyed every moment of it.

We finally trudged off with our prize and I promised to return the next morning to clean up the debris we had left. The morning was to provide a further surprise.

In the early light, I came upon a little bird sitting on the branch of the tree, close to the hole in which a few desultory bees still hummed. At first, I thought it must be a bee-eater catching an easy meal, but it soon became apparent that it was still a little fledgling and a very sad looking little fellow, too.

'A little bird, fallen out of its nest,' I said.

'Two,' he replied.

'Two?' I echoed in surprise.

'Two!' He was very adamant about it.

'Two,' said a third voice and a second little bird popped its head out from behind the branch.

I soon realised that our efforts of the previous day had driven away the parents of these two little birds and they were clearly very distressed and hungry. It did not take much effort to catch them and carry them home in the folds of my now obsolete protective suit.

Although I had no idea what species they were, the longer beaks proved that they were not seed eaters and they made quick work of the concentrated recovery diet for dogs and cats, mixed with baby cereal.

Over the next few weeks, they grew rapidly and started to develop a colourful plumage. No matter how I tried, I could never get them to mimic me as I coached them to say 'one'. They were clearly an indivisible pair, two parts of a whole. They would always remain 'two. Two…two…two…two.'

They were very endearing little birds and would hop towards you, make their plaintive little call of 'two' and then cock their heads hopefully, as if waiting for a response. It never seemed to satisfy them if I mimicked their call.

I gave them the freedom of my room and eventually I let them out into a large Loquat tree just outside the house. For a few days they bounced around happily, catching the insects that came for the fruit.

Late one afternoon, I suddenly heard a raucous outburst of sound from the direction of the tree: 'Two-puddely. Two-puddely. Two-puddely. Two puddely. Two.'

I rushed around just in time to see the magnificent colours of a male, black-collared barbet sitting on the same branch as the two of them. A happy trio of joyous singers, finally finding the other member of the choir.

At each 'two' uttered by the little birds, the newcomer would reply 'pud-dely', the sounds so perfectly timed as to sound as if uttered by a single bird. They were ecstatic and shortly afterwards they flew off and I never saw them again.

I felt bereft. My two little ones had gone. I told myself not to think of it as losing two daughters, but as gaining a son.

Throughout Southern Africa I sometimes hear the distinctive call of these barbets and each time I wonder anew at the perfect timing the pairs show as they make a perfectly united call.

Anton enjoyed his mastery over me as a beekeeper. I recognised his experience, and we made several further trips to catch wild bees, but I was always conscious of our unpredictable impact on the wild.

His careless confession to me concerning the illicit brain-enhancing drug he was taking gave me a wicked idea. I photocopied a page from a well-known medical journal but blocked out the text of an article. Then I typed in my own version of a supposedly scientific warning titled 'The Male Feminising Side Effects of Nootropil'.

The fictitious author warned that it had been shown that a single dose of the drug would in every case result in men developing female characteristics as the years wore on. The only prevention was daily injections of a painful male steroid in a very painful site for a full ten weeks.

A lot of students earned a little money by working after hours for researchers at the Onderstepoort Institute. Anton did a regular stint for one professor each week, and the prof proved more than willing to leave the article near Anton's workbench and allow him to stumble across it.

Disappointingly it proved to be a damp squib. Anton seemed unperturbed and showed no reaction at all.

Then his brother phoned a week later in obvious agitation, and Anton was forced to reveal all. His sibling was studying pharmacy and had procured the product, not only for the two of them but also for an extended circle of male friends from the body-building class, none of whom were acting very friendly toward them just at that moment.

The entire group of gym members were considering a lynching, but the originator of their problem had been entertaining the thought of jumping first to make their quest obsolete.

Revenge, I decided, is sweetest when it has time to mature.

Chapter 18

ADRENALIN RUSH

In 1984, the Parvovirus that causes feline enteritis in cats suddenly began killing off dogs. A worldwide epidemic spread within weeks, with young dogs dying from heart failure and severe gastro-enteritis and dehydration.

The university realised that they had no facilities to cope with a pandemic. All the patients needed intensive nursing but admitting them into the wards was not an option. A clever solution was to convert a stable in the large animal hospital into an isolation unit with three portable cages.

Only select students on isolation duty were allowed in, and they were not allowed to go near any other dogs. Before entering, they were required to don protective clothing, boots, masks and gloves. They closely resembled the astronauts that featured regularly on the TV during that era.

The university surgery specialists frequently had extremely valuable bulls referred to them for surgery. Many of these were giant mastodons that held little respect for handlers or handling facilities.

To offload them as they arrived in farmers' trucks, they had two long ropes looped over their heads and six men were assigned to pull on each rope. As the bulls came out, they charged towards one group of men, who ran as if their life depended upon it. The men on the other rope dug their heels in and tried to slow the juggernaut down to allow the first group to flee. Frequently the bull would turn and charge the second group of men, and the roles would be reversed, with the first lot playing the role of human anchors while their colleagues ran for their lives. By directing the progress of the bull to some degree and partly by luck, the patient would eventually be manoeuvred into a holding pen.

Students got used to seeing these bizarre versions of tug-o-war charging about the campus. They rarely got used to the rush of adrenalin they felt when called upon to treat the bulls.

Four of us were assigned a Brahman bull that breathed fire and ate maidens for breakfast. The only way we could administer the daily treatment was to drop a loop of rope over his head and then thread the loose end through the door of his stable, down the passageway between the two rows of stables and then through the handling facilities just outside the huge sliding doors.

Three of us held the rope and ran with it when the fourth opened the stable while standing on top of the wall of a neighbouring one. The bull ran in tandem with us until he was brought up short by the strong metal bars of the crush pen. The same procedure was used to get him back into his stable.

On the fifth day, we had become a little blasé about the job and even the two women on the team were relaxing just a little. As the bull exploded from the crush cage, he tore the rope from three pairs of hands and charged down the passageway and past his door and on towards the end of the line of stables.

All thoughts of ever graduating fled in his wake. How would we explain it if this valuable animal ran off, or worse still, ran off with a couple of students impaled on his horns?

The farthest stable had a prominent sign on the door announcing: 'PARVOVIRUS – NO ENTRY'. The bull unfortunately could not read English. There was a protective plastic sheeting over the bars and the door was closed but the bolt had not been sent home. The bull unceremoniously smashed the door open and charged in, looking for his china shop.

Unlike the bull, all the students were bilingual in English and Afrikaans and some of them had a wider range of vocabulary than I did, as I learned that afternoon.

As the bull entered, a bulky figure exploded through the plastic sheeting covering the gap between stable wall and roof, cocooned in boots, boiler suit, mask and full-length gloves.

She landed agilely on the floor of the passageway and sprinted in full garb up the length of it. Not even the bull could compete, which allowed us to push the heavy sliding door closed just after she exited from the passageway.

The bull took no notice of the door, but hit it at full tilt, rocketing it off its hinges, and then charged off down the road.

Four students lay on the ground convulsed in laughter as the fifth one sprinted off in a completely different direction to the bull, who eventually circled around and made his own way back into the confines of the stable which had been his home for the past two weeks.

The following day we handed over our charge to the next group of students. Eyeing the bull warily, they asked if they needed to know anything in particular about the patient.

'Oh no,' we reassured them. 'Just give us a call before you get around to treating him. We would love to come down and see how you get on.'

Chapter 19

LIGHT IN THE DARK OF NIGHT

The long years spent in lecture halls, learning minutiae that often seemed irrelevant, were interspersed with small highlights that gave a glimmer of the future, although went nowhere near preparing one for the harsh reality of the outside world.

Staring through the window of the prefabricated hall, we would see senior students going about their work, handling, testing, and treating the patients we so longed to be introduced to. During the short intervals between the lectures, we would occasionally wander down to sneak through one of the large animal wards. On our first visit, we noticed a diminutive student dozing in the corner of a stable while an impressive stallion snuffled in his food manger. We assumed that an overworked trainee had found a place to hide from the rigors of a demanding schedule and was catching up on some shuteye.

As we started to walk away, the stallion planted both hind feet firmly on the floor and lifted his tail before ejecting a stream of pungent urine. The figure in the corner leaped to his feet and charged forward, arm outstretched to catch a sample in the little bottle he held in his hand.

A few seconds later the stable door swung open, and the tired student stumbled out, prize in hand.

'Stupid horse refused to pee for hours,' he grumbled as he stumbled down the passageway. 'Five years of study and I end up holding the bottle while a horse does his business.'

A few years later and we in turn would become very familiar with every brick in the wall of the same stables, but at the time we envied our future colleague his freedom to work with something other than the thick volumes of text and the interminable droning of the lecturers.

Our little group of four students was doing our equine rotation when four of the top racehorses in the country were offloaded and led into the medical department's stables. All were showing severe signs of horse 'flu, with streaming nostrils and puffy sinuses. Their personal value earned them a stay in our comfortable facilities until deemed fit to be sent back to the trainer's yard.

Under the tutelage of Johan Gerber, the equine specialist, we set up drips and began the exhausting procedure of recording every change they showed, however small it seemed. Sleep was going to prove elusive as we worked out a rota to make sure at least one of us was always present.

Of particular concern was their temperatures that spiked repeatedly, hovering a few degrees above the normal for equines. The referring vet had sent them through in alarm, after the domineering owner threatened to sue him for not producing a miracle cure to get them back on the racetrack.

For six days we slept in snatches, stumbled around in the dark stables, and changed drips repeatedly. In the seventies there were no patent intravenous fluids on the market that were big enough for a patient as large as a horse; instead, the medicine department had worked out the electrolytes required to replace those lost in a dehydrated patient and mixed up a formula which they packaged in little white envelopes. Purified water was sterilised in an autoclave and then poured into a sterilised plastic bucket and the powdered electrolytes were mixed into the fluid.

We worked as automatons, tiredly feeding the incessantly thirsty sterile buckets and administering a host of drugs either intravenously or in the powerful muscles of the horse's necks. It was exhausting but enthralling. We were at last doing what we had studied for so long. Except for us, these magnificent animals would never survive. Sleep was vastly overrated.

I noted that Mark was in a small animal group together with the attractive Karen and two other students, who both exuded confidence and regularly earned the respect of the lecturers with their stellar wit and sharp intelligence. For the first time since we started the course, I felt a faint tinge of envy towards my younger sibling.

There were other students who wandered the corridors between wards in the dark hours, tending to the smaller domestic animals or the magnificent bulls that came in for surgery. It was common for groups of students on different wards to barter with others to perform their nocturnal duties. Ashley was one of four students who were on out-patients, treating patients brought into the faculty by members of the public. Each night, two of them would man the after-hours clinic.

'Just give my patient an injection of amoxycillin tonight at 2 a.m.,' Lisa begged, smiling at Ashley beguilingly. He agreed without much thought. Since he would be awake anyway, a short walk over to the bovine surgery department to inject a cow would be no hardship.

At the appointed hour, Ashley strolled down the corridor of the stable block, past a dozen empty stalls, until he reached the three at the end that housed overnight patients. Number 28 was a darkly masculine shadow asleep lying down. If Ashley had been in full control of his wits, he would have hesitated at the realisation that the bull covered most of the floor of the large pen.

Opening the gate, he pondered the rear of his patient, wondering just how to inject the thick liquid into the bulging muscles with least effort. The bull was lying in a position that made it difficult to easily reach his hindquarters that were pressed against one wall. Ashley decided that he needed a bit of co-operation from his client and nudged his rear with a boot.

The startled bull leapt to his feet and bounced around on four stiff legs to face his unexpected assailant. Large, vicious horns were suddenly directed towards the student, who hurriedly backed off, only to find himself between the gate and the wall closest to the hinges. The bull lunged.

Only the fact that this ferocious animal was so well endowed with his magnificent weapons saved Ashley from serious injury. One horn thudded into the wooden gate while the other dug a deep groove into the paintwork of the adjacent wall. Ashley was trapped between the horns, with an angry pair of nostrils snorting retribution in his face.

A young, agile student is capable of a dexterity unknown to most of us. Ashley squirmed up the wall, using the slats of the gate and the coarse plasterwork of the wall for his boots to find purchase. He reached up into the rafters and pulled himself out of danger's way.

Unhurt but in danger of succumbing to shock, all he could manage to do was stumble back to the out-patients block and phone Lisa to come and deal with the dragon herself. He later went on to graduate close to the top of the class and became a renowned vet specialising in chickens.

The adventures in the bovine department gave the four of us in the equine department a little light relief but the interminable slog was beginning to take its toll. The temperatures of the five horses continued to reach alarming heights. It was with immense relief that we greeted Prof Gerber on the final morning as he announced that we could cease our labour. In fact, we should disconnect the intravenous drips and discard them immediately.

His suspicions had been roused by the fact that he noticed how the temperatures of the horses seemed to peak a few hours after each new drip was administered. Submitting a sample of the electrolyte mixture to a pharmaceutical laboratory, he was stunned to learn that the mixture had been found to contain pyrogens – factors that caused a rise in body temperature when they were given intravenously. Far from saving our patient's lives, we had been the cause of the problem once the effects of the initial equine 'flu had worn off.

It was a lesson to use our wits when we went about our work, rather than just blindly accept the current thinking of the experts, who were, after all, only one more opinion. Nowadays, whenever we take on young graduates, their slavish adherence to the training they were given at the respective universities brings back memories of just how wrong current opinion could be.

After all, who first thought that it would be a good idea to work through the night for a full week, anyway?

Chapter 20

CHICKEN MAN

Overhead projectors and chalk boards were the only visual aids employed by the teaching staff at the university. Professor Adams, although one of the more elderly staff members, took it upon himself to produce a short film of a postmortem on a chicken. It was a progressive step, even more progressive than he suspected.

As the only lecturer in poultry, he had earned the nickname 'Chicken Man' from the students. His course was not very extensive, but it covered the essentials required by any student who intended to specialise in poultry.

A small handful of graduate vets each had their own clients or, more commonly, worked for one of the very big producers. The usual protocol was to visit each farm on a regular basis to analyse any problems and try to resolve them. On arriving at a farm, the vet was made to shower and don protective overalls and sterilised boots. Transmission of viruses from site to site by unwary vets was a real danger.

The first task, once in the complex, was then to do post-mortem examinations on any birds that had died within the past 24 hours. With tens of thousands of birds in each house, there were always a few deaths.

If a lot of birds die, the producers will often find one that is showing typical symptoms or the same malady and sacrifice it for the good of the rest of the flock. Fresh samples with microscopic histopathology and culture were invaluable to the consultants.

It was a wet and miserable day when I slipped into the auditorium to eat my lunch. There were a small handful of other students with similar minds.

Chicken Man arrived with a projectionist and together they set up the projector and screen. They critically watched their creation and then nodded at each other with satisfaction. It was a creditable production.

Chicken Man signalled his intentions to his co-worker and left the room. The projectionist began rewinding the film onto the large spool again.

On the screen, Chicken Man grabbed the various organs and stuffed them into the open carcass, which he closed by reversing a stout pair of scissors down the breastbone. Gathering a handful of feathers, he replaced them on the bare breast and then lifted the hapless bird onto its feet and allowed it to wander about, walking backwards.

The students all cheered and clapped in delight.

Chicken Man's prowess as a miracle healer was marred only by the fact that the re-incarnated bird looked as severely ill as it had before the post-mortem and possibly would not have welcomed its revival.

Chapter 21

Treating Aphrodite

The pedigree Ayrshire cow had the unlikely name of 'Glenmuir's Gorgeous Aphrodite'. The breeder obviously had a sense of humour. We were to learn that Aphrodite did too.

Steve and I were treating the hospital patients in the large animal medicine stables when we became aware of the higher-pitched tones of young women outside. Neither of us said anything but our shoulders straightened, and our heads were raised as we made sure we presented a professional image to our audience.

The very first group of veterinary nurses in the country had reached their third and final year of studies. In a male-dominated profession, they were a disconcerting and yet enchanting distraction. Since only ten female student vets were admitted each year, they were vastly outnumbered by the ninety men. The young nurses helped to balance the overt masculinity of the profession in the late twentieth century.

Aphrodite needed her hoof dressed daily and the two of us led her out each morning to the handling facilities to secure her before attempting it. She had obliged without demurring every day of the week and we had no reason to expect a problem as she walked sedately out of her stall. We had not considered the alarm she would feel when suddenly confronted by a bevy of green-clad young women, all waving sheets of paper.

Steve suddenly found himself being pulled along the passageway joining the stalls as he manfully hung onto the rope looped over the cow's head. I rushed forward and grabbed the end of the rope behind him to add my weight, hoping to stop our errant patient in her tracks. The cow hardly faltered but instead continued in her headlong rush for the large open door.

The grouped nurses scattered in alarm as a large brown animal suddenly rushed into their midst, dragging two red-faced men who dug their heels into the turf, only to be pulled off their feet, stumbling along, at times on our knees, and in between gaining our footing and then tripping to fall almost prone on the ground.

Angry comments began to fly through the air when the cow suddenly realised she had nowhere to go and turned around to retrace her steps, still at a rapid pace. Steve and I were once again subjected to stumbling behind our charge, trying to duck our heads and maintain just a shred of anonymity, while the young women began to jeer.

Aphrodite ended up back in her stall and the two of us decided that the bandage change could wait until the nurses finished their practical session and returned to their lecture hall.

A week later, we moved on to the small animal surgery section and our small group of four was joined by the four that included both Mark and Karen. It stuck me that Karen had passed the selection board despite the limit on women being accepted. I noted too that she and a fellow student seemed inseparable whenever I stole a glance at the couple, occasionally catching them staring into each other's eyes with obvious emotion.

There was, however, little time to sit around entertaining the green Imp of Jealousy. The surgery department had a number of very different and distinctive lecturers but was headed by Professor Du Preez, who was very knowledgeable and very opinionated, quick to offer criticism and seemingly oblivious to the successful efforts of his colleagues or the students. We learned to avoid his attention.

Professor Van der Merwe had a far more relaxed and positive attitude, which proved fortunate for Mark. The surgery department had just taken delivery of a new electrocautery unit, delivering a current through a probe that could be used to either seal blood vessels or cut through tissue.

The Prof worked meticulously at preparing a fractured bone before applying a stainless-steel plate. Just at the last minute, a tiny artery began to spout a thin stream of blood onto everyone close enough to be involved.

'Cauterise it,' he instructed. 'Touch the probe on the artery.'

Mark leaned forward and pressed the end of the probe against the errant blood vessel, while standing on the foot pedal to complete the circuit.

What Professor Van der Merwe had forgotten was that he was holding onto an artery clamp and a needle holder, both shiny metal and both excellent conductors of electricity.

The current surged through the leg of the patient and through the unfortunate clinician, who yelped and shook violently but was unable to let go of the surgical instruments.

The Prof was fortunately able to join in the laughter, and tolerated the ribbing from his junior assistant, Dr Basson, who was demonstrating a common operation of that time, the amputation of a femur head.

When patients experience severe pain in a hip joint, removing the ball in the socket allows the leg to move freely without bones grinding on each other. It is a salvage operation but had given thousands of ageing dogs and cats immediate relief from agony. The development of synthetic hip joints would only occur years later.

'There are several ways to take off the femur head,' Dr Basson instructed, pointing to the exposed white cartilage covered bone. 'Using a chisel is very effective but you need to get the angle right and make sure you have the bevel of the chisel on the correct side.'

He continued to stress the point: 'You have to be a real Numpty to get it wrong, but I have heard of surgeons splitting the whole shaft of the femur along its length. As I say, you have to be a real idiot to make that mistake.' He spent some time positioning the sharp instrument perfectly and then picked up a surgical mallet to tap the end of the chisel, just as Professor Du Preez walked in.

'No, no, no. Don't do that.' Prof du Preez pushed between us importantly. 'You must never use a chisel for this operation. Last week my chisel went right down the centre of the femur.'

He grabbed the instrument out of his junior colleague's hand and then walked off, still offering advice as he left. Silence greeted his departure but many of the students were suppressing their smiles and even Dr Basson had caught the humour of the situation.

Later in the week, the self-important Professor was performing a particularly taxing operation. We were all clad in the prescribed long white trousers that always reminded me of pyjamas, and a tunic over our torsos. Hands were adorned with gloves and masks covered our faces. Halfway through the operation, Professor Du Preez' thin pull-on trousers sank down to form a sad little heap around his ankles. No-one moved a muscle; each student seemed to be concentrating fiercely on the surgery.

The Prof coughed a few times and his normally precise surgical technique wavered. No-one paid any attention to his obvious discomfort. Eventually he turned to Karen, the only woman in the room, and asked her to help him.

Over the years I have seen other surgeons have difficulty with the femur head amputation, but never again have any of them ended up half undressed.

I once saw a poster that read 'Be kind to those who you tread on as you climb the ladder of success; you may meet them on the way down.'

In the case of the Professor, he could have changed it to 'Be kind to those under you; you may need them when your trousers fall down.'

Chapter 22

MILK WITH A KICK

The degree course attracted a wide range of students and understandably, we had a fair share from farming stock. Many of them showed an extra degree of toughness bred into them by their inheritance.

Michael Barber was a wiry individual who had grown up on a sheep farm in the arid Karoo near Grahamstown. He had a ready smile and an endearing humility, until it came to the field of agriculture in which he felt, quite rightly, that he had more experience than most of us.

Mike had a natural athletic ability and each year he would romp home in the long-distance faculty run, without ever feeling the need to do any training beforehand. It was a sore point among many of the other students and staff who joined the daily run on the road outside the university. They dubbed the wiry young Mike Barber 'The Barber-ian'.

The need for a daily rush from endorphins created through exercise was experienced by many of the group of athletes, who longed for a release from the stress of the lecture hall or the operating theatre.

One gloomy, rainy day on which the heavens seemed to pour misery on the earth, Professor Castle, a prominent leader among the more energetic group, felt the desire for exercise very keenly. The rain bucketing down would not have deterred him had it not been for the speeding traffic on the road that sent sheets of icy water over anyone foolish enough to get close to the edge of the tarmac.

The Prof had an ingenious idea. He knew that the equine research centre had just recently purchased a state-of-the-art treadmill to put their horses through their paces and monitor the effect of a range of variables. He made his way over to the centre and begged the use of the oversized piece of equipment. The staff agreed readily, hiding smiles of malice as they showed him the controls of the machine. What they failed to let him know was that they were able to alter the settings remotely from a hand-held responder.

The unwitting prof started his run gently, allowing his muscles to warm up slowly. The speed of the treadmill seemed a little too fast for him and he leant forward to press a button on the control bar, but then had to sprint as he found the ground beneath him speeding up. Thinking he had pressed the wrong button, he increased his stride to reach forward again, but his finger never quite made it to the button, as once again the treadmill belt increased in velocity. Soon he was running at breakneck speed, desperately trying to keep his balance and avoid getting shot off the rear of the contraption.

The end was inevitable, and the poor man ended up in a heap at the back of the laboratory. Peering round in a state of exhaustion, he was surprised to find a sea of faces watching him from every angle, some bearing mild looks of anxiety but most of them on the verge of raucous laughter.

The group of students that included Mike-The-Barbarian joined Mark's group on the outpatients' rota. One of their tasks after hours was to feed a very young calf in the Gynaecology department. Strolling over to the block, they found the milk left out for them had soured into a thick lump of curd and sharp-smelling clear liquid. The infant patient had begun a plaintive calling for its mother, hungry after recovering from extensive surgery. The students were at a loss as to what to do.

Mike noticed three silent shapes in the paddock next to the stables and realised that they were all milking cows and from their shapes, they had more than an adequate supply of milk for the little one. He picked up a clean bucket and walked towards the perimeter fence of the paddock. No-one needed to teach him how to milk a cow.

No-one, however, had taught him the vagaries of an electric fence. As he put one hand on the top wire of the barrier, 8000 volts of energy coursed through his body, sending him reeling backwards in shock, his feet coming off the ground and the heavy metal bucket cracking him on the shins and then giving him a sizeable lump on his head.

The calf got its meal that night, but only after the other students had found and de-activated the fence mains supply. The cow no doubt must have wondered why the hands that coaxed the milk from her udder shook so noticeably.

Mike had a second brush with death a month later and again I was party to the event. Mark, Mike and I had taken to cycling to and from the university each day and foolishly, the three of us took it in turns to lead while the other two stayed just behind, allowing the slipstream to pull us along almost effortlessly. You can teach students convoluted biochemistry pathways, but they are unable to absorb the fundamentals of common sense.

A large earth-moving truck came to a wheezing stop from a side road that joined the road the three of us were speeding along. From his vantage point, he must have seen a lone cyclist approaching rapidly and he paused to allow the bike to pass, while looking the other way for oncoming traffic.

As Mark passed the front of the truck, the monster engine revved and the front grille caught my rear wheel, sending me spinning into the undergrowth. Mike was not as lucky; he came off his bike and slid down the road, touching ground every ten feet or so. Each landing elicited a yell of anguish that made me cringe in sympathy.

The truck driver took one look at the mayhem he had created and sped off as rapidly as he could. We never gave him a second thought but rushed to the aid of our willowy colleague, who was hobbling about with all four limbs at odd angles and multiple grazes oozing from every site.

We all made it through the course and none were left with any permanent scars, but in the years following graduation, Peter had an ear ripped off by an angry Rottweiler, Simon spent six months in hospital when he obligingly climbed into the back of a car to get out a large dog that was refusing to budge, Helen was left paralysed from the neck down after a horse she was working on reared up and then came crashing down on her, and Jeffrey died when he contracted Ornithosis from a Macaw he did an autopsy on. Sadly, Jeffrey's one-year old son also died from the disease.

Most of us bear the scars inflicted by our patients, but the physical wounds are often a lot more bearable than those inflicted by the patient's owners, who each carry the most destructive weapon known to man: the human tongue.

In a typical day, a vet will deal with fifteen grateful, caring people, a few who grumble about money, and one who is aggressive enough to destroy any vestige of faith in humanity. In the early hours of the night, only the viciously nasty individual remains in the subconscious, and the effects can last for years.

Chapter 23

THE HEART OF THE MATTER

The Faculty of Veterinary Science at Onderstepoort had, for reasons known only to a few administrators, changed the admissions policy and in 1979 they no longer required applicants to have completed one year at another university. For this year only, they admitted a hundred students into second year plus a second intake of a hundred students into first year.

With the increased numbers of students at the faculty, the authorities announced that there would not be enough space for everyone in the dormitories and encouraged us to seek alternative lodgings. The thought of a university residence held no appeal, and I was quick to look elsewhere.

A friend of a friend knew of two elderly Italian ladies who spent each winter in the sunnier climes of Italy, and they were keen for us to house-sit for them. It proved an ideal situation for us and apart from the time their son arrived unannounced and found us trying to pick the lock of their wine cellar, not for the contents but for the challenge of getting it open, our stay was uneventful.

At the start of the second year, I learned of a small farm near the faculty, with two houses on the property, which was for sale. The property market was in a slump and the owner had gone insolvent due to a bad business decision. Mark and I twisted Dad's arm to act as surety and we were given a mortgage from the Standard bank to cover almost the entire cost. Spreading the word among the students resulted in ten of us moving into the two houses.

On our first day in the house, I was trying to hang a curtain over a window when, to my amazement, I saw two of the male students sprinting across the lawn, frantically pulling their trousers off as they ran.

Living with other students exposed us all to their idiosyncrasies but this behaviour went a little beyond the realm of acceptable. I ventured out to find out the reason for their mad race across the grass.

They had spotted a wooden kennel next to the shed that the previous owner had left behind. Since both owned dogs, they were keen to explore the possibility of a new shelter for their pets.

A faithful old crossbreed dog belonging to the previous owner had spent most of its life chained up near the kennel, acting as sentry to warn of intruders. The poor dog had obviously had a very severe infestation of fleas and on his departure, his little passengers had left behind thousands of flea eggs and pupae. Without a host, they had lain dormant until two unsuspecting young men appeared.

Warmth, movement, and carbon dioxide from an animal's breath are all triggers that cause immature fleas to explode from their pupae cases and jump onto a new host. The unfortunate students had suddenly realised that their legs were black from thousands of fleas crawling upwards. Modesty was overcome by horror and frantic activity, resulting in a flight of panic across the lawn, leaving two pairs of trousers halfway across.

The three female students who had joined us must have wondered if they had made a wise decision, particularly since they were outnumbered in the faculty by nine to one.

As landlord of the property, my studies suffered, not because I had too much to do, but because of the fact that I preferred running the tiny farm to spending hours with my nose in a textbook.

I seemed always to achieve a grade ten points lower than Mark did, apart from one memorable day when the reverse happened, and I scored higher than he did. The lecturers decided they must have made a mistake and swapped the marks over, so that he was awarded the higher grade. Mark enjoyed my chagrin and indignity for a day and then informed the incredulous staff of their error.

I never again scored higher than my younger sibling and in the final year, Mark was awarded the bulk of the prizes on graduation day. I was impressed beyond words, but I could not help thinking that the academics did not know what they were doing; this was my mischievous near-twin who had inherited more than his fair share of grey matter but was nevertheless still the boy I had grown up with.

In our last year in the house, a miracle happened in that Karen, the demure brunette from Zimbabwe, moved into a room in our house that had recently become vacant, together with a pair of budgies, a rabbit, a blind cat and a dog.

She was still being pursued by half the male students on campus, but she had chosen to share the house in which I was fortunate to be one of the half dozen occupants.

Karen had not been able to get any money out of Zimbabwe to pay for her studies and as a result had to work at various part-time jobs. I made the mistake of not cashing her cheque for the rent out of sympathy, and she reprimanded me sharply for it.

I saw very little of Karen, who had been placed in a different clinical group to the one I was in, but my chief delight was that the two of us were the only early risers in the house and I would often encounter her in the kitchen in the early hours, wrapped in an old pink flannel dressing gown. She never stayed any longer than she needed to make a cup of tea and retire once more to her room on the opposite side of the house.

The neighbour on the farm next door was a young part-time farmer from an Afrikaans family who had a good job in the city. Although we came from different cultures his affinity for all things growing struck a chord with me and it was easy to get to know him.

Hendrick proudly showed me his young Friesland cow that was in calf to a champion bull. He was expecting great things from the next generation once it was born.

Katy, a student a few years our senior, approached me to see if I would be interested in working as a nurse at a prestigious veterinary clinic in Sandown on weekends and during the holidays. I jumped at the chance. Regarded as the elite practice in the wealthiest part of Johannesburg, the practice had three vets and was one of the first clinics to employ a qualified nurse who worked on weekdays. They also had three Sotho men of varying ability who taught me more practical knowledge than we learned at university in the six-year course.

Of the three vets, only Dr Rose did surgery, which took up most of his day. Sophie, the nurse, would supply him with a steady stream of recumbent patients under the pacifying influence of barbiturate anaesthesia and the three assistants would then return those who had been neatly sutured up to their hospital cages and monitor them as they recovered.

The oldest assistant, a grizzled man by the name of Ganong, would invariably bring the patient to Sophie and hold it on the Prep Room table with one foreleg held out for the intravenous needle to be inserted.

When Sophie took a few weeks' leave, I found myself in the role of anaesthetist, a role I cherished but one at which I failed miserably at first. The elusive cephalic veins that run on the tops of the forelegs of dogs and cats seemed adept at moving out of the way whenever a needle was aimed at them. The harder I tried to pierce the wall of the vessel, the more they seemed to disappear.

After one harrowing ten minutes of struggling, I had to admit defeat and with slumped shoulders, I let go of the dog's foreleg and prepared to go and ask Dr Rose for help. Without any comment, seventy-year-old Ganong, still holding the dog with one arm around its chest, stretched forward with the other hand and neatly slipped the needle into the patient's vein, all the while coming at it from the wrong side of the patient. As blood welled out of the hub, I gratefully jumped forward and attached the syringe full of thiopentone.

I hardly felt any humility, but instead a wave of relief and amazement swept over me. Ganong said nothing but rolled the sleeping dog over on its back and began clipping the fur from its abdomen. No gratitude was expected but I knew he was aware of the respect I already held for him and the unspoken astonishment at his ability.

Working as a part-time vet nurse for three years, I picked up a lot of skills both through observing and by carrying out my duties. When we entered our final year at the university, in which we had to actually treat patients, I had a few unrehearsed moments of glory.

Entering the medicine ward, I was surprised to see seven students clustered around a patient on the table. All of them seemed intent on their subject. As I approached, the central figure stepped back and lowered his arm.

'We'll have to ask for a clinician to help,' he stated glumly.

In his hand he held a Teflon-coated Jelco catheter that he had obviously been trying to insert in the patient's vein. The number of angry little red marks on both forelegs of the dog made it obvious that each student had tried in turn.

'Go on, Stuart,' Mark urged, handing me a fresh catheter. A little apprehensively, I took my place in front of the dog and stroked his head.

'I'll call Doctor Francis,' announced one of the others, who made for the door.

I lifted the limp foreleg in front of me and slipped an elastic band around it just above the elbow. The vein was all but imperceptible under the skin. Taking a deep breath, I gently pushed the catheter forward and a bright flash of blood appeared in the hub.

Willing hands moved to help, but I disdained them all, instead attaching the end of the drip tube to the catheter and then taping them both to the leg with adhesive bandage.

The patient was hustled away into a hospital cage and the team began injecting, writing and generally caring for their charge. I stood and watched for a minute and then walked away, victorious and happy. Too bad we were never awarded grades for practical ability.

'Stuart has been doing this for years,' said Mark, and I could detect the generous pride in his voice.

Hendrick Swart called one afternoon in great distress, just as we had arrived back at the house. His prize cow had was dying from poisoning caused by a toxic plant they called *Tulp*, which translated meant 'tulip', although it is indigenous to the African highveld and contains cardiac glycosides which cause several symptoms, the most severe being cardiac arrest.

I rushed over, not at all confident that we could help in any way. Although there are drugs that act on the heart and others that help trap the toxin in the stomach before it is absorbed, once severe symptoms are apparent, the prognosis is very poor. Added to that was the fact that as students we had neither equipment nor pharmaceuticals.

Hendrik was deeply distressed. The cow lay on the rough lawn to the side of the house and to me it looked decidedly dead. We rushed over and examined it and then looked at each other. There was no sign of life at all.

We had all been given stethoscopes by the Eli-Lilly company as a promotional gesture. I spent some time trying to hear a heartbeat, without any luck.

'Is the calf also dead?' asked Hendrick.

I was about to answer that of course it would be, but instead made a show of placing my stethoscope on the bulging abdomen. Incredibly, there was a distinct, if faint, sound of a heart.

The look of delight and intent on Hendrick's face made me feel even more hopeless. How was I going to persuade him to accept the inevitable?

Instead, the reverse happened as he over-ruled my objections and pleaded for us to get the calf out. We had no time to think it through and found ourselves with sharp post-mortem knives at the ready.

Since the mother was no longer alive, we did not need to use anaesthetics and since we were not using any pharmaceuticals, technically we were not infringing any laws. Even so, the ethical conundrum perplexed me, and I could see it on Mark's face as well.

A few confident cuts with the ultrasharp knives and we were able to pull the motionless little body free. It was lifeless, and I felt uncomfortable at having separated it from its mother. Once again, I made a show of listening to the little chest and once again was astonished to hear a clear rhythmic beat.

We began pumping its chest and wiping mucous from its nostrils. There was no reaction. I could not detect any sounds from the lungs.

'They are probably filled with amniotic fluid,' commented Mark. 'We need to swing her as we do the pups after a Caesarean.'

Students are taught to support the little new-born puppies or kittens between the palms of their hands as they are delivered by the surgeon and to swing them in short arcs, with heads facing outwards, to expel the fluid in their lungs. It was not possible with a large calf.

I picked up the lifeless little calf by the hindlegs and swung it slowly around in an arc. A small amount of fluid streamed out, enough to cause all the others to retire backwards quickly, wiping at their arms in protest.

Exhaustion forced me to lower the patient to the ground after two full circuits about my head. The mouth of the calf opened fractionally, and it took a breath. Astounded, the pair of us managed to wipe away more mucous from the nostrils and to pump the chest vigorously, all the while being rewarded by a slowly responding little wail.

We left half an hour later, while Hendrick continued ministering to his miracle orphan, still pondering the events of the afternoon.

The calf survived and even grew a little in the following two months, but in the end, it succumbed to pneumonia. The weakened lungs and the absence of colostrum, the antibody-rich milk that mammal mothers produce shortly after giving birth, meant that the calf had no resistance to the ubiquitous bacteria that normally live in mutual harmony with all of us.

I did not feel that we had done it a favour by operating. Given the time to consider the options, I think I would have declined to interfere with the inevitable. Hendrick, on the other hand, expressed his gratitude that we had at least tried to save her.

Our final exams proved to be a nightmare for those of us who had introvert characters. They consisted of three weeks filled with sporadic trips to the offices of the lecturers to be grilled for half an hour or longer in the individual subjects.

When the list of students was organised into a timetable, I managed to trade my place with a student who did not want to be first on the list. I just wanted the agony to be over as quickly as possible, whereas he preferred to hear the questions others were asked and to prepare answers in the hope of being given the same thing. To my surprise, I found that Karen felt the same way as I did and had secured the tenth place in the queue.

We began to compare notes as we studied for each ordeal, and we found ourselves free very quickly after the start. I nevertheless found it incredibly tough and at times struggled to speak coherently when faced by two or three learned professors, probing to decide if we should be allowed to join their hallowed ranks.

The medicine department organised a system whereby we would each have to face three consecutive panels in turn, with a bell that rang each half hour to urge us on to the next panel. I waited apprehensively at the first door, almost beside myself with fear. The second door was next to the first and then there was a cloakroom and finally the third room of inquisitors. The three examination panels had large numbers stuck to the doors.

To divert my growing panic, I prised the number off the third door and stuck it to the door of the cloakroom as a joke. My intention of replacing it was interrupted when the bell rang and door one opened abruptly to allow a white-haired professor to beckon me inside. I forgot about my prank as I fought for my existence during the next hour and a half.

Leaving the final room in a state of shock, I was surprised to see the student second in line dutifully standing at the door to the cloakroom, waiting to be invited inside. He looked at me in amazement when I tore the number off the door and ushered him along to the next one in line. His protests ended when the door I had pushed him to opened and the examiner called his name.

Contritely, I replaced the number on the correct door and stole away, hoping that my mischief had not caused any serious harm.

The immense sense of anti-climax after each exam was difficult to dissipate. I tried to immediately throw myself into preparing for the next subject, but it proved impossible. I arrived back at the communal house and noticed Karen pacing about distractedly. She was clearly feeling the same.

The latest James Bond film had just been released and I diffidently suggested that we both go and see it. She agreed placidly and we spent the next few hours living the high-octane life of the super-hero, slowly allowing the tension of the morning to fade.

The ritual became entrenched and for three weeks we alternated between mind-sapping preparation, interspersed by short periods of intense trials, followed by a few relaxing hours at the local theatre. I was keenly aware that the relationship had two very distinct interpretations. I placed a much higher meaning on our regular visits to the cinema, whereas Karen accepted them as having little significance. She had broken up with her current boyfriend and decided that she was not interested in pursuing a new relationship at all.

Chapter 24

SOME OF HIS OWN MEDICINE

Students are not allowed to perform operations unless supervised by a qualified vet. It can be very difficult to get much experience before graduating, but we hit the jackpot.

The Vet Faculty was on one side of the main road and the Research Institute was on the opposite side. Many students took part-time jobs at the Institute in order to help put themselves through the course. One of the research veterinarians offered to mentor a number of us if we would neuter the growing horde of feral cats that roamed the Institute grounds. We leapt at the chance.

By the time we graduated, I had done several dozen operations, for which I was extremely grateful.

In our final year, we had to do rotations on various clinics, including a two-week stint at the Outpatient Clinic of the university. The procedure was for us to examine a patient and devise a treatment plan. Then we would consult with the qualified vet on duty and if agreed, we could go ahead with our plan.

A commonly used product was hydrogen peroxide, which bubbled fiercely if poured into a wound and looked very impressive. Today it is regarded as a bad idea since it actually kills off a layer of cells in addition to killing off the bacteria in the exudate.

Baster was a powerful Labrador crossed with a Ridgeback. He had shown off his power in a fight but had not come away unscathed. He had a small puncture wound on his rump, from which a small trickle oozed. I had suggested using peroxide and had been given the go-ahead.

Filling a 20cc syringe with the clear liquid, I pushed the spout into the small wound with difficulty. As I worked, the owner leaned over to get a better view. A hard push with the plunger sent the liquid into the pus-filled cavity under the skin. The peroxide reacted with the exudate and the resulting pressure caused the foul mess to squirt out, drenching the owner within seconds.

I stood back worriedly, wondering if I was going to receive a reprimand, but all he said was, 'Where can I buy some of that stuff?'

We were required to spend the night at the clinic to attend to emergencies, and only trouble the lecturers if a serious case came in.

A little after twelve, a dog was brought in with a nasty would to the leg. Two hours later, a ewe that was having trouble giving birth arrived. My fellow student, Simon, asked if he could do both procedures, aware that I had done a lot of surgery while working at the clinic in Johannesburg on weekends.

I was not really competent to act as a mentor, but pride kept me from voicing my fears and together we managed to do a credible job. The lamb was duly delivered by Caesarean section and the nasty wound on the dog was stitched up.

In the morning, Simon proudly displayed his handiwork to the clinician in charge of the clinic for the day and to our surprise we both received a stern warning.

'Closing the wound was not an emergency. Treating the patient for pain and shock was,' he angrily admonished. 'Forget the heroics. Do what is best for the patient at the time.'

He seemed a little more accepting of the successful Caesarean but again advised that we should have consulted someone more experienced.

The senior clinician for the day was a tall, willowy professor who had spent some time in the USA, qualifying as an international diplomate in medicine. He had returned to his alma mater and very quickly proved himself to be several decades ahead of the rest of the faculty.

I was presented with a dog in obvious pain. His owner had castrated him with a penknife and the wound had gone septic. Although I respect farmers deeply, having grown up among them, some of them can show barbaric tendencies.

I duly called the professor to get permission to proceed with treatment of the case and he came and examined the wound. Straightening up, he towered over the client and spoke with an icy fury.

'Did you do this?' The owner nodded. 'Did you use any anaesthetic?' The owner shook his head.

The lanky, aesthetic professor reached into his pocket and pulled out a penknife of his own. Unfolding the large blade, he turned to me and said coldly, 'Grab him and hold him down. We'll see how he likes it.'

The poor man turned an ashen grey and then sprinted out of the room in a panic.

I was tempted to laugh but one look at the fury on the face of the professor made me hold it in. Instead, I set about collecting the painkillers, antiseptics and antibiotics that I would need. The tethered dog watched as I worked, while the professor stalked out in anger.

Chapter 25

HOARSE WHISPERER

I suppose every student carries nuggets of wisdom with them that were gleaned from lecturers or clinicians they were privileged enough to learn from.

In our final year we were required to do two weeks at a time at different clinics and institutes. I was fortunate enough to be allowed to spend some time with the vets at Summerhill Equine Centre near the Durban racecourse.

On the first day I accompanied Dr Fleming as he made pre-race visits to a large number of horses due to race at the Wednesday meeting.

'We have found that blood potassium levels can be used to predict the performance of a horse in a race,' he instructed. 'Today we will take samples from thirty or so horses for analysis and any of those deficient in potassium will be given an intravenous supplement tomorrow.'

As we toured the area, visiting a dozen stables, Dr Fleming kept up a running commentary on the student who had been with him the previous week, a Rhodesian girl who had clearly captivated him. I wondered if he knew just how much she had captivated me, or if he knew that she had left a string of broken hearts behind over the past five years until finally a dashing young blade, who she had thought was finally the one for her, decided that he really only wanted the girl he had left six months previously. Karen had then buried her head in her books and tried to ignore the multiple admiring looks from many of the male students and several of the lecturers.

'If a horse is spooked at all, their potassium shoots up,' Dr Fleming instructed, returning to more serious issues. 'I will go in and catch the horse by its head collar, as quickly and as quietly as possible. You come in afterwards with the syringe and needle and when I hold out my hand behind me, pass them over.' I looked at the huge syringe and the thick eighteen-gauge needle and was grateful that it was not going to enter my jugular vein. 'Karen, the last student, was perfect at it,' he added.

The first horse was a magnificent bay, but Dr Fleming was unimpressed. 'Full brother to the reigning champion, but this fellow has never won a race and is unlikely to ever do so. Far too placid and uninspiring.'

Moving quietly on the balls of his feet, the doctor smoothly grabbed the horse's halter with one hand then held out his other hand for the syringe. I leaned forward just as his hand swayed and plunged the thick needle deep into his palm.

Dr Fleming screamed, his mouth inches from the horse's ear, causing the animal to rear up, ears flattened back on its head, with wide, frightened eyes. A string of invective poured out with words that neither the horse nor I were totally familiar with. It was an impressive tirade, and neither of us was to forget it quickly.

For the rest of the morning, I was relegated to carrying the equipment from stable to stable, but I never set foot inside the doors.

The following day I witnessed a scene that has remained permanently with me and has possibly saved me from serious mistakes a few times. A skittish black mare arrived at the hospital with a large round lump, the size of a man's fist, on the under-surface of its neck.

'An abscess,' announced one of the vets. 'They get them from splinters on the stable doors when they weave back and forth from boredom.' He went off to get a scalpel and disinfectants.

Returning a few minutes later, he had me hold the young mare while he lined up the scalpel blade and made a neat slash through the skin. I moved my feet, expecting a gush of foul-smelling pus to pour out, but nothing happened. Then an apple dropped onto the floor.

The lump turned out to be an unripe fruit that had got stuck in the oesophagus of the patient. The tragedy was that the continual production of large amounts of saliva prevented the cut from ever healing and the mare never made it to the racetrack.

I learned two invaluable lessons from the equine centre: First, always stick a needle into a lump to see what it is, even if it seems obvious, and second, never stick it into a colleague's hand if you want to retain their respect.

The first horse we had seen never did have his blood sample taken, due to the distress felt by Dr Fleming. We did however see him run two days later.

Dr Fleming had the task of examining each horse before they raced, but when he approached the bay gelding, its ears flattened once more and with huge eyes it began to prance about the ring, threatening to throw the diminutive rider off its back. It went on to win its first race, to the delight of its owners and dismay of the crowd, all of whom had written it off as a loser.

I found myself wondering if anyone had done any work on the value of screaming in a horse's ear the day before a race to motivate it to win.

I wondered, too, if Dr Fleming's potassium levels had soared the previous day. I could confidently vouch for the fact that mine must have.

Chapter 26

Uniform But Different

Every time I hear the opinion expressed by well-meaning parents that 'Everyone should be made to do national service. It makes a man out of them,' I cringe in horror.

National service dehumanised and destroyed. It was a breeding ground for drug and alcohol abuse and made a virtue of brutal initiation and bullying. The strong made it through and were often better for the experience, but the vulnerable were spat out as detritus.

As the new intake of young men collected at the station in Potchefstroom, we were introduced to the primary tenet of the armed forces: 'Hurry up and wait.' Eventually most of us sank down to the ground in exhaustion. The small group sitting in close proximity included a graduate who put his hands on the ground behind him and leaned backwards. A uniformed non-commissioned officer seemed to be waiting for his chance and stealthily walked over and then jumped with both boots on the unfortunate hands.

'Do you think this is a holiday camp?' he screamed as the injured recruit writhed in agony, tucking both hands into his armpits.

The humiliating depersonalisation began as each of us had his head shaved. Anyone unfortunate to arrive with long flowing locks was further humiliated by having half his head shaved and then had to return the next day for the rest to be removed. All clothes and personal items were surrendered and placed in a bag, while we dressed in a shapeless khaki overall and tennis shoes. It seemed to amuse the older troops passing out the kit to mismatch the items, forcing a hasty trade among the newer intakes as they swapped items with each other to get the correct sizes.

The enforced discipline and arduous physical training were bolstered by endless hours marching up and down the parade ground. It was six weeks before we were allowed our first weekend pass. No-one was allowed to have their own car or motorbike but had to be picked up and dropped off by relatives or friends.

The physical imprisonment we faced after years of striving to master both the skills and knowledge of an exacting profession was made almost unbearable by the knowledge that Karen had begun a very successful career in a top Johannesburg clinic. The partners had sung her praises on the few times I had visited, and she could spend hours talking about the cases she had seen and the clients she was growing to know. In the few weeks between graduation and reporting for national service, I made the trip through to see her as often as I could. She seemed to welcome a friendly face and since I passed a pizza shop with its own clay oven, I took to picking up two offerings to share.

It struck me how dedicated Karen was to both her employers and to her patients. Each evening we would have a quick meal and then she would return to check on the inpatients at the clinic, allowing me to tag along to help hold and restrain the more fractious ones. It was clear that many of her charges occupied a more prominent place in her heart than any suitor could hope for.

Wednesday afternoons were set aside for a sport of our own choice. Mark and I began a weekly long-distance run. During one of these excursions out of the camp, we realised that we could possibly find somewhere to keep a vehicle out of site of the camp and after a little while we found a friendly elderly lady who obligingly allowed us to park my little white Nissan 'bakkie', or pickup van, on her property.

Wednesdays became a day in which we could run out of the gate at noon, drive home to visit family and return to run in the gate just before evening rollcall. We also began to extend our excursions to weekends while the rest of the camp washed their kit or played sport.

Other servicemen tried sneaking out of camp through the back way, and several were caught and severely reprimanded. In contrast, we often passed one or more officers as we trotted through the gate and several times, we were given a nod of approval for our enthusiasm to keep fit.

Brian Watson surprised us by asking us to smuggle a canoe out of the camp. A medical doctor, Brian had very high ethics and was a man I came to admire intensely. His father was a missionary doctor in Swaziland, the small highland country completely surrounded by South Africa. Brian had grown up among the Swazi nation but was a South African citizen, and the government had put him through medical university. He felt duty bound to fulfil his obligations by serving his country in defending it, albeit as a medical officer. On his first weekend home, he was devastated by the way he was ostracised by his boyhood friends. Wearing the uniform of the South African defence force had not meant as much to him as it obviously did to his Swazi friends. On his return to camp, Brian asked to see the Commanding Officer and explained that he wished to be a conscientious objector.

The scorn heaped on him and the pressure exerted to get him to change his mind was intense, but he stuck to his guns, and he was eventually discharged from the defence force. As a result of his decision, he would be forced to work as a state doctor for six years, earning only the nominal salary that servicemen were paid.

Brian had yet to make his startling announcement when he asked us to get the canoe out of the camp. Mark and I donned our running gear, picked up the canoe and ran out of the front gate. Loading it into the back of the bakkie, we delivered it to the address given and then spent the evening at home.

At the end of 'Basic Training', we were told that we were to be transferred to Pretoria to do an officer's course. Our kit was packed, and we formed up on the parade ground, only to be told that due to civilian riots in the areas we were to travel through, they had decided to cancel the move to Pretoria, and we were dismissed.

The captain of the platoon was heard to remark that this was the perfect time for anyone to go AWOL, or 'absent without leave', since they had nothing scheduled for the whole weekend. To this day, I do not know if it was a test, but Mark and I took the bait and were out of the camp within half an hour.

Spending the weekend at home was an immense relief from the stress and boredom of the barracks. Seeing Karen was an enormous joy. She spoke about her work at the clinic in Johannesburg and the progress she was making, while I was spending hours doing nothing of consequence. I felt both an impatience to be finished with the enforced games dictated by politics and a rush of reassurance that Karen was doing so well.

At four on Sunday afternoon, we received a call from the camp. It was one of our fellow inmates, warning us to come back as soon as possible. The camp was moving to Pretoria after all. I suspected it was a hoax, but wiser minds urged us not to take a chance and we sped back to Potchefstroom.

As the car drew up at the front gate of the camp, we could see the long line of trucks, engines running, all ready to depart. Together we sprinted in, both still in civilian clothes and ran up to the tailgate of the truck at the rear. Willing hands pulled us up the seven-foot into the back of the truck and we surfed over the heads of all the other men until a space was found for us at the front. Uniforms appeared miraculously and we changed as the trucks sped off to the capital.

Slowly the full extent of the lengths to which our friends had gone became apparent. When the announcement was made to disembark, each soldier was made to present his rifle to the quartermaster and show his identity document to prove who he was. Anyone found to be missing would not be allowed to do the officer's course.

Our colleagues dug through our bergens and found our identity books. Danie Beytel, a medical doctor, risked both his military promotion and a smear on his medical career by presenting himself with my rifle and my identity. I never saw Danie again, since the medics and the vets parted ways after basic training, but over the years I have often thought back to the huge risk he took and the enormous gratitude I still feel for him. Danie, if you read this, please contact me.

The trip to Pretoria held no further surprises and we eventually tumbled out of the trucks and lined up to claim a bed in the officers' training quarters, a white band attached to each shoulder strap to signify that we were aiming to have it replaced by the two stars of a lieutenant.

Chapter 27

A.M.Bush

At the ages of four and six, respectively, Mark and I were experts at warfare. There was no-one who could defeat us.

I had found a plank that had split diagonally in an uneven pattern, one half of which resembled a rifle with broad stock narrowing down to a barrel. A nail served as the foresight and a second one, which bent obligingly when I hammered it in, made a perfect trigger. The rifle was deadly accurate and best of all, never needed to be reloaded.

Tennis ball-sized lumps of clay, hardened in the sun, bounced and shattered when thrown at the enemy, the pieces shooting up to resemble a minor explosion. We alone could hear the noise of battle even if no-one else could. We were merciless victors, and we never lost a war.

Mom spoilt it all by insisting that we include little sister Sharon in our games. It was a travesty. What did girls know about fighting? A wise general, however, knows when to fight and when to walk away. We had no hope of victory against such partisan maternal authority. Mom was a superior power. Sharon joined the ranks, but she had no weapon, so she would not be a consideration in our planning. She promised, however, to provide her own armoury.

The ground behind the house rose sharply in a low bank, perfect for surprise attacks on unwary enemy patrols. Mark and I decimated the ranks with our grenades and then laid down a withering hail of bullets. Victory was almost ours when a small figure scrambled up the bank with a garden spade twice her size and began to viciously decapitate the soldiers with sharp chops to the neck and bloodthirsty yells.

We froze, slightly horrified at the unwarranted violence and gore. As the youngest soldier returned to her position, we looked at each other with horror and decided we did not want to play anymore. She was frightening us.

Twenty years later, we found ourselves in uniform and once again playing the same games as we were subjected to the misery of 'Basic Training' during our compulsory military service. The officers this time were not as experienced as we had been, and we certainly did not have any spade-wielding women on our side. The game was just as serious though.

The enemy had surprised us in an ambush, or so we were told. The protocol was to drop down on our haunches and all shout in unison, 'Hurk! Lokanval!' For some reason all commands in the army were in Afrikaans, a far more expressive language than English.

The Bren machine gun operator would then take off with two compatriots and run at right angles to the enemy. The rest of the patrol would do the same, only going to the opposite side of them. Once the Bren machine-gunner had covered several hundred yards, he dropped to the ground and began spraying the enemy with bullets, giving the other arm of the patrol a chance to outflank them. The enemy, we were told, was to be a large rock in the far distance.

I could have taught the lieutenant a few things. First, enemy rocks were a lot smarter than he imagined and did not always play fair, and second, the rock he had chosen had a side at 45 degrees to us.

For some reason the lieutenant decided that I should carry the Bren gun and as a result I was sent sprinting off into the veld, bravely dodging the enemy bullets. Out of breath, I crouched down and began shooting at the lump of granite in the distance.

I have never been good at team sports, largely because once I get the ball, I am totally unaware of where the rest of my team are, and I fail to pass it on effectively. It was the same with the game we were playing against the rock. I was vaguely conscious of someone shouting off to the left of us, but my job was to annihilate the enemy, not pay any attention to distractions.

It was only when two pairs of rough hands grabbed the Bren gun from me and pulled me roughly away from my quest that I realised that something was wrong.

'Your bullets are hitting the rock,' they shouted in my ear.

'I was told to aim for it,' I protested.

The lieutenant lifted an arm and pointed angrily in the direction from which we had just run. 'Your bullets are ricocheting at the rest of the men. If you carry on, there is a good chance of some of them getting hit.'

In the distance I could just make out a crowd of soldiers hugging the ground, while others behind them were running for their lives.

I smiled in delight and then quickly composed my face at the scowl from the lieutenant. He was no doubt thinking of the repercussions if one of his men put several of the others in hospital or even worse. Mollified, I followed him sedately back to the rest of the patrol.

A month later, we got our own back on the enemy rock, or so we planned. The officers led us out into the veld, supposedly to lay an ambush of our own. I wondered if a large rock with a sense of humour might walk into our trap but in fact it soon became obvious that the purpose of the exercise was purely to make us endure another form of hardship, with little pretence of teaching any skill.

The commanding officer chose a night with a forecast of heavy rain. Three hundred and fifty soldiers were led out into the bush and arrayed in a huge semi-circle. Made to lie down facing the centre of the circle, we were instructed to stay motionless and silent until a flare and thunderflash were set off, at which time everyone would shoot an entire clip of rounds at the flare.

The evening dragged on, punctuated only by light showers of rain, but the thick black cloud that obscured the moon and the stars threatened a far heavier downpour. The officers were undoubtedly going to make us lie motionless all night, only triggering the attack in the early hours, once we had experienced the full lesson in patience and endurance.

I had been surveying a dense clump of bush a few yards in front of me. In a real ambush, I would not have been able to see the enemy as they approached. The bushes looked a lot more snug and secure and when the patrolling officers had moved farther down the line, I crawled forward and under the low branches.

The heavens opened up soon after I reached my haven, and I was grateful to find very little of the flood penetrated through to me. It was snug and warm, although still a little uncomfortable lying on my stomach. Slowly I drifted off to sleep.

At four o'clock, my heart exploded with panic when the flare drifted over my hideout, driven by the gale facing us and the sudden shock of bright light and the boom of the thunderflash was instantly followed by 349 rifles erupting in unison. If my legs had not been paralysed I would surely have run for my life and would probably have been mown down by a murderous hail of lead. As it was, I lost my rifle and had to search for it in a panic.

The cacophony had died off when I realised that I still had a full magazine of bullets and would surely be found out. In desperation, I pressed the trigger and the pitiful sound of a single rifle pattered away, hardly even resembling the massed roar of all the others.

'*Wie skiet daar? Korporaal vind daai donderse troep.*' The shout came from the dark as officers scrambled to find the errant soldier, but in the dark following the bright flare and the muzzle flashes it was impossible to see anything. I scrambled back to join the line of soldiers to the rear and then stood up among the milling crowd.

It struck me that I probably stood out as the only dry uniform, but since it was still raining, that rapidly changed. Besides that, someone with less control than I seemed to have relieved himself down the front of my trousers. There must have been a pool of it under the bush before I crept in.

If the commanding officer had been a medic, he could have found the culprit by checking everyone's pulse rate. It was a minor point. I had survived the night and slept most of it in the dry. Too bad my heart was still pounding away in my chest.

Chapter 28

MAD DOGS AND ENGLISHMEN

As students we were all vaccinated against rabies, since the disease was very prevalent in some areas of South Africa. Although it was rife in the Transkei, it had never been diagnosed in the sister state of the Ciskei. The vets nevertheless decided it would be wise to vaccinate all the local dogs as a precaution.

The extension officers did an amazing job in spreading the word about free vaccination clinics and on the first few days we were overwhelmed by long queues of patients. On the second week, not a single dog arrived. With a little patience, the extension team managed to find out that one of the dogs that had been vaccinated had died the following day.

This was serious, not only in terms of the safety of the vaccine but also relating to the confidence of the public. As word spread about the dog's death, every dog owner decided not to take the chance of losing their closest animal companion. The vet team set about tracing the owner of the deceased dog.

It took a few days to locate the elderly woman who had walked miles to the clinic for the vaccination only to have it die within twenty four hours. The bush telegraph had spread the news to the entire state within hours. We were keen to find out more and she was unperturbed at being questioned.

'Inja ifile izolo.'

I understood enough to know that her dog had died the previous day, but then I got lost as she continued. Linde translated for me. 'Mrs Dinigswayo says her dog died after the injection.'

'Tell her we are very sorry,' I instructed, 'Ask her if it showed any symptoms.'

The two of them exchanged a few sentences and then Linde turned to me with a rueful shake of his head. 'She says it was killed when it was hit by a car on the road as she walked it back home.'

The South African Defence force operated in the same way many military and street gangs do: Demoralise, humiliate and brutalise until personal identities are reduced to the primal building blocks and then re-assemble a group of men into a unit that functions as one. A key to survival was to preserve your individuality. This was easier said than done when faced with a commanding officer screaming in your face.

I had bought a camera a few years before being called up for national service and made the mistake of taking it along when enrolling. The lieutenant spotted it one day and asked a few questions, which I answered without any realisation of the dire consequences.

With the entire 350 soldiers on parade the following day, I was singled out and told that I would be the official photographer for the parade which the platoon had been training for over the past four months. I was both flattered and more than a little apprehensive. I should have run for my life.

While the commandant screamed commands at the exhausted soldiers as they marched, centipede-like, from one end of the dusty parade ground to the other, I was made to stand twenty feet behind him. As the hours dragged by, I began to daydream, drifting away from the harsh reality of two years in uniform.

The sudden appearance of the commandant's face in my field of vision as he screamed at me from a few inches away froze my brain and brought my heart to an abrupt halt. Spittle sprayed from his braying mouth and I could clearly make out the gold caps on two of his teeth. I thought wildly of the muzzles we used on vicious dogs and at the same time felt grateful that my rabies shots were up to date.

'Do you think you are not part of this platoon?' he screamed. 'Stand at attention. Who gave you permsission to slump like a @%$^&* ?' I straightened up but said nothing. 'Captain. Take this man's name and put him on charge.'

The spittle moved on and so did the volume. A younger officer curtly demanded my name and number, but as the commandant moved off, he shook his head and winked at me. I never heard any more about it, although I very quickly nearly found myself in far more serious trouble.

On the day of the parade, I stood stiffly to one side until a curt command brought me in front of the commandant and the dignitaries. As they posed, I levelled the camera and took the shot. The commandant changed places and put his arm around a second comrade, once again posing in front of me. I obliged and then had to repeat the action a number of times as he worked his way through the group.

I took the chance to change the spool of film in the camera while the officers refreshed themselves from a nearby table of drinks. They returned in a decidedly more jovial atmosphere and the routine of poses and clicks of the camera shutter continued.

The third roll of film was my last and I began to feel a little apprehensive. We were not allowed out of the camp and there was no means of buying photographic film inside it. The assembled crowd had changed and the commandant kept finding new subjects to be his compatriots in poses that became increasingly bizarre. Every now and then, they would sidle off to the liquid refreshments before returning again to model in front of me. I had no choice but to continue clicking the shutter of the empty camera, blanking my mind to the consequences as the long afternoon dragged out.

Gauging by the level of aggresion expressed when I was not standing at attention, I did not want to poke a stick at this rabid man by telling him I had no more film.

With the amount of alcohol consumed by my nemesis, I thought he would not remember a thing, but the very next week the captain of our barracks delivered the scarcely concealed demand for the photos. I had no choice but to explain the situation and he wisely reported to his commanding officer that the camera had failed after the first three dozen exposures.

I duly handed over the developed photos and shortly after that we were bussed out to a second camp before being assigned our posts.

I was born fifty years too early. Life would have been a cinch with digital cameras.

Chapter 29

THE ART OF WAR AND DIPLOMACY

For a platoon of qualified doctors, dentists, pharmacists, psychiatrists and vets to be grouped together under the control of unqualified but experienced army officers was a surreal situation. The latter group used harsh discipline and humiliation to great effect in controlling their charges.

In a country with eleven different language groups, the dominant tongues among the ruling white section were English and Afrikaans. Many were bilingual and even trilingual, being able to converse in the language of at least one of the indigenous tribes in the area in which they lived.

The unofficial language of the armed forces was Afrikaans, largely because members of this nation were more likely to go into the defence force, but also because it is a much more expressive, harsher language that makes shouted commands and expressions a lot more distinctive.

Misunderstandings nevertheless occurred. The word 'sit' has an obvious meaning in English, but in Afrikaans it means 'put'. The pronunciation is identical. Morkel, a highly intelligent university graduate, would find out how easy it is to be trapped by the parallel languages when he respectfully approached the captain of the platoon in the first month of our training. In deference to the three stars on the officer's shoulders, he politely removed his army helmet, a cardinal error in the defence force.

A corporal standing next to the captain jumped to the defence of his superior officer's honour by screaming at the unfortunate private, 'Sit op jou hoed!' (Put your hat on!)

The bewildered young man hesitated for a few seconds, causing the corporal to repeat the command with even more venom: 'Sit op jou hoed!' at which Morkel threw his hat upon the ground and sat upon it.

The two officers stared at the spectacle in front of them in bewilderment and then, as realisation came, two pairs of lips crinkled upwards at the corners. Strict decorum must be observed and the two managed to bark out a few more withering commands before hastily retiring to fall into helpless laughter.

Not so amusing was the high incidence of drug abuse among the servicemen as they struggled to cope with the endless pressure both physically and mentally. The psychiatrists were known to indulge in many of their supposed therapeutic products and would lag at the back of many exercises, in a dazed stupor.

The health inspectors, grouped together with the medical graduates, suffered the most. Isolated among people they did not understand, many of them found themselves unable to cope. Isak, a vertically challenged young man, was found in his bed having taken a hefty overdose of medication and promptly disappeared from our barracks, to be cared for by the professionals in the military hospital in Pretoria. At the time of his breakdown, all the conscripts were wearing a plastic helmet at all times. A few weeks later, steel outer helmets were issued, which would fit over the plastic ones; the steel supposedly provided more protection from flying metal, while the plastic inner protected the skull from the harsh metal against flesh.

When Isak suddenly re-appeared in our ranks, he unfortunately arrived just as we were summoned to form up and go out for a long run, in full kit including metal helmets. No-one thought to inform the unfortunate young Isak that he needed to wear his plastic helmet under his steel outer.

After a short period, I became aware of an ominous clanking that came from the health inspector jogging next to me. He was much shorter than all of us, but by ducking down, I was able to see that his metal helmet was lifting off his head with every stride, only to slam down again with a jolt. The poor man had just returned from the psychiatric ward and was now being subjected to treatment over and beyond the harshness dealt out to the rest of us.

I tried to draw the attention of the corporal to the situation, which resulted in a good deal of shouting in my face and then a similar treatment for Isak, but he was made to step out of line, and we never saw him again.

After our basic course, we were given a short officer's course and then sent out to our respective billets throughout South Africa. I found myself headed for the Dog School in the idyllic surrounds of Bourke's Luck. Site of a gold rush in the late seventeenth century, this isolated part of the Eastern Transvaal has a unique beauty, including the Blyde River Canyon with huge potholes, gouged out of the rock by massive boulders in the churning water during times of strong rains. The area is a favourite tourist destination for many, but for the five hundred servicemen trapped inside the barracks, there was nothing of interest to occupy us when given a short pass.

There were four vets assigned to the dog school and between us we saw one patient every second day. Within a very short period I became bored beyond words. Appeals to our commanding officer for a transfer fell on deaf ears. It suited him to have as many men under his control as possible. We worked a full day each weekday and half a day on Saturdays. Sundays were off, but we were expected to attend a church service.

The downfall of Apartheid was chiefly economic. The country thrived with its vast agricultural resources and mineral wealth. The industrial plant, Sasol, became the first unit in the world to convert the hydrocarbons in coal into more valuable petrol for thirsty engines. When Rhodesia and South West Africa both succumbed to international pressure and became Zimbabwe and Namibia, the economic pressures on South Africa increased, aided by the strict economic sanctions forced on the country by the rest of the world.

Our commanding officer was sent an order from Pretoria, demanding that he come up with ways to save money in a cash-strapped defence force. The top officers of the camp held a serious meeting and came up with a startling decision. Whereas up to now we had worked five and a half days and seen on average three patients a week, we would now see the same number of patients, but we would work six days a week. I decided that the enemy could dispense with their weapons; all they needed was to leave our decision makers a free hand and we would annihilate ourselves within a short period.

Given two weeks' leave from the defence force, I had spent many evenings visiting Karen in her shared accommodation in Rivonia, a suburb of Johannesburg. Since she was working during the day, I busied myself on my parents' farm.

Karen had kept her menagerie of animals with her throughout university and into her first job. The cage that housed two noisily happy budgies was becoming a little worn with age. I decided that they deserved a larger, more opulent home and set about making one from a plywood packing case. It was a thoroughly enjoyable task, and the result pleased me no end. I placed it in the back of my pickup truck and raced off to deliver it in time.

I had unfortunately not considered the vortex of wind that cascades over the cab of a pickup truck and swirls with some force in the open back. As I sped off, the lightweight box caught the full force of the wind and became airborne, flying out of the vehicle and smashing down on the bonnet of a police car behind me. Fortunately, the officer satisfied himself by delivering a stern warning about transporting unsecured items and the fact that he was at liberty to impose a heavy fine or even to make me accompany him to the cells at the police station. I would have been a lot more apprehensive had I not just survived the onslaught of fury from the camp commandant a few days earlier.

One of the veterinary orderlies had a pot-plant that succumbed to his inexpert ministrations and became a brown, dry stick. I noticed an empty drip bag and giving set that had been used on a patient lying on the table next to the unfortunate plant and stuck the end of the tube onto the broken end of one of the pot-plant's dead branches. The weak attempt at humour did little to relieve the boredom.

The following day it was announced that the entire camp would be subjected to an inspection by the commanding officer. The staff scrubbed and polished and we eventually had a neatly presented hospital unit. The inspection started at the far end of the camp, and we were left waiting for our turn, unable to do any work for fear of destroying the perfection created by our hard work. In the late afternoon one of the orderlies gave in to the temptation and got out a chess set and challenged me to a game.

I was pondering a complicated move when I suddenly became aware of a deathly silence about me. A second later a furious order was barked in my ear, and I turned to find the commanding officer towering above me, face red with rage at the site of a junior lieutenant playing chess when he should have been standing to attention for the inspection.

I endured a withering tirade, which was just beginning to abate when the CO noticed the drip attached to the dead plant.

'Who did this?' he shouted at the assembled troops and ten pairs of hands immediately pointed at me.

'Captain, put this man on a charge for misuse of military property!'

'Sir!' The captain turned to demand my name and identity number. I was told to report to the captain the following day, but on doing so, I learned that he had forgotten about the issue, and it was not mentioned again. My plant patient unfortunately did not benefit from the drip and was consigned to the bin.

In desperation, I put a telephone call through to the General in charge of the Medical Corps, using a phone that was made available to troops after hours. A junior officer took the call and reluctantly promised to pass it on up the chain of command. I shrugged in frustration, desperate to express my feelings at being kept idle for the duration of our miliary service.

The camp dentist was similarly bored to tears by his enforced inactivity. Whenever he could, he would find an excuse to make his way down to the veterinary unit for a chat. One morning, our entire staff were engrossed in removing a broken canine tooth from a guard dog. Trained to use his fangs if the need arose, this dog had snapped the tooth off by biting into a protective suit worn by a trainer who acted as a suspicious character to entice the guard dogs to attack. The dog handler reported that his charge was now ineffective since he would bite and then immediately release his victim, probably due to the pain from the broken tooth.

Veterinary dentistry had no answer in those days to the immense forces subjected on a dog's canine tooth, and conventional methods of repair had proved to be of little value. The current approach was to remove the tooth to relieve the pain.

The canine tooth of a dog has a massive root, three times as long and a lot thicker than the tapering exposed portion. It is an extremely difficult operation to remove and requires a flap of gum to be lifted away and the outer layer of bone to be removed with a dental bur. A single vet and a nurse could normally manage the operation but there was a fight among the assembled staff as to who got the patient to work on. In the end, we took it in relays.

Marcus, the dentist, walked into the clinic on the pretext of collecting developing fluid for the dental radiography section and was appalled to see ten eager faces with chisel and mallet, electric dental drill, and a host of smaller implements at the ready.

'What are you doing?' he demanded.

'Taking out a tooth.'

He surveyed the assembled crowd and shook his head. 'Let me show you how to do it,' he offered.

We took a collective step back and allowed him to take centre stage.

Clive caught my eye, and I could see the expectant humour buzzing. It was not every day that we managed to put another profession in the shade.

Marcus worked for several hours, growing ever more frustrated and bewildered. Eventually we took pity on him and showed him the X-ray of the tooth he was working on, a mammoth structure ten times the size of the human counterparts he was used to.

The laughter and jibes were taken in good spirits and Marcus suggested that he borrow our surgical chisel and mallet to use on Steven, a vet nurse who was booked in to have a wisdom tooth removed two days later.

'At least we don't give our patients a full general anaesthetic,' he remarked. 'We work at a higher level of skill and do it with only local anaesthetics.

The following day, I was summoned to the offices of the Commanding Officer of the camp, to find that the General's Adjutant was returning my call from Pretoria and wanted to know what was going on. I very quickly managed to convince him that I needed to discuss my role and was surprised when he scheduled a meeting for me to speak to the General the next day.

Replacing the receiver, I turned to see three of the camp's senior officers looking at me in consternation. 'What did the General want?' they demanded.

'He just asked me come down to speak to him,' I said nervously, wondering if this time I had overstepped the mark.

They watched me, unconvinced. 'You will have to tell us everything he says when you get back,' they warned ominously.

It was with immense trepidation that I reported to the miliary headquarters of the South African Medical Services, SAMS, in Pretoria. Fearing the worst, I was unceremoniously ushered into an office in which a figure sat in a comfortable swivel chair, exuding power. I expected to face a barrage of demands and was surprised when he began to tell me how his weekend had gone. He was clearly itching to share it with someone, although I guess he had already bored his junior officers by relating it repeatedly to whoever would listen.

He and his brother-in-law had gone hunting in the bushveld with several comrades in arms. His brother-in-law had proudly demonstrated his new, expensive BMW that had cost over a year's worth of his salary. That evening the hard liquor had been poured liberally and the campfire had burned late into the night. Eventually the group retired to their tents but sleep soon proved elusive when a hyena that sounded as if it were only yards away had struck up a chorus, laughing soullessly into the dark. The general had tried shouting at the noisy neighbour, to no effect.

The brother-in-law had finally decided he had suffered long enough, and he staggered out of his tent and let off a couple of shots with his high-powered rifle. The hyena decided he had met his match and kept quiet, at least long enough for the men to doze off.

In the morning, the General had stumbled out into the dazzling sunlight to relieve himself and was greeted by the sight of the new vehicle standing just to the side of the tents, but now sporting a jagged, round hole in the passenger door. When throbbing headaches subsided enough, the two brothers made their way to the far side of the car, only to find a similar hole in the driver's door. I wondered if the brother-in-law found it as amusing as the General did, but I laughed dutifully, amused but still full of apprehension.

Finishing his lengthy tale, the General seemed to realise that I had not come merely to appreciate his wit and demanded why I was there. I explained that there were four vets at the Bourke's Luck camp and that we only saw one patient every few days. I was desperate to be moved to a post where I could do something useful. To my horror, the general picked up the phone and called our Commanding Officer at the camp. This poor man, one rank junior to the General, but ten ranks my senior, was put through the mill, and had no choice but to confirm my statistics.

Putting the phone down, the General angrily denounced the system that could prove to be so inefficient and eventually said threateningly to me, 'You will be out of that camp before the end of the month. I cannot have you doing nothing for your two years' service. You have to pull your weight like the rest of us.'

Leaving the General's offices, I was amazed to see Marcus striding down the corridor towards the operating theatres. He seemed just as surprised and then more than just a little embarrassed.

'What are you doing here?' I asked.

'I brought your orderly down for an operation.' he said sheepishly. 'I started at 8:00 this morning and that wisdom tooth just proved impossible to remove. I gave Steven a hefty dose of local anaesthetic before starting but I have had to repeat it three times during the day. I just cannot win with the tooth. Eventually I bundled him into my car and drove down this evening for the surgeons to have a go here under a full anaesthetic.'

My mouth felt sore at the thought of the trauma the young soldier must have undergone at the hands of an inexperienced new graduate. I wondered, too, how much pain I would cause my patients as I slowly became more adept at the multiple skills required for our work.

My transfer documents arrived the day before Easter and as the Commanding Officer handed them to me, still looking decidedly suspicious about my trip to Pretoria, he commented, 'You have to get every department to sign off that you have handed back all equipment and they have no reason to detain you. It is already just about mid-day and many of the officers will already have knocked off and will be at their private quarters with their families. I am afraid it looks as if we will have you for the weekend at least. You can always leave on Tuesday.'

The general knew nothing of my desperation to get out of the camp and to spend the weekend in freedom. The lure of seeing Karen again proved irresistible. Some of the officers were surprised when I knocked on the front doors of their houses and explained that I had to get their signature urgently. None of them questioned it, with wives and children already enjoying the weekend in the background. By four in the afternoon, I was on the road and heading for sanity.

One of the final calls I made was to say farewell to Marcus, who looked decidedly downcast, not because I was leaving but because he had taken a look at my wisdom teeth the previous week and pronounced that I needed at least two removed. If nothing else had driven me to hasten my departure, the threat of finding myself in his chair again would have.

Chapter 30

CITY OF GOLD

Karen and Malachi were two of the four foreign students admitted to the university. They had overcome enormous odds to be accepted. On graduating, they both applied for a position at a progressive small animal hospital in a wealthy area of Johannesburg.

Malachi hailed from Israel, and he became a minor celebrity at the university. After he delivered a seminar on Salmonella in his final year, the Professor leading the course had commented, 'It has been an honour to listen to you, Malachi.'

Both of them were taken on by the two partners at the hospital, who then informed them that they were both going to take some much overdue leave. The two new graduates found themselves in charge of a busy upmarket practice. The fact that they coped admirably says volumes about the abilities of these two colleagues. I in turn listened to their exploits and itched to get involved.

Malachi later returned to Israel, a few years after working with Karen in Johannesburg. Five years later, I was vaccinating a dog belonging to a lady who had moved from Israel to South Africa, and I noticed Malachi's signature on the vaccination certificate. I commented that I knew him and asked if she'd had any dealings with him.

'Oh yes. He's useless' she said dismissively. 'He cut my dog's nails and made them bleed.' With such little thought, she condemned one of the most gifted and capable clinicians out of hand on a trivial criterium.

Now that I was stationed in Pretoria again, I was able to visit Karen freely in Johannesburg, an hour's drive away. It struck me how hard she was working, coming home to her shared bedsit late each evening and then returning at 9 pm to check on her patients. I wondered how long she would be able to keep it up. She had no life at all outside of work.

Her numerous talents did not, unfortunately, include culinary expertise. Not that she was incapable; she just did not put much value on domestic life when faced with a world of challenging and rewarding patients every day. I had passed an excellent pizza takeaway with a genuine clay oven on the road between the two cities and I took to ordering and collecting them on my way through.

Checking up on her patients late one night, Karen commented that in our final year at university, she had always felt as if she was second best. The three men in her clinical group had always rushed in to tackle any challenge and after they had mastered it, they stood back to allow the weaker sex a chance.

Mom had graduated *cum laude*, at the top of the university in her day and then gone on to become a teacher, but after a year in the classroom, she left to raise a brood of children. Her contribution to the lives of all her offspring was immense and in addition she effectively worked with a team of farm labourers every day, but at times she felt she had been relegated to third class. As a teenager I had made up my mind that any partner I ended up with would be treated as an equal or better. I silently hoped that Karen would be appreciated for her obvious skills and empathy now she had graduated.

Arriving back at Onderstepoort was akin to being released from prison. The Dog School at Bourke's Luck had been located in idyllic surroundings but the prospect of spending two years in enforced idleness was purgatory. At least at the university I would be practicing the profession I had trained for so many years.

I was further surprised and delighted to be asked if I and Stephen, a close colleague, would mentor the final year students doing their stint in visiting the farmers of the area. We were ecstatic.

Six months earlier, we had been students, desperately cramming information into our heads and frantically working all hours in the hope of eventually graduating. Now, we would be putting our skills into practice, while watching others, only a year younger than us, who were going through the agony of final exams.

It was a daunting prospect to act as mentor for some of the students, who were clearly a lot more astute that I was and would attain greater heights than I could ever aim for. The allure of getting out to the farms and putting our theory into practice was almost intoxicating.

Chapter 31

GOING THROUGH THE MOTIONS

One huge advantage of no longer being stationed in the middle of nowhere was that I could do locums on weekends. Given the opportunity to look after a well-established practice owned and run by Dr King, an elderly vet, I grabbed it with both hands. It proved to be a lesson I could not have learned at university.

Dr King showed me around and then made a startling statement. 'We have two assistants, Charles and Innocent. They will do any surgery, so you don't have to worry about that.'

I was taken aback. The two Sotho men seemed very pleasant and capable, but they were clearly not qualified. Perhaps I had misheard. I wondered if he meant they would prepare any patient for surgery.

On the first day, I walked through to the back, only to find Innocent garbed in surgical gown, gloves, mask and cap, busy with a scalpel and forceps. I watched for a while and was deeply impressed by his ability. I left, wondering at the need for six years at university to master the art I so cherished. I was also feeling very insignificant. If Innocent could manage a complex procedure without ever once attending a lecture, what did that say about the need to such extensive training?

Later on in the day, Simone, a Siamese cat arrived with an abscess on her face, a common problem in felines. Simone was being plagued by a Tom next door who liked to pick a fight. Cats' claws carry dirt from the litter tray or the soil outside, and when they penetrate the skin, they hardly leave a mark, but inject a load of bacteria into the body, which then rapidly grow and fester. Simone was going to need surgery to open the pocket of infection and allow it to drain.

I carried my patient through to the Prep room and gave her a tranquiliser as pre-medication for the anaesthetic. Innocent looked up from the surgery table to ask what was wrong with the cat and then walked over, still with a pair of forceps in his hand. Digging the tip of the forceps into the putrid infection, he grunted at the yellow ooze that spilled out.

'Yes,' he announced. 'It's definitely an abscess.'

Returning to his patient, he resumed his surgery, still using the forceps that had been pushed into the pus. I was staggered. Innocent had clearly mastered the mechanics of basic operations, and even went to the length of gowning up, but he had no understanding of the reason for aseptic technique.

My thoughts would be an easy target to label as racist, but I have since worked with many qualified Sotho men from the same tribe as Innocent and they would be horrified to hear of his actions.

I was still pondering this the following morning when I returned to Dr King's surgery to start another day. Rachel, the receptionist, let us all into the practice and then I noticed her picking up the seat of a stool from the floor and balancing it on its metal legs, before sitting on it. She saw me watching and explained:

'Dr King has a hang-up we have all learned to cope with. He had a breakdown when the practice very nearly went insolvent, and for a long period, his staff carried him. He had moved the business from the high street to an annexe at his home to save the rent and his clients did not all follow him. For six months he made a huge loss and ended up in hospital due to stress. When discharged, he was still the face of the practice, but the receptionists did most of the work in the front of the practice and his trusted but untrained staff took over the operations.'

They pointed out a lot of other signs I had not noticed, such as the surgical scrub brush that had no bristles left, the teacups that had long since lost their handles, and of course the receptionist's stool. Dr King was petrified of spending money.

I decided not to allow the assistants to work on any of the cases under my care, a move which they took with good grace and continued to be amazing in the work they did.

Chapter 32

PUT A SOCK IN IT

Mentoring the students on their farm visits placed me in a position way out of my comfort zone. Having only graduated six months earlier, I was now dealing with minds far sharper than mine. They had been selected as the top applicants from a wide pool of candidates, whereas I had sneaked into the faculty in the one year in which it admitted twice as many students. I was keenly aware of my more modest abilities.

Thirty years later I learned that most vet graduates are subject to the 'imposter syndrome' and I was not alone.

The overpowering feeling that we just are not up to the job is all too easy to believe. Being entrusted with the care of multiple species, keeping up with new techniques that surface almost daily, and trying to keep abreast of medications that change rapidly has a distinctly disorientating effect.

Having grown up on a small farm, basic diseases and conditions had been part of my early years and as with many farmers, I knew what to look for in a sick animal. I quickly learned that the superior minds that could recall the life cycle of a parasite that only occurred in fish in Siberia were often stumped when faced with the most basic of common-sense problems.

Among the most prevalent diseases in Africa must be those caused by the protozoan *Babesia*, among which are several species that affect different hosts. Cattle develop the disease aptly named 'Redwater', when infected with the Babesia bovis organism. The rapid breakdown of the red blood cells causes the haemoglobin to turn the patient's urine red.

Most farmers kept a bottle of one of the drugs that treated the condition in their fridge, a precaution that has saved numerous lives over the years.

The group of eight students arrayed around the drooping cow were known to be the smartest of the class and orbited in a stratosphere that I was no part of. I bravely faced the group and indicated our patient, inviting comment.

I had learned very quickly to put up a front by asking each of the eight students in turn what they thought of the case we had been presented, and then choosing the one that seemed most likely. So far it had stood me in good stead.

Our previous patient had been an ostrich with a long gash in its neck. I had been taught that to subdue this largest of birds, it was a good idea to put a sock over their head. One of the students volunteered their foot covering, and after a lengthy fight, we managed to get it in place and relaxed, expecting the powerful bird to give up the fight.

The ostrich had clearly not read the same books that I had, since it made no impression on him. The two students holding its neck had to fight just as hard to prevent it from breaking free and using its powerful legs to lash out at us.

In the end, we had to rely on a liberal administration of local anaesthetic to numb the area. Several of the students had jostled for the privilege of doing the needlework, but I was surprised in the end to find out how awkwardly the victor handled the instruments. I silently blessed the opportunity I'd had to work part-time at the surgery for three years. I had not realised that I had at least picked up some essential basic skills.

We managed after half an hour and several changes of surgeon to finally have one bird with a fairly neat row of stitches running half the length of its neck, like a zipper on a stuffed toy. The patient was by no means as ecstatic about the result as the six students were. Few of them would ever again be asked to deal with an ostrich.

The cow in front of us was even less ecstatic. It was, in fact, heading for an early grave unless we made the correct diagnosis and gave the right treatment.

'What symptoms do we have here?' I asked. All of them had been allowed to examine the cow.

'A very high temperature of 41 degrees, pale mucous membranes, rapid pulse and heartbeat, laboured breathing. The patient is depressed and not eating. The owner has noticed blood in the urine.' The leader of the pack was confident and accurate.

'Excellent.' I nodded. 'What are our differential diagnoses?'

The replies surprised me as one by one they offered possible causes of the red urine: 'Oak poisoning, Chronic copper toxicity, Leptospirosis, Post-parturient haemoglobinuria, *Brassica poisoning*, Bracken fern, Renal infarcts, Kidney stones, Rhubarb ingestion, Renal lymphoma.'

I looked at them in astonishment. I would have been hard pressed to come up with some of the possibilities that had rolled off their tongues so effortlessly. Ironically, none of them had mentioned the most obvious candidate.

'Er… what is the most obvious symptom?'

'Red urine.'

'And what is the most common cause of red urine in cattle?'

'Postparturient haemoglobinuria.' The red-headed student sounded as if there really could be no doubt of his opinion.

'She last calved six months ago. Postparturient would denote having given birth recently,' I commented.

The student was unabashed. 'It could be copper.'

I began to wonder if they were pulling my leg. Nine out of ten farmers would have known the correct answer in a flash. Were they being deliberately obtuse?

I thought back to the lecture delivered by an esteemed elderly professor who was known for his eccentric utterances.

'When you hear this ….' He commented, drumming with his fingers on the microphone, 'Think of horses, not zebras. Common diseases occur commonly. Eliminate the obvious first.'

The erudite collection of attentive minds in front of me was chasing after the zebras as they scattered over the plains. I tried another tack:

'What would you do next in order to work out what the cause was?' A simple blood smear would rapidly show up the little teardrop shaped paired organisms in many of the red blood cells. Any vet from Africa can make a blood smear, since it is so often part of the diagnostic workup.

'We could X-ray the kidneys. That would show up any kidney stones.'
'There's a test for Renal lymphoma; I was reading about it last week.'
'What about a urine culture?'
Exasperated, I decided they must be pulling my leg.
'Of course you all know it is Redwater. The clue is in the name.'
I looked around at the group, waiting for them to break into laughter at my expense, but instead, a few of them ducked their heads, abashed at their oversight. I was incredulous. Constantly living in the realm of the super-intelligent must make it difficult for them to function in a simple world.

I shook my head and set them to working out a dose of the drug required, but I made absolutely sure that they were capable of this mean task before allowing them to inject it into our patient.

The cow survived, the farmer was very grateful, and the average score in the final exams of this group was a good third higher than I had achieved. Many of them went on to become respected specialists, but I still remember the one time when the farm boy knew more than the cream of the crop.

Chapter 33

THE BIG QUESTION OF HOME HUNTING

Dr King had instructed me that if a complex operation came in, a local practice around the corner would do it for me. I bridled a little at being thought of as not capable, but I did not want to go against the wishes of my employer. I had grown to respect Dr King despite his eccentricities. When Rascal came in with an obvious cruciate ligament rupture, I duly called the nearby practice and arranged for the operation to take place the following day.

Dr Bryson was another sole practitioner and he welcomed me warmly but seemed a little put out when I asked if I could watch him operate. He agreed reluctantly.

I had noticed a huge jar of white tablets on the reception counter, with a label that read simply 'Salic'. The labelling regulations for medications today are very strict, but in the past, some practitioners got away with serious infractions. When I got the chance, I asked his receptionist what the tablets were.

'I have no idea,' she responded, 'but almost every patient gets a handful of them. Many clients swear by them.'

Dr Bryson made a great show of opening up the knee joint, and I waited for him to perform one of the several options we had practiced before graduation, and which I had assisted with a few times at Sandown as a student, but he seemed to ignore the vital structures I could just identify and after a while he merely sutured the wound together and commented, 'Sometimes all these joints need is to be traumatised and they then lay down a lot of connective tissue which stabilises them.'

Once again, I was staggered. I took the patient back to Dr King's surgery and the owner duly collected him. On discharge, he was handed a small envelope of antibiotics, and another filled with the white 'Salic' tablets. As I was leaving Dr Bryson's surgery, I had noticed the receptionist filling up the huge jar from a paper bag. I moved over and picked up the bag to read the ingredients. On the side of the packet, it proclaimed clearly 'Salicylic Acid 300mg'. Dr Bryson was giving all his patients aspirin.

I got the opportunity to speak to several of Dr Bryson's clients and they were all invariably deeply impressed by his skills.

'Do you know,' Mrs Gladstone commented, 'he just lays his hands on his patients, and they get better.' I thought she was pulling my leg, but several other clients verified her story. I struggled to accept that he had supernatural powers and felt convinced that his judicious use of 'Salic' might just explain his reputation. Perhaps there was not much difference between Innocent and Dr Bryson after all.

My feelings for Karen had grown to the point that I felt I was prepared to nail my colours to the mast. She, in turn, seemed oblivious of everything other than her all-consuming work.

Her parents had moved from Zimbabwe to South Africa, bringing only the very basic essentials with them under the strict emigration laws of the new independent state. With incredible acuity, her mother was managing to earn more than double our salaries through her work as an estate agent, and her father had just landed a job with Epic Mills as an international agricultural advisor. They needed to be near the airport in

Johannesburg and asked Karen to look for a house they could rent. She in turn elicited my help in visiting properties whenever she was free.

I had dithered for weeks making the decision and finally paid a visit to a jeweller and came away with a ring that cost half a year of my pitiful army income. I began to feel much as I had while standing outside the university professors' rooms waiting to be summoned in for a cross-examination.

Late on Friday evening, I nervously broached the question and waited even more apprehensively for a response. Karen shook her head in disbelief and then stated simply, 'I'll think about it tonight and tell you tomorrow.'

As I left her tiny shared flat, I hid the ring behind a hefty tome on *Anatomy of the Domestic Animals* on her bookshelf, praying that no-one would decide to read up on 'Viborg's triangle in the horse' before the following day.

'Don't forget we promised to go and see that house on Marlborough Avenue tomorrow at ten,' she commented as I slipped away into the night.

I am not sure if any of us got any sleep that night, but I had watched the hour hand of the clock as it made its tired, repetitive circuit around the clock until the early hours of the morning.

The following day, I arrived at the flat an hour early, only to be greeted by Karen, wearing a flame red dress I had admired on her in the past.

'It's a long drive so we better be going,' was all she said.

My buoyant heart sank slowly as we searched for the house. Was her wearing of the dress a way of saying 'No' in the kindest way she knew or was she immune to the feelings of a tongue-tied introvert who had not even known how to frame the question?

All morning we searched for our quarry and then dutifully followed the landlord of the house, as he showed us the extra bathroom and the sunny living room plus a well-established garden complete with a thatched garden room and tennis court. The family was bound to be more than happy in this up-market abode. I, in turn, was rapidly becoming disheartened.

Eventually the house hunting was over, and the family had listened to Karen's enthusiastic description of her findings, and she had signed the lease on their behalf. I wondered how I was going to retrieve the ring from her rooms and whether the jeweller would buy it back for a reasonable amount.

As we stopped outside her flat I said simply, 'I guess the answer is "No".'

She smiled and said, 'Didn't you realise that the dress was my way of saying "Yes"? I knew you liked it, so I chose it in honour of you.'

I shook my head as I took her in my arms. Would I ever understand the fairer sex? *Nothing fair about them,* I thought. *They play to their own rules.*

Chapter 34

STAND AND DELIVER

Horses and humans share the ability to sweat, unlike many other mammals. Horse sweat has an almost pleasant odour, whereas human perspiration has overtones of dirty socks that can be acrid and cloying. I came to experience both, one warm afternoon.

The five young stallions in their loose boxes rippled with muscle as they tossed their heads and snorted great plumes of moist air. Glistening coats and overt machismo, their testosterone-fuelled bravado was matched by the four students arrayed in a semi-circle facing me as I squinted into the warm morning sun.

'We'll walk them out over to that patch of grass under the big tree and knock them down there,' I announced in a voice that denied my inner trembling. 'You can watch me do the first one and then you can each operate on one stallion in turn.'

I spoke with a fragile confidence buoyed by the fact that I had gelded several stallions in the past. Although I had only graduated six months earlier, I'd had the good fortune of working as a volunteer for a charity in a deprived area and had been allowed to do a wide range of surgeries. Castrating stallions, though, still brought a rush of adrenalin to my brain as it tried desperately to remain calm.

Unless the young colts were neutered, they would fight viciously among each other, nature driving them to compete to be the herd stallion. Serious injury and even possibly death could result. Left to nature, only a few would lead successful lives herding a harem of mares and fighting off all opposition until a younger, more agile stallion arrived to challenge them.

Six months previously I had been the student, watching as more learned minds demonstrated the intricacies of removing the manhood of a thousand pounds of powerful equine muscle. Today I was the lecturer. I tried not to show that I was scared witless.

Kobe de Bruin, a powerhouse himself, destroyed any vestige I had of self-confidence by asking scornfully, 'Why knock them out? They do them standing at the race-track studs.' We all turned towards him, three enquiring minds and one feeling the panic rising.

'I did my equine rotation last month with Dr Baker down in Summerfield and he did dozens of them standing. The risks are lower, it is much quicker, and it is so much simpler.'

The four heads turned to face me. I would not call myself a coward but even I had my limits. There were some things I could not cope with. The censure of colleagues was one of them.

'We'll do them standing then,' I said.

I was no match for four aggressive students already competing for their positions in the world of veterinary professionals. I was, I admitted to myself, a shameless coward.

A month earlier, I had been trying to save myself from mindless boredom as I watched the six young servicemen who had been volunteered to be veterinary nurses sweep the clinic for the sixth time.

It was at Bourke's Luck that I began to go running each evening. Enforced idleness had the advantage of getting me to the peak of my fitness, a level I have never again achieved. My running companion was Clive Christy, a fellow graduate with superb skills and an endearing sense of humour.

Clive shared my frustration at not being able to put our hard-earned skills to work. We were hungry to hone and develop the six years of theoretical knowledge stuffed into our minds, translating them into practical application. Clive had begun a thriving voluntary clinic in the small towns that surrounded the army dog school, treating the animals of the local Sotho tribe. A young horse had been presented to him for gelding and Clive rose to the challenge. Although he had never done the operation on his own, there were enough willing hands to assist in holding the horse and he knew the recipe by heart. Three men expertly looped a rope over the horse's neck and tied it to a convenient branch, making sure it was secure and tight.

Clive drew up the calculated dose of the anaesthetic agent Thiopentone and managed at the second attempt to insert the needle into the bulging jugular vein on the neck of the horse, just an inch south of the rope. The horse rolled its eye, trying to see what was happening, clearly apprehensive but seemingly unaffected as the powerful barbiturate flowed into its vein.

This eventuality had not been discussed in our lectures. The stallion was not playing by the rules. He should have swayed and then collapsed, hindquarters going down first, while several men pulled hard on the rope attached to his head collar to prevent him cartwheeling over backwards and breaking his neck.

Clive remembered the instructions delivered by an earnest young lecturer, to repeat the full dose a second time if a horse did not respond. In all other animals, we increased the dose by increments, watching carefully as the effects became more obvious.

The second dose had no more effect than the first.

If Thiopentone is injected into tissues or leaked out of a vein that had been punctured, the strong acid of the product could cause large areas of skin and muscle to die off, turning black and shrivelling up. Clive was clearly in trouble, least of all because he was doing the operation as a favour and was unprotected by any insurance policy.

'Let him go,' he told the puzzled men holding on tightly to the fractious animal. Obligingly, they loosened the rope from the branch and the horse dropped as if pole-axed.

Understanding hit Clive with a wallop. The restraining rope had acted as a tourniquet. None of the anaesthetic had managed to reach the brain until they removed the rope that was compressing the jugular as it strived to pump blood up the neck. The operation was successfully carried out without further complication, but the patient was still groggy twelve hours later from the double dose of anaesthetic, much to the chagrin of the men forced to stay up all night to care for him.

I remembered Clive's relating of the tale and wished fervently for the powerful advantage of being able to render my patient asleep and unable to retaliate. Pride kept me from admitting it.

Kobe gave his very authoritative opinion loudly as he marched knowingly about the stable yard. Under his directions, we injected a single millilitre of Acetyl Promazine into the jugular vein of each stallion. I was sceptical; we routinely used a half to one ml in dogs and a quarter in cats. Surely the minute dose would not have any effect on the prancing, eye-rolling centaurs?

After ten minutes had passed, we filled two large syringes with local anaesthetic and injected it into the operation site. Maintaining close contact with the horse, left shoulder and head pressed against its flank, gave an early warning of muscles flexing before pandemonium could erupt, and being so close meant that invariably you would be pushed violently away as the horse gathered itself to launch a kick. This was the theory anyway. Since that day, so many colleagues have been seriously hurt by the powerful equines and many wear crash helmets and back protectors when working with them.

Once the local anaesthetic had been injected, Kobe made it clear that the surgeon had to retire for a cup of coffee. This presumably prevented anyone

from giving in to nervous impatience and operating before the operation site was fully numbed.

Kobe was the first to operate. I shamelessly allowed his superior knowledge to shine, and I accepted second place. A single cut into the skin and underlying tissues exposed the testicle, suspended by a thick spermatic cord, within which a thick blood vessel ran. Cutting this vessel inadvertently would cause death within a very short period. Past surgeons had developed a clamp which crushed the cord tightly and had a blade below the clamp to cut off the organ to be discarded.

To my amazement, each of us managed to successfully relieve his patient of its manhood and together we leaned against the pole fence of the yard and allowed the adrenalin coursing through our veins to express itself in excited conversation. Our patients walked about peacefully in a nearby field, no doubt feeling the effects of the operation, but it had been done with the minimum of trauma and we had taken every action we could to make it as painless as possible.

I began to feel deep gratitude that as one of five males competing to show our abilities, we had not had to show the same aggression that stallions were capable of, and we had not been subjected to the same surgical solution.

One of the young geldings walked over to the fence and stretched out his neck, nuzzling at my pocket, nostrils flared as he exhaled deeply, sniffing to find if I had any treats hidden in the overalls. As brutal as nature could be, she was also supremely forgiving when the aggression passed.

Chapter 35

Solomon's Folly

The slow-moving reptile on the branch in front of us was very thin. With the unlikely name of the richest king to ever live, Solomon looked like a pauper.

A detailed discussion with the owner revealed no clue as to what the problem was. Medical knowledge concerning the ailments of chameleons was still very limited, but from experience, we had learned that in many cases, transferring skills used in other animals could bring results in 'exotic' patients. Our knowledge was about to be increased by one more fact.

Few owners will pay for extensive diagnostic procedures on small animals, feeling that the cost should be relative to the size of the patient. I have often been tempted to point out that I am not small and I have a need to earn a living commensurate with any normal-sized person. I know I am wasting my breath.

Solomon's owner was prepared to pay for an X-ray, but this proved to be less than conclusive. We examined a stool sample to look for the eggs of worms or evidence of protozoal disease.

In the end we tried a number of drugs in the attempt to make a difference and finally the owner was forced to concede defeat and request that Solomon be allowed to end his suffering.

It was only as the final injection was being prepared that Karen noticed a sharp outline in his mouth. Another look at the X-ray made us suspicious that there might indeed be something hard inside the poor animal's mouth. It did not show up on the radiograph, so it could not be bone or metal, but it did seem to give the digestive system a peculiar look, with intestines in very straight lines.

After a long examination in the mouth it was possible to see something right at the back, in the pharynx. A gentle pull produced a plastic leaf, almost as long as the chameleon itself.

Solomon had not proved as wise as his ancestor who famously differentiated between real and fake flowers when a bee settled on the genuine ones. Solomon the chameleon had not been able to discern a fake leaf from a living one. Later we realised that the fault was not his. Spotting an insect on a leaf, he had used his prehensile, extendable tongue to shoot out and trap his prey on the sticky end of the appendage. The plastic leaf had unfortunately come as well.

Ever since, I have advised hundreds of reptile enthusiasts to watch out for this danger and peered into the mouth of just as many chameleons, but have never seen a repeat of this danger.

Solomon lived for several years afterwards and later came back to be examined after his wife, Bathsheba, bit his tail in a disagreement.

At least he had the sense to only have one wife, whereas his ancestor had a harem of hundreds of women. I was reminded of the advice given to my father-in-law by a Zulu colleague who was intrigued that he only intended to take one wife.

'Stay as you are, or marry three women,' he was told. 'Two will join together to give you a hard time, whereas with three, two of them will always be arguing with each other and you will be left in peace with the third.'

Chapter 36

DOUGAL AND THE DELINQUENT

Life, for me at least, seemed filled with promise as a newly married couple. Still only earning the pitiful salary of a national serviceman, I blithely assumed that things would run smoothly once I was demobbed and could start working as a private veterinarian.

Karen had resigned her position at the up-market practice in the wealthier part of Johannesburg and together we moved into a tiny cottage in the garden of a widow, close to the university where I was still enjoying the freedom of training final year students.

Finding a new job proved far more difficult than either of us had expected. I just accepted that Karen would eventually find the perfect position once they learned of her skills and charm, unaware that she was finding our limited income increasingly stressful. Eventually she accepted a post in a newer practice in the growing Western suburbs of Johannesburg.

I managed to come up with the minimum deposit for a small new-build in a neighbouring area, intent on starting my own practice. I felt that having spent more than the average time at university doing two degrees, I needed to really get going with my career. Plunging in at the deep end had both the advantage that I got to do everything and the disadvantage of not learning from older, more experienced minds, while still not set in my ways.

Karen's ability very quickly earned her the respect of her employer, who asked her to take sole charge of a brand-new clinic in an area that was still largely undeveloped, called 'Weltevreden', roughly translated 'Well Satisfied'. The owner of the practice, who had a larger branch in Helderkruin, closer to the more established areas, promised to sell the practice to her if she made a success of it.

As the houses multiplied and grew almost overnight around the practice, so did the clientele. Within a very rapid time, Karen was once again working all hours around the clock and thriving. I understood just how much her work meant to her and accepted the total dedication and unrelenting workload that dominated our lives. While she dealt with a heavy workload, I concentrated on setting up my embryo practice and finishing the last few months in uniform.

The law at the time dictated that we put up a brass plate and wait for the clients to find us. Large signs and advertising were strictly forbidden. I duly set aside three rooms of our house, nailed our plate to the wall and sat down to read endless journals while hoping for a client to venture in.

Karen, in the meantime, decided that we needed a second dog of our own. She already had Sindi, a crossbreed with an endearing habit of smiling as her tail stump wagged vigorously and then sneezing when her whiskers tickled her nose. Karen went off to the nearest rescue centre and returned with Dougal, a three-month old delinquent Ridgeback who seemed to have a dozen legs and yards of tongue. Dougal was enough to break any vet.

On the third day, just as I was settling down with a pile of journals, a furious uproar erupted at the front door. I leapt forward with valour and alarm, only to be whacked on the arm by a stout, middle-aged lady wielding an umbrella and an empty cat box, who was determinedly slashing at Dougal as he pranced about in delight.

As he dashed past, I hooked a hand under his collar and dragged him into the depths of the house before racing back to help our first and only client. The client was still at the front door, bristling with indignation and fury; the patient was nowhere to be seen. The empty cat box lay upside down at the foot of the tall eucalyptus tree in front of our house.

'Er … Can I help you?' I asked, not sure how to proceed.

The stout lady gave me a look that left no doubt as to her opinion of my intelligence and pointed up into the lower branches of the tree. 'Get my Florence down.' she commanded.

At the sound of her name, Florence chose to climb even higher into the leafy refuge.

It took a further hour, a precarious climb up a rickety ladder and a dozen scratches on my arm before Florence, a clearly frightened long-haired tabby cat in immaculate condition apart from the twigs in her fur, was safely back in the box. Throughout the procedure, Dougal shouted encouragement through the closed windows of the house, appearing in turn at each of the windows facing the front garden.

I took a deep breath and asked Florence's owner the reason for her call.

'I brought her to have her nails clipped,' she announced with heat. 'I don't think that will be necessary now. She will have worn them down as she climbed your tree.'

Client and patient stalked angrily down the pathway. I lacked the courage to ask for payment and besides, I did still put some value on my life.

Dougal had in the meantime started to devour the carpet in the hallway. He enthusiastically joined in the game of tug when I tried to rescue both the carpet and his intestinal tract from the consequences.

I had barely got the impromptu meal away from him when the doorbell rang, setting him off on another frantic bout of barking. In desperation, I locked him in the bathroom.

A florid man stood at the door with a cat in his arms. I silently uttered a prayer of thanks that I had managed to incarcerate Dougal before he sent another patient up our tree.

'My wife made me come,' the red-faced man announced. 'I told her to give the cat an aspirin, but she said no. Waste of money if you ask me.'

I assured the man that he had not wasted his money. Aspirin was a particularly dangerous drug in that cats are very sensitive to it; it could cause life-threatening haemorrhage. Florid man snorted but did not protest when I gently took the ginger cat from his arms.

I began possibly the most thorough examination of a patient ever and the results got me buzzing with enthusiasm. Simba had a heart murmur, but even more interesting was the fact that the pads of the lame foreleg were as white as his eyes. The paw was also ice-cold. The opposite foot had healthy pink pads and a reassuring warmth.

As I worked, I became aware of a disconcerting fact. Dougal was ominously silent. I excused myself and went to investigate quickly. The wretched dog had destroyed the bathmat, two towels off the rail and unrolled the toilet paper, which now festooned every surface on the room. He wriggled with delight at my scolding and tried to join in as I desperately gathered up everything moveable and then pushed him back into the room, but not before he had liberally lubricated my face with saliva.

Back in front of the increasingly suspicious client, I began to explain.

'Simba has a heart murmur,' I began. 'A murmur often means the blood flowing through the heart is sent swirling because of altered structures in the chambers. The turbulence can damage the red blood cells, which in turn set off a cascade that results in small blood clots, or thrombi. These thrombi can float freely in the heart or the larger blood vessels, but when these vessels divide into smaller tubes, the thrombi block the opening to the smaller vessel.'

My audience seemed unimpressed with my scintillating expose. I considered but quickly discarded the thought of digging through the journals to show him the article I had read only two days previously on this condition.

'Most commonly, the thrombi block the vessels going down the back legs, where the big aorta divides into two. Simba is unique in that the thrombus has blocked the brachial artery, in the foreleg. That is very rare.'

I turned over both forepaws in turn to demonstrate the bright pink healthy pads and the deathly white pads of the blood-starved right leg.

'What are you going to do about it?' he demanded, unimpressed with my explanation.

'Well…..' I hesitated. 'The ultimate workup would be to run some blood tests to see if any of the organs are affected, and it would be wise to arrange for a cardiologist to check his heart.'

'Waste of time and money,' he responded. 'What are you going to do to treat him now?'

'I would suggest both a painkiller and a blood thinner. Fortunately, there is one drug that will do both.'

'And what is this drug?'

'Ah, well… It has to be the correct dose and only given every three days. This will mean that the extrinsic coagulation pathway is blocked while the intrinsic pathway is preserved. The blood clots will be controlled but he will not bleed to death.'

'What is the drug?' he demanded again.

My voice dropped to just above a whisper. 'Er… Aspirin.'

He gave me a long look filled with disillusion.

'Not just any aspirin,' I hurried on. 'It has to be the 75mg tablets. Not the 300mg that people take, and it must not be given more often than every third day.'

He picked up Simba unceremoniously and walked stiffly to the door. 'Aspirin,' he muttered. '*&^%$$ aspirin.'

The door slammed behind him.

At the end of a harrowing first day, I looked sadly at the metal box of change I had so carefully arranged, and which was still in pristine order, untouched by the busy hands of commerce. I was not going to survive if I did not do better than this.

Sadly I walked through to the rest of the house, reflecting that the score to date was: Dougal – 2; Vet – zero. I opened the door to the silent bathroom, secure in the knowledge that there was nothing that he could have destroyed in the room.

Dougal lay in the bath on his back, as if enjoying a luxurious soak. In his mouth were the half-chewed remains of the bath plug, sticking out like a short cigar.

It was probably my imagination, but I am convinced that he winked at me.

Chapter 37

A THIRST FOR THE TRUTH

In the mild climate of the South African highveld, Dougal was expected to sleep in a warm kennel outside and patrol the garden to keep us safe. We unfortunately forgot to explain the small print in the contract when he arrived from the rescue centre.

Dougal loved everyone and loved life. His strong tail never ceased to beat from side to side and even the smallest noise had his attention instantly. Unknown to us, he had the reputation of being the life and soul of the party. The dark hours of night were filled with reverie as he toured the neighbourhood, rounding up all the dogs in the area and creating havoc. We slept on, exhausted from a heavy day treating many of his friends from their scrapes and bruises after a night on the tiles.

The first indication of his nightly escapades became apparent one morning when I went out to my faithful little car. I had parked my white Nissan pickup truck, or *'bakkie'*, in front of the garage, next to the garden wall. All thoughts of work were erased from my mind at the sight of a maze of brown streaks criss-crossing the windscreen from the roof of the cab down onto the bonnet of the van. I swore softly and meaningfully. Closer inspection revealed the obvious prints of a large dog haphazardly dotted over the vehicle. The grit and mud, together with Dougal's nails, had made deep scores in the paintwork.

Enclosed in the garden, he had found a way over the wall, using the van as a means of escape. Climbing on to the bonnet and then up onto the roof, he was able to hop over the wall. His return journey allowed him the thrill of sliding down the windscreen. He had clearly spent most of the previous night glorying in his newfound means of escape.

This was the final straw, I told myself. Dougal had committed his last offence. It was time for him to go, either back to the rescue centre or in a box. I'd had enough. Karen unwisely chose that moment to join me as we got ready to leave for our respective jobs.

'Have you seen what Dougal has done?'

Karen's face softened immediately. She would defend the devil if he had four legs and a tail. 'He's just a pup,' she said.

'Just a pup that has destroyed your computer and my van, to say nothing about all the other items he has chewed, buried or sicked-up on.'

Karen chose to ignore my anger, bending down to pat Dougal, who had rolled over onto his back, but we both knew that as dog parents, we were failing miserably.

Karen had left, together with her inseparable shadow, Sindi, before the first client of the day appeared. Mrs Blake pulled a reluctant black Labrador bitch behind her into the consulting room. Dougal announced their arrival with hysterical barking from the far side of the house. Attractive and well groomed, it was difficult to believe that Fiona Blake had two teenage daughters.

'Megan has suddenly started to drink enormous amounts. She has also begun to wee in the house, which she never did before.'

I smiled in relief. It was always so much easier when a patient had clear-cut symptoms, rather than the fact that they 'just weren't themselves.' Polydipsia-polyuria was a well-known syndrome with a string of twenty or so causes. A few simple tests would hopefully bring us to a diagnosis.

'We'll have to get a urine sample and test her blood to rule out the common hormonal problems,' I said as I checked Megan over. No temperature and all clinical signs normal. A faint smear on Megan's tail made me pause. 'When was Megan last on heat?'

'She hasn't come into season since you gave her that injection,' replied Mrs Blake. 'It was the best suggestion we had ever had – no more hassles with messy seasons and no cost of spaying.'

Her words made my blood run cold. Megan was the fifth young bitch to have developed signs of pyometra, a serious infection of the womb. The fifth to develop it three to six months after being given an injection designed to prevent her normal reproductive cycling. The drug had been hailed as a breakthrough with none of the side effects of the normal hormones on the market. Even the section on effects of overdosing in the textbooks glossed over the possibility of a womb infection.

'I'll just take some blood to send to the lab and then if you could collect a urine sample, I'll give you some antibiotics to start with while we wait for the test results.'

There was a fifteen-minute break between Mrs Blake and the next client, time enough for me to call the drug company that made the product. An enthusiastic young voice assured me that they had tested the drug thoroughly and were confident that the risk of pyometra was extremely low. He shrugged off the fact that out of twelve that I had given the product, I had seen five dogs develop the condition.

'Pure co-incidence,' he assured me. 'I understand that you only graduated a short time ago?' His insinuation was obvious.

'Pyometra is not easy to misdiagnose,' I countered.

'Our rep told us that you still only see one or two patients a day at your new practice. Perhaps with a large sample of patients a more accurate assessment would be possible.' *Or perhaps,* I thought, *most busy vets just do not make the connection between the injection and the condition, since the latter normally takes six months to develop.* Only the fact that I knew each of my small pool of patients so well had allowed me to link the two.

By chance, the rep from Coopers, the company that marketed the new injectable drug, was an old friend of mine and was coming around the following day to peddle his wares.

The developments in medicine occur so rapidly that it is impossible to keep abreast of everything and, although we had to attend on-going courses and lectures, drug company reps also played a key role in letting us know of new products and changes. They were also unfortunately adept in subtly manipulating the profession.

Marcus, the Coopers rep, brought his own cat in for a vaccination the next afternoon and we had a discussion on the possible side effects of his company's new drug that was being used extensively by vets all over the world. He assured me that I need not worry about my concerns.

'We keep a close eye on all reports submitted regarding our products, as you well know. We have not had many complaints at all.'

I decided not to use the injection again until I was satisfied that my fears had been groundless.

Five years later, Coopers was bought out by another company and ceased to exist. Marcus was among the casualties, his job evaporating overnight. A few months later I saw him again and he was quick to apologise.

'We are aware of the risk of pyometra developing in dogs, and coincidentally in other species as well. I knew it a long time ago, but we were instructed not to spread it about.'

His frank admission did nothing to allay my distrust of big industry. I should have known better from the start.

Chapter 38

GAURDIAN OF THE VULNERABLE

The birth of the Information Age enveloped us without our realisation. The media were hailing the new technology of microchips, and preaching that our lives would be altered forever. I could not see how they could possibly have any effect on us.

On graduating, Karen's parents had given her one of the first generation of desk-top personal computers. Karen's sister had been employed to sell the machines and seemed vastly knowledgeable about them, spouting words such as 'Basic' and 'Fortran'. Karen's parents felt sure that we would be able to use the new machine to diagnose problems in animals with ease. We in turn looked longingly at the cream coloured electronic gizmo and wished fervently that we knew how to drive it.

The cost of the new technology was not insignificant and, aware that her parents had put out a considerable sum to acquire the machine, we gave it pride of place on the desk in the spare bedroom intended for use as an office.

The new-build house was comfortably well finished and had a reasonably sized garden, still sprouting a forest of weeds, but enticing me to start planning and digging. The only downside was the heavy traffic. We had chosen the house because it was on the major connecting road between nearby amenities and a 'T-junction' faced our house with an side road leading off to an industrial area. I planned a prominent sign on the wall nearest the junction.

Although my new clinic was still only just ticking over, I put as much as I could into every day in the construction of the building and in setting up vital services and supplies. We fell asleep very quickly in the evenings, exhausted from the day's labour.

It was well after midnight when Karen sat bolt upright in bed and said 'What was that?'

I had vaguely heard a scream and then a loud thump, but the thought of getting up in the cold was unappealing to say the least.

'I think it must have been owls.' I commented. Two days previously we had marvelled at an Eagle Owl that soared effortlessly over our garden and then perched in some neighbouring trees.

Karen was having none of it and urged me to get up and investigate. I grudgingly complied, sleepily opening the door from the bedroom to the garden and stepping out into the crisp night air, hoping to be able to be able to return after a cursory look around.

The sight of a car's headlights beaming at me from the region of the T-junction jolted me awake. There had been a solid wall at this point when we retired for the night. The sobbing of a young woman drove all vestige of slumber from my foggy brain and I rushed over to the hapless car.

A young man, clearly under the legal age to drive and reeking of alcohol, staggered out of the vehicle and stopped me from going any closer. His companion, an equally young woman, managed to control herself and joined us to stand at his shoulder, sniffing loudly.

They both pleaded for me not to call the police and promised repeatedly to repair the damage, the young man assuring me that his father was a builder and would make good what he had destroyed. I took down their details and made no promises but foolishly did not get the authorities to record anything. Still only just older than the young and reckless, I felt a distinct sympathy for the couple.

I was allowed back into the house but Karen had a few scathing, if slightly amused, comments about the 'owls that had woken us up'. I noticed that her dog Sindi had been kept indoors while I had been sent to investigate, but I was not brave enough to comment on it. Dougal was nowhere to be found and we later realised that he must have been rounding up his friends in the neighbourhood.

A few nights later, both feeling jaded from a heavy schedule, we opened the door to the office and were greeted by the sight of the new computer, with chewed cables and a key board that had lost most of the keys. Canine teeth marks were visible on some of the keys that festooned the area. Dougal came to join the party and wagged his tail furiously at the sight of his handiwork until the sudden realisation hit him that he was not appreciated by all and he slunk off to hide in the kitchen while Karen tired hard to find it in herself to forgive him.

Although we had two dogs who had both been assigned the role of protector, neither seemed to take their job description seriously. Sindi knew that she could rely on her owner to keep her safe instead of the reverse and Dougal had an attitude that would have made the young man who used his car as a battering ram seem decidedly responsible.

A few months later, Karen once again sat up in alarm in the dead of night. Knowing better than to ask my opinion on whatever had disturbed her, she got up and padded over to the window without turning on the light. Parting the curtains a few inches she peered out into the back garden and immediately gave a small gasp.

'There's a man climbing over our wall.'

'Hurrumphh.' I replied and rolled over.

'Stuart, there's a man in our garden and he's walking towards the house.'

I rolled out of bed and cracked my shin against a cupboard. Holding onto the wardrobe, I stumbled over to join her at the window. Sure enough, there was a dark figure walking very gingerly directly towards us.

Bravado had less to do with it than a brain that had not yet caught up with the actions of my body. I unlocked the door and stepped out into the dark. Sindi made as if to follow me, pressing against my leg, but a hand shot out and pulled her back. Behind me I heard the ominous sound of a key turning in the lock. I suddenly had no means of escape.

The intruder seemed twice my size and infinitely more aggressive. His hands were held loosely at his side and I wondered if he had a concealed weapon with him. I searched fruitlessly in the shadows for the outline of any potential means of arming myself without any result.

'What are you doing here!' I demanded in a voice the belied my fear.

I have no idea what I would have done it he had produced a knife in response and charged. He certainly seemed to be unfazed by my sudden appearance. Almost reluctantly, he turned and trotted lightly back to the wall and was over and gone within seconds.

I followed his example and retired from the battlefield, but then had to suffer the humiliation of begging to be allowed back inside. Karen spent a few minutes shining a torch through the window to convince herself that I was indeed alone, before reluctantly unlocking the door. She pulled it closed rapidly as soon as I was in and once again made it secure.

'Why,' I asked, 'Did you stop Sindi from coming out to help me?'

'I did not want her to get hurt, of course.' Her reply carried a tinge of surprise that I should have to ask.

My position in the hierarchy had been made clear. Nevertheless, I did not have to share the glory of being the one who vanquished the foe with anyone else, least of all a dog who needed protection from the fair maiden about to be ravaged.

Chapter 39

SOUTH OF THE RIVER KEI

Karen gave all she had in developing the embryo veterinary practice in Weltevreden Park, and after a year it was bursting at the seams. The clients loved her, the staff sang her praises, and the patients responded with enthusiasm.

The owner of the practice offered to sell the business to her for a sum that left us gasping. Karen was incensed. She had created the good-will and had put the place on the map. Now she was being asked to pay for her exemplary work. She angrily declined the offer and also refused to go on working at the centre.

I was taken aback at the strength of her determination. It concerned me that she could be liable for costs if she broke her contract with her employer. Diffidently, I volunteered to work her notice period and surprisingly, both her employer and Karen agreed.

Woody, a friend who had been at university with us, rang to say that he was working in the Republic of the Ciskei and the little state was desperate for veterinarians. Karen was buzzing with enthusiasm, while I clung to my dream of a clinic in the wealthier suburbs of Johannesburg.

In the end I had to admit that it had been extremely difficult for Karen to find a job in a chauvinistic profession and my little embryonic practice would hardly support the two of us. The Ciskei government, in contrast, was offering an enviable salary for anyone willing to make the long trip south. I was no match for female enthusiasm and cold logic. We left our modern, newly built house and drove down to a promised state-owned bungalow that evaporated before we arrived.

With our worldly belongings in transit and due to arrive in King William's Town, we had an afternoon to find a place to stay in a town that was bursting at the seams.

It was late afternoon when we met Millie Tinker. She listened to our tale of woe with bright-eyed interest, concern growing visibly at our plight, before enthusiastically suggesting that we extend our search to include the small village of Kei Road, thirty kilometres away.

'The house next to ours is empty. It's prefab, mind you, and cold in the winter. It belonged to a bachelor so it's small and the water comes from a pond when the borehole dries up, but we love it out there among the mist and the farms.'

In desperation we agreed to have a look at the house. From King William's Town, the road entered the Republic of Ciskei and wound northward, climbing steeply until half an hour later it once again passed back into South African territory. A small border post had been erected on the Ciskei side after an abortive coup attempt by insurgents from the Republic of the Transkei, which lay even farther north. Tired and dejected, we were stopped by an armed guard and made to troop into a tiny brick building to show our passports and sign a logbook.

Just after the border post, a sign directed us eastward to Kei Road, a tiny hamlet forgotten by time. The roads were untarred, with pools of water collected in the crook of each turn bearing testimony to a recent shower.

The house was small and simple, asbestos-cement walls shedding strips of white paint into the untended flowerbeds. The view from the porch overlooked a small pond fringed with willow trees in which white egrets sat immobile, intent on the life in the water below. Green farmlands stretched away to the hazy purple hills in the distance.

In comparison to the house we had left in Johannesburg, the building was depressingly old and cramped. I watched the look of dejection on Karen's face for a moment before mentally accepting the inevitable.

The lure of the surroundings had yet to take effect that first day as we rushed back to King in order to sign the lease, and then it was back to the post office to await our errant pantechnicon.

The van never arrived. By seven that evening we decided to call it a day, trundling wearily back to Kei Road, where we unhooked a couple of curtains, under which we spent a very uncomfortable night on the floor.

The second day was once again spent in front of the post office until at two o'clock an unrepentant van rolled to a stop beside us. No explanations were offered, the trip merely having taken longer than they had expected. The driver was genuinely surprised at our agitation, following us in bemusement as we led the way to our new home.

The true character of the area only became apparent with the arrival of the moving van. Within minutes of drawing up to the little house, the townsfolk began to arrive.

"I thought you might be a little hungry," said Millie Tinker, carrying a tray piled high with the makings of a picnic lunch. A small crowd slowly gathered to welcome us or help carry furniture in. The contrast to the big city we had left, in which none of our neighbours had ever met each other, left us a little breathless.

The van and the crowd had departed when a two-wheeled cart drawn by a pair of oxen entered the street, slowly and sedately rolling to a halt beside our gate. A gnome-like figure hopped off his perch just behind the oxen to lift a garbage can, which he emptied into the cart. Flashing a gap-toothed grin at us, he cheerfully led his charges down the road to the next house, leaving us watching in bemusement at the combination of ancient transport and modern-day services.

The sun rested temporarily on the rim of the distant hills, turning the water in the pond a brilliant orange as a trio of turtles sent ripples expanding over the surface. Two horses came to the fence to snuff inquiringly at us, tossing their heads as we approached.

Ornate streetlamps from a by-gone era suddenly came to life, creating pale cones of light in the mist that faded before ever reaching the ground. Slowly the hectic events of the past forty-eight hours faded into insignificance as the ethereal beauty of our surroundings gradually revealed itself.

Chapter 40

FIERY WATER

Graham Tinker, our neighbour in Kei Road, was known to have a sudden temper, although he generally got over it very quickly and was not known to cause anyone harm.

As an estate agent, he joined forces with a builder and bought two houses in disrepair, with the aim of renovating them and flipping them back on the market for a quick profit. The two employed several itinerant labourers to help with the work and as tradition dictated, a flag was hoisted on the roof of the building. It would come down when the work was finished, and a party had been thrown for all the workmen.

The housing market unfortunately dropped before the entrepreneurs could capitalise on their venture. Graham was visibly upset but accepted that he could not expect to always win. His generosity and good nature came to the fore when he supplied the workmen with several cases of beer to celebrate the end of the project. Unknown to him, the weak liquor was fortified before the party with several bottles of strong, home-brewed alcohol supplied by a local *shebeen*.

Graham paid a visit late that evening to the two newly repaired houses to see that all was in order. As he neared the buildings, the raucous noise of the celebrations became obvious and then a glass bottle exploded on the pavement only a few feet from him, carelessly tossed by one of the workmen.

Pent-up frustration and anger exploded into action, and the diminutive man rushed in among the revelling crowd to demand who the culprit was. Several fingers singled out the hapless individual, sitting on a bale and watching owlishly. Graham grabbed a nearby roof strut and chased the rapidly sobering individual out of the house and down the street, managing to land a cracking blow on the top of his head before the longer legs of his prey outpaced him.

The speculation houses were sold just before Christmas, albeit at a loss, which Graham bore stoically. In the days before the festivities, a range of tradesmen and service providers knocked on doors, asking for their 'Christmas Box', and received gifts ranging from a few coins up to much larger amounts. When an unknown face appeared at Graham's door, asking for his share, he shook his head.

'Why should I give you a Christmas Box?' he asked. 'Who are you?'

For an answer, the stranger lifted his cap to show the neat little scar on the top of his head, left by Graham's roofing timber. The two men laughed, and the labourer collected a sizeable gift before leaving, no doubt planning a repeat act the next time the opportunity arose. A whack on the head was a small price to pay for a large sum and the friendship of an ex-employer.

Chapter 41

LOVE BEFORE LAWS

On our first day as state vets in the Ciskei I found myself watching through a window into an enclosed courtyard attached to the clinic in Zwelitsha. Two dozen young boys, ranging from six to young teenagers, were milling about in the yard, each one attached to a non-descript dog. In the corner of the yard stood a forty-four-gallon drum on end. At first I thought it must be a rain-water collector but Vuyu, one of the vet assistants, informed me that it was filled with an organophosphate solution, aimed at killing ticks on the dogs.

None of the dogs would have won at Crufts, but they had the unique ability to not only survive, but thrive in the harsh climate of the homeland, where other canines tend to succumb to the potpourri of infectious and parasitic diseases. Most were never actively fed, but scrounged the leftovers thrown out after family meals and caught small animals and birds to keep themselves from hunger. Few of them were vaccinated and even fewer sterilised, but to think of them as uncared for was a short-sighted view. The close bond between the people and their animals was vividly displayed that afternoon.

As I watched, the dogs were caught one by one by several boys and unceremoniously manhandled and dropped into the drum of liquid. A spout of grey inevitably shot upwards and drenched all the boys close enough, evincing a wave of laughter from everyone watching. It crossed my mind that none of them would have any ectoparasites.

One young boy hesitantly approached the door of the clinic and spoke briefly to Vuyu.

'He wants a vet to look at his dog,' Vuyu informed us. 'It has a lump under its tail, and it is bleeding.'

Doug, one of the vets who were shortly to leave the area, nodded and waited for the dog to be lifted onto the table. His fears were confirmed almost immediately.

'It's a TVT, a transmissible venereal tumour,' he announced. The mood among all the staff dropped noticeably.

This cancer is one of the few that can be passed from one dog to another. It was rife in the Ciskei and there was a concerted, if futile, campaign to eliminate it.

Vuyu dropped to his haunches and spoke to the young boy for several minutes. The lad began to shake his head and then to protest loudly. The message being relayed was that his dog had to be put down to prevent it spreading the cancer to other dogs. Doug was already busy filling a large syringe with Pentobarbitol to inject into the patient.

Tears began to flow down the face of the boy and all of us began to feel decidedly uncomfortable. Vuyu's tone became stern and yet his compassion was clear as he put his hand on the boy's shoulder. His words had no effect other than to increase the obvious distress in the young face. Suddenly the boy broke free and turned to run out of the clinic and up the hill. He seemed to have abandoned his dog and reason had triumphed, albeit a hollow victory.

Halfway up the hill, he turned, put his fingers to his lips and uttered a shrill, piercing whistle. His dog shot out of the hands of the assistants and off the table before sprinting after its master. The two of them disappeared over the brow of the hill and were gone.

Vuyu sat back on the floor and laughed in delight. The assembled staff erupted in glee. Rules had been challenged and flouted and not a single person cared. Tears and laughter were everywhere as Vuyu and Doug clapped each other on the shoulders and shook their heads in disbelief, amusement and admiration.

Chapter 42

SUBSISTENCE FARMER'S HIGH

The house in Kei Road place had been empty for a few months and the garden was a mess.

I decided to grow a bed of flowers just inside the front border, a post and rail fence that served only to keep the cows from the neighbouring small farms out as they passed by when herded to and from the common grazing land.

I bought a '*bakkie*' load of horse manure from a farmer, which infuriated Meg next door. She came over to complain that the 'pile of poop' was attracting flies and to keep the peace I dug it in the next day. Two packets of California Poppy seeds were sprinkled on top.

The seeds sprouted and so did every weed seed in the digestive output of the horses. I managed to pull out a few but they tended to uproot the poppies so in the end I left them.

Gloria, a maid who came to help several times a week, saw me kneeling at the flowerbed and politely asked if I would take her to town to visit the Optometrist.

'My eyes are getting really bad.' she said, 'In one week alone they have got much worse.' I readily agreed and duly drove her down to King William's Town and her appointment with the eye doctor.

The next day, as I was about to leave for work, I noticed that some animal had leaned over the fence and eaten a few of my poppy plants. I made a mental note to stack thorn bushes on the road-side of the fence that night.

That week, I was introduced to the 'Keiskammahoek Irrigation Scheme'. It was an impressive, multi-million-rand development in the fertile corner (*hoek*) where the Kei and the Kamma rivers joined.

In 1820, the British soldiers, returning from giving Napoleon a bloody nose, found that the industrial revolution had made their cottage industries obsolete and them unemployable. The British government had to come up with the solution to the surge in unemployment.

The Cape Colony in South Africa was plagued by raids from the Xhosa nation. The East India Company in essence ruled South Africa and persuaded the British government to send out hundreds of families to settle in the 'border area' and act as a buffer against the marauders.

Each family was given a plot of land, a cow, some instruments to till the land and seed to sow for the first year. They were not allowed to leave their farms.

Most of the settlers died within the first few years and almost all of those left ended up migrating to the local towns, where they contributed enormously to the history of the country.

The pen-pushers of Whitehall had assumed that anyone could farm; even an itinerant weaver could produce a crop from virgin land that had erratic rainfall and hostile raiders who slaughtered the livestock at night. One hundred and sixty years later, the greatly enlightened South African government decided to do exactly the same thing with exactly the same results.

A huge swathe of farms owned by white ranchers were nationalised and their owners forcibly moved off. Over a hundred Xhosa families who lived in an area the government had decided would be white South Africa were uprooted and settled in Keiskammahoek. Each family was given a small house, four cows, free veterinary and extension officer support and the communal use of a modern dairy parlour.

The ruling National Party, bastion of Apartheid, would have been scandalised if their actions had been likened to those of the Politburo in Communist Russia, but they were in fact identical.

Farmers survive because they have a deep passion for their work and their way of life, because they are prepared to work eighteen hours a day when needed and go without when times are lean. It is not possible to make a successful farmer by just putting him on the land. Within two years, all but 27 farmers had become bankrupt and were paid by the scheme managers to leave.

Each remaining farmer was then given three of the farms, with their three little houses and twelve cows. When I arrived on the scene, only two of the farmers were making a go of it. The rest eked out a subsistence and lived on what they could scrounge from the environment. We watched as the womenfolk of the community walked over the pastures collecting edible plants.

Wild spinach, or *Amaranthus*, grew all over the eastern half of South Africa and in spring was harvested by many of the tribes. I had heard it called by many names but *Marog* or *Imifino* were common.

Mr Makena was a surly individual who had taken a dislike to vets after a run-in with my predecessor, but he was a good dairyman. Peter Tsusi, on the other hand, was a young man who had made an incredible success where the masses had failed. I later learned that he earned more than any of the vets, extension officers or managers. Peter became a good friend. Years later I watched his bitter grief at the death of his 18-year-old son and then was humbled to see him coaching his 12-year-old daughter to take over the business when she left school.

Within that first month, Peter would, however, test my resolve to the limit, which gave Mr Makena endless delight. Or almost endless.

When I arrived home that evening, Gloria accosted me and begged a lift to collect her new glasses. As I waited for her, I noticed that even more of the poppies had disappeared into a cow's wide mouth. With an effort I dragged some thorn branches from a nearby pile to the front of the fence.

The following day Gloria once again met me as I drove up. 'These glasses are very bad,' she announced. 'They make me feel very sick and I cannot see because everything is moving.'

I agreed to make the journey once more for her, but then noticed that all the poppies had been chomped off. 'Those darn cows. Look what they've done.'

'What is it, nKosi?'

'Those cows have eaten my plants,' I said, pointing to the destroyed bed of would-be flowers.

'They are not imifino?'

'No, they are not imifino. They are my poppies.'

'Ah-weh,' said Gloria and ducked her head.

I noticed her discomfort and the truth slowly dawned on me. 'Gloria, have you been eating my plants?

'I'm sorry nKosi.' She squirmed uncomfortably. 'I thought they were weeds.' A glimmer of humour gave the lie to her contrition. 'They tasted very bad, but I thought it was just because you put all that manure in the ground.'

I slammed the door of the car. 'You do not need new glasses, Gloria. You have been eating opium. It is a wonder you are not a lot sicker.'

As I walked away, I noticed her looking speculatively at the remaining plants.

'No Gloria,' I said. 'You cannot have any more.' I made a mental note to drag the thorn bushes around to our side of the flowerbed in the morning.

Chapter 43

FIGHTING A REARGAURD ACTION

It was a hot Friday afternoon and the guest speaker from Texas Agricultural and Medical University droned on, threatening to wake any of the audience of vets by tapping on the screen with his stylus. The lecture just after lunch was impossible to be enthusiastic about, but we had to attend a certain number of hours of CPD to remain licensed to practice.

Very little penetrated my brain until suddenly I realised that he was discussing the very operation I had done a month earlier.

'The strangest thing about repairing an R-V laceration is that every time you place a suture, the cow coughs. It makes it very difficult indeed.' A few hardy souls laughed faintly, but I was captivated.

I had not imagined it then! It was not something I had done wrong.

'We do not know why it happens, but the suspicion is that it is direct stimulation of the vagus nerve.'

Peter Tsusi had brought half a dozen cows to be examined at the monthly vet visit to his section of the Keiskammhoek Irrigation Scheme. His cows were in superb condition and most of those presented for inspection were just post-calving checks and pregnancy tests. One was very different.

'My cow calved yesterday,' said Mr Tsusi. 'The calf was very big and when it came out it damaged her.' The young cow's birth canal had a huge tear that would prevent her from ever having another calf unless it was repaired. It was a very challenging operation, one which I had only read about and had never even seen performed. In the remote area at the bottom of Africa, there were no specialist referral centres and no-one to call upon to help me out. Fortunately, I had only recently graduated and had spent years stuffing often useless knowledge into my aching cranium. I could at least give it a go.

While an assistant held the tail out of the way, I washed and then disinfected the entire rear end of the cow. Then I scrubbed my arms and hands rigorously as we had been taught and finally pulled on sterile surgical gloves. My instruments were neatly laid out on a drape covered bale of hay. The cow obviously approved since she added a plop of manure to the row of instruments. A cow's rear end is no respecter of status or occasion.

In frustration, I cleaned off what I could and replaced the most critical ones from a second set kept in a sterile surgical pack. I once again sterilised the back end of my patient, but not before I had wedged a thick wad of cotton wool in the offending aperture facing me. I donned a fresh pair of gloves, my last, and set to work.

Cattle and horses often require several large bottles of local anaesthetic to be injected and I had got most of the drug into the operation area when the cow gave a gentle cough and the wad of cotton wool, now with a soggy green end to it, was projected outwards and over the instrument table, leaving a green stripe in its wake.

Mr Makena, arch-nemesis of the vets who served the dairy scheme, had just arrived and he laughed at the sight. Peter turned to remonstrate with him, but he shrugged it off and took up a ringside seat at my shoulder. I had long accepted that the personal space of a Xhosa man is less than half that of us prissy Europeans, but his juxtaposition was not welcome as I fought to maintain my professional bedside manner that was rapidly becoming smeared with green.

A much larger wad of cotton wool was forced in, while the patient remained unperturbed, stretching her head to try and get a mouthful of the grass growing beside the handling facilities.

I remembered the complicated 'Six-bite suture' required to repair all the layers of the damaged area, bringing in strong connective tissue that, once healed, would prevent the tear from recurring next calving. As my needle made the third bite, the cow coughed again and this time we all ducked, even before the organic missile was launched over our heads.

Mr Makena's chuckle had now given way to a delighted roar of laughter. Even Peter had to turn away for a few moments to compose his face before once again urging me to carry on with the operation.

By the fifth unguided missile, I had had enough. Working on the butt of a cow was one thing but being the butt of the joke was more than I could take.

Peter's earnest, almost pleading face was not enough to keep me going but suddenly I found an unexpected resolve while watching Mr Makena stagger about, holding onto the shoulder of a crony while they laughed uncontrollably. I was not going to let him claim victory.

By now my once-sterile instruments had become camouflaged in various shades of green and my table and I could both hide in plain view inside a bush and be invisible. I guess we might have been detected by the odour.

With determination, I stuffed all the remaining roll of cotton wool into the offending launching tube in front of me and set to work once more. The cow did not seem to even notice it and certainly took no offense. Perhaps the local anaesthetic prevented her from feeling anything.

With great difficulty I managed to close the gaping wound and restore a semblance of order, even though the cow gave a few desultory coughs that had no impact on the tight roll of cotton wool. Mr Makena grew a little impatient. He had thoroughly enjoyed himself and he did not want the merriment to end. As I worked, I was aware of his intense interest as he leaned more and more into my field of vision. I was about to ask him to move away when the cow gave a violent cough and I sensed rather than saw the movement of the cotton wool plug.

I had the advantage of being able to aim and I had the trigger in the form of the suture needle. Mr Makena had no prior warning as the foot-long missile was launched straight at him. It hit his shoulder and side of his face, dropping him to his knees.

The assembled crowd held their breath for a split second and then the delight erupted as my detractor cautiously removed his glasses to reveal a figure of eight devoid of slime while the rest of his torso had taken on a distinctly Martian hue. He spat with disgust a few times and then dug in his pocket for a handkerchief to wipe some of the detritus from his mouth and nose.

I held my breath, waiting for the verbal assault. He lifted his eyes until they met mine and Peter's in turn, and then he laughed. Peter relaxed visibly and joined in. The only one of us unaffected was the cow, who seemed to be bored with the whole procedure and wandered down to the pasture to join the rest of the herd.

Mr Makena never really accepted me and rarely brought his cows to the vet visits, but he would wave whenever I passed by and then turn to make some ribald comment that had the rest of the farmers chuckling but was beyond my linguistic ability.

The cow went on to produce a calf the following year and was expecting again when I finally left the Ciskei to start a private practice in King William's Town.

Chapter 44

Tukulu

Apartheid was the status quo for most of my life. I grew up on a farm alongside four black families and although there was a mutual respect, our social lives never crossed. Moving to a state populated and governed by the black Xhosa nation exposed us to a view from the opposite side.

The culture was clearly very different to ours, but they were gracious in their acceptance of us for our skills and as fellow humans. I was never exposed to the violence and hatred that erupted after we had left.

The Xhosa nation lived in a large area that had once been the frontier of the original Cape Colony. The Xhosa clans were divided into two groups by the Kei River, and the enmity between the two groups was the stuff of legends. The smaller, South-eastern Ciskei was given separate independence from its larger neighbour across the river, the Transkei. A narrow strip of land between the two countries was retained by the South African government and became known as the 'Border Area.'

All the white farmers in the area, designated to be the Ciskei, had their land expropriated. A parastatal agency, Ulimocor, was set up to improve the farms and to establish indigenous owners on the land.

We had arrived to test the herd of 400 cattle for TB and Brucellosis, both serious infections that affected cattle and humans.

The manager of Tukulu, Baron Umlumbe, met us at the stock handling pens. A huge man with a disturbing falsetto voice, Baron had shown me a side of his nature that was deeply reassuring. As chief of a nearby village, he had the welfare of all the villagers at heart.

Baron left to mobilise the team of stockmen to bring in the herd of cattle. As I waited for the arrival of the herd, I noticed a flash of orange and then caught site of a hoopoe landing at the entrance of a cement drainpipe under the loading ramp attached to the cattle enclosure. Every few minutes one of the parent birds would land with an insect in its beak and then hop into the opening to stuff it into one of the gaping mouths that were just visible from my vantage point. The birds had impressive crests which they raised in display. Called *Amatekwane* by the locals, they will forever represent the African savanna in my mind.

In a bush nearby, a dozen red-billed hoopoes flapped about, noisily gabbling in a raucous fashion. Baron had informed me that the Xhosa called them *Hlekakhazi*, or 'laughing women'. The name very aptly described the sound they made. I had yet to find the courage to describe it to Karen, but she would no doubt find it just as amusing.

I wondered over to a fenced paddock in which close to a hundred young goat kids pranced about on stiff legs. Only a few days old, the little miniatures were exact replicas of their mothers, apart from their pristine, shining coats and coal black hooves.

In the centre of the enclosure was the top half of a car, bonnet, roof and boot, standing on the ground and giving the impression that the rest of the vehicle must lie under the soil. A little kid stood proudly on the highest part of the car roof while around the edges of the metal a group of his rivals took short run-ups and then bounced as high as they could onto the car, only to slide back down. Eventually one of them managed to keep his feet and immediately the two little goats turned towards each other, lowering their heads to tussle vigorously until one of them slid unceremoniously off the roof. The victor bleated triumphantly, prancing on his straight legs, only to be challenged almost immediately by another contender. I watched entranced until the sound of the men herding the cattle interrupted my reverie.

Baron had no reservations in talking about the past while we waited for the herdsmen to drive the cows into the wooden pole race, ready to be injected with tuberculin and have a vial of blood extracted for the laboratory.

His father had worked for old man De bruin, the wealthy farmer who had owned vast tracts of land. Each year the farmer had toured his farms to inspect the cattle and record the numbers on each bit of land. The stockmen dutifully presented the cattle and that night they drove them over to the next farm, which De Bruin would visit the following day. The farmer's records became increasingly fictitious year by year. Baron laughed at the memory and made sure that he not only counted the cattle in his care but recorded the ear-tag number of every single one of them.

At the end of the day, Baron asked if I would see two of his own goats at home that tended to walk in circles and were becoming increasingly emaciated.

His village was a disorganised collection of circular mud huts and square cement block rooms. It was clear that he was very highly regarded by his clan, as the men and women greeted him warmly while a crowd of children formed a comet's tail that followed him as he moved about.

The goats were a pitiful sight, and it was clear that they suffered from serious brain damage. Chief suspect for the condition was *Echinococcus*, a worm that occurred in dogs but in sheep it formed a cyst in the organs.

The sheep picked the parasite up from grazing on pastures infected by dogs, who in turn became infested when eating meat containing the parasitic cysts.

I described the parasite to Baron and he responded by confirming that they had slaughtered a goat the previous week with the same symptoms and had been amazed to find it had almost no brain tissue in the skull at all.

'What did you do with the damaged brain?' I asked.

'Why? We fed it to the dogs.' He pointed to the motley pack of hounds that formed a fringe around the accompanying bevy of children.

Walking back to the van, I commented on the haphazard arrangement of the houses in the village. Nestled in an attractive fold of hills, there seemed to be no provision for roads or amenities.

'Who decides where to build the next house?' I queried.

'I do,' he replied. 'If a man gets married and wants to build here, he comes to me and gives me a gift, such as a bottle of whiskey. I tell him where he can build.'

The arrangement seemed to suit everyone concerned and if it offended my cultural need for straight lines and ordered numbering, the inhabitants seemed perfectly happy with the system, and they were the ones who lived here.

Chapter 45

BUSH SURGERY

The owner of the first patient I saw at the Alice Clinic greeted me in English. I smiled with relief. I felt a surge of brotherly love for the elderly Xhosa man as he stood before me, coupled with a deep humility that a black man, without the advantages of first world schooling, could speak my language fluently while I struggled to use his.

'What is wrong with Spot?' I asked.

Spot looked vibrantly healthy. A non-descript dog, roughly the size of a spaniel, she was pitch black from her coal-dark nose to the tip of the tail she kept tucked between her legs. I wondered idly if she had earned her name not because she had a spot but because she was 'the spot'. A black spot.

'She needs an operation,' the old man replied.

'What kind of operation?'

'One to stop her getting chickens.'

I looked at him, puzzled. Thoughts of wiring her jaws together or extracting her teeth flashed through my mind.

'Do you want us to stop her from stealing chickens?' I queried.

'Oh no. The operation to close her up. To stop her getting chickens.'

The two of us stood in silence, neither able to able to make any progress. I sighed silently and, admitting defeat, called for Doris to interpret.

'*Asifuni Ntontsho,*' the old man said when she came.

A faint light glowed dimly in my mind even before Doris had explained. 'He wants us to stop her from having little ones. Puppies.'

In Xhosa the young of any animal was called the same, *Ntontsho*. The old man had merely chosen the incorrect diminutive in English. I nodded with relief. I knew how to spay her. I was immensely grateful that I didn't have to do anything more drastic to prevent her from getting chickens.

After attending to the rest of the patients, Doris and I lowered the tailgate of the van and spent the next half hour operating on Spot in the shade of two enormous Cape fig trees, whose massive trunks had sent suckers down into the earth over the decades, reminding me of mangrove trees. Spot would never have puppies, and hopefully no chickens either.

As I was about to leave, one final tardy patient arrived, a tired-looking horse with a large growth just above the fetlock on the near foreleg.

'It looks like a sarcoid,' I informed Doris. 'It probably should be removed since it looks like his offside hoof is catching it when he walks.'

There was a small stream of blood running from the inner edge of the growth down to the hoof, with a tiny pool of red oozing into the dry dust.

'Unfortunately I don't have the right equipment to tackle that today.'

'Oh yes. The vets use *bloudraad,*' Doris instructed me triumphantly.

I thought I had heard incorrectly. *Bloudraad* was the Afrikaans name for the thick, heavy gauge wire used by farmers to fence their land.

Doris disappeared into the room with the lowered ceiling, only to return with a stout length of fencing wire. Despite my mild protests, she rapidly collected the makings of a fire and soon had the makeshift surgical instrument heating up in the flames.

With strong misgivings I anaesthetized the patient, the willing hands of several bystanders helping to pull the horse to the ground as the drugs took effect.

Doris carefully handed me the wire, now with a glowing red tip. Cautiously, I applied the searing end to the base of the tumour on the horse's leg, while pulling the mass away with the other hand. A nauseating cloud of noxious smoke drifted into my eyes as I worked.

The wire cooled rapidly and had to be reheated a dozen times before the task was complete. With a feeling of unreality, I surveyed the neat scar on the leg of the horse. Despite having given the maximum dose of painkiller to the horse, I also injected local anaesthetic just above the wound to block the nerve running just behind the strong cannon bone.

'They must not ride him for a week,' I instructed, 'and then I want to see the horse again.'

Doris nodded dubiously and conveyed my instructions to the owner. As the horse struggled upright, the owner agreed to return the following week, although Doris was clearly not convinced.

We packed away the equipment and when I turned to check we had everything, I noticed the horse we had just operated on walking down the road, with its owner astride its back.

'They have no other way of getting home,' Doris explained. I shook my head in disbelief and hoped that the horse was not in any pain after the ordeal and that the local anaesthetic would last until they got home.

Chapter 46

SAVING THE SEA LION

The only veterinary practice in King William's Town was owned and run by Gill Johns, a graduate for the Royal College of Veterinary Surgeons. She had a smart little building on the outskirts of town. A few weeks of after arriving, I decided to stop and say hello.

The waiting room was empty when I walked in, and the receptionist gave me a decidedly unfriendly glare.

'Dr Johns is operating,' she informed me coldly, 'You will have to come back after 4 this afternoon when she starts consulting again.'

I explained who I was and asked if I could go through to say hello; I would not be able to come back later that day. The receptionist looked doubtful but disappeared into the bowels of the building, only to return a few minutes later.

'Follow me,' she said economically.

Dr Johns was busy with a routine dog spay when we walked into the neat little prep room opening into the theatre. There was a long list of operations written on the white board on the wall, most of which had a line drawn through them.

'I have three more to do, so it is unlikely that I will be finished long before afternoon surgery,' she informed me. I nodded but introduced myself and then commented on how quick she seemed with her surgery. Dr Johns seemed not to have heard.

The receptionist returned just as the operation finished to say that a client had walked in with his dog and wanted to be seen immediately.

'He says his dog has biliary.'

Gill stalked through into the waiting room and stopped a few inches from the client. She only came up to his waist but bristled with indignation. At his side, a magnificent black pointer drooped in obvious ill health.

'What university did you graduate from?' she demanded.

'What?'

'What university did you graduate from?'

'I never graduated from any university. Look – Pavla here has got biliary. He is very anaemic and has a very high temperature. I know what biliary looks like, but I have run out of Berenil to treat it with.'

Dr Johns drew herself up to her full height, still way below the client's shoulders.

'I will decide if he has biliary. I will examine him when we open again this afternoon and then I will decide what to treat him with.'

For a moment the suave gentleman looked as if he was going to hit her, but then he turned abruptly and stalked angrily out of the practice.

The coastal area of the Ciskei was sparsely populated and had a wealth of wide, pristine beaches and mammoth sand-dunes rising up to meet the open grassland of the farms that lined the Southern border of the country. Karen and I had been invited to lunch at the home of one of the managers involved with the pineapple project in the area.

Miles of straight, prickly rows of these tough plants had been planted over multiple hectares of land, their precise lines creating a crosshatch pattern over the hills.

Chris and Adi met us as we drove up to the house they had been given, perched on a small rise with a 180-degree view of the sea. They lived in a paradise that was only marred by its isolation. Visitors were more than welcome.

As we walked to the front door, a lion cub emerged from the shadows and ran clumsily towards us in an uncoordinated stumble. I soon found out that there was nothing affecting her jaws as she playfully mouthed my hands and arms when I bent down to pat her.

Chris and Adi's little toddler Coral appeared and claimed her pet by putting her arms around its neck. The lion cub seemed to instinctively know to be gentle and rolled on her back, nibbling at the Coral's shoes as the little girl allowed herself to roll on top of the cub.

'*Ingonyama* comes from Mpongo Park,' Chris informed me. 'There is something wrong with her legs. We are fostering her and trying to find out how we can help her, to prevent her being put down.'

The reason for our invitation to lunch became clearer with the next sentence. 'You couldn't X-ray her legs for us, could you?'

I was glad to be involved and pleased that we had something to offer. I only wished we could have adopted the cub. Reason told me it would be foolhardy, while pride and a love for all animals, and in particular young animals, warred with common sense.

Little Coral tried to run off down the path, but Ingonyama immediately pounced on her and the two rolled down the grassy slope amid playful growls and childish chuckles. The rest of us watched with delight on our faces. The little cub would never have thrived in the middle of suburbia, I realised. I would have to settle for treating her when I got the opportunity.

Chris and Adi spoke of their enthusiasm for scuba diving and had an immediate audience in Karen. She had always loved marine life and the thought of getting up close to it enthralled her.

'I know a professional diver who was in the Special Forces in Zimbabwe. I'll ask him if he would teach a group of us when I see him on Tuesday,' Chris offered. Karen responded enthusiastically, unaware of what she was getting herself into.

The next client looked a little familiar, but I could not quite place him until he picked up the black pointer at his side and placed her on the consulting table. Suddenly the scene in Dr Gill Johns' waiting room flashed back into my mind.

Niko Palexis had arrived at Dr Johns' practice on the day I visited her. He had left in a huff when she challenged his diagnosis of biliary in his dog.

'What can we do for Pavla today?' I asked.

'She has something in her paw. We went hunting yesterday and she charged after a bushbuck in a thick forested area and when she came out, she was limping. She will not let me examine it.'

Pavla was certainly favouring her left hind leg. She was not happy when I made a move to touch it, and I had to resort to putting a muzzle on her and took the opportunity to inject a strong painkiller in the scruff of her neck at the same time.

By moving gently, I was able to support her body with my shoulder while I lifted the paw. There was nothing to see and she did not react when I gently pressed each toe and then the web and pads of the rest of the paw. I moved my hands higher up the leg, flexing and extending joints, feeling for heat, swelling, or signs of pain. When I reached her stifle, Pavla seemed to tense.

She was obviously guarding her knee, or stifle, not too happy when I straightened it out. Holding the femur in one hand, I used the other to hold the tibia and gently moved them in relation to each other. There was a small amount of laxity in the joint. Laxity in a joint that was critical in supporting her weight and propelling her forward when she walked.

I lowered the leg and then compared the joint on the opposite leg. There was a distinct difference.

'I think she may have ruptured her anterior cruciate ligament,' I informed him.

Niko looked puzzled. 'There's nothing in her paw?'

'Nothing that I can find. I would suggest that we knock her out to take some X-rays of both hind legs and when we do so, we will be able manipulate the stifle joints without worrying about hurting her and at the same time we will spend some time examining the entire paw very closely in case we have missed a fine foreign body that is not easy to see.'

Niko agreed reluctantly. 'She is a working dog,' he stressed, 'but she means a lot to me. All my dogs do.'

'How many do you have?' I wanted to know.

'I have eight dogs. They are all used for hunting. I keep them in tip-top condition.' He looked at my face and misinterpreted my expression.

'A lot of people do not approve of hunting,' he challenged.

'I was just thinking that eight dogs must cost you a lot. The food alone must set you back a lot.'

'I have five café's.' He used the term for convenience stores in South Africa. 'I bring young men out from Cyprus to run them and then after five years, I give each of them their own café. They make me a lot of money.'

I had heard of these young immigrants sleeping behind the counters in their stores, prepared to work for very little, but in the end reaping a large reward as they are set up for life. Many of them return to Cyprus and then bring a young wife back with them.

Niko returned to his defensive stance. 'How much have you paid towards game conservation in the past ten years?' he challenged.

'Not much,' I admitted. 'We have spent some time in several of the reserves, but apart from that, we have not been involved.'

'I have spent hundreds of thousands,' he said with a sincerity devoid of conceit. 'When we go hunting, we pay large sums to do so, and we are strictly regulated in what we can hunt. If no-one was prepared to pay to be allowed to hunt, there would be no income to support the game and the land would probably be converted to grazing for cattle or sheep.'

I nodded at his logic, prepared reluctantly to see his point of view. Large-scale international tourism was not a big industry in apartheid South Africa. Apart from the big, government-owned reserves, very little land was set aside for the rich fauna of the subcontinent.

Pavla did turn out to have a ruptured cruciate ligament and we operated on her the following day. She made a full recovery, although it took six weeks before she used both hind legs in perfect synchrony.

Niko became a regular client at the practice, and I made a point of treating his dogs as patients, ignoring their job descriptions. They were always in perfect condition and clearly doted on their owner.

Chris arrived at the clinic with Ingonyama, the little lion cub from Peddie.

'She's no better. Possibly even a little worse. Her owners are talking about having her put to sleep,' he said sadly. 'You can understand their point of view. Sometimes it looks as if she is in pain when she tries to keep up with the dogs or with Coral.'

Disabled or not, little Ingonyama was no pushover as she batted my head with huge paws and grabbed at my arm with her mouth.

'You have to be firm with her, or she takes advantage of you,' Chris advised. 'Funnily enough, she seems to know that Coral is not strong enough to take any rough stuff and she is very gentle with her. Even so, she sometimes hurts our daughter without meaning to. I guess sooner or later, we are going to have confine her so that the two of them can only play together while we are watching.'

The radiographs showed typical broad physeal lines, characteristic of rickets.

'What does she get to eat?' I asked.

'Well, we are weaning her off cow's milk and she gets mostly fresh meat. Nothing but the best for her.'

'Do you give her any supplements?'

'Yes.' Chris was adamant. 'She gets a vitamin mix that Mpongo give to all their lions.'

'Does it have any calcium in it?' A deficiency of calcium was the cause of rickets, and it could be caused either by a lack of the mineral in the diet, or the absence of ultraviolet light required by animals to convert vitamin D to the active form, which in turn was necessary for calcium to be absorbed. A lack of UV light in the harsh sun of Africa was unlikely.

'I'm not sure,' Chris admitted. 'I don't think so, actually. Surely there is enough calcium in the meat. I mean, it's what they eat in the wild.'

'Not really. They don't selectively cut out meat from their kills. They eat the skin, the organs, some of the contents of the organs, the cartilage and most importantly, they gnaw on bones and ingest anything small enough to swallow.'

Chris nodded but was far from convinced. He was wanting a more dramatic diagnosis, preferably something that could be instantly cured. I knew that I could be wrong, but even if it was not rickets, providing a source of calcium was just good husbandry.

Years later, I found myself relegated to treating most of the 'exotics' or pets other than dogs and cats in a town in England. I soon became aware that a lack of calcium was the most common cause of a wide range of symptoms, from paralysis and deformities in reptiles to convulsions in parrots. Keepers of these less common pets often refer to 'Metabolic Bone Disease' or more commonly MBD.

Ingonyama responded partially to the calcium supplementation and seemed to improve but some damage had been done and she would never recover fully. Sadly, Chris took her back to the reserve that had bred her and we never saw her again, although he assured us that she was being looked after and treated as a favourite attraction as she rolled about on the grass, no doubt remembering her soul-mate Coral with deep nostalgia.

Chapter 47

DO AND DIE

Dave was in his fifties but still as fit as ever. He had served in the Special Forces in the Rhodesian army and had been persona non grata after independence. I got the feeling that he had more than a few skeletons in his closet. And in his fridge, and dresser, and bathroom cabinet. It puzzled me that a land-locked country like Rhodesia needed a squadron of deep-sea divers.

At one stage, he had been called upon to descend a 30-foot column of brick, at the bottom of which a snapped chain that raised a sea barricade had fallen. Since the column would not allow him to turn around, he would have to ascend backward to get out. In the event of getting stuck, he had a thin tube attached to his belt in case they had to feed him soup while they worked to free him.

We later heard from a friend of his that Dave would occasionally cadge a lift from fishermen, to be taken out to an exposed outcrop of rock, where he would spend six hours diving on his own. On their return, they would find him standing on the rock, which was no longer exposed, holding his gear up around his head and waiting for his lift.

Dave had the gift of blunt reality.

'When you are thirty metres deep in the water and you start to ascend, the air in your lungs will expand rapidly. Unless you breathe out, your lungs will burst, and you will die.'

We looked at each other a bit apprehensively. I tended to take his advice with a pinch of salt, but Karen listened intently. I realised that I had better make sure I didn't get anything wrong.

'If you do not keep your wits about you and you come up under the boat, you can knock yourself out or get badly hurt by the propeller, and then you will die.' He was filling us with enthusiasm for the endeavour.

A written exam completed the course, and then we moved on to the practical. The course had been held at the Mpekweni Resort since they had a deep pool in which we could practice. The manager informed us on the day that the pool had unfortunately been drained for routine maintenance and could not be used.

In order to qualify on the course, we were required to swim three laps of a 100-metre pool in a set time and then stay afloat for fifteen minutes. We were also going to have to show our ability to remove and replace all our kit while deep under water.

'I know of a suitable site we can use,' Dave announced. For six people who were all of sound mind to trust the judgement of a Special Forces veteran as to what was suitable proved to be one of many bad mistakes of the day. Dave drove us to an old quarry, filled with ice-cold green water.

The steep sides of the abandoned quarry prevented the sun from ever reaching the water, and the floor of the pool was sharply jagged rock. We hobbled painfully down to the water's edge in tightly constricting wet-suits, some of us resorting to putting on our 'fins' or flippers to try and reduce the pain on our feet, while others preferred not to lacerate the rubber soles.

We made it across the water once but on the second lap, Karen turned a deep blue and just stopped moving, while still in the middle of the lake. She had not the slightest atom of fat on her, while I was fortunate enough to be more closely related to the roly-poly seals on the beach front. Even so, I was painfully cold and found it difficult to inhale.

I had to put an arm underneath Karen's shoulder and swim backwards, slowly pulling her towards the edge of the quarry. Dave stumbled down the rocky edge and together we carried her up to the waiting van and wrapped her in the inadequate warmth of every piece of clothing I could find.

To my astonishment, Dave seemed to regard Karen's ordeal as sufficient to graduate and even more amazingly, she was game to carry on with the course.

We had found a more suitable pool down at the Fish River Resort and drove down to perform the second-last test.

'You need to fill your lungs with air and then descend to the bottom of the pool, while slowly exhaling to allow yourself to sink.' Dave made it sound as simple as going for a walk. 'On the bottom, you must take off all your diving gear and leave it on the bottom of the pool. Then you ascend to the top, take a breath, and go down again to put your gear back on again.' It sounded daunting.

'When you get down the second time, find your respirator and take a breath before you do anything else. I will be on the bottom, watching you, and if you do not breathe out when you start the final ascent, I am going to hold on to you until you do, so that no-one damages their lungs.'

We all slowly sank to the floor and sat in a circle. Dave pointed to Karen and then pointed upwards. She moved to the centre and took off her gear, neatly placing her mouthpiece on top of everything to be able to find it easily on her return.

Karen floated upwards and paused while she caught her breath before upending and swimming vigorously downwards. The fact that her weight belt lay on the floor made it extremely difficult for her to descend, since the body naturally tends to float.

In desperation she finally made it and grabbed at the respirator to take a big breath. The extra air in her lungs threatened to force her upwards until she managed to use her other hand to find her weight belt.

A second frantic breath and desperately paddling legs dispersed all the kit and left her spiralling upwards. Without hesitation, she put out her arms to swim upwards, when Dave suddenly grabbed her around the waist.

The match was totally unequal.

Karen closed her fist and socked him in the face. Dave reeled back in surprise while five other contestants on the floor of the pool rocked about in glee. Karen shot to the surface.

We all graduated. Dave was too afraid of my demure wife to suggest any other option.

Our first deep-sea dive was in the Port Elizabeth harbour and could not have been more disappointing. Grey-green water with a visibility of almost zero. It was enough to make anyone abandon the idea of the sport forever. Karen gave up fairly soon on the dive, with very good reason, and we all returned to the boat.

If that had been the end, we would have forever recoiled at the thought of scuba diving. Fortunately, a week in the Comores and later in the Maldives firmly entrenched our enchantment for the world beneath the surface of the waves.

We learned that skin-diving, swimming close to the surface while wearing a mask and breathing through a snorkel, allowed us to see almost as much as the deeper scuba diving, with the exception of the very large fish, eels and sharks. Karen would happily spend most of the day with her face in the water, and our only injury tended to be severe sunburn on the backs of our legs.

Chapter 48

THE BULL STOPS HERE

'This bull cost more money than you will ever see in your life. You better not mess things up.' The powerfully built and impressively wealthy tycoon was clearly used to being obeyed, the implicit warning clear in his aggressive manner.

Woody eyed the owner impassively, but I knew that inside he was anything but calm. Both of us had travelled down to the southernmost tip of the Ciskei on a mission to vaccinate a Brahman bull that had just arrived in the country from Texas. It only required one person to administer the vaccinations required but I had found the chance to see this impressive animal irresistible.

The bull was reported to be the most valuable animal in the world. He certainly had the carriage and aloofness of royalty. It had been whispered in the corridors of Ulimocor that the animal was merely a pawn in a game of subterfuge by its wily owner. By going into business with a member of the Ciskei cabinet, they had together purchased a prime tract of land at the mouth of the Fish River, which divided the Ciskei from South Africa.

Gambling was illegal in South Africa, but casinos flourished in the homelands. There was little doubt that the land supposedly purchased for agriculture would soon be home to an army of one-armed bandits and blackjack tables. The clientele would drive over from South Africa to indulge in their passions.

The bull was also reported to be a ploy for the mega-rich owner to get his millions out of South Africa, at a time when there was a strict limit to the money you could take out of the country. A third string to his subterfuge was the tax rebates he had managed to manipulate. Rumours were rife, but then they could just have been rampant envy. The bull was indeed an impressive symbol of machismo.

A large, imposing head, the size of a coffin, was lifted high as he surveyed the crowd around the pens, blinking every now and then from the camera flashes. His massive shoulders carried a large hump, and the enormous body had the appearance of a rhino on long, powerful legs. He was not an individual to take lightly.

'Are you ready, Mr Phil-yoon?' A smartly dressed ranch-hand, complete with ten-gallon headgear addressed the new owner of his charge, the drawl in his accent making his Afrikaans guest flinch at the pronunciation of his name. I wondered if the bull had a Texan accent and whether the cows watching with interest from the paddock in the distance would find it attractive.

Two herdsmen had entered the bull's enclosure and were approaching him warily. He eyed them loftily and then dropped his head, pawing angrily in the dust with a fore hoof. The men faltered and then turned and ran as the huge beast exploded into action, charging towards them with lightning speed.

The man closest to the rails dived under the lowest rail, while his companion raced down the chute through which the cattle were driven to be inspected individually. The bull followed close on his heels. Several of the men on the outside of the rails turned and fled but one man was made of stouter stuff. As the fleeing herdsman passed him, he rapidly pushed a thick pole across the narrow chute, supported by the rails on each side. The bull skidded to a halt and eyed the pole. Behind him, a second pole was quickly inserted, while two more were added at differing heights to the front of the bull. He was now imprisoned in the high walls of the race.

Woody approached cautiously, talking softly as he neared the bull. Slowly and meticulously, he reached out and ran a hand over the huge shoulder. The muscles under the skin twitched but the bull stood immobile, allowing the gentle attention as Woody began his examination.

For twenty minutes Woody worked silently, inspecting his patient with an impressive thoroughness. Finally, he turned to the man at the front of the race. 'I need to inspect his teeth and the rest of his mouth,' he said. 'We'll need two of you to help hold him.'

The crowd thinned rapidly as the men moved aside, trying not to catch his eye as they did so. After a minute, one of the men plucked up the courage to step forward. His fellow herdsmen called out raucously as he climbed onto one of the rails and leant over in front of the bull. As his hand latched onto the muzzle of the bull, the bull's heavy head swung viciously against the rails, scraping the skin off the back of his wrist. In agony, he dropped to the ground and clutched his hand to his chest. The rest of the men took a step backwards.

Woody turned towards the owner. 'I cannot examine his mouth unless we sedate him. I haven't found any sign of a problem elsewhere. Do you want me to give him something?'

'Nee wat,' the owner protested, 'He was given the all-clear before he left the USA. He's healthier than the rest of us here. Just go ahead and vaccinate him.'

Woody nodded and strode off towards the van, reappearing after a few minutes with my vaccine gun. He positioned himself on the second highest rail and, taking care not to get between the bull and a rail, he plunged the needle into the animal's withers. The bull lurched forward against the restraining poles, causing the entire structure to shake. Woody pressed the trigger to inject the vaccine and the bull dropped as if shot with a gun.

Stunned, Woody jumped down and peered anxiously at the prone form lying between the poles. I stepped forward, nerves on edge, as I too examined the silent mountain of bovine flesh.

'He's not breathing,' shouted Woody. 'Get some adrenalin and that big ET tube.' As I raced off, he yelled at the frozen audience to start dismantling the wooden crush.

The bull was beyond hope even before I returned. Woody went through the motions of resuscitation but the futility of it all was apparent to everyone.

'You killed him,' Mr Viljoen stated bluntly. 'I'll sue you for every cent you've got.'

Woody looked at him speechlessly, ashen-faced with shock. I noted that the big farmer had not expressed any concern for his animal apart from anger at the cost.

'The vaccine couldn't have killed him, even if I got it in a vein by mistake,' said Woody defensively. 'We'll do a post-mortem examination on him to see why he died.'

'You killed him. I have thirty witnesses, and you are going to pay.'

I belatedly voiced my support for Woody. 'Let's do an autopsy in front of these witnesses, before deciding on the cause of death.'

There was a snort of disgust, and the big man kicked the carcass lying between us in anger. 'You're wasting your time…and mine.'

Woody walked stonily over to his van and returned with two large butcher's knives. He handed one to me and together we set about opening the massive body on the ground. We worked silently for an hour and a half until suddenly I sensed a stiffening in Woody's frame. Wordlessly he pointed to the heart as I peered over his shoulder. The cause of death was patently obvious.

The huge heart was normal, apart from a thin wire, blackened with rust and blood, protruding from the thick wall of the left ventricle.

'What is it?' demanded Viljoen.

'Wire,' said Woody shortly.

'Yes, I can see that. Where did it come from?'

Woody turned and walked tiredly over to his van and began packing away the equipment. Viljoen glared angrily at his departing back. I stepped into the void.

'The wire must have been swallowed by the bull with his food,' I explained. 'Cattle are notorious for picking up small pieces of wire as they graze since their flat muzzles allow them to crop the grass so close to the ground. It would have gone into the bull's forestomach and as the stomach contracts to mix the contents, the wire would have been pushed through the stomach wall and then migrated towards the heart.'

'But then why did he drop dead from the injection?' Viljoen demanded, unplacated.

'If the wire was sitting close to the heart, it would have penetrated the heart muscle when the bull lunged forward against the pole in front of him.'

Viljoen stared at me for a few moments and then gave a vicious kick at the dead bull before stalking off, followed by his retinue of photographers and reporters.

In silence I mourned the magnificent beauty of the huge bull, his massive regal mien and proud attitude. He had travelled halfway around the world, only to die a pointless death. Instead of roaming the African veld and staking his claim as a king among lesser animals, he was in an instant a lifeless pile of bones and meat. It was a tragedy. His owner roared off in a cloud of dust, no doubt mourning his losses just as keenly.

Chapter 49

ALL IN VEIN

The cow lay flat on her chest, with her head under a thick, impenetrable thorn bush. I could only see the rear half of her, and so far it had told me very little apart from a normal temperature and a flaccid tail and hind legs. I was unlikely to get any more information unless we trudged back to the farmhouse and returned with a tractor and ropes to pull her out.

She had recently calved and she was producing large amounts of milk each day. Her history made the diagnosis of 'milk fever' very likely. This is in fact an acute deficiency in calcium. Milk is extremely rich in the mineral and cows struggle to mobilise enough from their diet and their skeletal system. The hormonal balance of pregnancy is just not geared up to the demands of lactation.

A deficiency in calcium causes extreme weakness in cows, whereas in dogs it often results in tremors, shaking and full-blown fits.

A month earlier, I'd endured a back-breaking day collecting blood from a herd of over 400 cows with Woody, chief vet for Ulimocor.

Woody had collared me to help him 'bleed' the herd of Bonsmara cattle down on the Peddie coast of the Ciskei. I greeted the idea of a day in the sunshine close to the beautiful sea with enthusiasm. Four hundred seemed an awful lot, but Woody appeared unfazed. It was clearly going to be an enjoyable outing.

The assembled Xhosa men herded the sleek, dark-red cattle into the long chute that held twenty of them, stacked at an angle which allowed their tail ends to face us, while the wary heads were pressed against the rump of the cow in front of them. A herdsman lifted the tail of the first cow and Woody deftly inserted a thin needle into the vein running along the under-surface of the tail, while he pushed a vacuum-filled sampling tube onto the opposite end of the needle. A bright spurt of crimson rapidly filled the tube to the neck. The cow never moved, the operation hardly causing any sensation at all to the bovine nervous system.

'You start at the back, and I'll work from the front,' instructed Woody. I complied apprehensively and approached the last cow in the chute.

The needle in my hands seemed cumbersome and unwieldly. I pushed it into the tail and paused, but nothing happened. Pulling it out a fraction, I redirected it at a slight angle. Still nothing. I continued for the next ten minutes, by which time Woody had done all nineteen cows in front of me.

'Come on, Phillips. Get a move on.'

I glowered under my hat but stood back to allow him to take over. I had hurt the poor cow enough.

In retrospect, I should have known better from the start. In the army we had rapidly got to know that when it came to taking our blood, the enthusiastic, newly qualified medics could produce tears in even the most hardened soldier, while the long-serving nurses did the job without causing the slightest sensation.

I managed to extract blood from two cows in the next score, before once again Woody was back to gloat and heap derision on my efforts. By the tenth batch of cows, I was managing six and by the end of the day, I could almost keep up with him, although my back ached, the palms of my hands felt crippled with arthritis, and the sun had set off a blinding pain in my skull.

Woody stood back and handed the last tube of blood to Chris, the assistant, who was returning the filled tubes to the polystyrene tray holder. 'Four hundred and twenty-four. Not bad for one vet and one beginner,' he announced.

'Four hundred and twenty-three,' replied Chris.

Woody whirled around to confront him. 'Where do you get 423 from?'

'That is the number of tubes I have listed on the form.'

Each tube had a number in numerical order. As each cow was sampled, Chris had entered the identity of the cow on a form, corresponding to the number on the bottle. The number of cows he had written down did not match the number of samples we had.

'Where did you go wrong?' demanded Woody.

'I never went wrong. You got the samples wrong.' This was serious. If any of the cows proved positive for Brucellosis, they would be culled. No-one wanted to condemn the wrong animal. The two of them argued back and forth for fifteen minutes, but neither could solve the conundrum.

Suddenly Woody stopped and then stepped forward to pick up the trays of blood samples and unceremoniously drop them into an open half oil-drum.

'We'll have to do it again tomorrow,' he announced. 'Let's hit the beach before the sun goes.'

I was aghast. My entire body protested. This was madness. Woody saw the look on my face and demanded, 'Got a better idea?' I shook my head.

As the cows moved off into the pastures, I hoped they would forgive me, particularly the first cow, who had so patiently endured my fumbling apprenticeship.

I did have the chance to swap places with our patients during the year in which I worked at Allerton Laboratory. Part of our service was to analyse brain samples from deceased animals, including the occasional human, for rabies. All the staff had to be vaccinated against the disease and when they tested my antibody levels a few weeks after the second vaccination, I proved to have the highest level on record. The blood transfusion services decided that I would make a good guinea pig and provide serum for them to treat people bitten by rabid animals.

Every second Wednesday, I made my way down to the library in the complex and spent an hour while a nurse performed the same procedure as I had subjected my patients to. Too polite to stick a needle in my tail, she instead pushed one the size of pencil, or so it seemed, into the vein in the crook of my arm and the bright red fluid rushed out along the plastic tube and into a transfusion bag. I thought I would get used to it, but despite the number of times that nurse Dracula visited, I never quite managed it without gritting my teeth as the sharp metal entered my skin. I did, however, get to know a great deal about this kindly soul, despite the tough job she had, since each session found us chatting for the hour, patiently waiting for the life-saving fluid to exit my arm.

While at the laboratory, I embarked on a research project that required taking blood from a flock of nearly three hundred sheep. I once again plunged in, unaware of the task I had set myself. The sheep had no tails to speak of and the vein running on the ventral surface was not easy to find. They also had no cephalic vein in the foreleg, in which we had inserted the needle into the dogs. Sheep needed to have blood taken from their jugular veins.

The trouble was that the neck of each of these sheep was covered in a thick layer of wool. Try as I might, I could just not find the vein. Once again, the first patient endured my attempts, while I grew increasingly desperate. This time there was no Woody to do the bulk of the work while I practiced.

My assistant was once again an old man, this time from the Zulu clan. Simon was bent over almost double from childhood polio. Despite this, he deftly caught and held the sheep with ease. I remembered Ganong and wished he was with us. I wondered if he knew how to get blood from a sheep.

Simon coughed softly and when he caught my attention, he produced a short length of rope, which he looped over the head of the sheep he held.

A quick twist of the loose ends and the tightening pressure on the neck made the jugular vein stand out like a cord on the neck of the animal. I inserted the needle with ease and seconds later, we released the first of our subjects and dropped the tube into the first empty space in the rack of tubes. Once again, I had been 'shown the ropes' by an illiterate, but imminently competent, fellow African.

The cow sticking out of the thorn bush back in the Ciskei had been a challenge, but I'd had a plan. It would be extremely difficult to get to her jugular vein too, but the memories of drawing blood from the tail vein, however, gave me an idea.

With practiced ease, I managed to insert the largest bore needle into the vein running under the tail, and I quickly attached a 'flutter valve', a thick rubber tube designed to allow air into the bottle as the fluid runs out. A bottle of Calcium Borogluconate was on the other end of the flutter valve tube. Standing up, I held the bottle as high as possible to make it run into the cow as quickly as it could.

The bottle gave a little burp through the flutter valve and then began to fill with blood flowing up the tube. I stared at it in amazement. This just could not be happening.

I remembered the time when Mark had attached a drip to a dog and then watched in bewilderment as the blood flowed up into the drip bag, but he had quickly realised that he had failed to remove the tourniquet used to raise the vein from the leg of the dog. The cow had no tourniquet or obstruction to the flow of blood.

Just as the bottle reached its maximum capacity, I pulled the needle out and pressed hard on the site to stem any bleeding.

Sitting back, I thought about it for a long time. The huge aorta coming from the massive bovine heart was as thick as a garden hose. It divided into two branches to travel down the back legs, and it had numerous smaller branches diving off to feed other parts of the body; however, a thick artery carried on from the end of the aorta and ran the length of the tail. With no diversions or joins, the pressure in the tail was far greater than in other parts of the body. I had connected my bottle almost directly to the heart.

I managed, fortunately, to find an easier vein to use, one that drained the blood from the large milk-factory of an udder. Two bottles ran in uneventfully.

I was just thinking that I had perhaps jumped to the wrong diagnosis, or perhaps this was one cow that was going to need a Phosphate supplement as well, when she gathered her legs underneath her and gave an almighty heave, to completely disappear under the thorn bush.

The herdsmen on the far side of the bush were talking animatedly among themselves and suddenly darted away as a large bovine body came crashing out of the foliage directly towards them.

Our patient walked unsteadily towards a clump of lush ryegrass and bent her neck to bite off a bovine sized mouthful of greenery. She was back to the task of consuming as much energy as possible to convert it to milk. Our job was done, apart from giving advice to the farmer concerning the need to dramatically increase the calcium content of her diet while she was in high lactation.

I also made a mental note not to try and be too clever next time an anatomical conundrum presented itself. Physiology and Murphy's Law had to be taken into account as well.

Chapter 50

TSOLWANE

The Ciskei Agricultural Corporation managed several small game reserves, the largest being Tsolwana, a pocket of land near Queenstown in the Eastern Cape. As employees, Karen and I enjoyed a small discount when we booked one of the few chalets in the reserve for a weekend.

Pete and I had discussed some of the issues in the reserve, but he got to do more of the work than I ever did. The top brass had introduced Mouflon and Himalayan Tarr, both cliff dwelling species that defied gravity. It was a strange decision since neither was indigenous to Africa, and it soon became apparent that the move was purely to attract international hunters who wanted to put another tick on their personal score card, an action that impressed only themselves.

After ten years of successful breeding, both the cliff dwelling sheep, or Mouflon, and the antelope started falling to their deaths from cliffs. Pete was presented with a few dead animals and, on doing a post-mortem, found that they had been infected with Gedoelstia fly larvae, which caused a severe inflammation around the eye, often resulting in blindness.

After a peaceful night, we woke one morning to find three white rhino only a few hundred yards away, peacefully grazing in the rapidly warming sun. Misguided machismo, partly born out of my extensive experience of one encounter in the Umfolozi, had me walking slowly closer to the lumbering beasts to get a photograph, trying at the same time to encourage Karen not to be afraid.

It was only when I realised that she was crying that I knew I had gone too far, and I retraced my steps with contrition. Far from impressing her, I had unwittingly frightened her.

On a later trip to the Etosha pan of Namibia, the wealth of wild animals remains a highlight in my memory. Chief delight was watching the animals come down to drink in strict order. Predators crouched at the water's edge but rapidly gave way when the elephant lumbered in. The rhino waited until their larger cousins moved on before venturing down, and then the lower orders took their turns one by one. The giraffe waited until the end before lowering their long necks with front legs widely spread to enable them to reach the surface of the water. Having to undergo such contortions left them vulnerable to attack, even though a kick from these giants could kill any predator foolish enough to tackle an adult giraffe.

As we watched, a very young elephant calf cavorted around its mother, who was slowly walking down the sloping bank of the water hole. Two rhino moved aside and waited for the elephant to pass. Junior chased after some guinea fowl that moved quickly out of his way and then he ran up behind the rhino and slapped one with his immature trunk.

The rhino bounced around angrily on stiff legs and junior suddenly seemed less sure of himself, darting behind mom and keeping out of sight of his indignant victim.

After satisfying their thirst, all the elephants moved off, apart from two teenage bulls who remained, reaching to pull swathes of reeds into their mouths. The herd moved off and five minutes later the leader returned agitatedly and trumpeted at the two tardy individuals, who rapidly rushed off to join their family.

Chapter 51

IF FISH COULD FLY

When we accepted the offer of jobs in the Ciskei, we took advantage of the fact that the tiny country was desperate for vets and we made it a stipulation that we would be allowed to fly the thousand kilometres to Pretoria once a month in order to do an honours course in animal medicine. Our cheeky request was agreed to without hesitation.

Occasionally other Ulimocor personnel asked us to act as couriers on our monthly trips up north, and none were as unique as the fingerling trout that we were coerced into taking up to Professor Huchzermeyer, specialist in fish diseases at the University.

Tiny Visser, in charge of the Peddie Trout Hatchery, showed us around his domain: a series of large circular ponds of placid water which erupted into frenzied churning of the surface as he broadcast pellets of fish-food over the surface. Each pond contained fish at different stages of their development.

'The little fingerlings are dying in large numbers,' he announced. 'The Prof has a suspicion that they are dying from a condition called Infectious Pancreatic Necrosis. He has asked us to send up some living fish or those that have just recently died for him to perform autopsies on them.'

I was unprepared for his next sentence: 'I told the Prof that you would take some with you when you next go up to your course.'

'How?' I asked.

'I took a few up last year in a plastic bag inside a strong suitcase.' Tiny smiled. 'Caused no end of a stir at the airport, but they let me take them.'

Reluctantly I allowed him to persuade me.

On the day of the flight, we arrived at the hatchery at 4:00 in the morning, the ponds steaming sleepily in the heavy mist just before dawn. Tiny was waiting with our cargo, a large suitcase that was ominously heavy. Opening it, he showed us four large, heavy-duty plastic bags filled with water and air, cosily nesting among polystyrene packaging material.

'I put each bag inside a second one to prevent them leaking and I filled them up with oxygen, so they should survive the journey.'

'There must be nearly a hundred in here,' I protested. 'You told me we were taking a few fish.'

Tiny shrugged, embarrassed. 'There was plenty of room, so it seemed sensible to send as many as we could.'

Arriving at the airport, I hurriedly commandeered a trolley and man-handled the heavy suitcase onto it. The mad dash to the check-in counter was made more difficult by the weighty trolley that had a mind of its own. Silently I offered a little prayer of thanks for arriving safely. We were going to make it.

'*Amanzi ayavuza lapa.*'

I looked in surprise at the elderly porter, who was pointing agitatedly at our luggage. Following his gaze, I found myself staring at the offending bag that by now was letting out a steady stream of water.

'What have you got in there?' demanded the woman behind the check-in counter, who had paused in her punching in of the data on the tickets.

'Er ...fish.'

She looked at me in exasperation, as if dealing with a child of low intelligence.

'I meant,' she said slowly, 'what have you got in that suitcase?'

In answer I manhandled the luggage off the weighing platform, laid it on its side, and opened the catches.

The bags had all burst, releasing their contents into the spacious cavity of the case. The porter and check-in official stared in amazement at the myriad of tiny forms darting about in the shallow depths. A small crowd collected behind us, peering over my shoulder in fascination.

'Fish,' said the woman.

'*Inhlanzi*,' said the porter.

'Yes,' I replied, looking around helplessly.

With the help of the elderly porter, who had clearly decided he was not going to let such an interesting subject disappear, I dragged the suitcase to one of the gutters just outside the door of the airport, where we tipped out the water, salvaging as many of the fish as we could. Returning to the counter, we placed the soaked case on the scale once again. As we ran to the boarding-gate I turned to see the grizzled old porter watching us curiously.

The flight to Johannesburg was uneventful. Arriving at Jan Smuts airport, we still had an hour's drive through to Onderstepoort on the outskirts of Pretoria. We arrived just in time to deliver our charges before rushing off to the lecture. By now the expression of amazement on faces was shrugged off.

'Been on a trip to the underwater city of Atlanta, have you?' quipped the young technician as he scooped up the fish into a deep plastic tray. 'You know that we only needed half a dozen at the most.' I made a mental note to have words with Tiny when we got back.

We landed in East London the following morning, feeling jaded and hopelessly jetlagged. The same elderly porter helped to wheel our bags out of the building. We conversed in a mixture of Xhosa and English.

'You still have the fish?' he inquired.

'No, we left them up in Pretoria,' I replied.

'They eat them there?'

'No, they just looked at them.'
'But they were dead.'
'*Ewe*,' I agreed. 'Yes'.
'They have never seen fish before?'
'No, I mean yes. They have seen fish before. They just wanted to see if these fish were sick.'
'But the fish were already dead.'
'Yes,' I said. 'They wanted to find out how to treat the sick fish.'
'Can they heal the fish if they are dead?'
'No.' I searched futilely for the words to describe the process of an autopsy. 'The dead fish can teach them how to stop the rest of the fish from getting sick.'
'The fish teach them?'
'Yes. No. Yes, they learn from the fish.'
'From the dead fish?'
I nodded and hastily pushed the trolley bearing two half-empty bags, no longer packed with fish, out towards the parking area. He watched expressionlessly as we drove away, his thoughts hidden behind an inscrutably bland face. I in turn felt both humbled and frustrated by the gulf between us.

The elderly Xhosa man had a fair grasp of English, acknowledged as one of the more difficult languages to learn, whereas I had only a smattering of his native tongue. Put to the test, I suspect he also knew more than I did concerning dead fish that could teach people about disease.

Chapter 52

THIS LITTLE PIGGY

The cattle owned by the men in the Ciskei represented their pride and their wealth. The vets and the extension officers worked fruitlessly to persuade them to sell or slaughter their unproductive sterile beasts and concentrate on keeping only animals that provided milk or a calf each year. To the Xhosa man, one cow was one unit of wealth, irrespective of its productivity.

In contrast, the chickens that scratched in the dust around the huts were regarded as a source of food, as were the little black pigs rooting in the undergrowth and spreading the garbage piles in their search for sustenance. An agriculture graduate at the University of Fort Hare told me of his doctorate on indigenous economics and his findings that the annual income from the few chickens and pigs far exceeded that from the families' prized cows.

We had just finished the morning clinic in Zwelitsha when a piercing shriek became audible in the distance. A few minutes later, a bicycle crested the hill and then descended towards the clinic. The noise seemed to emanate from the parcel strapped to the front of the bike.

All the assistants collected around the new arrival and the noise was quickly unstrapped from the handlebars. On the ground it resolved into a pig with black and white patches. Dignity restored, he ceased his ear-piercing noise.

'Ah, it's a Summer pig,' announced Vuyu.

'A Summer pig?' I asked.

Surprised, Vuyu repeated the phrase. 'A Summer pig. All the black and white patchwork pigs are called Summer pigs.'

'Why?'

Vuyu looked at me as if instructing a complete novice. He shrugged his shoulders. 'They are,' he said.

Our porcine patient had a respiratory infection, and his owner was provided an antibiotic to dose him with. Before leaving, Doug drew up two syringes of drugs and injected one little black rump and one pinky-white one. The first started off the intolerable shriek and the second one raised the decibels considerably.

The protesting little pig was once again strapped to the bicycle handlebars and unceremoniously pedalled up the hill again. The agonising sound faded as the distance increased, until silence returned once more to the clinic.

One of the afternoon visits was by chance to see a litter of pigs in the village of Rai. In Xhosa, an 'R' is pronounced as a guttural 'G'. I found it almost as hard to pronounce as it was to converse with our patients.

We found the village and began the search for Flat 27. Vuyu had explained that a 'flat' in the Ciskei was a house with a flat roof, as opposed to the rondavels, or round huts with a pitched, thatched roof. The numbers never ran consecutively, but instead represented the age of the houses. The first house built would be Number 1 and so on.

Mrs Dembe's flat was eventually located, and she greeted us warmly as we clambered stiffly from the van.

'You called us about your pigs?' Vuyu asked, after the usual complicated and fulsome greetings were over. 'Where are they?'

'Ah, they will all be in different places by now. They roam free in the village.'

I was annoyed. We had given explicit instructions that patients had to be confined on the day of our visit. On a good day, we could treat six or seven patients, but if we had to spend our time rounding up animals, that was often reduced to one or two.

Vuyu correctly interpreted my scowl and was quick to tell Mrs Dembe that we would not be able to wait for her to catch the pigs and that she would have to call us on another day when she had them all in a pen.

'Oh no.' Mrs Dembe smiled. She picked up metal bucket and strode out into the sunshine. Banging on the metal container, she called out, 'Here, piggy. Piggeeee. Piggeeee-piggeee-piggeee.'

A barrel across the way suddenly rocked forward and a little black form erupted from it. The gate leading into a vegetable garden was knocked open and a second similar form came charging out. From various points in the village, five little pigs came hell-bent in answer to the summons. Within minutes all of them were confined within a rickety pen made from gnarled poles and thorn bushes.

Mrs Dembe smiled and stood back, inviting us to inspect our patients, all of them head deep in a trough into which the contents of the bucket had been emptied.

The next visit was to a Mrs Thembisa, who had successfully set up a backyard poultry business. After buying a hundred day-old chicks and raising them to the age at which they could be sold, Mrs Thembisa had decided that if she could do it with a hundred, why not a thousand? She got help to build a second brick building to house the enlarged flock and went into production.

As an entrepreneur, she was to find that it was not always smooth sailing. Her chicks were only three weeks old when a few started to make little 'snicks' as they breathed and began to lag behind the other birds in their growth. Within two weeks, most of the birds had succumbed to the respiratory infection.

I surveyed the neat little building and the organised yard with approval. Mrs Thembisa was clearly a woman of ability. She came out of her house to greet us and led us across to the poultry house.

There was very little we could do to help her current flock of birds, many of whom were stunted and sickly. A range of different organisms could have caused the outbreak and only by sending samples to a veterinary laboratory would we find out which of them was involved. The chances of it being a virus were unfortunately very high and we had no weapons against viruses, including AIDS and 'Flu. The less common bacterial causes and the Mycoplasmas would possibly respond to antibiotics but the condition of the chicks was unlikely to catch up to their previous state. We would send off samples and prescribe treatment, but more importantly, we would consider how to prevent a second outbreak if new birds were brought in.

With the help of an interpreter, I explained to our client the importance of strict biosecurity when raising chickens. Flocks should never be mixed with other birds and anyone going into the housing had to wear protective clothing to prevent carrying infections with them. Mrs Thembisa was encouragingly astute and her comments made it clear that she understood.

We then got onto the subject of vaccinations. Commercial producers make use of a host of vaccines that are given from the day of hatching up to adulthood in a complex program that involved multiple injections or the addition of the vaccine to the water.

Mrs Thembisa was enthusiastic. She nodded eagerly and it was relayed to me that she knew about vaccinations and used them already. Surprised, I asked if she had any in stock at the moment. She beamed and indicated that I should follow her, setting off to the chicken house.

Reaching the door of the structure, she stopped abruptly and pointed up towards the roof. At first I could not see what she was indicating but then I made out a dozen little vaccine bottles suspended from the eaves. I turned in surprise to Vuyu for an explanation.

'Mrs Thembisa has put the bottles there to keep the spirits away from her chickens,' Vuyu commented.

The two of us observed each other in silence. The gulf between us was almost tangible. I had no idea of communicating to her the complexities of biology, while she in turn knew just how little my culture understood about the spirit world that was so real to her nation.

It struck me how little I actually knew about immunity. I accepted that vaccination stimulated the body to produce antibodies because I had been instructed about it in a centre of higher learning. Scientific research had demonstrated the effect of the protocol, but in truth I knew only what the most learned researchers had tried to explain to us, and they in turn had a very strict limit to their knowledge.

There are many drugs that work but we do not understand how. There are many diseases that we have very little grasp of. We did the best we could with the information we had, but over the years, new developments often showed the flaws in our reasoning.

We had been taught that dogs developed skin allergies by inhaling pollens and other allergens, triggering off a hypersensitivity reaction in susceptible animals. It was accepted by the veterinary profession all over the world. Only when more astute minds began to question this mechanism did they learn that in fact, the pollen particles landed on the skin and were actively taken into the body by Langerhans cells, moving through gaps between cells that occurred due to a lack of the phospholipids that made up the 'cement' that sealed this junction in normal, non-allergenic dogs.

Our knowledge is very limited and future generations are going to laugh at our misconceptions, just as we shake our heads at the beliefs of the past. Mrs Thembisa was doing the best she could with the knowledge and understanding she had of the subject. I had no idea how to bridge the gap.

'Tell Mrs Thembisa that we will try and get her some fresh vaccine if we can,' I instructed Vuyu.

Mrs Thembisa smiled happily and enthusiastically agreed to wait for it to arrive. In the meantime, she would have to reply on the older bottles that were clearly losing their potency in deterring the spirits causing the sickness in her chickens.

We drove off with the grateful smiles of both Mrs Dembe and Mrs Thembisa in my mind. I sincerely hoped I could make a difference and help both of them with their ventures.

Chapter 53

A FATE WORSE THAN DEATH

When the government set up the multi-million-rand dairy scheme at Keiskammahoek, they also constructed a world class dual-carriageway to the remote town that was a pleasure to drive on.

As an employee of a parastatal organisation, I was given a government vehicle, a brand-new white minibus that I fitted out with cupboards, running water and all the mod cons required for treating animals in the rural areas.

Lingele and I had spent the day at the KIS Scheme and were returning home, only to find the road blocked with a row of large orange pixie-hats and white barricades, with a herd of yellow earth-moving machines digging up the pristine tarmac in the distance. A sign marked the direction of a detour, leading us onto a steep, winding dirt road running past and through several villages.

The two-hour journey had suddenly doubled in length. I tiredly put my foot down and concentrated on dealing with the corrugations that threatened to shake the van into its component parts.

As we rounded a sharp corner with a steep bank on the left, two young women came running down the slope, the impetus of their rapid descent making it impossible for them to stop before running into the road in front of us. I found out later that they had mistaken our van for one of the ubiquitous taxis that ply their trade throughout Africa and were intent in stopping us to get on board.

I swerved to the right, only to suddenly catch site of a dark black saloon car approaching up the opposite slope. I swung the wheel to the left to avoid the car, but the other driver swerved as well and we came to a grinding, shattering halt with the noses of both cars crumpled against each other.

The front of our van had squashed inwards, and both my knee joints had deep lacerations penetrating them. With an effort, I pushed the driver's door open, and half-fell, half-dragged myself onto the grass verge. Lindele joined me a few minutes later and when he smiled nervously, I realised that he had lost his two front teeth in the altercation.

The smoking vehicles gave a series of loud ticks, but nothing exploded and after a while I lay back and closed my eyes, trying to ignore the pain.

The sound of car doors slamming made me look up, only to see two men walking towards me, carrying a coffin between them. I felt a jolt of disbelief. I was not aware that I had crossed the river Styx.

For a minute I wondered if I was looking down on my dead body from a higher plane, and then my perfectly functioning brain informed me that I had better show them that I was alive or I might end up in a wooden box in a shallow grave in the middle of the African veld. I cautiously raised my head, but the men ignored me and hurried past.

I later learned that I had interrupted a funeral cortege and the directors were anxious to minimise the trauma to the bereaved. They disappeared and we never heard from them again.

I was one of the last patients to enjoy the old hospital in King William's Town, a charming single storey building with wide, almost empty wards. My knees had both been stitched up by a very young and supremely competent surgeon who was also one of the local GPs.

On admission, the sister had insisted that I supply them with a urine sample. In a state of near shock and having worked all day in the heat, I was totally unable to comply with her request. She left in irritation, telling me that it was hospital policy to get blood and urine from every patient on admission. I decided that she could get a good job in the local tax office.

During the operation, a much more approachable nurse inserted a thin catheter into my arm and ran a litre of fluid into my parched body. The drip was continued after I was trundled through into the ward. Worn out, I fell asleep in the warm sunshine flooding through the large picture windows that overlooked the small town.

I woke a few hours later to see several empty fluid bags on the drip stand, with a final one still filling me up to the gills. My bladder was urgently tapping on my tonsils and warning me that something dreadful was going to happen if I did not move. Quickly.

I swung my legs over the edge of the bed and winced in agony. From the doorway the strident tone of the matron barked out, 'And where do you think you are going?'

'The loo. I need to go to the toilet.'

''You are going nowhere, young man. Get back into bed.'

I started to protest but she pushed me back with one hand and with the other she grabbed what I had mistaken to be an aluminium water jug from the stand next to the bed and began taking liberties with the front of my hospital issue pyjamas. I would have protested further at the indignity, but my bladder gave up the unequal contest and I rapidly began filling the container.

A few minutes later, I had to endure even more humiliation as I called weakly to the matron for help.

'What is it?' she demanded crossly.

'Er...it's full. Can I please have another one?'

'What are you?' she exclaimed. 'A camel?'

As she bore away the two full jugs and placed a single one on the stand next to the bed again, I could only think with gratitude that at least I had not woken up thirsty and reached for what I took to be a jug of drinking water.

Chapter 54

The Colour of Empathy

South Africa is home to billions of ticks, and many of them carry the potentially lethal parasites that cause 'Biliary fever' in dogs.

The ticks inject the Babesia parasites into the dog when they bite. The protozoa enter the bloodstream of the dog and move from cell to cell, destroying each one as it bursts to release another cluster of organisms searching for new red blood cells to invade. Death is primarily due to anaemia, although a wide range of complications can occur.

Firenza was a magnificent Rottweiler brought down by the microscopic parasites floating in his blood. Under the lenses the paired, teardrop-shaped organisms were obvious in the red blood cells and the diagnosis was easy. His white gums and roaring temperature were simple clues even before the blood smear. An easy diagnosis but a challenge to treat.

He had too many parasites to kill them all in one go, since each red cell carrying a parasite would rupture as the parasite died and the resulting anaemia could be fatal. I chose to use Trypan Blue, a less effective drug that would give Firenza the chance to form new blood cells as the damaged ones died. A healthy dog can replace its entire stock of red blood cells in twenty-four hours.

Firenza's white gums took on a deep purple hue as the drug flowed into his veins with the drip fluids.

He stayed in the hospital overnight but by the second afternoon he was in serious condition and would possibly have died without intervention. Most of his red blood cells had been destroyed by the parasites and he urgently needed a transfusion. His gums were once more a deathly white, with a ghostly bluish tinge.

Blood groups in dogs are a little more complex than in humans, but you can often get away with one transfusion. A second administration frequently results in severe reactions. Firenza slowly turned pale pink again as the donor's blood flowed in. The pink, however, was short-lived.

On the third day, even the whites of his eyes had turned yellow as both his original blood cells and those from the donor ruptured, releasing their haemoglobin that was rapidly metabolised to the yellow pigments of jaundice.

A blood smear showed that many of the red blood cells were a lot smaller than normal and perfectly round, as opposed to looking like a doughnut. Large macrophages, a class of white blood cell, were also obvious, many with red blood cells that they had engulfed still visible within them.

Firenza was suffering from auto-immune haemolytic anaemia, a fancy name for a fatal condition. His white blood cells could no longer differentiate between normal and diseased red blood cells and were killing off all of them. His own immune system was finishing the job that the parasites had started.

A boring subject to most sane people but I found it fascinating. As I battled with the complexities of the disease and its complications, Firenza began to occupy a place closer to my heart than most patients. We had long chats while the drugs coursed through the drip lines and then into his veins. He allowed me to take liberties that I rarely risked with other Rottweilers as he moved closer to death, then farther away, only to swing back on the pendulum. He was a very special dog.

The science and medicine fascinated me. I read up as much as I could, and we made every effort to keep him going.

On the fifth day, Karen was busy with another patient when she passed the cage in which a very dejected Firenza lay. His eyes followed her desultorily but he looked close to the end.

'His nostrils are all blocked up,' she said with concern.

'Hmm?' I peered over to see what she meant. The dried mucous on his nose was all but preventing the movement of air.

Karen got a small bowl of warm water and a handful of earbuds. With care, she gently cleaned out each nostril in turn. Firenza watched her with widening eyes and as she finished, he gave a wiggle with his truncated tail and licked her hand.

I shook my head, perplexed. No matter what the touts of equality proclaim, men and women are not born equal. There is definitely something on the extra X chromosome that most men lack. I have since met a number of men with an equal if not greater sense of empathy and I have envied this special quality in every individual who displays it.

Firenza the rainbow dog, recovered under my care, but he saved his most effusive welcome for the women in his life.

Left to me, our son Peter would probably not have survived his childhood asthma attacks, since my diagnosis whenever he began to struggle to breathe was 'Give him a little time. I am sure he will be OK.' His mother's reaction was to race past ambulances while they struggled to keep up with her as she rushed him into hospital.

I was reminded of the special care that women give when the Grebor family brought their tiny little dog in after it had been unceremoniously rolled through the bushes and into a muddy ditch by a pack of larger dogs.

Mrs Grebor had wrapped Winston in a filthy towel that must have been pretty awful to start with but now bore the slime and foul mud from the ditch. Winston had also been unable to control himself in his fear, and the mess on the towel was extreme.

I gently disentangled the little dog and cuddled him as he shivered on the table. Rene, one of the nurses, came in to give a hand and lifted the little patient to whisk him off to the safety of a warm cage.

Mrs Grebor put out a hand to retrieve the foul scrap of cloth from the table, but Rene stopped her and picked it up herself.

'We'll put this in the cage with him,' she announced. 'It will make him feel at home because it smells like you.'

Mrs Grebor looked startled and then saw the compassion in the young nurse and understood. Nurse, dog and filthy towel left the room, and I was left facing a client who had just been unwittingly insulted.

A little twinkle appeared in the worried eyes, and she smiled when she realised that I had understood. The worry returned in full force a second later.

'Don't worry.' I reassured her, 'Winston will be fine. The girls will take excellent care of him.'

Chapter 55

THE GIFT OF LIFE

Christmas has always been a trying time for me. Giving and receiving gifts is the most stressful procedure I can imagine. I was always so conscious of the value of the gift and whether it was meaningful to the recipient. Thankfully Karen did most of the shopping, which meant I only had to get a gift for her, something I agonised over for months.

In our first year together, we had spent Christmas with my family. Six adult children and ten grandchildren, four dogs and three cats in a house that had never really known order among chaos and collected piles of useful things in corners. It was very crowded and noisy.

I always felt a little overwhelmed at such events, but when I found Karen crying in a corner, I knew it was just too much. We said our goodbyes and slipped away. From then on, we spent each Christmas in the hot, humid climate of the Natal South coast where her family had gravitated to.

It was a small price to pay once a year. I knew that for the week we stayed with her parents, I would not have a wife, as she reverted instantly back to their little girl. The conversation reverted to all the insider happenings that only those who knew their past intimately could understand. It was one week of the year in which I learned to be tolerant.

I took to going for long solitary walks and exploring the area, brimming with a natural world so different to the dry Highveld where I had grown up or the wide grasslands of the Eastern Cape where we had established roots and opened a practice.

I decided that to reduce the stress each December, I needed to buy things throughout the year that I knew she would like and hide them until required. When she admired a large brass urn, I slipped away and secreted it in our car, later hiding it in my wardrobe. A week later she chanced upon it and was so delighted that I lost my purchase as she happily displayed it next to the fireplace.

Karen took to dropping hints and close to Advent one year, she raved about a set of earrings and a necklace with sapphires in gold that she had seen in the window of a local jeweller. I paid a visit to the shop but there was no sapphire set that I could see. When questioned, the salesperson produced a lovely trio and persuaded me that it could only be the one, even though I knew it was not delicate enough to be Karen's taste.

On the day, she unwrapped the parcel and looked up in surprise. It turned out that there were two branches of the same jewellery chain and I had visited the wrong one.

The following Christmas I opened a card from her and came face to face with a message saying, 'We are going to have a baby.'

I was pole-axed.

The news was the most precious gift, but her whole extended family were sitting around opening parcels and I had no idea how to react. She expected ecstatic shouts of joy and I just wanted to share the moment alone with her.

Not for the first time, we had totally misunderstood each other. It would not be the last time either.

For our first four years together, I struggled not to complain when Karen cooked everything until it was black and crispy. On the rare occasions we had bacon for breakfast, I found it difficult to eat because when trying to spear it with a fork, it shattered and shot all over the plate and beyond. I in turn was offering her, on even rarer occasions, bacon that she could not bring herself to eat because it was still alive.

Other misconceptions slowly raised their heads.

I had established a routine of going out early the farms, while Karen took care of the clinic. At mid-day, I would return to the practice, while she went home. Unwittingly, I was being credited for all the operations she performed each morning, which I discharged in the evening. It did not make any difference that I told each client that she had been the surgeon; they just associated the work with me.

I was unaware of the state of things until a client came in to thank me for the fine work I had done on Shadow, a German shepherd with a fractured leg that had healed perfectly after Karen performed a delicate procedure in which she placed a stainless steel rod inside the shaft of the femur.

Mrs Gibson stood in front of Karen and peered over Karen's shoulder, addressing me while ignoring the surgeon who had saved Shadow.

'Thank you, Mrs Gibson. It's fantastic that Shadow is doing so well,' I responded. 'Karen here was the surgeon. I just admitted him the one evening and discharged him the following day. She did all the hard work.'

'Yes. Thank you, all of you,' Mrs Gibson replied. 'And thank you especially, Mr Phillips, for such an excellent job.'

There was nothing I could do to change things and eventually Karen had to arrange to discharge most of the surgical cases herself. It meant staying later, a move which troubled her, particularly as the bump grew while the pregnancy progressed.

Chapter 56

FINDING PREMESIS

The pending arrival of a tiny person, a chimera of me and Karen, was breath-takingly filled with drama. We had never been parents before and we had no training. How on earth were we going to manage it?

There was only one animal that Karen showed a lack of affinity for and that was a human baby. Oddly enough, babies tended to be drawn to her like a magnet and would crawl in her direction instinctively. Cats tend to show the same attraction towards people who do not really want them to curl up in their laps.

After only being together for a few months, I had noticed the largest preying mantid on the floor behind Karen. These aggressive predators hold their paired forelegs up and in front of the body, as if beseeching a deity for grace but in actual fact in preparation to strike at any prey that was foolish enough to get too close.

I had once gone searching for a wayward tennis ball in the long grass behind a court at a holiday resort, only to be pounced on by a massive mantid, who decided to make a meal of my leg. Fortunately I still carried my racquet and swiftly wacked the insect into a clump of bush. My heart rate had jumped a notch and then doubled again when the mantid immediately flew back to land on the same leg.

My swipes with the racquet became ever more frantic as I beat my little assailant off several times until I was able to make it back to the safety of the tennis court and the mockery of Mark who would not accept that I would admit to being afraid of such an insignificant opponent. I longed to be able to coax the mantid onto his leg as a kindness to both of them.

Karen was unaware of the tough little insect behind her and I expected hysterics when she came face to face with it. Bracing myself to rescue her and earn her undying gratitude, I called out to her and warned her that she was being stalked.

Karen turned and I held out my arms to catch her, only to have her bend down fluidly and scoop up the insect in her hand and lightly toss him through the open window into a bush and away from the danger of heavy heels. As delicate as she looked, there was a core of titanium under the soft exterior.

The biggest problem we faced when considering the arrival of the baby was Karen's work. No longer would she be able to travel the length and breadth of the Ciskei in a poorly sprung Isuzu pickup van. We considered the options and decided that a privately owned practice would be the most suitable path to follow.

It would inevitably be very quiet to start with and then hopefully grow with time. Karen could take it easy initially and have a lot of time to nurse our little sprog. I wasn't quite sure what had to be done for newborn babies but hoped that maternal instinct would triumph. Fortunately I was blissfully ignorant of the nights I would have to share, cradling a howling little boy while bouncing up and down to try and soothe him, or change his nappy over the next few years.

The most pressing need was to find a suitable building to convert into a veterinary practice. Our first option had been to buy the existing practice in town, but it was made clear to me that it was not for sale. I began poring over maps and driving past houses in prominent positions, knocking at doors of any potential site. Nothing seemed suitable.

A few houses seemed to be promising and I knocked on doors and got to speak to a lot of very interesting townsfolk. A vivid memory I have is a chat to a 95-year-old gentleman who was convinced that his longevity was due to him drinking two litres of water first thing every morning. He was not keen to sell his house.

Without realising it, I was spreading the word that we were in town and were intent on opening for business.

There were two sprawling doctor's practices side by side in Ayliffe Road. One of them was owned by two brothers who also had a second practice in the smarter part of the town. It appeared a little run down, whereas the second practice, owned by a second pair of brothers, had a smart entrance and seemed to be thriving. Karen urged me to find out if the first building was for sale.

'We could never afford such a large complex.' I protested.

After weeks had passed without finding anything suitable, I swallowed my pride and approached the doctors. The brothers Geldenhuys were more than just a little enthusiastic.

'We have been trying to sell for months. The only offer we have had is from the Botha brothers next door. If they buy the building, they will inherit all our clients that attend that branch.'

I diffidently explained that we might not be able to afford the amount they were asking, and the price was rapidly reduced.

At their urging, I visited the local branch of the Allied Building Society and was staggered to be offered a mortgage that covered the full price of the property.

'You will need your savings to purchase equipment and supplies.' the friendly bank manager counselled. I nodded, too taken aback to speak.

I was just about to leave when a thought came to me and I turned back to face me benefactor. 'We will also need to buy a house in town. Could you offer us a loan that would cover that as well?'

It was his turn to be surprised but after a few minutes hesitation he agreed, asking only for a small deposit for the house.

I returned home, my shoes hardly touching the ground as I floated along in sublime fulfilment. Not for the first time, I would have to admit that Karen had been right in her instincts. The building she had first spotted had turned out to be the one I should have chosen from the beginning.

When we did eventually open our doors, we did so over an easter weekend, thinking that most people would be enjoying the break and not thinking of trying out a new veterinary practice. By the end of the weekend, we had seen 34 patients per day and were exhaustedly wondering if we had done the right thing.

Although the rush of clients pouring in the doors at the new clinic abated somewhat when the town realised that we were there to stay, we had the unusual experience of thriving from day one. Plans of starting small and then growing the business once the baby no longer needed attention every minute of the day were thwarted by fate.

I unwittingly ended up with the ideal scenario in which I visited the farms and horse stables each morning, while Karen dealt with the rush of small animals at the clinic. In the afternoon, I would return to do the evening shift at the practice. I had not only a very fulfilling diversity, but many of the townsfolk came to regard the practice as mine, since even surgical cases that were operated on in the morning needed to be discharged in the evening by yours truly.

I arrived back at the clinic one day after a hot morning dealing with 400 cows on a dairy farm on the coast, to find a note stuck to the door. It read 'Gone to hospital. Baby on its way.'

I cancelled all appointments for the afternoon and raced to the maternity ward in expectation. The staff looked at me in surprise and informed me that it would be hours still before junior put in an appearance.

'You need not have been so hasty, Mr Phillips. The baby will come when it is ready.'

I had so often given the same advice when clients called about their animals going into labour. Somehow it seemed very different when it involved the two people most precious to me.

I returned to the practice and dealt with the patients too urgent to wait until the next day. The receptionist scolded me for making Karen work right up to the last minute, and I felt decidedly guilty. Karen, however had been stoic and accepting. Neither of us had been through a birth before and did not really know what to expect. She had attended antenatal classes, but I was unaware that I was expected to join her at the time. She said nothing, as our fledgling surgery grew rapidly and consumed both our lives in an endless rush.

Peter arrived the following morning, after a sleepless night for both of us. I had assisted so many domestic animals in the birth process that I was surprised at how traumatic it was for humans. Had I any inkling of the pain ahead I would never have tenderly held Karen's hand while she squeezed it until I could hardly bear the agony. I was convinced her fingerprints remained on the palm of my hand for weeks afterwards. Mothers have no idea what their husbands go through for them.

The squat little blue-grey Buddha-like baby was not what I had expected, but the instant I held him, I knew a rush of feeling that overwhelmed me. It was obvious that Karen felt the same.

Two other babies were born in the same ward that day, one of them to a delightful Taiwanese mother who delivered a handsome little Chinese boy. She was open and friendly, and Karen bonded with her from the start. The father insisted that his child be given an identity armband so that he would not be confused with anyone else. The staff smiled as they complied and labelled the only good-looking child with dark black hair in the ward.

Peter developed jaundice and was put under a phototherapy blue light to help his body break down the yellow pigment.

'Why is your little boy having the blue light on him?' the Taiwanese mother wanted to know.

'Because he is yellow and needs to be treated,' Karen explained.

'But my boy is also yellow,' she replied, with a twinkle in her eyes. It was clear that she understood and clearly preferred her baby to the insipid occupants of the cots on either side of him. It was a time of rejoicing for six parents, each couple engrossed in the new centre around which their lives would revolve for the next few years and hopefully for the rest of their lives.

Chapter 57

A WEE DRAM OF THE WARM STUFF MELTS THE ICE

Starting a veterinary practice from scratch after only being qualified for less than two years brought with it untold stress. Overnight I became architect, builder, equipment purchaser, accountant, decorator, and slave, without any prior training.

The practice was in the tiny hamlet of King William's Town, last outpost of the British Empire and a small enclave of white South Africa almost totally surrounded by the Ciskei, home to the Southern Xhosa nation.

The task of employing staff seemed both ridiculously easy and impossibly complex. There were only a dozen veterinary nurses in the entire country in '87, and none of them ventured down into our remote little town. I needed someone to fetch and carry, to hold animals and clean floors. More exacting tasks could wait until we had a steady stream of clients beating their way to our door.

With unrealistic abandon I took on a nervous young Xhosa man, purely because he was the first person to come looking for work. With such little forethought, I gained one of the most important assets of the business.

From the first day Cecil was hopeless. The problem was that he was petrified of me. I needed someone to jump to my every command because there just weren't enough hours in the day to achieve a tenth of the urgent things lined up for me. Cecil jumped but by no means in a useful direction. I decided fairly quickly to look for a replacement assistant as soon as possible.

In the very early hours of the morning, the Browns rang to say that Sylvestor was in trouble. Sylvestor the cat was crying pitifully and seemed unable to get up. I sleepily agreed to see him at the surgery.

As I examined the little body that lay on the table, Cecil unobtrusively entered through the back. He had rooms to the rear of the building. My hands gently felt the tiny waist and the problem was instantly obvious. Sylvestor had a cricket-ball sized lump in his normally soft and pliable abdomen.

'His bladder is blocked,' I announced to the two worried faces on the other side of the table. 'He cannot urinate, and the waste products are building up in his body.'

At their prompting I continued, 'Left like this, he will die.' I omitted any reference to the agony that he must have already been experiencing. 'We need to give him emergency treatment to try and stabilise him and then catheterise him.'

The anxious faces nodded, and the procedure began.

We had no quick access to blood tests in those days, but within a very short time, Sylvestor was sporting a drip line into his cephalic vein and the blessed relief of sedatives, painkillers and finally anaesthetics coursed through his veins. The crying stopped.

From my vast experience of two years, I had found that intravenous silicone catheters and washing up soap worked far better than the urinary catheters and Walpole's buffer designed for the procedure. Unblocking male cats was very common in the last half of the century, until it was shown that all the foods sold for cats were at fault. Almost overnight the incidence dropped from a weekly ritual to several cases a year. Sylvestor was a victim of the industry's ignorance of feline nutrition.

'Cecil, could you pass me that…' I began.

'Scissors!' he said in anticipation, gleefully holding out the instrument.

'No, Cecil. I want the…'

'Elastoplast!' Once again, the proffered item.

'No, Cecil. Just stop. Stop and listen.'

'Yes,' he said, chastened.

'Pass me a 10ml syringe and that bowl of solution.'

'Yes,' he said triumphantly, passing me a bandage and a drip tube.

Cecil and Sylvestor contrived to see me in an early grave over the next two hours. Try as I might, I just could not insert the hair-thin catheter. The urethra was blocked with sharp Struvite crystals, a composite of Calcium, Phosphorus and Magnesium that looked ominously like tiny chisel blades under the microscope.

As my cursing increased in volume, so Cecil seemed to shrink as he tried unsuccessfully to escape observation. In desperation I reached forward to feel the turgid swelling once again in the pitiful body in front of me.

I never pushed very hard at all. Hardly touched him. Sylvestor had no excuse for what happened next as a stream of hot, rancid urine squirted into my face and all over me, while I went rigid with shock and horror. Sylvestor sighed with relief while every cell in my body absorbed the negative energy he had bequeathed with his anointing.

To make matters worse, Cecil started with a full-blown epileptic fit. Of all times to choose. He started to twitch and writhe, leaning against the table in what seemed like agony with his eyes closed tightly and his lips drawn back in a rictus of pain. I had already learned of the abnormally high level of epilepsy in the nation just over the border—a tribute, I later learned, to the ministrations and treatments of the witchdoctors.

Suddenly Cecil dashed from the room and out into the darkness. My concern for him was tempered by my even bigger concern for Sylvestor. I could not abandon a patient under anaesthetic, particularly one in such a precarious situation. In desperation, I rushed to the window to see if Cecil was still alive. In the dusky rear garden, I could just make him out as he leaned against a tree, seeming to sob uncontrollably, and then suddenly it struck home. The little swine was laughing. Laughing at me. I returned, disillusioned, to my patient.

Slowly the reality and the irony of the situation seeped through my anger and irritation and my mouth began to turn up wryly at the edges, only to quickly return to stern solemnity as the taste of urea edged in.

Cecil returned quietly into the farthest reaches of the room and began to tidy up, his head bent and eyes firmly fixed on the floor. I had made Sylvestor comfortable in a hospital cage and he was slowly waking up and peering about, completely unaware of the cataclysmic trauma he had put me through.

As Cecil moved past me, I noticed him peering anxiously out of the corner of his eyes. I wagged a finger at him, and a little sparkle of pure delight lit up his eyes, a sparkle that never faded over the next five years as he grew and learnt and became the ever-reliant backstop, forever ready to do anything to help. I think in truth he was hoping for a repeat performance, something I was equally as determined not to take part in.

Chapter 58

ALIBI IN NAPPIES

At the age of six months, Peter proved to be a nocturnal animal, sleeping fitfully during the day and crying at night. After months of rocking him in the dark in hour-long shifts, his parents were considering the merits of adoption. We would have paid for an adoption. Anyone could have him, providing we did not have to pay them too much.

It was after eight months of age when a more than averagely observant doctor pointed to the skin over the windpipe just above the join of the breastbones that was sucked in with every breath and commented: 'Your little boy has asthma. Look, he is hardly getting any air at all.' Lying flat in a cot with a severely compromised respiratory system, it was very lucky that he survived. We felt unrealistically guilty.

Months earlier, after a particularly bad night, I had staggered tiredly off to work in the morning, wondering just how I was going to manage to get through the day. Fortunately, no arduous physical tasks had been scheduled.

I walked down the corridor of the headquarters of Ulimocor and found my office largely by feel, as my eyelids seemed to be sagging around my ankles. The telephone rang even before I found the chair, and the Director General firmly invited me to join him in his office.

This was the end of it, I thought. I knew I had not been performing very well over the past few months and no doubt others had also noticed. I was clearly going to be dismissed.

As I entered the office at the end of the corridor, two burly men in uniform stepped forward, one to each side of me. I looked at them owlishly in surprise. A third figure in plain clothes approached me from the front. He made no attempt to introduce himself, but instead asked curtly, 'Where were you last night?'

'At home,' I said simply. 'I spent most of the night trying to get our baby to sleep.'

'Do you have any witnesses to corroborate this?'

I smiled, which deepened the scowl of suspicion on his face. 'I guess my son can vouch for me.'

'Can you call your son and ask him to come into this office?'

I made the mistake of chuckling. 'No,' I confessed. 'He is only six months old. I was trying to get him to sleep.'

'And your wife?'

'I guess you could ask her. I think she was there last night. At least there was someone who took Peter when I passed him to them in the dark. Must have been her.'

My interrogator was unimpressed. 'I have three independent witnesses,' he announced, 'who all described your van and gave the correct licence number, as the vehicle that hit and killed a pedestrian in Zwelitsha last night at…' He consulted a sheaf of papers in his hand. '…2:35 a.m.'

I laughed. He was very good. I wondered who had put him up to this. I peered around to see if they had rigged up cameras to record an episode of *You've Been Framed* but could not spot anything.

'Dr Philips,' he said importantly, 'I am arresting you for the murder of an individual as yet un-named, on the night of the fifth of December 1988.'

I laughed again, which further perplexed him. At his command I followed him out of the building and curiously, he allowed me to drive between the two police vehicles as we made our way down to the squalid little police station in the centre of Zwelitsha.

I was shown into a room and seated on a straight-backed chair just inside the room and facing the far wall, which had a window through which a shaft of bright sunshine penetrated. The light was painful to the eyes and I moved to shift the chair to the side when a voice from the dark depths told me to stay where I was. I realised that there was a second person in the room, carefully positioned so that I could not see him against the glare.

He questioned me for several hours, at the end of which I was probably mumbling. I had never been so tired in my life.

I experienced no concern at the charges. I was innocent and at that stage of life I truly believed in the integrity of the police and the courts.

The truth was that I unconsciously held an extremely privileged position: I was a white male in a society in which white males had for over a century been at the pinnacle of command. In a different era, a different land and a different culture, the very characteristics that were my 'Get-out-of-jail-free' card could prove to be the exact opposite.

In the end they let me go, but not before my unseen interrogator informed me that he was required to incarcerate someone, and it was looking as if it was going to be me. I disloyally hoped they had a bed in the cell and that they would provide someone else to rock the baby each night.

As I drove off, it occurred to me just how negligent they were being in allowing me back on the road in my present condition. If the car had not known the way home, I am sure I would never have made it. Never before had the thought of bed seemed so enticing.

Chapter 59

INSPECTOR CLOUSEAU
I PRESUME?

Waking from the depths of exhaustion, I realised that while I was immobile, my brain had raced off like an unleashed dog going for a walk and doing twenty times the distance that its master does. It thought I had the answer to the puzzle. I was not so sure that the police would buy it.

I drove out to the garage where Ulimocor routinely had their vehicles serviced and spoke to the manager. He abruptly dismissed my request and let me know that he had only recently purchased the dealership and would have no records from the era I was talking about. Fortunately, the elderly woman who sat tapping her teeth with a pencil in the next office was able to help. I left, armed with the information I needed.

At the police station they informed me that the captain in charge of the case had left and would only be back the next day. I once again made my way down to the little station the following morning, ever more eager to share my thoughts with him.

'I think I know what has happened.'

He looked sceptically at me. I saw him glancing at my hands and wondered if he was visually measuring it for the cuffs.

'Six months ago, I had an accident in a van belonging to Ulimocor. Only the front of the van was damaged, but the insurance company wrote it off.' He sniffed but seemed a little more interested.

'They gave me another identical vehicle and since the new one was registered at the same time that the old one was de-registered, it ended up with the same licence plate. I remember at the time thinking that although I had cost the company R50,000 I had saved them R15 since the plates could be re-used.'

I definitely had his attention now.

'I went to the garage that handled everything yesterday,' I continued. 'They have a record of the van coming in and the assessment for repairs and they have a record of the sale of the new vehicle. They have no record of the damaged van being disposed of.'

I could see by the light in his eyes that I did not really need to carry on, but I was enjoying my role.

'I think that someone patched up the old van and carried on driving it without getting it registered. When they hit the pedestrian, they knew they were in an illegal vehicle and that is why they did not stop.'

The police captain was very reluctant to give any credit for my brilliant sleuthing but promised 'to look into it.'

I left and sadly, never ever heard anything more about it.

I was nevertheless elated, and in my mind, I had narrowly escaped the gallows. I often wonder if they caught the guilty driver. Perhaps there is still a warrant out for my arrest. There may be posters on the walls of police stations showing a man slumped at the steering wheel with his eyes closed and baby-sick staining the shoulder of his shirt. A very desperate man indeed.

I am probably safe in that a few years ago, I contacted the South African tax office, to be told that their computers only went back as far as the year 2000 and they had no records from before this. They are very wise in only keeping tabs on those under twenty years of age. We oldies never did anything wrong.

I could not wait to tell the rest of the staff at Ulimocor, a few of whom no doubt had been thinking of possible replacements for the second-best inspector in Africa masquerading as a vet. Some of them seemed distinctly disappointed that their recipes for 'Cake with a File in it' would no longer be necessary.

Chapter 60

COKE, MAGNETS AND WIRE

'Always keep a piece of wire in your pocket. Then you can produce it if you cannot find anything in the rumen." Sage words from an experienced surgeon, imparted to a lecture hall of attentive students. Owners of cattle were rarely sympathetic when faced with a large bill and a cow taken out of production because the vet was convinced it had a piece of wire causing problems deep within her body.

My patient, a black and white Friesland milk cow, was showing all the signs of having ingested a sharp piece of wire that had penetrated the walls of her stomach and was now heading for the heart.

Modern practice is to use X-rays to locate the wire and, in many cases, if the patient is given a large magnet to swallow, the wire will become attached to the magnet and rendered innocuous. In the eighties, working in a remote African country, neither portable radiographs nor magnets were available to us.

'Her rumen is not moving at all. She is showing extreme pain when lifted with a pole under her chest, and I could hear a faint tinkle when I listened to her heart.'

I had my doubts about the last point. The sound had been very faint, and I could not always hear it. However, the other signs all indicated the possibility of Dorcas having a foreign body piercing the rumen wall.

"Can't we just give her some Coke?" Mr Mantinda asked.

I sighed at the common fallacy. So many farmers had expressed their unfaltering faith in the ability of the popular soft drink to dissolve anything in the digestive tract of their animals. It amazed me that they were all too happy to drink the stuff themselves.

I shook my head, but Mr Mantinda dispatched a young boy, or *kwedien*, on some errand which I later learned was to purchase a large bottle of cola.

In our final year at university, a small group of students had been given an opportunity that we jumped at. A herd of eighty prize Bonsmara cattle needed our help. Even more amazingly, the breeder, his private vet and the university were all keen to encourage us.

In one of the more severe droughts that plague Africa, this enterprising farmer had taken measures to preserve his herd of sleek brown cattle with their characteristic stocky, muscular conformation and, in doing so, had sentenced them to certain death.

Hay, alfalfa and silage were not cheap, but they could see the cattle through to the Spring rains. The farmer found a ready source of supply and then set about enclosing the cattle and creating a means of feeding them without allowing them to trample the precious fodder.

South Africans are fond of the saying 'Boer Maak 'n Plan': Farmers find solutions. The word 'Boer' also refers to the intrepid Afrikaans nation who gave the mighty British Empire a run for their money in the two Boer wars.

This Boer bought a load of used telegraph poles from the government, and long lengths of old, unsheathed cables. The cables were the problem in that they were comprised of multiple smaller strands of steel wire, twisted tightly around each other. Innocuous in their pristine condition, the years had taken their toll and short lengths of individual strands had broken and dropped to the ground.

The hapless farmer had constructed a *kraal* or pen using the poles to hold up the lengths of cable. The cattle were able to push their heads between the cables and reach the fodder spread on the ground, just outside the kraal. The short pieces of wire were easily ingested by the cattle, with their broad mouths and strong tongues.

The wire travelled down the oesophagus and into the first of the four stomachs, or rumen. This large muscular sac contracts roughly once a minute, mixing food, bacteria and fluid in a huge fermentation vat. Smaller amounts are pushed through into the second stomach, the reticulum, with a net-like layer lining the walls. Wires that got stuck in this stomach would with time penetrate the wall because of the repeated contractions, and many of them would get pushed forward into the sac surrounding the heart or even the muscles of the heart itself. Death was a common result.

The private vet had operated on a dozen cows and removed a score of embedded wires. Several others had died before he could get to them. Faced with a further eighty patients in a critical state, the farmer and vet had turned to the university and a small group of us had been enrolled as embryo surgeons. We were in the right place at the right time.

Working in pairs, we confined each massive bovine in a crush, or chute, constructed of wooden poles. The animals were fortunately benign and placid, used to being handled by their keepers. Experience had taught us that an aggressive Bonsmara could either leap out of the crush or use their powerful neck muscles to seriously hurt an unwary arm caught between head and pole, or kick viciously between the bars.

One student injected several bottles of local anaesthetic into the skin and muscle layers over the area just behind the left rib cage and below the spine, effectively blocking the nerves that ran down from the spinal cord.

The second student scrubbed up ready for surgery and then made a long incision running downwards, parallel to the last rib. Several incisions were required to penetrate through all the layers into the abdomen. The bulging, grey sac of the rumen was easily identified, and it too had to be cut open, all the while preventing any of the contents from spilling into the abdomen.

A scrubbed arm, covered in a long blue stocking-glove would then be inserted through the opening in the skin, muscles and rumen. Digging around in the contents and slowly finding the opening to the reticulum was an indescribable occurrence. Rumen contents have the sweet, aromatic smell reminiscent of freshly mown lawns and fermenting beer, with a hint of ammonia that is not unpleasant at all.

Finding the elusive wires and removing them gives a feeling of euphoria that could possibly be partly due to the fermentation fumes, but nevertheless was immensely rewarding. We had saved one more life. We each got to operate on eight cows and after two days we were all both exhausted and walking on air.

Around the campfire in the evening, the experienced vets were encouraged to relate the most memorable events of their careers. Beer in hand and illuminated by the flickering flames, Prof Coetzee told how his practice had been built on a very steep slope, with an entrance at the level of the passing road, but the rear of the property falling sharply downhill.

Late one evening, he had been called upon to help with a nursing bitch that had given birth ten days earlier and was now showing signs of a calcium deficiency. As the thirsty pups drained her of milk, the calcium resources in her body rapidly became depleted and she collapsed and started shaking, finally going into full-blown seizures. The prof fortunately had both the knowledge and the remedy. He set up a drip and ran in a large volume of Calcium Borogluconate. The result was almost immediate, but the side effects took a little longer.

The rapid reversal in electrolyte balance in the body had widespread sequela, the most obvious being extreme nausea. The poor mother stopped convulsing and instead began to heave. The watching owner, full of empathy for his dog, began to feel sick himself. After a short while he put his hand to his mouth, but the undulating motion of his shoulders gave the game away.

With explosive suddenness, the owner rushed towards the back door, mistaking it for the bathroom, and then found himself treading on air as he tumbled down three stories to the gulley below. Professor Coetzee spent the rest of the night patching his second patient up and taking him to the local hospital for care. The mother dog took less time to return to normality than her caring owner.

A few years later, now working in the remote Ciskei, I eventually prevailed upon Mr Mantinda to allow me to operate. We tied the forlorn animal against the side of the crush, after which I infiltrated the site just behind the ribs on the left-hand side with a local anaesthetic.

Twenty minutes later, I gingerly I put my hand into the opening on the side of the cow. The moment of truth had arrived. I silently began to wish I had taken the advice and kept a piece of wire handy to produce miraculously if all else failed.

There was no wire. At least none that I could find. I swept my hand over the floor of the huge stomach, pulling carefully at the walls to feel if they had adhered to other organs, all to no avail. Mr Mantinda correctly interpreted the look on my face.

"There's nothing in there," he said crossly.

At that moment, the young boy dispatched to the local store returned triumphantly bearing his bottle of Coke. Mr Mantinda's scowl deepened. Not only had he suffered the cost of the operation and the loss of production from his cow, but he had also spent money on a remedy that clearly was not going to be needed, because of this idiotic vet who had made a misdiagnosis.

I was about to withdraw my hand when my little finger brushed against something hard. Desperately I moved my hand farther back, groping for the object I had felt. The opening to the smaller stomachs was totally obstructed by a large mass. I grabbed a free end and pulled.

Slowly, from the depths of the animal, a long, green piece of material was produced. Only when I had most of it out and had shaken off the adhering material was the dark blue cloth visible. A belt with a buckle at one end tinkled as I threw it over a pole.

"My overalls!" exclaimed Mr Mantinda. "They went missing last week." He picked up the pungent mess, shaking it out ruefully. A hard lump of extraneous material had become enmeshed in the cloth.

'Never mind," I advised. "Soak it in Coke and it'll all come off." For a moment he looked at me quizzically and then gave a generous smile and chuckled ruefully.

An array of mugs was produced and as a group we happily consumed the cold beverage. At least we could sleep peacefully, knowing that any hardware we had inadvisably consumed would be digested by the sweet, caffeine-laced liquid.

Chapter 61

BACK TO FRONT

'Worsie can't stand up. He was fine last night but this morning he hasn't moved, and he bit me when I tried to make him get up. He seems to be paralysed in his back legs.'

Worsie was a Dachshund, or *Worshund* in German. His elongated backbone made him a prime candidate for a spinal disc prolapse. It was not good news.

'We will need to get him to the practice to assess him and probably take some X-rays. Can you bring him down now?'

I gave instructions on how to gently tie his mouth with a stocking and then support his entire body on a board when they lifted him into the car. I had a waiting room filled with urgent cases, and it would be hours before we could consider doing a house-call.

Joe from the SPCA had brought in three feral cats for neutering. Joe and his wife were retired farmers from Zimbabwe. Having lost everything in their country of birth, they had taken on the thankless task of running the local animal rescue centre, which they did with simple efficiency and an endearing love for their inmates. I could not but help feeling humble in their presence.

'Remember to cut the tip off their left ears when they are under anaesthetic,' he asked. 'I don't want to spend hours catching them again in a couple of months' time, only to find that they have already been done.'

Feral cats are generally returned to the site where they were found and released again. They are rarely happy in a house and if an area is suddenly devoid of cats, others merely move in. Clipping the ear meant that they could be identified as sterile and left in peace.

The couple with the Dachshund arrived far sooner than I expected. They had to be very concerned about Worsie to have travelled so fast. I took them straight into the consulting room ahead of three other cases that had been waiting for some time. As they disappeared into the room, I apologised to the small crowd, who were gracious in accepting the need to get the little dog some pain relief.

Worsie looked at me from the side of his eyes, almost daring me to allow my fingers close enough to snap at. He lay on the consulting table watching me warily but seemed very alert and in no risk of going into shock.

'Be careful,' the wife warned. 'He is well known for being aggressive.'

I took her warning seriously, even though I had been subject to far too many little canine crocodiles before to have not approached him with care from the beginning. I needed to test his pain reflexes in detail, but that could wait until we were ready to give him an anaesthetic prior to taking some radiographs. It would no doubt upset him to have his crooked little legs handled to insert a catheter, and it did not make sense to upset him twice by manhandling him now.

'I will just give him something for the pain first,' I started to explain.

'Will that be necessary?' The couple seemed surprised. I, in turn, was amazed at their reaction. I am sure that if they had been suffering from a slipped disc, they would want some pain relief.

'Then we'll take him through to the X-ray room and get some radiographs of his spine.'

'But that will cost a fortune.' The husband was almost apoplectic with anger.

'It is the only way to assess his back, I'm afraid.' MRI and CT scanners were a long way off from being developed. If we could not make a clear diagnosis from survey X-rays, we would inject a contrast medium into the space around the spinal cord, to see how far it flowed up the spine until it stopped at any obstruction, but I did not mention it to the owners. They seemed upset enough as it was.

It is possible to get a good idea where the damage in the backbone is by doing a detailed clinical examination and working out where the nerves are damaged by checking all the reflexes. The examination would be done regardless but X-rays could give us so much more information as well.

Corrine, the receptionist, opened the door and seemed about to interrupt me. I ignored her for a few minutes while I delivered the final part of our normal preamble when admitting patients for surgery.

'Before we give an anaesthetic, we always give owners the option of having blood tests done. If there is any evidence of damage to a vital organ, particularly the liver or kidneys, then we either do not go ahead, or we take measures to support these organs while under anaesthesia.' I made the offer, not expecting them to accept it after their angry reaction to the suggestion of anaesthesia to take radiographs.

The wife looked as if she could not believe her ears, while the husband stepped forward and picked up his dog, carelessly allowing the back legs to slip from his grasp and stormed out of the room.

'Nothing but a money-grabber,' I heard him say over his shoulder. His wife gave me a look of fury and followed her partner from the room.

Corrine spoke before I could react to the unwarranted criticism.

'Worsie the Dachshund has just arrived' she announced. 'They are in the next consulting room.'

'But then, who was…'

'That was Alex. He came in to have his nails clipped.' She looked apologetic. 'Sorry, but you met them at the door and took them straight in. I never had a chance to warn you.'

The owners of the first sausage dog refused to believe my apologetic explanation when I phoned them later, while the second little Worsie went on to have a spinal operation, which required the owners travelling almost a thousand miles to get to a surgical specialist. It was a total success, and we saw him for many years afterwards. The neat little zipper of a scar running down his back never quite disappeared.

The final patient of the day accompanied Mr Brown, a neighbour from the same street we lived in.

'I got Millie from the rescue centre,' he let me know. 'She has one ear that has the tip cut off. They said it was to sterilise her.' He paused and looked puzzled. 'How does cutting the tip of the ear off prevent her from having kittens?'

Chapter 62

X-Ray the Wallet

I like to think of myself as having at least average intelligence but there are many fields that completely bewilder me. I have, for instance, never understood how women can spend an hour chatting to a friend on the telephone; surely there are not enough things in the whole world to discuss for so long?

Another field that I felt I should have at least a basic grasp of is business finance, and yet I have repeatedly been humbled by my lack of acumen in this area.

Working for the government in a very remote area in which expensive diversions were decidedly lacking and having a vehicle at our disposal, our only large expense was the rent of the house, which was very modest indeed. As a result, we began to accumulate a tidy balance in our bank account. This had been bolstered by the fact that before our wedding, I had been led to believe that I would be footing the bill for the ceremony and had cancelled plans for a honeymoon on the Greek Isles and instead accepted a low-cost cottage on the coast. At the last minute, Karen's parents had come up with funds that covered almost all of it. The funds I had collected for our honeymoon had not yet been spent.

For a student of nine years, living as cheaply as possible, the slowly rising heap of shekels seemed enormous, and I nervously decided it needed to be invested wisely. Brian Tyrell, a friend who ran a large accounting firm that advised the Ciskei government, graciously offered to advise me where to secret my small fortune and I was only too keen to listen. I arranged to visit him in his plush offices in Bisho.

Each morning, as I prepared to leave the house to drive to the area I was to be working for the day, I would notice an old man in a long black coat, walking slowly past the house, with a decided stoop to his shoulders. All he needed was a scythe to make him an exact copy of the Grim Reaper. So morose was his attitude that I felt deeply sorry for him. A little Jack Russell stuck faithfully to his heels, intent only on following its master and oblivious to all distractions.

One Sunday afternoon there was an urgent knocking on the front door, and I opened it to find the sombre old man standing in the fading sunlight with his little dog in his arms.

'Two big dogs attacked him,' he said in a tone so low I had to strain to hear the words. 'He never had a chance. All he wanted was to defend me.' The tremor in his voice and the moist eyes were testimony to his trauma.

I gathered the mauled dog in my arms and took him around to the little lean-to at the back of the garden. We stored excess equipment and medications in the depths of the shed, and I had set out a small stainless steel table just inside the door. It looked like a rudimentary veterinary surgery, even if it had yet to see any patients.

Without the luxury of inhaled gas anaesthetics, I relied on the injectable Pentobarbitone in a syringe, needle inserted into the vein that runs on the upper surface of the foreleg. Worried about shock, I set up a drip in the other leg and began the task of repairing our patient's injuries.

I love stitching up wounds. The patient arrives in pain and often covered in blood. The skin and sometimes deeper layers are ripped open untidily, leaving gaping, jagged deficits in the integrity of perfection. Repairing the damage and putting everything back in place is infinitely satisfying. A happy, pain-free wag of a tail is worth far more than any monetary fee.

I found it hard to set a price for the work. In any veterinary hospital a lot of the costs are due to the economics of staff wages and overheads for rent, drugs and equipment. In our situation it had cost me a Sunday afternoon, but I could think of worse ways to spend the time. In the end I charged the old man a nominal fee, conscious of his humble appearance.

A month later, I was once again called out on a Sunday. As I drove out of the driveway, Elizabeth, the maid from next door, held out a bundle of letters.

"Your dogs wanted to bite the postman every time he tried to put these into your box."

I thanked her and drove off.

Mr Ntefu was a man of stature. He greeted me warmly and then produced two young puppies who looked extremely sorry for themselves.

'I have a litter of eight. They were all doing really well and then this morning these two are vomiting and have very bad diarrhoea with blood in it.'

My heart sank. Parvovirus had exclusively affected cats up until a few years previously, when almost overnight it had crossed the divide between the species and began to rapidly kill off susceptible young dogs. There are other causes of similar symptoms, but the rapid spread of the disease throughout the world only a few years prior to this put it high on the list of differential diagnoses.

'I think your pups may have Parvovirus. If they do, then the whole litter will probably get it and they may all get very ill. Parvovirus often kills young dogs.'

Mr Ntefu regarded me expressionlessly. 'Can you treat them?'

'Well…' I hesitated. 'There is no cure for viral diseases yet, including the common cold or AIDS. We have, however, managed to pull a lot of them through by putting them on a drip to replace the fluids and electrolytes they lose as a result of the vomiting and diarrhoea. We do use a lot of other drugs and hospital care, but it is the drip that makes the difference. If we can keep them going until their own immune system fights off the virus, they stand a chance of surviving.'

'I would like that,' he agreed.

'It can become very expensive,' I warned. Keeping fluids running into a litter of puppies around the clock for a week can result in a hefty bill.

'I will pay.' He smiled.

I wondered if he knew what he was letting himself in for. Although he was well-dressed and assured, there was no knowing what his financial status was. With more than a little trepidation, we admitted the two pups and spent the evening setting them up in the isolation ward.

I was on my way home again when I passed Elizabeth walking in the same direction. As I sped by, the irony of the situation struck me: Here I was, a privileged motorist, ignoring the plight of a fellow being, even after she had earlier gone out of her way to help me. I braked hard, pulling off the road and reversing back towards the lone figure.

It was only when she climbed into the car that I realised my mistake. Where I had expected a neatly dressed Elizabeth, the woman who flung herself into the seat was dirty, with a torn, stained dress. Worst of all, she did not look like she was going to get out in a hurry.

'Where are you going?' I asked, accepting the inevitable. Better to take her there than create a scene.

'Nowhere,' she said, leering at me.

'What do you mean, nowhere?'

'I know what you want.' She nodded knowingly. 'It will cost you twenty rand.'

The realisation hit with a jolt. My surprise was even greater because of my preconceived ideas: In my mind a lady of the night wore a long scarlet dress and stood in the light of a streetlamp, exuding an expensive scent while coyly showing an ankle.

The slovenly woman on the seat next to me had none of the above qualities. In fact, it struck me that a man would have to be really desperate to feel anything but revulsion.

'I think you had better get out,' I said.

'No. I want my money first.'

It crossed my mind that I should just drive home, but the thought of Karen coming out to find this creature in my car flattened any burgeoning courage.

Perhaps I could drive to the police station.

A picture of Captain Joubert, whose dog I had treated for a skin condition the previous week, flashed through my mind. It would be hard to bear his amused grin while trying to salvage some pride.

'You must get out,' I repeated, tempted to give her a shove. She remained seated, regarding me impassively, sure of her power over the weaker sex.

A solution finally occurred to me. 'I'm sorry,' I said, 'I have AIDS.'

Her composure faltered for the first time. 'AIDS?'

'Yes, you know. The disease that kills you. There is no cure.'

'You don't look sick.'

'Do you want to take a chance?'

She looked at me hesitantly before slowly edging off the seat. Slamming the door, she let rip with a string of four letter words, while I gratefully drove off as fast as I could.

'What took you so long?' asked Karen when I finally got home.

I was sorely tempted to make up a story, but in the end I told her everything, expecting a frosty response. To my chagrin, she laughed delightedly, questioning me in detail, before phoning everyone she could think of to relate the sordid details.

For weeks afterwards I would pass one of her friends in the street who would greet me with stiff composure, only to break into muffled giggles the moment I was supposedly out of earshot. I decided there and then to be more selective who I gave lifts to in the future.

My judgement was brought into question shortly afterwards when I learned that the elderly man in the black coat who had brought his dog to me after it was mauled was not at all as I had assumed.

'He owns three factories in Mdantsani,' I was told. 'He just looks as if he is penniless, after he was attacked by a group of men one evening in his factory. They took a lot of money but more importantly, they broke his spirit. Now he just lives for his dog, even though he is worth a fortune.'

Ruefully, I remembered a partner in the practice I had worked at as a student warning me never to try and judge how much a client could afford. 'Just do the work and charge it fairly. Never try to X-ray a client's wallet.'

The conversation came back to me as I faced the rest of the litter of puppies when Mr Ntefu brought them all in. They were clearly in various stages of debilitation, the havoc wrought by the Parvovirus as it stripped the cells lining the intestines and purged the poor patients of mucosa and a large amount of blood, leaving them dehydrated and listless.

'The first two are a little better but still have a long way to go,' I informed him. 'The costs are mounting up, even if we only charge for the materials.' I mentioned a figure.

Mr Ntefu did not bat an eyelid. Instead, he asked me to carry on and left the whole litter for us to nurse for a week, at the end of which the whole building reeked of the pungent odour of Parvovirus and bloody diarrhoea.

We pulled all but one pup through, and Mr Ntefu collected them with obvious delight. I diffidently handed him a bill that had been pared down to the minimum. We were going to suffer a big loss in this case, but the amount owing was nevertheless staggering.

'I thought it would be much more than that,' he said gratefully. I smiled and nodded. Little did he know just how much we had done for free, even if the account came to thousands.

As he opened his wallet, a card fell to the floor and I stooped to pick it up.

'You can keep that if you like,' Mr Ntefu offered graciously. 'It is my company in Dimbaza.'

I turned the card over to read 'Bisho Beer Wholesalers.' It took a few minutes for the image of the large warehouse to come to mind, a complex that occupied most of one side of the town.

'We made five million this year and the Christmas period is not finished yet.'

I felt stunned. I had once again judged a person and got it horribly wrong. I watched as he counted out the money, wishing I could take back the statement he held and replace all the bits I had cut out. His grateful smile and the sight of seven happy puppies play-fighting in their pen should have made up for it but sadly, I resented my largesse and promised myself I would not do it again.

Later in the week, I paid a call on Brian Tyrell. As he showed me into his office and offered coffee, I was overwhelmed by the opulence and air of success that seemed to hang in the air. Banks of computers stood in silent deference along one wall, eager to comply with their master's requests.

'Gold.' Brian gave the word a reverence uncharacteristic for his reserved nature. 'Gold shares are everything at the moment.'

He tapped on the keys of the nearest computer and a colourful graph appeared on the screen. Even I could see that the gradient of the tracing was consistently upwards.

'Gold has outdone the FTSE and the Dow Jones every year for seventeen years now. You can't go wrong with gold.'

He could have told me to invest in snow and I would have accepted his advice. Finance and economics were a closed book to me.

The next day I confidently walked into the office of the manager of the Standard Bank to arrange the purchase of the gold shares.

'A good move. A very good move, if you don't mind me saying so,' he commented. Mistaking my hesitation for doubt, he said more forcefully, 'I have taken out a second mortgage on my house and invested it in gold shares. That is how certain I am that they are a winner. You won't regret it.'

The shares would be mine by Thursday afternoon. On Friday, Karen and I flew up to Johannesburg and then drove to the University of Pretoria for our monthly lectures for the medicine honours degree. That evening we made our way to my parents' house, halfway between the two cities.

Dad, as always, made us welcome and asked how our careers were progressing. I smiled inwardly, happy at the news we could pass on to the effect that we had joined the financially savvy elite that knew their way through the maze of economics.

'I bought some shares today,' I announced casually. I failed to add that we had invested every spare cent to our name.

Dad's interest was immediate. 'What were the shares?'

I resisted the temptation to inspect my fingernails as I casually replied, 'Gold.' There was an unexpected silence, which puzzled me. 'Western Durban Deep Mine, actually.'

'How much did you invest?' Dad asked cautiously.

'Fourteen thousand.' A sum that would have paid for two years at university. More money than I had ever seen. A tenth of the value of a house.

Dad slowly reached for the newspaper on the coffee table in front of him. Turning it over, he held it out to me, with the headlines in bold black print on the top:

'GOLD PLUMMETS: BLACK FRIDAY ON THE STOCK EXCHANGE'

I held the paper and felt sick. Could this be an elaborate joke? One look at the concern on Dad's face and I knew that it was genuine. The article went on to summarise the events of the day with a little more decorum. No matter how I looked at it, we had lost one third of our investment overnight.

Distraught, I looked over at Karen. She would surely despise me for the fiasco. Half of the money had been hers. Her lovely features were taut, as if the tears were about to well out. Catching my eye, she struggled to contain herself and then gave in, as she allowed the laughter to rush out happily.

I sighed, not sure whether to be offended or to join in. Watching the humour in her eyes at the catastrophic news, it hit me that I was indeed fortunate. Blessed to have a partner who was able to react with such a positive response to a significant loss of wealth. *After all, it was only money,* I thought ruefully and gave her a hug. If only I could shrug it off so easily.

Chapter 63

AIR AND WATER

As new parents, we stumbled through the first few months trying to follow at least a few bits of the deluge of advice heaped on us by everyone we knew. As time went by, we discarded most of it with the realisation that each new-born baby arrives having had a different schooling in how to reduce adults to tearful exhaustion.

Peter never slept at night. We listened to endless advice and tried every idea we could, but we were no match for the prowess of a tiny three-month-old. Whenever he was placed in his cot, his eyes would start to open, but they were never as fast as his mouth that almost immediately seemed to open with a wail.

No medication seemed to have any effect, nor did timing of naps or the hours he was kept awake. Changing to goat's milk and then soya only made those who had to prepare the bottles long for a simpler solution. The only action that seemed to give our little charge any rest was to be held in the arms of a parent, or in a baby carrier strapped to a chest, and for the tiny tyrant to be bounced up and down endlessly. The moment you stopped and tried to gently lower him down, he would revert to the wailing persecutor sent to try us.

Watching a recent episode concerning the SAS training, it struck me that when being schooled to resist torture, trainees are subjected to endless tapes of a baby crying. The only reason I have not applied to join the SAS is that this inhumane treatment would instantly reduce me to a quivering wreck, only too ready to join the enemy.

At the time, guilt ruled our every moment of life. How could we be so bad at parenting? Several well-meaning friends counselled us to put him in his cot and just leave him to fall asleep eventually. 'If he knows you will come and pick him up, he will continue to play up.'

Since lying flat in a cot triggered instant protest, we had resorted to placing him in a pushchair, which kept him in a semi-sitting position, a state which he seemed to find easier, and which gave us a few minutes of rest at a time. I placed him in the chair and strapped him in to prevent a tragedy. As I left the room, his mouth opened, and his lungs began their nightly chorus of anguish. Resolutely, both of us closed the bedroom door and moved into the next room.

The heart-wrenching wail continued for nearly half an hour and when it finally stopped, neither of us could resist the temptation to immediately open the door to check that Peter had not been spirited away, out of earshot.

The sight that greeted us shocked us both to the core. The little boy had slipped out of his cosy bed and his neck was tangled in the restraining straps of the buggy. Fear and guilt surged as we rushed to free him. Unhurt, our little boy seemed only too glad of the rapt attention he was given for the next 24 hours.

The local doctors in town tried everything they could: removing tonsils, placing stents in the eardrums to relieve pressure in the inner ear, even suggesting tiny doses of brandy before bed. Sadly, even large doses did not dull our hearing enough to give us any peace. We could not help but feel useless in our roles are mother and father. Peter was nearly two before a paediatrician pointed out the obvious to us.

'Your little boy has asthma.

Look – he's hardly getting any air at all. See how his chest sucks in with every breath.'

Sudden realisation hit. One of the first words Peter had learned was 'Open', a plea he often made in the early hours of the morning, pointing to a nearby window. Allowing a cold breeze of air seemed to reduce his desperate crying, even in the icy depths of winter.

The diagnosis went a long way to both reducing my sense of guilt and increasing it. Peter had spent most of every morning at the surgery, among a wide range of animals. Now tests showed that animal dander was the chief allergen, along with house dust mite.

Our lives changed progressively as we tried in vain to deal with our little boy's symptoms. We took to changing clothes before going home, in order not to carry animal fur with us. His mattress and pillows were covered in plastic, curtains replaced with similar impervious sheeting and sadly, stuffed toys were banished, apart from his beloved and bedraggled pink panther. Nothing made any difference.

As he grew, he was introduced to a nebuliser, which he used several times a day, sitting in front of the television and watching Scrooge McDuck and the Beaver boys. At the age of two, he was adept at using the Video Cassette Recorder and we shamelessly allowed him to watch the box for hours.

The hour's drive to the hospital became a well-known route and we spent many nights by the bedside of a pale-faced little boy struggling for air, unresponsive to the increasingly powerful cascade of drugs the specialists ran into his veins via the drip.

On one memorable occasion, Peter had developed cystitis, which necessitated frequent bouts of urination. Although he had become almost potty trained, the urgency of his need often overrode any hesitation and he would step outside into the garden to relieve himself.

Such an incident coincided with one of our visits to consult a leading asthma paediatrician, who examined Peter for some time and then sat back and shook his head. I noticed the tired pot plant in the corner of the paediatrician's office and was distracted by the thought that it needed a little tender care, or at least more frequent watering.

'The only recourse we have left is to use drugs intended to treat cancer. They will hopefully counteract your son's over-active immune system,' he pronounced.

The two of us were silent, more than a little horrified at the thought of pumping an otherwise healthy little boy full of extremely potent chemicals with all their side effects. The specialist nodded, aware of the turmoil we were experiencing. Only Peter was unaffected by the news. He had other pressing needs.

As we stared in turn at the paediatrician, the ceiling and then the backs of our hands, a sudden tinkling from the corner startled us and caused Karen to spring to her feet. She rushed over to Peter, who had looked for and found the only greenery available and was relieving himself in the doctor's pot plant. She looked around desperately for a more suitable receptacle, but Peter calmly finished his ministrations and returned to play with the wooden toys on the carpet in the middle of the room.

There were seven of us in the room and only two were happy; the thirsty pot-plant had received a welcome drink and Peter was a lot more comfortable, but the medical professionals were clearly taken aback, and the parents were looking decidedly red in the face. Even the carpet seemed a little ruffled at the unexpected shower from a little boy whose aim was not yet perfect.

It crossed my mind that I experienced much the same scenario from my patients on a regular basis, but the affronted specialist did not seem to be in any frame of mind to appreciate flippant comments, so I kept my silence, smiling inwardly at the range of emotions displayed by the others present in the room.

Chapter 64

LOST IN TRANSLATION

When we first flew down to the Ciskei for the job interview, the director of Ulimocor, asked if I could speak Xhosa. I diffidently replied that I could not, but that I had done a year of Zulu at university. I did not add that I was still at the Pidgin-Zulu stage and struggled to talk the language.

'Xhosa should be no problem to you. If you can speak Zulu, then you should be able to cope. All the Nguni languages are very similar; only a few words differ.'

I was soon to learn just how wrong this assumption was. Although the syntax was the same in both languages, the meaning of the words often differed markedly. *Kusasa* in Zulu means 'tomorrow', while in Xhosa it means 'in the morning'. The Zulus use the greeting *Sabona* (We see you). The greeting in Xhosa is *Molo*. Fortunately, I was given an interpreter-guide Lingele was quiet and unassuming, a young man still caught in the remnants of boyhood. Determined to learn as much from him as possible, I chatted to him in my Zulu-Xhosa while he humbly corrected me in monosyllables, occasionally shaking his head in total lack of understanding.

We were on our way to *Tukulu*, a cattle ranch managed by Ulimocor, when, rounding one of the bends, we suddenly found ourselves in the middle of a small flock of sheep, milling about aimlessly. Three goats on the edge of the flock of sheep darted off into the bush.

'Why do goats have the sense to get out of the way, when sheep don't seem capable of understanding?' I mused aloud.

'They are waiting for their change,' replied Lingele.

Surprised, I turned questioningly towards him.

'Long ago,' he began, 'a sheep and a goat took a ride in a taxi and each of them paid the same fare. On the way, the taxi took a sharp turn and the sheep fell out, while the goat continued on to its destination. Ever since then, sheep have been waiting in the road for their change from the taxi driver.'

I grinned at the snippet of modern folklore and hooted until the sheep finally parted enough to allow us to pass.

The heat of the day was slowly growing oppressive when we suddenly came upon a small village store. I braked hard and pulled off the road. Opening the van door, I asked Lingele if he would like a cool drink. '*Ufuna ukuphuza?*'

Lingele turned his head away and looked through the window.

Rebuffed, I entered the shop, wondering at the reason for his rudeness. The store was divided into a narrow entrance for the customers, separated from the rest of the shop by wire mesh, leaving only a small opening through which the storekeeper could pass the purchased goods. I asked for two Cokes in English, my confidence as a linguist shattered by Lingele's reaction. The storekeeper smiled and retired to the rear of the shop, returning with two ice-cold bottles. Back at the car, Lingele accepted one of the cool drinks without a comment. I shook my head in bewilderment and started the engine.

The divide caused by my lack of fluency in the language severely limited my ability to fully understand this nation and made it harder to do my job effectively. The problem was even greater for Dori Diggs, an American veterinary surgeon, sent out by a missionary society to lecture at the Agricultural College of Fort Cox.

As the most recently employed vet, I was given the duty of collecting Doctor Diggs from the airport. Among the small crowd of passengers that disembarked from the plane, she was instantly identifiable from her strong accent. She in turn recognised a fellow colleague from my down-to-earth working clothes.

The first hour involved many requests from each of us to repeat what had just been said. Our nations both had their roots in the British Isles but somewhere along the line, the languages had diverged considerably.

Arriving at Fort Cox, I was greeted by a stockman who assumed I had arrived in response to a call sent out regarding the pigs, many of which exhibited a serious skin problem. Dori enthusiastically jumped at the chance to meet her first patient on the African continent, while I went off to find out where she would be staying.

Dori was led down to the complex of pigsties, beside which a tall, statuesque Xhosa man was standing, dressed in a neat suit.

'Hi y'all,' she greeted.

He in turn frowned and seemed puzzled but nodded politely.

Many of the sows had red patches on the skin, worst wherever a crease occurred. Top of the list of causes was mange, an intense itching of the skin due to a microscopic mite. The red rash was often caused by the pigs rubbing against walls and other structures.

Turning to the local man, who was watching her intently, Dori ventured to find out more about her patients.

'D'ya hawgs scritch?' she asked. The man said nothing but indicated for her to repeat the question.

'The hawgs. Are they rubbin' agin the walls n'suchlike?'

The inscrutable expression on the face of her audience remained in place.

Crouching down, Dori imitated a pig rubbing itself against the wall of the sty.

'I-hawgi scratchi?'

A sudden clearing of understanding flooded into the face of the Xhosa man in front of her. 'Er… yes. They are pruritic, if that is what you are asking.'

Abashed and taken aback, Dori got to her feet. Her complexion was rapidly becoming more like that of the sows as a pink flush spread from the creases of her neck.

'I am Zola Gebeda. I'm the dean of the College. You must be the new American vet?'

They exchanged greetings and spent the next fifteen minutes trying to converse with mixed results. Arriving at the site, I was greeted by Mr Gebeda, who had shared the office next to the vets in Ulimocor before his promotion to head of the college. Dori, in turn, seemed relieved to see a friendly face, albeit only slightly more able to understand her instructions.

At her request, I provided the trade names of the various drugs suitable to treat Sarcoptic mange and the sows were scheduled for treatment as soon as sufficient Ivermectin pour-on arrived.

That evening, I asked Baron why Lingele had ignored my offer of a Coke earlier on.

'What did you say to him?' he asked.

'I asked if he would like a drink – *ufuna ukuphuza?*'

Baron roared delightedly. 'A Zulu might understand what you mean but those words in Xhosa, with your accent, mean something totally different. You were asking him if he would like a kiss.'

Chapter 65

PIGEON PAIR

The birth of a first child had seemed to me to be an experience of indescribable delight. It was only matched by the day, two years earlier, on which I watched his mother walking up the aisle towards me. On both occasions I thought it would never be possible to experience anything like it again.

When I cradled our little girl Leigh, shortly after she had chosen to enter the world, I was rocked by the intensity of my love for this tiny, elongated little human who could not possibly have been called beautiful by anyone other than a besotted father.

Leigh was clearly a feminine activist in that she too cried non-stop for three months. Not that she had any reason to that we were aware of, but clearly, she felt that she had to be the equal of her elder brother. At one stage our nearest neighbour came over out of concern that perhaps this young couple were mistreating their new baby, since she wailed almost continually.

Peter was a serious little man with a thirst for knowledge and a never-ending curiosity that I so often failed to satisfy. I still have no idea what answer he expected to his repeated question as to which was stronger, an atom bomb or a volcano? He later solemnly informed his befuddled parent that a volcano could carry on for years whereas an atom bomb was over in seconds. I had no reply to his wisdom.

He puzzled, too, over why mammals, at least the more advanced ones such as humans, had not existed at the same time as dinosaurs. After considering it for a few days he announced that he knew the answer; it was clearly because the dinosaurs would have eaten the people.

Leigh, in contrast, was a bundle of delightful mischief. She cared nothing for deep scientific discussion but had a heart that responded immediately to any animal that she came across. She presented me with a jar full of garden snails with strict instructions on how to care for them, just at the time when I was trying to salvage the last of the Hostas in the garden from the ravages wrought by these gastropods. I hoped she would forget about them after a day or two but fortunately I was wise enough not to dispose of them unceremoniously since she asked to see them two days later. Most of them escaped from the jar within a week and no doubt spread their numerous offspring throughout my garden.

I had purchased a video camera for the sole purpose of recording the early years of two of the three most precious people in my life. Sadly, the two of them soon became adept at recording programs from the television on tapes in the VCR and the priceless episodes of tiny people were overwritten with episodes of Scrooge McDuck.

One surviving tape has captured a serious discussion between the two of them. As they sat at either end of a cot, Peter related how much his cat had loved him and always lay on top of him. Leigh was not to be outdone.

'He also loved me,' she insisted.

'No. You were not there then. It was only Mommy and Daddy and me and Bandit.'

'Well, where was I, then?'

Peter looked at her in exasperation. How could he explain that his younger sister had not yet been born? He settled for an easier option.

'You were still in Mommy's tummy.'

'Why was I in Mommy's tummy?'
'I don't know. But Bandit loved only me.'
'Well, Simba loves me, and Dustin and Sindi.'
'Yes,' Peter conceded. 'They all love you.'

Chapter 66

ELIJAH AND THE CHARIOT OF FIRE

Every veterinary practice seems to have a member of staff that can unerringly break anything. Elijah joined us a year after Cecil started, and the two of them could not have been less similar.

With an open, friendly character, Elijah became a good companion who shared my days on the road and opened a window to the complex culture of the Xhosa nation I had so much to do with. After eighteen months, I learnt that he was supporting his parents and six younger siblings on his meagre salary as a veterinary nurse. His father received a state pension that survived only as long as a trip to the bottle store.

Elijah was a man who could put his hand to anything. Sadly, as soon as he did so, it would crash it the ground and invariably send sharp splinters shooting into everyone in the vicinity. Nothing fazed him and as a result, we suffered a good deal from his enthusiasm.

I booked a day to test a herd of cattle for TB, which required the cows to be herded into a race, where they were held like neatly stacked sardines, to have a small square of hair shaved from the neck and a minute amount of tuberculin injected into the skin. Two days later, we would have to return and measure the resulting thickness of the skin. Any cow with a marked reaction would be reported to the government authorities.

A weekend farmer had asked me to test his lone cow as well, and I had arranged to stop at his smallholding on the way to the large cattle farm.

'I cannot be there on that morning,' he informed us. 'But my wife will show you where everything is.'

Although strictly speaking I did not need any help on the trip, things were slow at the clinic and Cecil could manage without his protégé for a day. It would be nice to have a bit of company on the long drive, I told myself. If only I could have heard the gods of mischief chuckling to themselves at my naiveté, I could have saved myself a heap of trouble.

I had fitted out a microbus with cupboards for equipment, running water and a second battery wired in parallel to power the headlights should they be needed for emergencies at night.

I loaded up the van, installed Elijah in the passenger seat, and drove to the hardware store on the edge of town to purchase a tin of enamel paint and a plumber's plunger.

Steve, a friend who practiced in the small town of Vrede and spent most of his time on cattle, had scoffed at my tales of shaving patches on four hundred cows and told me to use a plunger dipped in paint to mark the spot where the tuberculin was injected. I decided to use his method to save time, and as a result I spent an extra day on a job that nearly cost me my life.

Daisy was nonchalantly chewing her cud and enjoying having her back rubbed by her owner's wife when we arrived. Both Daisy and the owner were both clearly in advanced stages of pregnancy. My misgivings grew as I searched in vain for some structure in which to confine our patient.

'No need. No need at all. She will just stand for you to do what you have to,' Mrs Jackson announced.

I compromised and looped a long rope around her neck and tied the end to a stout telephone post near the driveway.

Opening the paint tin, I dipped my unlikely new instrument in the bright red contents and then pressed it against Daisy's neck. A snort of bovine displeasure showed just what Daisy thought of her new tattoo. She began to walk sideways in protest. Mrs Jackson rushed to comfort her as I returned to the van to load the automatic syringe with the tuberculin.

Behind me, I was vaguely conscious of Mrs Jackson's rising levels of verbal anxiety, which ceased abruptly. On turning back again, I was startled to see that far from having succeeded in calming her charge, the reason for Mrs Jackson's silence was the twenty-foot rope that was now wound tightly around her and the telephone post, with one loop around her neck and another just below her ample bulge that now seemed about to rupture from the tension.

Elijah was manfully pitting his fifty kilograms of strength against Daisy's five hundred as the pair circled the hapless Mrs Jackson, who was rapidly turning a violent shade of puce. The neat circle of red had now multiplied in ever-decreasing shades, adorning both Elijah and Daisy, who sported red circles all over their bodies.

I ran to join the fray and together we managed to cajole the spooked cow to reverse her direction and unwind her owner, who resembled a bunch of plump purple sausages, joined but constricted at each junction. She staggered off and did not re-appear before we had packed up and driven away.

I made another appalling error of judgement in entrusting Elijah to put the paint tin in the van. After a bumpy journey of close to two hundred miles, we arrived at the cattle farm to find the staff had the animals corralled and awaiting our ministrations. It was when I opened the back door of the van that I was greeted with a sight that almost broke me. Elijah had stored the paint tin upside down and half of it now covered every surface within sight.

A lot of cursing, some perfunctory cleaning and some more cursing followed. We started the TB testing an hour late and as a result it was nearly dark as we drove out of the farm. This time, I had firmly hammered the lid of the paint tin on and wedged the tin firmly on the floor between other items of equipment. If only I'd had the sense to throw it away.

I had not counted on Elijah stowing the last few items and deciding that the paint tin was not secure enough and instead placing it inside the cupboard on top of the second battery, the metal of the tin neatly bridging the two terminals and setting up an electrical current that slowly turned the metal red hot until it melted, allowing paint to drip down onto sizzling metal.

We had only gone a few miles when we were suddenly engulfed in choking black smoke with the toxic smell of burning chemicals. I swerved off the road and we tumbled out onto the ground. The jolting ride over rough ground fortunately dislodged the metal tin and with the current cut off, the impending inferno subsided.

Elijah sat on the hard ground, shaking his head, with smudged red rings of paint covering his head and torso. In the gathering dark I could hardly make out his features when suddenly he smiled happily and the brilliant arc of white neatly split his face and glistened in the headlights of each passing vehicle.

Two days later, I had to return to the cattle to measure the skin thickness at each injection site. Elijah was dutifully ready and waiting at 7:00 am sharp. I had forgotten to let him know that I in fact left at 6:30, since I needed the extra time if I was going to manage without an assistant for the day.

Chapter 67

DIGITAL SYNTAX ERROR

Computers formed no part of my childhood and I graduated just as the first PC's were becoming readily available. My elder brother Fred had a far greater exposure to the mainframe computer at the University of Witwatersrand, which occupied a whole floor of the building and was kept alive and awake all hours of the day and night by students who punched out little squares from cards that were then fed by the hundreds into the workings of the machine. A single mistake on a card would render their program invalid.

Fred was enlisted to help when prospective students from schools in the area visited the Engineering faculty and were given a chance to ask the machine any question they liked. The visiting scholars typed in their requests on one terminal in a room and the university students typed back the replies from a terminal on the other side of the wall. Digital Duplicity had arrived.

The PC that Karen had been given on graduation had sadly, been consigned to the scraphead after being mauled by Dougal, but we replaced it a few years later with an even more advanced version of these new wonder machines.

An enthusiastic engineer later showed us one of the most amazing aspects of our machine. 'If you want, for instance, to change all the letters 'A' to an 'E', then you just type in this command,' he instructed wisely. 'See how every 'A' on this page of writing is now an 'E'. Isn't it just fantastic?' We both nodded and eagerly awaited his next party trick.

'You can reverse the process by doing this. It will make all the 'E's go back to 'A'.' He pressed a few keys and then proudly pointed to the text on the screen which should have reverted back to the correct original spelling.

All the 'E's that had originally been an 'A' had been changed back, but then so had all the original 'E's that had been 'E' all along. The result was still garbage.

A long, drawn-out afternoon ensued as he battled with the wilful machine to try and get it to obey his wishes, until he finally had to admit defeat and deleted the entire text and slunk off, looking very deflated.

Some time later, a second person produced a 'floppy disc', the latest development in computers, and pushed it into the slot on the side of the PC. Playing around with the program that he had created, he commented, 'I'll leave this with you for a week or so. Have a go with it. There is nothing that you can do which I cannot correct later. Try anything you want.'

We dubiously kept an eye on the machine, but it took a week before Karen was brave enough to attempt the impossible and turned on the softly humming plastic box. The early PCs had a button on the keyboard which has since disappeared from modern machines, labelled 'FORMAT'. Karen gave it a tentative poke. Nothing happened apart from a soft whirring of cogs as the brain of the machine responded. She pressed it again and then again, several times. Still nothing happened. Giving up, she tried to call up other sections of the program that the boffin had shown us, but nothing seemed to respond.

Eventually she tired of the sullenly silent gizmo and called the engineer, who gasped, 'You did what? You pressed FORMAT ten times. You could have done anything you liked apart from that. FORMAT wiped everything off the computer.' He ended in an almost whimper. 'Oh dear.'

A few years later, I used the computer to write a book in the program called WordPerfect. With the limited memory capacity of computers at the time, I soon used up all the space that was available and an ominous warning appeared on the screen. I shrugged it off and finished the section I was writing before saving it. The following day, when I tried to open the document, I was greeted with another message to the effect that the file I was trying to open was too large for WordPerfect to handle.

I tried everything I could think of and then enlisted the help of several professionals, who informed me sadly that the 300-page book was lost forever. I was distraught.

A colleague who had graduated in the same year that we had, had married a Swiss national employed by Nestle, the chocolate makers. He was fascinated by the machines that were slowly beginning to dominate everyone's lives. On the off chance that he might be able to help, I explained the problem and then took our PC over to their house. He was unable to offer any encouragement but promised to have a look at it.

A month later, Luca called to say he had made a breakthrough. After hours spent playing with the overlong document, he'd had the insight to eliminate all the 'white space', which he explained was the open line between paragraphs and the half-empty lines at the end of a sentence. The resulting piece of work was now retrievable but needed weeks of work to restore the correct spacing. This time, I divided the chapters into two sections to prevent a repeat of the catastrophe.

Working with dairy farmers in the Eastern Cape, I was frustrated by the lack of accurate record keeping of their herds. Efficiency required that a farmer knew which animals were in calf and which were barren, which cow was producing vast amounts of milk, and which needed to be 'dried off' to build up reserves of energy and calcium for the next calf.

A simple dairy management program came onto the market, and I peddled the program to a handful of producers. For the first time I could help them organise their records effectively. The problem was that it meant spending multiple hours in the evenings typing in the data. Since I was doing it for free and only charging for the work that resulted from the records of which animals needed to be checked for pregnancy and which needed help from injectable hormones, among other applications, it was hardly cost effective, but it was my baby, and I was proud of it.

The end of each month proved to be particularly stressful as I worked hard to get a report out to each farmer. Finishing late in the evening of the 31st of March, I had finally managed to do it and turned the machine off. I had grown careless about backing up the data, despite warnings from multiple professional keyboard tappers.

Coming home for lunch the next day, I was met with a clearly apprehensive Karen, who apologetically told me that she had inadvertently wiped off all the data on the program that had taken me eight months to input. I was devastated. Our previous experiences in computer-related catastrophes gave extra credence to her confession.

It was only when I noticed the tell-tale little creases of amusement at the corner of her eyes that I realised that something was up. Unable to control herself, she impishly pointed to the date on the calendar, and I realised how neatly I had been made a fool. She was incredibly attractive when happy and very easy to forgive, even if it made me invest in a stack of 'floppy discs' to keep the records safe.

Chapter 68

AVE CAESAR

'You remember me, Doc? I brought my Maltese to you three years ago.' The elderly woman eagerly searched for a spark of recognition in my face. It was tempting to pretend that I did in fact remember her dog, but I had been caught out before when I asked how Fido was, only to see the shocked realisation in a client's face as she quietly reminded me that I had put her dog to sleep at that last visit.

Every second person in King William's Town seemed to have a Maltese Poodle, energetic little dogs covered in dense white curls and attitude. There must be thousands of them in South Africa. They have no nasolacrimal duct to drain tears from the eyes into the nose, so instead each one has little brown stains below each eye. They also have the worst teeth in the canine kingdom and a breath that would send dragons into hiding. I could not tell one little Maltese from the next.

Debbie had recently joined us and ran a grooming business in the rooms behind the surgery. Her memory and recognition abilities left me in awe. As I walked through the door with a wriggling bundle of white fluff in my arms, she commented, 'That's Roger, isn't it? Mrs Peterson has two of them, Roger and Daphne.'

I nodded, impressed.

'Daphne's mother is Adele, Miss Peterson's oldest dog. Adele has diabetes and Daphne's father, Peterkin, was run over on the road to Bisho two years ago.'

She could have told me anything. I had no ability to contradict her, and I had learnt to trust her recollections.

'You promised to call me the next time you had a Caesarean to do.' Debbie said accusingly. I knew what was coming. 'Cecil tells me that you operated on Flex, Mr Stein's retriever, last night.

'Sorry Debbie. It was at two in the morning. I really did not feel comfortable calling you at that time. Your husband would not take kindly to me waking you both up.' She was unmollified. Debbie longed to witness the birth of a litter of puppies by Caesarean section.

Admittedly, it is the most rewarding of operations. A bloated, uncomfortable mother, straining and in pain, is relieved of her burden and presented with a bundle of new life when she wakes up.

The surgery is no more challenging than a normal spay. The skill comes in reviving the often still, lifeless little bodies freed from the bag of fluid that has been their home since conception and handed to the waiting nurses. The surgeon must remain sterile and can only drop each puppy into waiting arms before returning to the task of finishing the surgery. The nurses begin the vital task of vigorously rubbing life into them. Victory is seeing a little pink mouth open and utter a tiny cry of protest.

'Farm Granny' had given Leigh a fluffy toy dog that became her all-time favourite. It had a zip running the length of its plump tummy which when opened, revealed half a dozen identical replicas of the mother squashed inside. It started the cogs in my brain whirring.

I placed the little toy on the surgery table and covered it with a surgical drape. It took a bit of effort to arrange the surgical instruments, the drip line and anaesthetic tubes and for some unknown reason, Cecil and Elijah were nowhere to be found. I had to enlist the aid of June, our receptionist, to call Debbie from the grooming room. She responded with endearing speed.

'Who is it?' she wanted to know. I realised that I had not prepared the cover story adequately.

'It's a new client,' I told her, trying not to give the game away.

'What breed is it?'

'Er ... She's a Jack Russell. Flicker van der Merwe.' I hurried on, 'She started giving birth last night, but the pups are too big.'

'Jack Russells don't normally have problems giving birth.' Debbie was right. I realised that I had to get the show on the road before she rumbled me.

'Would you get a sterile towel ready, Debbie?' I pointed to a pile of them on a stand. 'I'll pass them to you one by one and all you have to do is clear the mucous from their nostrils and mouth and then rub them, just as the mother licks them after a normal birth.

I picked up a scalpel and a pair of forceps. With exaggerated care, I took hold of the zip and pulled it gently down, exposing the sleeping cloth puppies inside. Gently, I lifted out the lifeless form and dropped in into her waiting hands.

Debbie started to rub and then stopped to look more closely at her patient. A deep frown was slowly replaced by a look of anger and disgust.

'You beast. You absolute beast,' she commented with heat. I grinned and ducked as she tossed the puppy at my head.

A week later we had a huge black Labrador rushed in by a local farmer. Bess produced sixteen robust black sausages that were squirming in Debbie's hands seconds after being released from their confinement. Each delivery widened the smile on her face until I wondered if her mouth would stretch right around her head and cause it to fall off.

What was precious to me meant so much more to her. Not for the first time, I realised how privileged I was to be able to do the work I did. I felt a warm glow as I watched the delight on her face, knowing that her boundless love and maternal instinct was something I would only really experience vicariously.

Years later, after practicing for five years in the South of England, a client marched into the consulting room triumphantly and placed a little white, curly-haired dog on the table.

'I bet you've never seen one of these before,' she challenged. I smiled. No, I had not seen one before. A couple of thousand Maltese poodles perhaps, but not just one. There are indeed differences to the work in different countries; they just aren't always what you would expect.

Chapter 69

NOT A GOOD IDEA

Karen demonstrated her ingenuity and business sense when she suggested we turn our garage into a flatlet and let it out. The house we lived in was on a slope, with the garage below the rest of the building. It had never housed a car but was filled with a range of items that I 'knew would become useful one day.' It also contained a wide range of tools, collected over the years from Dad's hardware business. The potential of the tools greatly exceeded my prowess as an artisan.

A particularly valued power tool was a small radial arm saw, the motor of which could rotate 180 degrees and serve as a router. Dad drove home the point that in his 50 years in the trade, most of the injuries he had seen on the hands and arms of workmen who frequented his store were from routers, the blades spinning at speeds that made them invisible to our eyes. A router clamped to a fixed base was the ultimate tool of self-destruction. I decided never to use the router, but the little saw was used regularly.

One feature included in our plans was to open up our lounge by incorporating the porch into the room. I was sceptical, but Karen assured me it would make a big difference.

A problem that seemed to concern only me was that the ceiling in the lounge was at a different height to that of the porch. The architect assured me that it would be a simple thing to correct. He rescued owls and was more intent on seeking my help to nurse them back to health than to discuss the intricacies of construction. The builder too assured me that it was well within his abilities to deal with the problem.

The builder noticed my cherished table saw and decided that he would borrow it to do the edges of the cupboard doors, and he made a quick trip to the hardware store to purchase a router bit.

Karen was startled by a blood-spattered young man at the front door, begging for a trip to the hospital. He had used the router on the saw and then when he came to cut a piece of wood on the same machine, the spinning router blade was forgotten as it spun into invisibility. The wood was neatly sawn by the saw blade, and the base of the workman's thumb was almost taken off by the router blade in the same few seconds. Karen obliged with horror and rushed the unfortunate man to A&E.

I arrived home in the afternoon to find a note explaining where everyone had gone. I hoped the workman would recover, and in the meantime, I set about making myself some lunch. While it warmed in the oven, I wandered down to the garage and noticed the radial arm saw in the centre of the room. I had been putting off the job of cutting a small piece of wood for a project because the saw had been pushed to the back of the garage under a lot of items. This was my chance to complete the work.

I turned the machine on and held the length of wood against the brace at the back of the table, pushing the blade away from me and through the wood. The router blade on the opposite side of the motor neatly cut through the base of my thumb on the hand holding the piece of wood. A spout of blood preceded the jolting pain.

Half an hour later, I joined the row of invalids at the hospital, sitting next to the workman who had just had his hand sutured closed.

Later in the month, I watched the progress of the builder as he and two men broke down the wall dividing the lounge from the porch. It intrigued me since it appeared as if the load-bearing wall held up the roof and everything would surely come crashing down once the support had gone. I watched them work until most of the wall was reduced to rubble before stopping them from going on.

'Surely that whole structure is going to come down if you remove the rest of that wall?' I protested.

Exasperated, the builder stopped and walked over to where I stood, before turning to look at the wall they were working on. He paused for a few pregnant minutes and then said quietly under his breath, 'You're right. There is nothing to support the roof if that lintel comes down.'

He disappeared and came back twenty minutes later with the architect, who also took one look and turned a paler shade of white.

I shook my head in disbelief, while the four men raced off, only to return with stout metal supports which they propped up under the sagging structure.

We lived in a half-finished house for several weeks, during which it became obvious that the builder was not going to return to finish what he had started. I managed, fortunately, to find another company to complete the job. They were at first perplexed with what to do with the heavy concrete lintel that spanned the original dividing wall. Breaking it up would need serious machinery. Karen tentatively suggested that they could possibly dig a hole in the floor underneath the lintel and lower it into the ground. The suggestion was eventually accepted but only once I had owned it and the misogynistic loss of face in accepting advice from a woman was avoided. The beam was duly lowered into a shallow grave and lives there to this day. I wonder what the archaeologists of the next century will make of it when they excavate the house of a pre-digital family in Africa.

The enlarged lounge that was eventually finished sported a bow window and seemed almost double the size of the original. Karen had been able to visualise the change while I had to wait until the work was done to realise just how much better it would look. Together we set about finding a tenant for our new flatlet beneath our house.

Mark and Aimee were a young couple who lectured at the University of Fort Cox. Aimee was a cellist and Mark composed music on a computer. Together they brought a new lease of levity to our lives.

Aimee frequently knocked on the front door, eager to spend an hour discussing her day with Karen. We delighted in her company but found it trying when the knock at the door so often woke an infant just as he had been coaxed to sleep.

'Don't bother to knock, Aimee,' Karen instructed her. 'You are always welcome, and we never lock the door. Just come in any time you like.'

She did mention it to me, but it never registered in my mind.

Late one evening I tiredly got out of the bath, only to find that I had forgotten to bring a towel. I had also left my clothes in the bedroom. The only other item in the bathroom was Karen's dressing gown. I impishly pulled it on, leaving a pair of hairy legs exposed, while it did not quite close around my waist. I opened the bathroom door and began the descent to the ground floor to share my amusement with Karen.

The opening front door galvanised me into lightning action as I leapt down the second half of the staircase and raced through the door into the kitchen. Behind me I heard Aimee's distinctly high voice.

'Stuart? Was that you, Stuart? Is everything okay?'

I cowered at the far end of the kitchen, desperately hoping that she would not venture into the darkened room.

Karen appeared from the far side of the house and at Aimee's prompting, she investigated, only to laugh uncontrollably at the sight that greeted her. The two women left me trapped in the room for a further fifteen minutes, until Aimee took pity on me and left, no doubt to amuse Mark with her tale of my discomfort.

Chapter 70

ONE GOOD TURN TAKES YOU DOWN THE WRONG ALLEY

Driving a microbus in the Ciskei, I was often mistaken for a taxi, with many of the people standing beside the road trying to get me to stop. With time I even learned the codes used to indicate destinations: A finger held horizontally meant Zwelitsha, two pointing downwards was Bisho and so on.

Occasionally I gave a lift to a single individual, although I avoided groups out of fear for my safety. It was only when two tyres of the van were punctured at the same time on a lonely stretch of road that the plight of the pedestrian in the dry African countryside was brought home to me.

I stood beside the road, looking as forlorn as I felt, watching the cars appear on the horizon, only to flash past unheeding. It was over an hour before a taxi pulled off the road, bumping slowly to a halt behind my vehicle. The Xhosa driver climbed stiffly out from the driver's seat, calling a cheerful greeting as he walked around to the rear of his van to detach the spare wheel.

"I'll collect it from you tomorrow," he said airily, waving away my thanks as he sped off.

A few days later, with the incident fresh in my mind, a young man approached me in the street.

"I have just got out of hospital and need the fare to get home to Alice," he said. I looked at him with a jaundiced eye, ready to brush him aside, when the generosity of the driver came back to me.

"Come," I ordered, marching off to the taxi rank, where rows of blue vehicles stood patiently waiting for passengers.

"How much is it to Alice?" I asked one of the drivers.

"Five rand," he replied.

I counted out the money which I handed to the driver. "Please, will you take this man to his home?"

"Sure," he responded.

Pleased with myself, I left the two of them, walking off towards my car. Even if the beggar had only been looking for drinking money, I had managed to show compassion without being taken for a ride.

Driving around the corner I passed a bottle store. As I sped by, the image of the beggar and the driver entering the shop was indelibly imprinted on my mind. The driver even had the cheek to wave cheerfully as I passed, caught in the relentless surge of traffic.

Chapter 71

TWO BY FOUR RULE

We were both besotted with our little boy and even though he could only just crawl and pull himself up on the sofa, I paid for a local man to make a video of our rising star. After filming him for fifteen minutes, the cameraman asked if he did anything other than crawl, and we found ourselves at a loss for an answer. Wasn't that precious enough?

The minister from the local Baptist church paid us a visit, ignoring Peter completely. We in turn kept one eye on our offspring the whole time. He managed to get himself to the wicker laundry basket and tried to sit on the rim, with the result that he fell in and got stuck with his heavy nappy filling the opening. Two of us found it highly amusing. Peter was annoyed and the minister hardly seemed to notice.

At the end of the visit, the pastor suggested a prayer and we duly closed our eyes and bent our heads. Puzzled, Peter climbed up onto the sofa and prised open Karen's eye with two pudgy little hands. The explosive laughter in the middle of the prayer did not amuse the man of the cloth, who left shortly afterwards.

The man was an excellent preacher and could elucidate scripture to a very high standard, but he clearly was not a people person and definitely not a toddler person.

For the first few years Peter, and later Leigh, would accompany us to work. Peter had found a wheel under the theatre table that when turned, would tilt the top surface. He would sit on the floor and drive the table in his imagination while his parents carried out less skilled work on the tabletop.

I was examining a dog on the consulting table when the couple who had brought him in began to smile with delight. Confused, I looked around for the source of amusement, to see Peter with stethoscope plugged into his ears and listening intently to the dog's leg, his little arm having to stretch as high as possible just to reach the top of the table.

The ophthalmoscope and otoscope disappeared one day and were only found when one of the staff noticed Peter and Leigh digging in the mud outside the back door of the practice with the little metal cones from the scope. Neither instrument worked very effectively afterwards, and we eventually had to resort to buying a new set.

At times when we had a short break, the kids would often climb into small cardboard boxes, which I attached to each other with dog leads and pulled the resulting train around the practice until my back could not take it anymore.

The two of them took great delight in climbing into a large, walk-in dog cage and pulling the gate closed behind them. There they barked and growled while I alternately told them off for being bad dogs, or gave them titbits of biscuits or chocolates, which were appropriately referred to as dogfood.

One afternoon, a young man accosted me in an overflowing waiting room and gabbled something about his car. I tried to shake him off so that I could attend to the next urgent patient, but he persisted until a more authoritative gentleman informed me that the young man was trying to tell me that our children were throwing stones on his new BMW. I rushed outside just in time to see them both scoop up double handfuls of pebbles from the driveway and toss them gleefully into the air. The fact that most of them were raining down on the expensive car in front of them was lost on them as they egged each other on.

They were both perplexed to be scolded and it dawned on us that we were the ones at fault. Our darling little angels needed more supervision.

Grace was duly employed as nanny. She was plump and jovial and spent most of her day laughing at the antics of her charges. They adored her and we were able to continue our work without worrying about the cost of their next bit of mischief.

Chapter 72

RAINING CATS AND DOGS

It is very tempting to adopt all the waifs and strays that pass through our doors. It is also easy to imagine that we will be able to handle problem animals when others have failed. Although we do learn to deal with aggressive, shy or overly playful patients, coping with long-ingrained behavioural conditions is clearly out of our remit.

Karen adopted Sindi, her crossbreed dog, for a number of reasons, one of them being protection. The problem was that Sindi loved everyone.

She did frighten the uninitiated when she ran up to them with her mouth open and sneezing every few breaths. She smiled happily when greeting and her moustache tickled her nostrils, triggering off a reflex sneeze. It tended to be a bit unnerving to some visitors.

A client brought in Sam, a huge Rottweiler, and asked amid tears for him to be put to sleep.

'Sam is very difficult to control. He belonged to my father, who passed away last week. I live in a very small flat and we are not allowed to keep animals. I have tried every avenue I can think of to find him a new home, but very few people have the space or the time for him.'

I should have known better, but the thought of ending Sam's life was just too much. I decided to give him one last chance. I would take him home and see how it went.

We had learned that these big black, roly-poly dogs that resemble bears could be very aggressive indeed and a number of our colleagues had been seriously injured by them. Most of them were not overtly vicious, but they showed marked fear when faced with the unknown and often bit in self-defence. No-one wants to be bitten, in self-defence or not, by a Rottweiler.

Sam was delightful but a real handful. He showed no restraint at all and rushed in to investigate the cats, earning a sharp scratch on his nose as a result. He made no attempt to bite his assailant, but it was easy to see how a single snap from his powerful jaws could spell tragedy.

It was difficult to tolerate him indoors, but we had a large garden, with a lot of shelter, and the weather was forecast for a long warm, dry spell.

Two days later, I was watching Sam through the kitchen window, wondering how we could find a more suitable home for him. Although he responded to affection and interaction, we just did not have the time to do him justice. As I pondered, a more pressing danger suddenly loomed.

The postman pushed a few letters through our door and then walked around and onto a pathway between our house and the neighbour, whistling softly as he went. As he walked, his little red cap was just visible above the garden *domcrete* wall. With each step, the enticing red item would show briefly for a few seconds and then disappear, only to show itself again a few feet farther along.

Sam was entranced. He watched the tempting red spot for a few paces and then he began to bounce on his crouched legs, keeping pace with the unsuspecting postman as he progressed along the length of our garden. The jumps were getting higher with each step and the awful possibility suddenly became acute. Sam was very likely to jump over the fence onto the poor postman.

I rushed to the door and burst out, just in time to see Sam in mid-air as he cleared the fence with ease.

'No. Sam. Sam, come here boy.' I rushed to the wall and pulled myself up to get a better view.

The postman probably saved his life that day by not running. Sam would have taken him down within a few paces. The huge dog had fortunately landed just in front of the once-jovial man, who looked as if he was facing Armageddon, legs buckling and mouth hanging slackly open. Sam was looking at him curiously but showed no aggression at all.

'Here boy. Here Sam.' The big dog looked up at me and wagged his hindquarters on which a tail had once been attached.

I clambered over the wall and landed awkwardly between the two of them. Sam licked my face and the little man behind me sank to the ground.

'Blixem,' he muttered in awe.

'Are you okay?' I asked. '*Hy het jou nie gebyt nie?*' He did not reply and once I had wrestled Sam back to the gate and inside the property, the red-capped gnome had gone. We never got any post for the rest of the month.

Karen's aunt gave Sam a home and doted over him.

I thought I was going to have to go and explain to the postmaster if we ever wanted to get our mail delivered, but after the month a new man appeared. He had clearly not been warned, as I watched his head bob up and down above the garden wall. Sam, fortunately, was dealing with an excess of loving cuddles in his new home.

I never did learn if the first postman suffered any permanent damage, physical or other.

Chapter 73

THE EYES HAVE IT

I thought Jasper's owner had travelled over five hundred miles to consult me because of my prowess, but it turned out that he was related to our receptionist and was hoping for mate's rates. Jasper the Chow was a huge ball of brown fur, with a black nose at one end and a curled-up tail at the other. Very little of his features could be seen but on parting the fur, two sticky, pus-filled eyes could just be made out. Jasper spent his life in pain and shadows.

All four eyelids were slightly rolled inwards, with the result that the eyelashes rubbed on the sensitive surface of the eyes. It must have been a daily agony. Jasper had become a grumpy old man before his time, both because of the constant irritation and the fact that he felt vulnerable in that he could not see.

We had operated on a lot of dogs with entropion, but Jasper was extreme. Clipping away the fur from around his eyes produced two bins of brown matting. Once the goo had been delicately washed off, the full extent of the problem became apparent. To correct the problem, we had to remove a large sickle-shaped crescent of skin all around the lower and outer edges of the eye. Suturing the loose ends pulled the eyelids into shape. Jasper was given a face-lift.

He went home with his head in a bucket that had the bottom cut out and with two swollen eyes in the middle of puffy circles of bare skin. He was Halloween all on his own.

I was still musing about the mammoth operation on Jasper when Mrs Miles brought in Tico, her tiny Yorkshire terrier, with very similar, painfully mucky eyes. This time it turned out to be a deficiency of tear production. In the 21st century we now know the cause and the control of this syndrome, but thirty years ago treatment was aimed at either putting artificial tears in the eyes ten times a day, or a revolutionary operation in which the duct from the large salivary gland just below the ear was moved to open at the top corner of the eye, washing the eyes in saliva.

Mrs Miles had persisted with the drops for six months, but she had grown tired of the responsibility that would never end. She was keen to try the operation. I in turn, was extremely hesitant to venture where angels had only left fleeting footprints.

There were no private surgical specialists in that era and the Internet was not even a twinkle in someone's eyes. I resorted to reading my university notes before attempting the operation.

The duct from the gland was as thin as a hair. It ended in a tiny, raised blimp, a few millimetres in size, just under the lip near the large cheek teeth. It was not possible to isolate the duct, so a larger swathe of tissue that included the duct was dissected free and moved up on the face and buried under the skin, with the little opening ending just under the upper lid of the eye. A lot of the operation was done in blind faith, and I found it hard to believe that it would be a success.

It was only when I squeezed a drop of lemon onto Tico's tongue that we could see a small amount of saliva flowing from the duct and over the surface of the eye.

Two weeks later I phoned Jasper the Chow's owner to find out how he was doing.

'Never seen him so happy,' was the report. 'For the first time he could see where he was going, and he has been racing about like a puppy.' I was thrilled. There is nothing more rewarding than stepping out of your comfort zone and not falling flat on your face.

'He's back in hospital though.' The thrill faded rapidly. 'I took him to the local practice, because we did not have enough time to come down your way again.'

'What's wrong, then?' I asked.

'Oh, Jasper was unstoppable. We never used to worry about him going on the road in the past, but now that he can see, he's taken to jumping over the fence and running over to greet anyone that passes. Yesterday he hopped over just as a truck was approaching and got knocked on the leg. Broke his femur, he did. Silly mutt.'

Apprehension rose markedly the next day as Mrs Miles, the owner of Tico, the little Yorkie, entered the consulting room with little Tico tucked under her arm. I noticed that he seemed to have put on a lot of weight since the operation.

'How is he?' I asked, dreading the answer.

'Watch this,' she replied, putting the tiny dog on the table. He sat obediently, watching his mistress expectantly as she rummaged about in her bag.

Holding up a small dog treat, she brought it close to his nose, his gaze never leaving her hand. His tail quivered in delight and then a tear rolled across his eye and down his face.

Mrs Miles laughed, and Tico received his reward. I could see that this little conversation piece was going to end up with a serious weight problem as his party trick was played out for the benefit of anyone who paid them a visit.

I smiled and rubbed Tico's head. I never thought I would be so delighted to see a dog cry.

Chapter 74

First Do No Harm

People are strange animals and difficult to communicate with. There are times I have spent an hour examining an animal, then discussed the problem with the owner and given advice on how they can solve it without medication. On leaving, they all offer the same comment of 'I don't owe you anything, do I?'

In contrast, a ten-minute consultation followed with an injection has them opening their wallets gratefully.

A wise old colleague once explained how he kept a bottle of vitamins on hand and frequently dispensed a handful of them with no charge, levying only the fee for the time spent examining the patient. Clients felt better walking out with a tangible result in their hands.

After Elijah had been in our employ for eight months, he started having fits, alarming full-blown, grand mal seizures. We urged him to seek medical advice and he eventually consented to allow me to drop him off at the general hospital. The imminently competent medics ran a series of tests and diagnosed it as epilepsy. They gave him Phenobarbitone, which controlled the fits completely.

Elijah's problem was that it cost him far more than he could afford to travel to the hospital each month to get the drug, even if it was provided by the government for free.

He announced that he was going to consult a local indigenous healer. All sorts of alarm bells rang in my head, but I had nothing to offer in the way of counselling. On his return, Elijah had obviously had his head shaved and walked with a renewed optimism.

He explained how the *Iqgira*, or medicine woman, worked. If she was worth her calling, she never asked what the problem was. Instead, she asked several seemingly unrelated questions and, together with a keen observation, told you what your problem was.

Elijah had been reliably informed that he had been cursed by someone he had offended and to release the spirits that were throwing him to the ground and making him twitch and writhe, he needed to shave his head to let them out. Elijah was cured.

Two weeks later, he once again had a serious seizure.

A local man in King William's Town had just retired from his job as a conductor on the railways. He was fluent in both Xhosa and in guile and bought a glass crystal pyramid and set himself up as a healer. Neighbours watched in disbelief as he made trips down to the Buffalo River to fill reclaimed glass bottles with muddy water and any plant life he could find.

The charge was ten rand and for that, he would suspend the crystal over his patient and by the way it swung, spiralled, or reflected the light, he would pronounce a cure for any malady. His patients had no interest in a diagnosis.

His reputation spread rapidly among the local community and soon there was a long line of customers at his door every morning. Elijah paid him a visit and came away with one of the ubiquitous bottles of water with a leaf suspended above a layer of silt.

I had tried to dissuade him from the quackery, but Karen pointed out that seventy percent of people who visit a doctor would get better even if nothing was done. The psychological benefit of being attended to and the placebo effect of sips of sewerage-tainted water had been well documented in medical science.

'What harm can it do?' she asked.

I only knew my paternal grandmother was a saintly, white-haired lady who had raised seven children on a shoe-string and had a string of homilies by which she faced the uncertainties of life.

'If you have 'flu, you need to cut an onion in half and put one half in the corner of your bedroom,' she advised. She was proved right time and time again, as the patient 'miraculously' recovered over a week or two. Oddly enough, anyone who shrugged off her advice and did not put their faith in the vegetable also recovered.

The medication sold to Elijah did not seem to do any harm, but it also had no effect on reducing the frequency of the fits in the young man.

Eventually, in desperation, I doled out the tablets to Elijah from the supply we kept in the drug safe for four-legged sufferers and for several years, he would accept them gratefully. He made a trip to the hospital every six months and dutifully showed me the receipt and the prescription issued on each visit.

Around this time I was woken one night in the early hours by a hysterical Mrs Pienaar.

'Doctor, what were those tablets you gave me for Chevvy?' she implored. I had no recollection of who or what Chevvy was. I asked her to describe the tablets.

'Big, round, brown tablets in a little plastic bag with L-O-P-4-T-o-I written on the label.'

'Lopatol.' The image of the big mastiff suddenly came to mind. He had come in the previous day, and I had given her a supply of worming tablets.

'Are they dangerous, Doctor? Will they kill a person?'

I assured her that they were perfectly safe if taken in moderation.

'I woke up with a migraine and I cannot see properly when I get them and in the dark, I swallowed two of his tablets.'

'Did they work?' I asked.

'Yes.' She paused to consider the implications of this. The placebo effect has its uses.

'Well, you solved two problems in one, then. At least you know that you don't have worms either.'

Mrs Pienaar had the grace to laugh, small recompense for being woken in the middle of the night.

Six months later, Elijah's sister arrived at work on his day off. She was as thin as a rake, and he announced that he was taking her to consult the pyramid-wielding healer. While waiting for him, she asked one of the other assistants for a glass of water and drank it thirstily.

I shook my head as the two of them left to walk to the other side of town, to the house of the man I regarded as a charlatan.

The reminders were going out to clients who had purchased wormers six months previously and I could not resist including one to Mrs Pienaar, encouraging her to come in for another dose of Lopatol, the dog wormer. After all, who knew when she would next have a migraine?

A few months later, Elijah came to tell me that his sister had been admitted to hospital with a diagnosis of sugar diabetes, complicated by severe ketosis, the result of delayed treatment.

I sympathised with him but felt relieved that she had finally ended up in the right place. Elijah shattered my thoughts with his next words.

'She died last night. She was in a coma when we took her in, and she never recovered.'

Chapter 75

POPEYE MEETS THE COOKIE MONSTER

"It's never going to go back. There isn't that much space inside her."

I hunched my aching shoulders against the words, wishing I could prove them wrong. I had unfortunately been moments away from voicing them myself.

Ulimocor had decided to phase out several schemes, which meant that the amount of work I did for them dropped sharply, enabling me to offer a better service to private farmers on the South African side. Once again, I found myself having to prove my ability to a new set of clients.

The Brahman cow lay on a slope among the thorn bushes, her drooping ears flicking listlessly in the fading light. Behind her lay the impossibly large mass of her womb, the organ that had enclosed the calf now standing a few feet from his mother's head.

The same process that had given birth to the little replica of its mother had inverted and rhythmically pushed the pink mass of her womb out after it.

The thin-walled veins draining the organ became shut off when folded over as the organ inverted, while the thicker-walled arteries remained patent, continuously allowing blood to flow into the mass, with the result that it grew in size by the minute, until at times it seemed as large as the cow itself.

The monstrous mass seemed to have a life independent of the cow, who continued to strain her neck to reach anything edible within reach. The sun was sinking rapidly behind an ominously dark hill in the distance. I had positioned the van so that the headlights would shine on the cow and as the natural light faded, the scene became outlined in shadows and harsh electric yellow.

I lay with my face in the dirt, my bare torso smeared and aching with exertion. After two hours of unrelenting endeavour, I had managed to reduce the size of the swollen womb by two thirds, but still it refused to return to where it belonged.

With sudden irritation I thought back to the conversations I'd heard among colleagues:

'Just injected 10 cc of oxytocin into it and then I had to move fast to look as if I was doing the work while the organ just contracted up and slipped inside.'

'Poured sugar over it to draw off the fluid and lifted it on a tray until gravity drained it and allowed it to slide back.'

I had covered the prolapsed womb with every hydroscopic substance I had and now I felt like a swamp creature after wrestling with the soggy mass, sticky with sugar and striped a fluorescent green from the acriflavine glycerine, alternating with dark brown Armorican powder.

Little pinpricks where I had injected the hormones that were supposed to cause the offending organ to retract leaked thin trails of blood to mingle with the rest.

The whispered horror stories that surfaced only late in the evenings after the stains on the counter had grown and the barkeeper had begun to direct impatient glances at the huddle of men and women as they bared their souls to the only people that could understand came back too.

Stories of four-hour battles ending in victory, only to have the cow push it all out again before the vet got back to the surgery, and the devastating tale of an amputation, requiring each engorged blood vessel to be tied off and cut, only to have the cow die as the truncated mass was pushed home.

"Nah, it'll never go back. Best to shoot her and be done with it."

The five men formed a semi-circle behind me. Old man Bester had been a provincial rugby player in his youth, the iron hard resolve still apparent in his powerful shoulders. His four sons had been cast in the same mould: gentle giants who together made the local rugby team a formidable force.

The lights of the car suddenly dimmed almost imperceptibly, a warning that the battery would not last much longer. The feeling of desperation grew as the light faded.

Two of the brothers knelt on either side of me, holding the ends of a large drape in which we had lifted the womb. The other three stood placidly, arms folded as they watched in silent judgment.

A feeling of Deja vu floated over me as I lay prostrate on the ground. I was back at school, undergoing the compulsory athletic testing as teams were selected for the various events. The master in charge held out the large round shot, waiting for a volunteer to start the trial. With a misguided desire to get it over with, I stepped forward to take the heavy weight.

My throw went a pitiful ten metres before thudding into the hard earth. I stepped back contentedly, sure that my days on the shot-put circle were over. I had not counted on the resourcefulness of the rest of the boys, nor on their well-developed acting abilities.

As each one heaved the ball, a grunt of impressive volume was followed by a flurry of limbs while the shot lazily lifted into the air to thump down short of my mark. In a daze I allowed myself to be coerced into representing the team, the rest of whom hurried back to the locker rooms in glee.

On the day of the athletics meet, a small crowd had gathered around the shot-put event, mostly young girls eager to see the rippling muscles of the most powerful young men in the region.

Several soft gasps of admiration fluttered out as one by one the young Adonis clones stripped off their tracksuits to begin their warm-up routines. I stood by hesitantly, not daring to impose upon the act. Several contestants had made their first throw before I was finally called.

"Number 16. Philips."

The master in charge of the event looked around inquiringly at the group flexing their biceps. I stepped forward and bent to pick up the shot.

"Philips," called the master, looking straight over my shoulder. "Is number

16, Stuart Philips, here?"

I raised one hand to catch his attention, the shot still clamped against my stomach with the other. "I'm Philips, sir."

He blinked at me in surprise.

A few titters escaped the crowd. I diffidently approached the concrete circle.

"But he's so skinny," I heard a female voice say. I braced myself and took up the classical stance with shot tucked in the crook of my neck, weight balanced on one foot. With an explosive heave I launched the missile forwards, doubling over in exertion. The shot slammed into the ground halfway between the crease and the little flags that marked the length of the other throws.

A couple of spontaneous laughs were smothered as I turned round, but the merriment shining in the onlooker's eyes was unmistakable. As inconspicuously as possible I retired to watch from a little way off.

Any hopes of being left in peace were shattered when the master called my name a second and then a third time, the laughter growing with each of my attempts until all pretence at hiding it was abandoned. With my last throw, the boy enlisted to place the little flags at the point of impact after each throw decided it was not worth moving out of the way, watching my effort land far short of his feet without flinching.

A roar of mirth rushed over me as I turned and escaped to the locker rooms.

The similarity between my present situation and the shot-put event caused a hot flush to creep up my neck. The Besters were influential cattle owners in the area, their opinions highly regarded by so many of my clients. I desperately needed to make a good impression on them.

Bracing my feet against a tree, I pushed with all my might against the prolapse, now reduced to about twice the size of a football. Although my hands sank into the drape-wrapped organ, it remained stubbornly protruding from the cow's rear.

With a grunt the youngest brother dropped his side of the supporting drape to stride away to his van. The other three followed with varying degrees of haste. Only the father remained motionless, impassively watching my contortions.

The car headlights gave a quiet pop and expired completely, leaving the old man and me in the gloom.

With a suddenness that bewildered me, the womb suddenly slid home into the depths of the cow, leaving the drapes to fall to the ground as I opened my hands in surprise.

The organ had gone.

Tentatively I probed the recess of the cow's womb, amazed at the unexpected resolution of my problem. The womb was back in place, exactly where it should be.

Rising awkwardly to my feet, I arched my back to undo the kinks while glancing over at the old man. He remained unmoved, betraying no sign of recognition of what had happened.

The youngest brother returned abruptly, carrying a revolver in one massive hand and a powerful torch in the other, stopping short as he got to the cow. Two of the others turned to watch, following his gaze until with a start the significance of what they saw hit them.

"What did you do?" asked the brother with the gun hanging from his hand accusingly.

I ignored the question, busying myself collecting the fluids to instil into the womb to ensure the complete inversion of the organ and help fight the inevitable infection that would result from hanging out in the dirt for several hours.

The five of them watched silently as I worked in the pool of light from the torch, inserting a pipette to run in the fluids and then injecting antibiotics into the cow's rump. None of them said another word, but two knelt to examine the area where the womb had been more closely.

Packing away the bits and pieces that had become scattered around the small scene, I commented brightly before climbing into the van that I would be back in the morning to check on the cow. As I glanced at the old man, I thought I saw him wink, but it probably was just the poor light.

Chapter 76

HARD TO SWALLOW

The horse lay on its side, neck arched backwards and lips drawn back in a ghastly parody of mirth. The legs seemed to strain as if intent on running, if only they could gain purchase on the ground. I had never before seen a case of tetanus and it took a few minutes for my fumbling mind to register what it was.

This apparition of horror shocked me. Shocked me despite the morass of pain and death I had seen pass before me in my short career. It was always an incredible blessing to be able to administer relief in any form, but occasionally we were left powerless.

'How long has he been like this?' I asked.

'Since the weekend.' Five days. Five days of growing torment.

I noticed a smear of blood on the horse's hind legs and on closer examination, the open castration wound became obvious.

'Who performed the operation?' We were the only private surgery in town, but there were three other vets employed by the government, plus two retired seniors, and occasionally locals preferred to use a practice from a neighbouring town.

'Sarah. Sarah Gilbey operated on him last Friday.' I felt a physical blow at the news. Sarah Gilbey openly operated on animals without a licence and without any training. She was vociferous in her denunciation of the 'money-grabbing vets' and had a following of animal owners and farmers in our area. She had been active long before we arrived on the scene.

'What did she use as an anaesthetic?' I wanted to know.

'She didn't. She drove four stakes into the ground and lashed his legs to them.'

I had not thought I could be even more traumatised.

'Had she vaccinated him for tetanus?'

'No. He has not had any vaccinations.'

If a vet gelded a stallion without vaccinating for tetanus, they would be in danger of prosecution and a serious reprimand from the veterinary council, if not suspension.

I could do very little to help the stricken horse. A simple penicillin antibiotic could have helped in the early stages, since *Clostridium tetani* is susceptible to the drug. I gave a large dose anyway. I also gave maximum doses of painkiller. I felt like it was much too little, too late. We had muscle relaxants, but they did not last for very long.

The owner refused to give up, despite the extremely poor prognosis. I instructed her to give the young horse small amounts of water every fifteen minutes and to make sure it could swallow. She had already said she could get him to eat small handfuls of grass. I left to order the tetanus antiserum, only too aware that we were closing the stable door long after this poor horse had bolted for the pastures in the sky.

Back at the surgery I telephoned the Veterinary Council and was again stunned to hear the verdict. Their job, the legal advisor told me, was to punish errant vets. They had no interest or jurisdiction when it came to members of the public, no matter how heinous the crime.

I asked who I should report this too and was told simply, 'You're on your own in this. You will have to sue this woman. Remember, however, that it is far from a sure thing that you will win the case and if you don't, it will give her a free licence to do as she wishes in the future.'

I mulled over the predicament and finally decided to try the SPCA.

I did not really get on well with the new SPCA officer, but perhaps that was because her predecessors had been an old farming couple who had decided on a less arduous lifestyle and taken up the challenge of caring for waifs and strays. They had lived a simple life totally dedicated to their charges, allowing the public to dictate things as they wished. The new officer quite reasonably refused to allow visitors after hours and stuck to the rules rigidly.

I drove around to the SPCA centre and was met by Roween, the middle-aged woman in charge of the centre. She looked less than pleased to see me and was immediately defensive.

'I've come to report a horse that has tetanus after being operated on by a lay person,' I announced, expecting a similar reaction to the one I had felt when I first saw the patient. Her response staggered me.

'Yes. I know.'

'Have long have you known?'

'I got Sarah to geld him,' she admitted, 'I helped her with him. I did not know it would turn out this way.'

A thousand questions flooded my mind, but the enormity of the situation made them superfluous, and I muttered a few words and left.

Nursing my pummelled brain once more at the surgery, I remembered the advice given by the legal arm of the Vet Council. 'Get the public prosecutor to help,' he had suggested. I would take his advice.

King William's Town had a population small enough for most people to be familiar with each other. I knew of the public prosecutor but had not exchanged more than a nod in passing before. She listened patiently for a few minutes and then completely destroyed my faith in the rule of law, at least in that corner of the world.

'It was my horse,' she said simply. 'Roween and Sarah said he would be fine. I don't know anything about the medical side; I just ride. He was getting too frisky, and they said a simple operation would sort him out.'

'But surely you must know that a lay person cannot carry out an operation like that?'

'They said it would be fine, so long as she did not use an anaesthetic.'

'You were prepared to let her cut your horse, without the benefit of any pain relief.' I was stunned.

'I didn't know. I have never been involved with an operation on a horse. I thought it was a common procedure.'

I duly took delivery of the antiserum the next day, but even as I injected it, I knew it was futile. The young woman I had taken to be the owner but was in fact just a groom, had done her best but clearly some of the food or water had ended up in the lungs, causing the horse to cough in a suppressed and painful manner.

This was one of the few times in my career that I insisted on putting a patient out of its misery. The young woman objected that it was not her horse and she did not have the authority to give consent, but the horse gave a soft gasp and sagged down to the ground, his tormented eyes glazing over.

I can remember every single patient that I failed. Every animal that I inadvertently caused to suffer. Every mistake I made that impacted on my charges. This horse lying prone, like a marionette with the strings pulled too tight, seared a pathway on my mind that will still be visible in a thousand years when the next civilization digs us up to learn how we lived, and comes across my tightly drawn features and the shoulders pulled up to ask the question:

'Why?'

Chapter 77

NO GREATER LOVE

Lindele opened the gate and then stood back to allow the calves out. After the first one had plucked up the courage to leap for freedom, the rest pounded after it. In response, sixty cows milling around the handling pens rushed forward to greet their offspring.

Not for the first time I marvelled at the way mother and calf unerringly knew exactly who they belonged to and managed to find each other among all the other bovine bodies.

I was reminded of this again a few months later as I stood at the school gate waiting for my two little ones to appear. Among the throng of noisy kids, I instantly spotted the serious little figure of Peter as he walked sedately, deep in thought, and a few seconds later Leigh appeared, irrepressibly trying to keep her feet on the ground while the rest of her threatened to lift off the earth.

Two pied crows watched the sea of people from the heights of a nearby tree and one cocked its head and then turned to the other. I could imagine it saying, 'It's amazing how they can pick out their young ones among all the others.'

When Leigh wanted a fifth chocolate one Saturday morning, I explained that she would have to wait until the short arm of the clock reached the number 12 before I would allow her one. Returning to the room after a short absence, I found her standing on the table, stretching as high as she could, to move the hour hand to its required position, while Peter watched in a mixture of delight and censure.

When told she could not take toys to school, she appeared at the car with an enormous croquet hat, bulging with an assortment of items hidden underneath it, looking distinctly like Paddington Bear or Dr Seuss's *Cat in the Hat*, while holding her hands out as a sign of innocence.

Both kids adored the young maid Bungi. Her real name was *Sibungile*, which in Zulu meant 'We give thanks for her', bestowed on her by her parents. She had shortened the name to simply 'Bungi'.

Bungi became an instant heroine to the kids when we arrived home one day and she proudly showed us a six-foot snake that had unwisely entered the house while she was present. Bungi did not believe in examining snakes to determine if they were harmless or not and had promptly and with considerable bravery despatched this one with a garden rake.

Leigh insisted on keeping the snake overnight and I made the serious misjudgement of encouraging the two kids to tie a length of fishing line to the reptile and then pull it along the floor while hiding in a cupboard when Bungi returned the following morning.

Bungi went a pale grey and staggered about for a good ten minutes while I panicked at the thought of the penalties for manslaughter.

The success of the trick galvanised Leigh and she refused to be separated from her prize. Instead, she scooped it into a plastic supermarket bag and carried it triumphantly off to school.

The teachers at the school were easy targets. One by one they spotted the little three-year-old carrying a bag almost as heavy as she was and came to ask what it was inside. None took her reply seriously until the bag was opened and they shrieked in shock. Leigh was ecstatic.

Later that morning the headmistress persuaded her to allow them to bury the by now foul-smelling body but then had to dig it up again when she howled for half an hour.

The little school was held in rooms adjacent a church, with John 3:16 inscribed above the door. As I watched the two little children of 3 and 5 years of age, it struck me how a God who gave his Son for our salvation must both take our transgressions very seriously indeed and have a love for us that surpasses all understanding. There can surely be no greater love than that of a parent for a child and to have that passed on to us is deeply humbling.

Chapter 78

CRY TWICE BELOVED COUNTRY

There were sixteen operations booked in for the day: six spays, two castrations, five dentals, including Sammy, the Maltese poodle with the choking halitosis that hung like a foetid green cloud around his cage in the kennel room, a bull terrier with a fishhook in his throat, a ruptured cruciate ligament and an assortment of lumps and bumps needing attention. I was as usual hovering between elation at the success of the practice and despair at coping with the unpredictable pressures thrust upon us.

Woody strode in the open back door with a casual glance at the bustle of pre-op preparations to borrow a cooler box to store the tuberculin he needed for a day testing cattle in the Kat Valley.

'I want to be as far from the madness of today as possible,' he announced.

I turned questioningly towards him while trying to inject a boxer that Zola was holding, his face averted skywards as the dog's tongue lapped the air in an attempt to lick him. A thick spray of saliva was spattered on his chin and chest.

'They're having a protest march from King up to Bisho today,' said Woody.

I shrugged noncommittally. There was too much to cope with at the moment to worry about the endless political manoeuvring that had become our daily fare.

I noticed Zola listening avidly to Woody, his face a passive mask. I wondered what he made of it all and whether his moral convictions forgave or condemned Woody's bias. I wondered if we would ever know.

Karen came through carrying a birdcage with a Cape Parrot huddled on a perch in the centre, feathers fluffed up as if cold despite the warmth of the room. Woody's attention immediately focused on her, professional interest and physical attraction easily drawing him away from my desultory lack of attention.

Pat stuck her head around the door and announced, 'Mrs Muller can't get through the crowds at the front. She phoned to ask if someone could collect her dog Amy from the shop in Amatola Road.'

'What crowds?' I asked, but she had already closed the door. Turning to Elijah, I asked if he would go over to pick up the dog and was startled by the sudden look of fear on his face. It dawned on me that perhaps I should find out what was going on and I made my way to the front of the practice.

The noise of the crowd was evident even before I stepped through the front door. The road in front of the practice was filled with people. While I watched, a bus groaned to a halt at the lower end of the road to disgorge a further fifty figures that moved into the assembled crowd as if drawn by strong cohesive forces. Several taxis were turning tight circles on the far side of the intersection, stopping only long enough to allow their cramped loads to disgorge onto the pavement before turning and racing back towards Mdantsani, only the driver and one other figure left on board.

Mr Mnondo passed the gateway to the practice, turning his head away sharply as he recognised me. Behind him his teenage son Lundi smiled happily, obviously enjoying the holiday atmosphere. He nodded in recognition when I greeted him.

'What's going on?' I asked.

He shrugged. 'I don't know. They brought us here by bus. When I got to school, they were waiting for us and loaded us straight on. The taxis are also bringing everyone they can find. There is a man in each taxi telling the drivers where to go and they have to go.' He smiled unconcernedly.

'Who are "they"?' I asked.

Lundi shrugged his shoulders.

'What are they protesting against?' I asked.

Once again he shrugged and then moved off in response to his father's angry scowl.

Without pausing further, I made my way into the mass of bodies, moving easily through them as they made way graciously, and then continued on to the little shop in Amatola Road. Amy was sitting on her owner's lap, happy at the unexpected attention.

'I didn't expect you to come,' Mrs Muller apologised. 'I thought you would send one of your staff. I just didn't want to risk trying to get through the marchers. You will take care of her, won't you?'

I smiled reassuringly and then paused as Mrs Muller continued, 'There isn't any risk of her getting hurt when you go back, is there?' Her concern was all for the dog and up until then I hadn't considered any danger to myself.

'I did not have any trouble getting here,' I offered and then left, with Mrs Muller unplacated and troubled.

Once again, the milling crowd parted but only just enough to let me pass through. Two of the younger children patted Amy on the head and then giggled conspiratorially behind their hands. Reaching the front door, I was surprised to find it closed. Juggling Amy onto one arm, I used the other hand to open the door. Two small bodies squeezed through behind me before I could close the door and with amazement I recognised Joy's daughters, apprehensively watching me.

The door on the far side of reception opened and Angelina called the two teenagers through. I followed more slowly to find them crouching nervously on the floor of the spare consulting room.

'They don't want to go with the marchers,' explained Angelina. 'The organisers brought them all here, children and teachers. No-one had any choice.' It was clear that the two girls feared for their safety, rather than having any political motivation.

'They can bring some chairs through from the back if they want,' I offered. 'I don't think we'll be having many more patients today.'

Zola walked through to the front, carrying a broom as I went through to put Amy in a cage. Most of the patients to be operated on had spent the previous night in the hospital, relieving the owners of the necessity of bringing them to us in the morning.

Karen was already busy with the first spay, assisted by Cecil, the green mound of draped patient lying motionless on the table between them. Elijah was shaving the second dog on the prep table.

'We'll have to get another surgery table if it stays this busy,' commented Karen. 'If we move this dog up to the top of the table you could possibly squeeze the next one on the end.' I nodded agreement, watching Elijah work with practiced care.

The door to the waiting room opened suddenly to allow Zola through, his face ashen and set. He put his broom down and then said softly, 'They are calling me. I was sweeping the front room when they saw me and told me to come.' He disappeared without further comment. Cecil and Elijah looked scared and indecisive.

I walked over to the table, picked up the dog and carried her to the theatre area, calling over my shoulder, 'We'll need another spay set, Elijah.'

The spell was broken, Cecil and Elijah returning to animation and competently helping with the operations. Together the four of us worked as a team, the two men efficiently holding and controlling the patients with gentle firmness until they slowly succumbed to the effects of the anaesthetic and then preparing the operation sites.

I was scrubbing my hands and arms when the sound of a Tannoy burst through the window. Dripping soapy water on the floor, I went through into the reception area and peered between the curtains.

At the upper end of the street, a group of men were facing the crowd, urging them to action. Abruptly the men turned and began walking slowly up the hill, chanting as they went. The crowd surged behind them.

Angelina closed the curtains as I returned to the prep room, putting the noise of the crowd out of my mind for the next few hours, until by mid-day all the operations had been done. Karen left to collect Peter and Leigh. Angelina and Joy's two girls made their way home and Elijah disappeared into his quarters for a lunch break.

Cecil was sponging off the blood from a poodle's foreleg when the unmistakeable popping sound of gunfire in the distance brought us to a standstill.

The sudden unwelcome thought that Karen and the kids were on the side of town closest to Bisho galvanised me into action.

'Stay until Elijah gets back, please Cecil. You can call me on the paging system if you need,' I instructed and rushed out to leap in the van and race up the hill.

The streets were deserted, apart from a few white people who came out onto the sidewalk to peer curiously in the direction from which the gunfire had come.

I had passed four blocks and was starting the climb up to Bisho when the road was suddenly blocked by fleeing figures racing down towards me, a mixture of panic and excitement on their faces. Forced to slow to a crawl, I passed groups of children shouting to each other with animated faces, older men and women fleeing silently, and one old man hobbling along in obvious pain.

It took a further ten minutes to reach the nursery school, where an agitated group of teachers and carers could be seen standing at the entrance to the school and tending to several figures sitting or lying on the grass.

I flung open the door of the van and raced towards the familiar faces, fear sending my pulse racing. One of the teachers looked up briefly and then returned to her task of bandaging the leg of a young man, lying on his back with one arm across his forehead.

'Peter and Leigh have gone home. None of the kids are here anymore,' she said shortly, without looking up.

'What happened?' I asked.

'The Ciskei police formed a cordon between the independence stadium and Bisho. The speakers urged the crowd to defy them. When some of the young men broke through the fence and charged the police, they opened fire.'

Not all the injured appeared to be young. An elderly woman nursed a shoulder while a grey-haired man grimaced in pain from a heavily bandaged foot that oozed blood onto the green grass. The young teacher noticed my glance and continued, 'The police then turned their fire onto the crowd, shooting indiscriminately at anyone.'

I was about to leave when she added bitterly, 'Those brave leaders who urged action were the first to run. I watched Kessel hiding behind a Land Rover while all around him the innocent were being shot. He and the other organisers were the first to run.'

Driving back towards home, I passed Mr Mnondo walking slowly down the hill, tears pouring down his face. I slowed the van, leaning out of the window to ask if he needed a lift to town. He ignored my question, walking on for a few yards before his agony welled over. 'They shot him. He's dead.'

'Who did they shoot?' I asked anxiously. 'Not your son. Not Lundi?'

He nodded his head and then turned abruptly, leaving the main road to walk through an open lot. I watched him go in helpless pity and anger, guilt and relief that the three people who made up my universe were safe. I knew that I would never begin to understand the grief of parents who lost their children to the senseless greed of the politicians.

Karen was at home when I arrived, the children noisily splashing in the shallows of the swimming pool. The world seemed surrealistically calm and serene.

'What was all the noise? It sounded like fireworks,' commented Karen.

I watched the look of horror spread across her face as I relayed the events I had seen. Sadness seemed to seep upwards, pulling the edges of her mouth and eyes downwards.

'Those poor people,' she said softly.

Whereas I felt anger at the senseless and costly power displays of the political rivals, Karen was filled only with sorrow for the victims. In the distance we could hear the wailing shrieks of protest from the ambulances racing towards Bisho.

Zola was back at work when I returned for the evening consulting, impassively finishing his task of sweeping and mopping the floors. He was noncommittal in his replies to my questions.

'I knelt down and prayed when the bullets came. Then the Bisho police came and told me to go before they arrested me. I walked back here.'

I asked him to carry Amy back across town, but her owner arrived just as he was leaving, overjoyed to see her dog and bubbling with the need to dissect the day's events. I excused myself to deal with the next client. The afternoon rapidly filled with clients leaving the safety of their homes and venturing out to bring their sick animals to us.

Driving home, I watched the setting sun, expecting it to light up the sky in a blaze of blood red colour, but the darkness seeped in quietly until the stars that had been in the sky all day long were once again visible.

Chapter 79

A Frozen Smile

Eve St Lawrence was an attractive, vivacious woman with a bubbly nature. Her husband John was a quiet, taciturn man of few words. Despite their differences in character, they were clearly devoted to one another. She in particular seemed to adore him. He reciprocated with introvert reserve. There was, however, one occasion late one night, or more accurately, early in the morning, when I saw a deeper side to his emotion.

Trying not to acknowledge the tinglingly frigid temperature as I walked up their driveway past the immaculate flower beds, feeling as brittle as the frost covered greenery that crunched underfoot, I made my way around the side of the house to the poolside at the back, where two blanket-shrouded figures breathed clouds of mist into the dark. Between them a bedraggled black nose was visible from under a third blanket.

'So glad you came.' Eve's voice juddered slightly as she shivered. Beside her the other two mounds of blankets were both shaking, and the dog's mouth was chattering loudly.

'I woke up to hear a loud noise from the garden: goof-goof-goof-goof.' Eve gulped and shook a little. 'I thought it was a break-in, so I sent John out to investigate.'

John raised his head and gave me a haunted look. I noticed the blue tinge at his gills and the slicked-back, damp hair.

'He came back to say there was a dog in the pool. We rushed out and tried to coax it towards the shallow end and the steps, but it just circled around the deep end. I was worried it was going to drown.'

'She pushed me in,' John added.

'Yes,' admitted Eve, unashamed of her actions. 'John helped to get him to the edge of the pool and together we lifted him out. Poor thing.'

I wondered which 'poor thing' she was referring to. Both looked about to freeze to death.

'I had just rushed in to get some blankets when you arrived. I haven't had a look to see if he is injured or anything. Why would he fall in the water? He is obviously a stray, and he isn't wearing a collar or anything.'

Eve leant over and gently pulled the blanket off the dog to inspect it more closely. It was a black Labrador with a grizzled, greying muzzle and rheumy eyes. Eve's eyes moistened in sympathy. John's face remained inscrutable from within the depths of the blanket hooded over his head.

The dog, freed from the shroud, took a couple of rapid steps forward and tumbled back into the water.

'He's fallen in again.' Eve panicked. 'He'll drown. Oh John, do something.'

John made a hesitant move towards the edge of the pool and then crouched down at the concrete lip. The dog was a foot lower than the edge and a yard out of reach of his outstretched arm. He froze, momentarily undecided, while the dog's head dipped under the surface. Behind him, Eve stepped forward and gently edged him forward, where he made a frantic whirling grab at the void of the night with both hands before crashing into the water.

The three of us managed to pull our patient out of the pool and this time carried him into the warmth of the house, leaving a damp trail on the plush lounge carpet. It was Eve's turn to remain silent, while John's face and the set of his shoulders spoke volumes.

On a more thorough inspection, it became obvious that the dog was blind. Thick cataracts gave the eyes a milky-white blankness. He had probably wandered into the garden, not knowing where he was.

There was little more that I could do for him that Eve had not put into operation the minute her charge was safely enclosed in the spacious kitchen. A warm bed, thick blankets and a heater drying the air nearby helped as we rubbed vigorously at the old body, trying to restore his circulation. He gratefully accepted a bowl of warm water and even wolfed down some leftovers that Eve warmed up gently in the microwave.

Catching a glimpse of John's grim features as he watched the dog, I wondered if they had a nice warm dog box, and whether Eve would be comfortable in it.

The following day the couple called in at the surgery to say that they had found the owner of their midnight caller and he was safely back in familiar territory. They in turn had found how he had let himself out through a carelessly unlocked door to relieve himself while the owners slept on, but then found himself in unfamiliar surroundings.

On a later visit I noticed that the St Lawrences had fenced in the pool to prevent a repeat of the incident. I wondered if it was John's intention to keep wanderers away from the water or to prevent himself from being pushed in with nothing to grab hold of.

Chapter 80

MAKE IT SNAPPY

The most convenient newsagent on the outskirts of King William's Town was owned by the Govenders, a middle-aged Indian couple. I was introduced to them by their dog, Snappy.

The couple worked impossibly long hours without a break for eleven months of the year and then took a trip back to India each autumn. Snappy was a regular fixture in the shop, dozing behind the counter, chasing rabbits in his dreams. Apart from a short walk twice a day, he never stirred. Until I walked in.

Each time I neared the counter I would place my purchases on its polished surface and extend a handful of money across, smiling a greeting but determined not to utter a word. The Govenders would nod and happily ask after my health or comment on the weather. Civility demanded that I answer and try as I would to disguise my voice, at the first syllable, Snappy's ears would prick up.

Slowly he'd lift his nose and sniff the air, moving his head from side to side, and then with a rush he'd spring from his comfortable bed and charge around the counter, barking furiously. Mr Govender was always ready for him and grabbed at his collar as he passed, but I could never help wondering what would happen if Snappy made it past the protective barrier.

The Govenders were on one of their annual holidays when friends of theirs brought Snappy into the clinic, as yellow as a canary but without the chirp. Snappy had very serious liver failure and was at death's door. We gave his carers the bad news and expected them to opt to put him to sleep, but they were understandably reluctant to take the decision. Could we, they asked, keep him going until the Govenders' return?

It was three weeks before his owners' return and in that time, Snappy made a remarkable if slow recovery. The Govenders came back to find a dog that looked much the same as the one they had left on their departure. It was difficult to impress upon them the tenuous bridge he had crossed in their absence. At his final check-up, Snappy was back to normal, or at least almost normal.

'He does not seem to be able to hear.' Mr Govender was clearly very worried. I could find no reason for his deafness and all other signs were encouraging. I advised a diet suitable for dogs with damaged livers and suggested they give it some time and see what happened.

The change noticed by the Govenders became more obvious to me the next time I stopped to buy a Coke. Snappy slept through the entire exchange, even though Mrs Govender made a point of repeatedly drawing me into a conversation. As I left, I could not help noticing the disappointment on their faces.

Snappy was back with us a few months later when he wandered into the road and into the path of a speeding truck. He had not heard the approaching vehicle or its blaring horn. In addition to multiple scrapes and bruises, Snappy had a broken radius in his foreleg. We operated the following day, and he was back home by the weekend.

A month later, I once again stopped at the little store and ventured inside with my new sense of confidence, which proved to be misplaced. At the first sound of my voice, the little dog launched himself into the air and tore around to the front of the shop, to tear a strip off the end of my trouser leg.

My clothing was the only victim apart from my dignity, but the Govenders were delighted.

'We have our dog back!' Mr Govender exclaimed. 'He can hear you. Oh thank you, Doctor. Thank you.' If Indian reserve did not exceed even that of the English, I am sure he would have hugged me.

Ruefully I made my way home, not sure just how I felt about their delight and gratitude. Weeks of dedicated care and nursing had been taken for granted, but a result I could not have predicted, nor claim any responsibility for, had resulted in effusive thanks. Perhaps, I ruminated, I should have taken all his teeth out when we operated.

Chapter 81

MAKING LIGHT OF IT

Great Danes have a deep chest and abdomen. The stomach is suspended, as in all mammals, from the spine by means of a strong curtain of tissue, but it is free to swing if the other organs give it the space. Filled with food, it has a tendency to twist on its suspension if the dog is overactive following a large meal.

Jason normally had an irrepressible spirit, but this evening he showed none of his joie de vivre. Obvious pain stretched the lines of his face, while his stomach was grossly distended.

"He ate his supper happily this afternoon and then played with my son. We only noticed his condition just before we phoned," Rev Tomlinson said.

Karen and I looked at each other. A gastric torsion in a dog does not have a good prognosis. All too often the patient dies soon after the condition is corrected.

"His stomach has twisted on its long axis, cutting off both openings," advised Karen. "The food inside the stomach has continued to ferment, which causes tremendous pressure, resulting in even more damage to the walls of the organ."

She never went into the details of toxins from the damaged tissue trapped within the twisted blood vessels, just waiting for us to unravel the veins and so liberate them into circulation.

"We'll try to empty the stomach with a tube first," I said. "Failing that, we'll have to operate."

Rev Tomlinson nodded worriedly and left sombrely while the team set about trying to help the dog that was larger than the smallest pony at the local riding club.

Jason sank slowly to the table under the effects of a barbiturate. While I set up a drip, Karen and Cecil tried to push a lubricated, pliable tube down the oesophagus. After several attempts we gave up, wheeling the silent form into the theatre. We would have to open up and reduce it manually.

Karen wielded the scalpel while I monitored the anaesthetic. Within minutes the angry red surface of the dilated organ was revealed through the incision in the abdominal wall. Trying to rotate the balloon produced no results; it was too enlarged to move.

"We'll have to deflate it first," suggested Karen, directing me and Cecil as we collected a large bore needle and a 50ml syringe.

Cecil was already proving his worth as an assistant. He seemed to have a natural affinity for the animals, although he was extremely nervous of me. Karen and Cecil seemed to be kindred spirits.

Karen gingerly slipped the needle through the thin wall of the stomach, drawing back the plunger of the syringe to extract the gasses. "This will take forever," she complained.

"Pull the hub out of the syringe and let the gas escape," I suggested. "Keep the opening away from the abdomen in case the contents of the stomach come bubbling out."

With a little trepidation, Karen did as I directed. A faint hissing was audible as the trapped gasses were released.

"If we lit a match now, it should burn like a blow-torch," I commented.

"No!" came the stern reply.

"Let's just see what happens." I held a lit match to the open end of the syringe. A blue flame spread merrily around the perimeter. "Come and see this, Cecil," I called.

Together the two of us chuckled happily while Karen crossly urged me to blow it out.

Suddenly the syringe began to buckle, the heat from the flame melting the plastic and causing it to sag tiredly.

"It's going to fall into the wound," shouted Karen. "Get it away from here."

In desperation I grabbed the hot plastic in a sterile drape, dropping it into a bin as it burned the tips of my fingers.

"If this dog dies it'll be your fault," said Karen angrily.

Cecil sneaked away while I checked our patient's vital signs in chaste submission.

The following day Jason bounded out of his cage, sweeping his owners off their feet.

"Not much worse for wear," commented Rev Tomlinson. "You gave us a fright last night when you painted such a grave picture."

"Jason had a good surgeon," I admitted.

Karen glanced at me over his head, but the smile never came. She looked tired after the late night call-out.

Rev Tomlinson noticed it too. He leaned across to whisper in my ear, "I think the two of you are working too hard. Remember, all work and no play makes Jack a dull boy."

Chapter 82

A CAN OF YOUR FINEST

Cecil had an endearing love for every patient. Several times, when the pressure of the job reduced my tolerance level and a fractious patient began to play up, I would find myself getting irritable. The animals seemed to sense my mood and became even less co-operative. Occasionally Cecil would wait for an opportune moment and spirit the patient back to the hospital ward, leaving me shaking my head in the realisation that he had noticed my growing aggravation and had acted in the interests of the cause of it. I generally went and got a cup of tea and took a break. I wonder if he ever realised just how much I appreciated him.

We were always working to perfect our service to our clients, while still with one eye on the bottom line. It is not easy to cover the multitude of costs involved in running a vet practice. Given the chance to attend lectures and courses on practice management, both of us attended eagerly. In one seminar, the American speaker mentioned powdering each patient with a small amount of perfumed talc before it was discharged.

'We forget how the chemical aroma and sometimes the smell of blood, and even fear, may linger on our patients,' he counselled. 'We are so preoccupied with curing them and relieving suffering that we are oblivious to the state in which they leave us.' It made good sense.

The staff were shown how to go about cleaning wounds and injection sites and then give a small puff of powder onto the back of the dog. It made a huge difference. South Africa possibly has more Maltese Poodles than all the other breeds together and owners so appreciated cuddling a nice-smelling little fluffy white lap-warmer.

On one busy afternoon I looked up from my conversation with Mr Visagie about his cat that was limping to see Cecil lead a stocky little Scottish terrier out into the waiting room. I froze, half-expecting the inevitable.

The little black dog waited until it was in full view of the packed room before shaking itself vigorously. A dense cloud of white enveloped both dog and Cecil, who started sneezing uncontrollably.

The owner rushed forward to rescue her dog while the assembled crowd chuckled at the antics of the by-now little grey waif as he shook himself every few steps.

In the early days, we cut costs at every opportunity. At that time, most vet practices sterilised syringes and needles for re-use. The glass syringes had been replaced by plastic disposables but they were too costly for us to discard after a single use.

I noticed that sometimes the needles were not very sharp, and Karen commented that she had experienced the same problem. Economising was one thing, but we did not want our patients to be adversely affected.

Karen showed Cecil how to run the tip of each needle across the ball of his index finger. The blunt ones could be felt to scratch the surface of the skin and could then be discarded. The sharp needles were then placed in the pressure cooker to be sterilised. Cecil was happy to oblige.

Over the next week, we had several animals develop nasty abscesses at the injection sites and at first, we wondered if the tops of the bottles had become contaminated. The previous year, extensive building refurbishments had filled the air with a fine cement dust. Having been a medical centre for nearly a hundred years, the bacteria harboured by the walls could tell many a tale. We had to discard several bottles of drugs and covered all new ones when not in use.

This time it transpired that cement dust was not to blame. Coming into the prep room one afternoon, I noticed Cecil picking up the already sterilised and needles and testing each one for sharpness before placing it in the plastic box on the counter. The walls harboured bacteria, but nowhere near as many as we did on our hands and clothes.

Mrs Van Driesel brought in a little black dog that was born with an attitude—an attitude that got it into serious trouble with a German shepherd. Little Mitch was covered with bite wounds over most of his body. The bigger dog had attacked it and turned it into a blood-leaking colander.

Our first reaction was to treat Mitch for shock. The pooling of blood reserves in the muscles, ready for fight or flight, could be catastrophic if not reversed once the animal is out of danger. Starved of oxygen, the vital organs begin to break down. The condition got its name from early observers who noted deaths among patients who were not physically hurt in any way.

Mitch then underwent extensive surgery, but bite wounds are notoriously infected from the bacteria in any animal's mouth. Bites from humans are very common on the large mines in South Africa, where powerful men work under very stressful conditions and fights can be explosive. A medic confided to me that if bitten, the men are immediately hospitalised and put on a drip with intravenous antibiotics.

Mitch recovered and became a firm favourite among the staff. He stayed for a week to have his multiple wounds treated before being discharged. At home he seemed to deteriorate, and Mrs Van Driesel begged for him to be re-admitted.

Cecil took Mitch under his wing and even changed his name to 'Patch-patch' in honour of all the little oozing holes in his skin. He was eventually discharged once the last one had closed, although he twice returned for other problems, and we always made sure that he and Cecil got a chance to rekindle their relationship.

After three and a half years of faithful service, I was pondering how Cecil managed to survive the full thirty days of each month. As soon as he had his salary, he would disappear for a weekend and come back the following week reeking of alcohol and looking like a wreck.

It had previously taken a long time before I had learned that he was one of a set of twins and his sibling had drowned at the age of eight. In the Xhosa culture, the spirits of long-past relatives influence their daily lives and are revered. I sometimes wondered if Cecil's departed brother had turned up for work to keep his place until Cecil was able to stand up.

On numerous occasions, I would respond to a call in the middle of the night and walk in to find Cecil comforting a patient in the hospital. He seemed unbelievably concerned for their well-being. On one occasion, I had to park the van far from the practice due to work being carried on in the street outside. Since I walked the short distance to the practice, my engine had not alerted Cecil to my approach, and I found him leaving the building with a dozen cans of dogfood in his arms.

Since we had done a food hygiene module at university, I knew that canned dog food in South Africa was in fact fit for human consumption, although the authorities kept it quiet. I was saddened to think that Cecil had to resort to eating it and had probably been stealing it for a long time.

My discovery stopped his tail from wagging and his head drooped. After discussing it with Karen, we sadly dismissed the young man.

Finding a suitable replacement for Cecil proved almost impossible. I even missed being passed the wrong instruments as I worked.

Six months later, he reappeared at the back door, looking even worse than he had after a monthly binge. Things were clearly not going well for him.

'Hullo Cecil,' I greeted. 'What brings you here?'

He ducked his head and mumbled under his breath. On the second try he managed to get the words out. 'I want my job.'

Watching the apprehension in his features, I knew that we would not have to worry about him stealing again. He had more than learned his lesson.

'I caught you stealing the dog food. Why should I give you a job again?'

'Because I cannot find work anywhere else.'

It was difficult to argue with his simple logic and we agreed, after reading him the riot act. I don't know if he ever resorted to a canine culinary experience again, but we were immensely grateful to have him back on the team.

Chapter 83

EXPENDABLE

Karen had given Sindi a home after bringing her back from the dog rescue centre. Part of the deal was that Sindi would act as personal body-guard, a job description Sindi did not understand. She loved everyone.

Rushing up to strangers, she bared her teeth in a grimacing smile, the body going into a tight curl with the stump that should have been a tail gyrating furiously. The sight was frightening enough but then the whiskers on her face would tickle her nose and she would go into a paroxysm of violent sneezes. More than one uninitiated visitor had slammed the door and retired in fear.

The trouble was that as an effective deterrent against aggression, Sindi failed from the start. In desperation, we consulted a behaviourist, who proved to be both effective and kind.

After observing her reaction and noting how she retired behind Karen's skirt when facing an assailant, Kit made several changes: Sindi was given a collar and a lead and secondly, Karen and Sindi were placed behind a large gate. A threatening, masked intruder then appeared, stick in hand and malevolence obvious in his intentions. Sindi growled, a little timidly at first and then as the assailant reacted by drawing back, she developed a deeper timbre, growing in confidence, while the masked man backed off hurriedly.

At one stage the collar slipped off her neck and she was instantly not so sure of herself anymore. It was far more comforting to be able shout insults and threaten aggression when it did not have out to be carried out.

Gill and John Johnston had served as vets on two continents before retiring in King William's Town. When Gill closed the doors of her practice, she offered to sell her stock of drugs to us, and I gratefully accepted. We inherited several items that spent years in a drawer but were never used, whereas most of the products were rapidly prescribed to our patients.

At the time I voted for the opposition political party, who campaigned for universal suffrage, but in common with many English-speaking South Africans, I was confident that it would never come about, since the apartheid regime had an ironclad grip on the country. We were free to express our disquiet about the unjust regime, comfortable that we would never have to cope with the situation should the collar slip from around our necks.

When FW De Klerk did an about-face and released Nelson Mandela from Robben Island, the liberal whites in South Africa were perhaps the most surprised. Suddenly we had to live up to our proclaimed ideals.

Despite being incarcerated for twenty-seven years, Mandela showed enormous forgiveness and statesmanship by leading the new country through a peaceful revolution. The wave of crime, corruption and bloodshed that would follow when he finally passed away remained in abeyance while he was in control.

The ruling political party was the African National Congress (ANC), who had been banned during the years of oppression. A more radical, violent splinter group had formed, called the Pan African Congress (PAC). With the onset of independence, most people regarded the PAC as a spent force and disregarded them.

A year after FW De Klerk had made his startling announcement, and the ANC had won the election, the King William's Town Golf club held their annual charity ball. Most of the town attended, apart from two young vets who staggered home each evening after an exhausting day at work and then supported each other through the night as they took turns seeing to the needs of two little babies.

The charity ball was well under way when the door at one end of the hall opened and a figure tossed in a hand grenade. The door at the far end of the hall was flung open a few seconds after the explosion and two men sprayed the shattered crowd with automatic rifles. The brave assailants then disappeared into the night, while their unarmed victims reeled about in horror, trying desperately to offer succour to the wounded.

In an act of senseless violence, two people who had spent their lives attending to sick and injured animals, had been at the forefront of the campaign for equality and who were trying in the last quarter of their lives to help needy people, were killed on the same night.

Gill died in the grenade explosion, while John, who had crossed the hall to collect drinks for both of them, was gunned down as he held the most dangerous weapon the assembled crowd possessed that night, a glass of wine.

Nelson Mandela was scathing in his condemnation of the attack, and the radicals dispersed into the bush.

A deeply unjust society had just experienced a foretaste of the ongoing senseless and vicious violence that would erupt once the calming sanity of a great statesman finally ended.

Chapter 84

LAND OF BIRTH

'We have exhausted every known drug and technique used to control severe allergies. Your son is getting worse all the time. The only thing we can do is use drugs that we normally reserve for treating cancer.'

The two of us looked at the specialist in disbelief. Surely he could not be suggesting that we resort to the very toxic drugs that we had occasionally used on our patients—drugs that suppressed blood formation, damaged organs, and caused severe side-effects.

I had just finished treating an old dog with a mast cell tumour and had decided that I would in the future try to discourage owners from going down this line. The poor dog had suffered more than was fair. He had lived for another six months, the average survival for a cancer victim.

Peter had been on cortisone for most of his life. The allergy specialists had advised that it would not affect any part of the body other than his lungs, taking it in via his nebuliser. In reality, we had noticed very distinct mood changes when he was given the drug as opposed to the brief periods without it. His growth was affected and for years afterwards he was plagued with joint problems.

'We are not giving him cancer treatment.' Karen was absolutely clear about it. 'Would it make any difference if we moved to a different area?' she asked.

'Not really. He may be a bit better for a few months, until he develops allergies to the new pollens.' The specialist was not very encouraging. 'Taking him out of school might prevent him from getting every cold and virus that is going around. Since the cortisone prevents him from fighting them, he is susceptible to all the bugs. The problem is that he cannot stay out of school for the rest of his life.'

We returned home in deep despair. Even little Leigh seemed to be affected by our mood.

'We are just going to have to move to a higher altitude, where there are fewer house dust mites. We cannot just stay here.' Karen was adamant. I thought of all the complications of selling the house and the practice and finding new jobs. Fortunately, one of us had her priorities right and she phoned around and found an isolated farm in the middle of Natal with a guest house for rent.

'I have noticed how many people in town have respiratory problems,' she informed me. 'The tanning factory belches out sulphur fumes all day, and the town is in a hollow, which prevents the wind from clearing it away.'

I knew better than to argue. Within a week, Karen and the two kids had packed up and left. The removal van arrived to take most of our furniture and follow them. As they loaded up everything, I considered how hard it was going to be for me to take anything that was left when I managed to sell the house, and in the end, we loaded everything into the large pantechnicon, apart from my own clothes. I would sleep on the floor and eat at the kitchen counter.

The practice had been on the market for some time, with very little interest from prospective buyers. A young couple had shown an interest in setting up in opposition to us and they seemed unimpressed when I contacted them about a possible sale.

Word spread through town that we were leaving, and our clients panicked. At the thought of not having any veterinary service in town, they flooded in to get all the work done that they had been putting off in the past.

I had no family to distract me, and I enjoyed working hard. A routine of very long days overloaded with cases began. Having done so many routine operations in the past, I had developed a lot of shortcuts that probably increased the risks to the patients and were less than ideal. The staff had learned to work with me, and they kept me at the sharp end while they took over a lot of the preparation, monitoring and settling down afterwards. We had a team that pulled together as one and I remember each one of them with great affection to this day.

The young couple called again and asked if they could see our financial books. I agreed readily; they were a source of great pride to me.

'No, not all the historical records. Just the past month,' Mike insisted. 'My sister is an accountant, and she is only interested in how the business is doing now.'

He seemed suspicious, and I wondered if he felt we were keen to sell because we were not making the grade financially. I handed him the daybook and the daily takings sheets, meticulously written out by our receptionist.

I wondered if I should tell him how the town was flooding in to get their animals seen to before we left, but he brushed it aside. He clearly trusted his accountant sister far more than he trusted me. I shrugged it off and returned to the salt mine, eager to keep occupied and stop myself worrying about the woman I loved and the two little people who meant the world to me.

Daily phone calls were not reassuring; Peter and Leigh had found the move very unsettling, and my absence further upset their security. Karen was finding it very hard on her own in a new house, in a new part of the country.

Mike called the next day and let me know that they wanted to buy the practice. 'We want to buy the business, but we do not want the company,' he informed me. 'We are also not interested in the building, since we have found a cheaper, if somewhat smaller, one nearby.'

I called our accountant, who assured me that the company could sell the business and we could do what we liked with the company afterwards. I called Mike to let him know we agreed.

The neighbouring building housed a medical practice. They had tried to buy the building we had ended up with when an opposition medical group had sold it five years earlier. The original owners had jumped for joy when we had arrived on the scene, since they were deeply concerned about losing clients to the opposition if they sold to them. They had a second, larger practice on the other side of the town. Our neighbours now enquired whether we would sell to them.

Our house had been on the market for a while with very little result. A neighbour called on me to find out how I was doing and made it clear that she was interested. The next day I had a call from a buyer keen to take the ramshackle little beach house I had managed to buy the previous year.

After struggling for months to interest anyone in our concerns, I had suddenly sold the business, the commercial property, our house and the beach hut within three weeks. I bought a small trailer to pull behind my van and loaded up the last of our possessions. As I drove out of the town, memories of leaving Bourke's Luck in one day when the Commandant had insisted it was impossible flooded back.

'He can get things done quickly if he is motivated enough,' Karen's mother commented. Driving into the farm at Mooi River in Natal, I noticed the three prime motivators standing at the door, and I knew exactly where I wanted to be.

Chapter 85

LED BY THE NOSE

Having worked every day of the year for seven years, apart from our week in the Comores, I decided that I was not going to find another job in the veterinary field. I had even done all the night calls since I shuddered at the thought of sending Karen out into the dark. She in turn had worked just as hard as I had.

For the first six months, we explored other possible means of employment. I was very keen to go into dairy farming and accepted a job as a manager on a very large farm owned by the Harts.

Getting up in the dark and trudging off to the dairy was very rewarding for me. Sadly, I became increasingly aware that Karen found it very isolated and had no possibility of finding work. Peter wrinkled up his nose whenever the wind changed direction and wafted the aroma from the dairy up to the house.

'It smells,' he complained.

Leigh was absolutely delighted by the little calves, the ducks and the rooster. She was in her element, but I wondered how long it would last.

A very attractive small farm came only the market, and I cajoled the family into having a look at it. I also asked James Hart, the farmer I worked for, to give his opinion. He spent some time showing me all the pitfalls and problems. In the end I had to walk away from it.

I sadly had to admit that I would be the only one fulfilled in my role as farmer. It would be very selfish to expect the rest of the family to give up their dreams to allow me to do what I wanted. I had prayed so hard for my dream to be fulfilled and in the end nothing came of it.

A year later, Mr Hart, who had advised me, bought the farm himself to raise his heifers on. I felt a little miffed but had to admit that he had the means and the experience. He would undoubtedly make a success of it.

Early on in my employment with the couple, I had raised the question of security. Since independence, the incidence of theft and worse on the isolated farms had quadrupled.

'We have been on this farm for many years now. The labourers are all friends, and we treat them well. We make sure they are happy and content. We never employ new staff who we do not know,' I was told. 'That is the best security we can have.'

In the end our family moved to the very pretty town of Howick, still at a high elevation, although we had to descend down a steep gradient to Pietermaritzburg for work each day.

Karen found a job with the SPCA, while I took on a part-time position at Allerton Laboratory, a government lab set up to provide a service to the agricultural entities in the area. It took me several months to find out what they expected me to do.

Eighteen months later, a veld fire started on the farthest stretch of the Harts' farm. James gathered all available hands and rushed over to fight it. On his return he found his wife dead on their doorstep and the house ransacked. Those responsible had arrived earlier in the day from a different part of the country. They had no experience of the kindness of the Harts, nor the loyalty felt by their many employees.

The Hart family moved to Zambia and once again took up dairy farming.

I thanked God that He had not granted me my wish in buying the farm I so coveted.

Chapter 86

LABORATORY RAT

After moving five hundred miles from the Eastern Cape Border to Howick in Natal due to the ill health of our son Peter, we found it impossible to get work. It was an enormous relief when I was offered a post at The Allerton Veterinary Laboratory in Pietermaritzburg. Karen in turn secured a post at the busy local SPCA rescue centre.

There were five other vets and a specialist in Rabies when I arrived at the laboratory, and they were all at the top of their game. After a few weeks I wondered just why they had taken me on, when there just did not seem to be any work for me. I felt distinctly like a spare wheel. Three months later, I learned that that was exactly the role I was to fill.

In the meantime, I regularly made the rounds of the various departments, watching the staff work with an effortless expertise as they monitored the health of the dairy cattle in the province, analysed toxins, feeds, and a range of inorganic materials, performed post-mortems on deceased livestock, poultry and birds from the bird parks, and coped with a steady stream of samples from suspected rabid animals and a few humans.

The local agricultural college sent their students to the laboratory once a year, and I was delegated to give them a guided tour of the facilities.

In preparation, I went around to each department and arranged for the white-coated boffins to put on a short display.

There was one section that proved to be more than a little challenging. No-one was interested in parasitology and the task of identifying worms in stool samples had been passed over to a disgruntled, disinterested young woman, who was more often than not on sick leave.

I looked around the dismal, smelly laboratory and wondered what I could show the students the following day. There was very little to stimulate their interest at all.

On a very dusty shelf were two dozen sample bottles that must have been in the same place for nearly a century. Each one was almost embedded in the powder of detritus around it, and the murky contents that had once contained an example of parasitic life had dissolved into a watery sludge. I opened a bottle with some effort and poured out the thin fluid inside to see if there was anything of interest hiding in the murk. There wasn't.

The label had been held on by an elastic band and the paper had darkened, making the writing illegible. The elastic band was so perished that it dropped off and lay on the shelf. I picked it up and popped it into the bottle and put the lid back on.

The perished rubber band had sections of fairly normal thickness interspersed with thinner, stretched portions. A little impish thought began to do a jig in my mind as I looked at the perished rubber band in the bottle. On an impulse, I opened the bottle again and half filled it with water from the tap on the lab bench.

With a smile I began to open all the bottles. Each of the rubber bands was unique; they were different thicknesses and had perished to differing degrees. Once inside the bottles, the collection looked a little more impressive than a shelf of ancient dirt and debris.

The following day the students spent several hours listening avidly to minds that moved in higher planes than mine, until the last door was opened, and they clustered into the parasitology lab. I said nothing as the bottles were passed from hand to hand and faces registered disgust at the variety of worms that lived in the livestock these young students tended daily.

The day was a resounding success. The students and their minders thanked us profusely and drove off in two minibuses. I was mentally patting myself on the back when I turned to see the puzzled face of the director of the laboratory looking intently at a sample bottle in his hand. Quietly I made my way out to the back door and slipped into the car-park unnoticed.

Chapter 87

THE TIGERS IN AFRICA

After having very little to do at the diagnostic laboratory for several months, I received a rude shock when told that almost all the other vets were going on leave at the same time. The Director and the Rabies specialist would be the only two on site for several weeks.

I was initially taken aback and filled with alarm but very rapidly became enthralled with the work. From being a nobody newbie, I suddenly had an intensely packed day, starting with reviewing the bacteria cultured in several thousand milk samples, followed by reports on suspected toxins and then analyses of pastures and feeds. I was suddenly the go-to guy, and I absolutely loved it. It was short-lived but enthralling.

The pinnacle of my short role as laboratory expert came when the SPCA arrived in a white van to announce that they had a dead tiger that needed an autopsy. I shook my head in disbelief. Tigers did not live in Africa. Surely they had it wrong.

It was a tiger. A very dead tiger with one leg missing.

I stared at the huge body in awe. The beautiful beast was at least twice my size, with paws the size of dinner plates. One swipe could clearly have disembowelled a man or taken his head clean off his shoulders.

Mr Boswell, the owner, was a retired circus performer who had a menagerie of ex-circus animals on his farm. The public no longer tolerated animals paraded around a ring, and many of them had left centre stage. Mr Boswell had decided to retire along with them.

'He should not be allowed to keep them,' an officious lady informed me. 'One of his tigers attacked and killed the other and this time we have got him. We are going to confiscate the whole lot, but we need you to support us.'

I wondered how they hoped I could help by performing a post-mortem, but they clearly were determined to prove negligence on behalf of the beleaguered man.

The autopsy revealed nothing. Nothing at all. The tiger proved to be in magnificent health. I took samples of every organ and their contents. A depressing thought slowly surfaced that perhaps if Rick, the usual pathologist, had been present, he would have exposed the cause of the uncharacteristic fratricide with ease.

On impulse, I telephoned Mr Boswell and was confronted by a wave of indignant anger. The two tigers had lived together peacefully for twelve years, and he had no idea why the one had suddenly killed the other. I questioned him further and wrote copious notes that did not help at all.

Mr Boswell mentioned that he had just fed the tigers on parts of a racehorse that had died following an operation. I got the name of the vet who had done the surgery and went to visit him.

Dr Baker was dismissive. 'It had nothing to do with the horse,' he stated firmly, 'and certainly nothing to do with the surgery or any of the drugs used.' He gave me a very short list of everything they had used.

My attention stopped at the word 'Morphine'. A little tickle started in my memory. Dr Baker was not impressed. 'Bah. Morphine is fine. I fell off a cliff ten years ago and I have more steel in my body than in my garage. I take morphine in quantities that would knock a horse out. Love the stuff.'

Back at the laboratory I dived into the extensive library in search of references to morphine. Then I made a second call to Mr Boswell. The dead tiger had eaten the liver of the hapless horse, while his assassin had only devoured some of the meat.

In the autopsy hall, Matthew and Dingi, the two Zulu men who had helped with the post-mortem, were busy cleaning up. The dead animal had been wheeled into a walk-in freezer with an impressive lock on the door. The entire hall was surrounded with thick steel bars, creating the impression that we were inside a cage at the zoo.

Matthew approached me hesitantly to ask if he could take parts of the tiger home with him. I was a bit startled and asked why.

'They are very powerful muti,' he replied. 'The *Isangoma* have asked me for them.' The witchdoctors clearly valued the supposed power inherent in the tiger's body.

I referred the request to the director, who vehemently opposed the idea and instead insisted on locking the freezer and the iron barred door and pocketing the key himself.

'We have had parts go missing in the past,' he informed me. 'Gall stones can fetch a fortune on the black market. Nothing must leave this site. It will all be incinerated once you have finished with it. As a diagnostic laboratory handling infectious and dangerous material, we have to be very strict in preventing contaminating organisms into the general public.'

I returned to my office to arrange the analysis of the various samples from the post-mortem.

The following week, a deputation from the SPCA arrived with a bundle of important-looking documents. They were keen to press charges, but my findings were not what they wanted to hear.

'The cat family is subject to variable responses to morphine. In small doses, it can result in the "Feline Manic Response", causing aggression or excessive fear. In large doses, it sedates the animals.

'In a group of predators, a weakened individual is sometimes attacked by the others in the group, possibly because it represents a threat to the safety of the group by attracting other predators, or possibly due to a shift in the hierarchy that is exploited by one individual settling scores with a previously stronger member.

'The dead tiger ate the liver and received a huge dose of morphine, sending it to sleep. Samples from the organs show very high levels of the drug. The other tiger, the attacker, only took in smaller quantities from the muscle meat, and it became aggressive enough to kill its own brother. Samples from the meat on the farm and from the surviving tiger confirm lower levels of the opioid.'

The assembled officers of the charity were less than impressed and Mr Boswell simply showed his disgust for all officialdom and left to attend to his beloved charges back home.

I returned to the autopsy hall with the director to instruct the assistants to begin the incineration of the tiger, but when we opened both locks and entered the freezer, it was empty. Not even a single multi-coloured hair remained.

Chapter 88

Duck Down and Hide

'Can anyone give these three a home?'

The head of virology held out a double handful of yellow fluff with three little orange beaks just visible between her fingers. A second later, a bright little black eye peaked over the top.

'We had too many embryonated duck eggs for virus isolation,' she continued, 'and three of them have hatched.'

I looked at the tiny, fluffy little bodies and immediately thought of Leigh. Her little heart was almost as soft as their down. Given the chance, she would adopt every orphan that happened her way.

I was proved right when I presented them to her that night, and it was an effort to prize her away from her new charges at bedtime. The next morning, she was up at dawn and busy with them even before I could get my eyes to focus.

A few days later, I spotted her on the lawn, washing their feet and brushing their fluffy little stumpy wings. I grabbed my video camera and sneaked out to film her unawares. The camera had been bought solely to record the early years of the two littlest people in my heart.

Leigh picked up a duckling and put it on her shoulder. 'Sit like a parrot,' she commanded. The parrot slid down her arm, lacking the claws to hold on. A second little duckling was placed on a shoulder with the same result. All three of them just wanted to cuddle as close to her on the floor as they could.

I smiled as I watched her dip their little muddy feet in a bowl of water and then scrub them with a toothbrush. A hairbrush then served to get the debris from their golden down. I was intrigued.

Then suddenly it looked a little too familiar. I realised with a shock that it was my hairbrush. My hairbrush matted with duck droppings and assorted flotsam. She had raided the bathroom cupboard and purloined my belongings. Suddenly everything was not so cute.

The soft brush used to moisten the dirt on the little legs was my shaving brush and the toothbrush to scrub the mud off was… Well, I was clearly never going to use that again. I was speechless. I should have been used to it. In a family devoted to fur and feathers, I had neither, and would forever fill the lowest order in importance.

A few years earlier I had purchased the video camera when I realised how quickly the two of them were growing. After being on duty 24 hours a day for every day for seven years, with a few sparse long weekend trips, we had finally booked a week in the Comores and shamelessly called on family to help. Mark was coming up from Cape Town to run the practice and Granny and Grandpa were going to look after the little ones on their farm in the Transvaal.

I fretted needlessly about leaving them. In the hopes of making our departure easier for them, I drew a treasure map, using my childhood memories of the farm we had grown up on. The treasure was a collection of gold-coloured plastic jewellery and cut-glass stones, together with a bag of chocolate money in gold foil, all in a realistic looking miniature wooden chest that had once held a presentation pack of toiletries.

Arriving on the farm, I stole away for a few minutes to bury the treasure in a shallow hole and, after covering it with soil, I placed eight bricks in the form of an 'X' over it. The pirates clearly did not want to forget where their booty was.

The Colour of Empathy

As we stepped into the car to leave, I handed Peter the map and suggested he get Grandpa to help him decipher it. I had expected tears and heartbreak as we left, but instead all attention was focused on a vision of untold wealth waiting to be discovered.

The Comores were pure bliss. The only small niggle was the ever-present worry as to whether the older and younger generations back home were coping. Returning a week later, I was surprised not to be met by tearful little faces, but instead two little people marched out of the kitchen door, wearing identical white caps bearing a logo for 'Toyota' on the front. Each of them had a small knapsack on their backs and carried a long stick.

'We're going tiger hunting,' they informed us by way of greeting and marched off down to the bottom of the farm. Granny tiger-hunter brought up the rear, wearing an identical white cap and carrying a small bag.

The trio marched an obviously well-rehearsed path until they found refuge among an outcrop of white quartz rock. Rucksacks were tossed aside, and the pair foraged around to produce a small pile of dried grass and three twigs, which was set alight by the oldest member of the party. She then proceeded to warm up two sausages in a jam-jar held over the flames. The tigers were clearly too cowed by this display of prowess and none of them came out of hiding.

Later that day, after a prolonged farewell session, we climbed into the car for the long trip southwards. Peter turned to Grandpa as he was about to embark and handed him a well-worn map.

'I made a treasure hunt for you, Grandpa, so that you won't be sad we are going,' he said.

Grandpa had to enlist Granny's help in deciphering the scrawled map, but the bricks placed in a cross once again helped them eventually locate it fifty yards from its original site. The treasure was very similar to that discovered a week earlier, but the chocolate coins had suffered from time and devaluation and were comprised solely of the outer gold foil wrappers. It did not matter; the value placed on the gesture by the finders was immeasurable.

Chapter 89

A HOLE IN THE DIAGNOSIS

I woke up in the early hours of the morning with the sure knowledge that I was having a coronary. The pain in my chest was piercing. I was clearly in the middle of a heart attack and my chances of making it downstairs and surviving were slim.

At least I could write my last thoughts to my loved ones with the pencil and pad next to my bed that I had started to use to record the deep and wise thoughts that came to me in the early hours (earlier than the wee hours that have a different need altogether). The scribbles on the paper that greeted me in the morning were, however, generally indecipherable or just plain nonsense.

I had tried using an iPad but by the time I had fired it up and focused my eyes on the keys, I was generally too awake to go back to sleep. A pen worked well until it leaked all over the duvet and resulted in a smudged black eye the next day. The value of having a means of recording my thoughts was brought home to me by the piercing pain in my left side; if only I could find the pencil that seemed to have gone missing.

Finding the pencil, wedged deeply between mattress and my side, resolved the issue. No tearful good-bye was necessary, only a prolonged session of gentle massaging of the deeply bruised chest and the consignment of the offending weapon to the bin. I wondered if perhaps a slate and chalk would be safer in future; the scribbles would be no less pointless anyway.

Operating on dogs that have ingested large sticks is a surprisingly common occurrence for vets. The worst offenders are the sticks used in kebabs that still have the remnants of the meat adhered to them after they have been discarded.

Jet was a dark black Labrador who fitted his name perfectly. He arrived with several inches of kebab stick protruding from his side. Despite his obvious problem, his tail never stopped beating for more than a few seconds as he enthusiastically greeted everyone.

It was very tempting to just pull the stick out, but in doing so, we would be leaving an open hole in the intestines for bacteria to leak out, and we could lose the location in the thirty-foot long intestines through which the stick had exited. The correct procedure was to open him up and assess the damage first.

An inkling of possible complications made us take an X-ray first and afterwards we felt intensely grateful that we had. Jet had two other shorter pieces of kebab stick, a handful of silver foil used to wrap the uncooked meat in, and a beer bottle cap. He had clearly enjoyed a three-course meal.

Several hours later, he went home with a new scar running down the midline of his tummy, plus a neat little stitch on his side. He had also been rechristened by the staff and grinned and beat his tail against the cupboard when they called him 'Hoover'.

A second patient, *nKosi*, was a crossbreed dog of uncertain parentage, but with the heart of a lion. His owner, an elderly Zulu man, lived in the more remote areas of Kwazulu and the journey to the clinic had taken half a day. nKosi arrived with a bandage made from an old sheet wrapped around his midriff.

'We were hunting two weeks ago when nKosi was attacked by a bush-pig that stuck a tusk into his belly,' the old man told us. 'I thought he was going to die but he slowly got better over a few weeks. Now he is fine, but he cannot drink water, or it pours out of his stomach.'

Scepticism rose unbidden at this diagnosis. It was not feasible to imagine that water drunk by a dog could pour out of a wound in his stomach. There had to be a mistake. For answer, the owner unwound the makeshift bandage to expose a modest hole just large enough for a man to be able to put a finger into.

One of the assistants brought a bowl of water and nKosi drank thirstily. Nothing seemed amiss, when suddenly a thin stream of water began to trickle out of the wound. nKosi turned around to look at it in puzzlement, licking at the last few drops as the stream subsided, before returning to the bowl in front of him.

Each time he took in enough liquid, it would begin once more to pour out of the wound.

The edges of the wound seemed to be adhered to the surrounding skin. After giving an anaesthetic and exploring the abdomen, we found that the wall of the stomach had fused to the muscle layer of the skin and a fistula had developed which allowed the contents of the stomach to pour out of the hole. Solid food seemed less likely to exit, but water had no compunction against spurting out.

The hole in the stomach was duly repaired, as were the holes in the body wall layers. nKosi went home with a neat scar on his side. Any possibility of making a living in a circus was dashed but at least he would no longer suffer from chronic dehydration.

Chapter 90

THE THIRTY YEAR HOLIDAY

Karen gave everything to her job, never settling for anything but the best for her patients and giving her clients as much time as she could. Coping with a child that never slept through the night for the first three years added to the stress. After five years of hard labour, she admitted that she was just not managing as well as she previously had. At that time, she picked up a nasty viral infection that resulted in a chronic cough for six months.

Eventually she found that she just could not continue to work at pace and slowly her energy reserves seemed to reduce until she had to admit that she was no longer able to get up in the morning.

Every conceivable test was run by the medical staff and only a handful of minor abnormalities were discovered. The final diagnosis was M.E., or Myalgic Encephalomyelitis, commonly called 'Yuppie Flu'.

She felt let down by the label attached to her, feeling that it was belittling. In turn, I worried endlessly about her condition and whether she would carry on getting worse. My heart went out to this dynamic, enquiring, motivated spirit that I loved with all my heart. I had no idea what to do to help her. I traipsed after her as she visited specialist after specialist.

We called on a rather pompous medic who announced that it was a deficiency of Magnesium that could only be treated with weekly injections, which only he could give. The fact that no blood test had shown any deficiency was dismissed out of hand.

'It is never that obvious or we would have known how to cure it a long time ago,' he informed us as he collected his considerable fee. I was angry at what I saw as profiteering at the expense of Karen's health and likened him to a prostitute, a statement that sparked off a serious altercation between Karen and me.

His injections had no effect.

Six months later, a 'micro-nutritionist' was consulted in Karen's desperate search for help. A very pleasant Polish doctor prescribed a small arsenal of pills, 90 of which had to be taken every day. Some had to be swallowed together with milk and others with orange juice.

I was sceptical, but Karen did seem a little better and I could see no harm in the products.

A more pressing problem was that we were rapidly running out of funds. My salary only just covered Peter's medical bills and the cost of driving from Howick to Pietermaritzburg and back each day. Our savings were rapidly being used up in our living costs and Karen's medication.

As always, I largely ignored our predicament, but Karen had experienced the acute penury of moving from Zimbabwe to South Africa with almost no money allowed out of the country at the time. She was well versed in economic hardship and was deeply concerned by our dwindling reserves.

To make matters worse, we had both taken out pension and medical insurance policies from a company even before graduating. They had an impressive marketing technique of delivering a lecture to final year students with the blessing of the faculty, most of whom also had policies with them.

We submitted a claim for medical costs, only to be told that M.E. was not a recognised condition by the medical profession and no payment would be made. We had both made monthly payments to the insurance company for over seven years, but they were not prepared to pay a cent.

'William called today,' Karen announced as I carried a tray of food into the bedroom. She made every effort to join us for meals but at times was unable to summon the energy. 'He was saying that although it is not possible for a vet to support a family in South Africa on a single salary, they are paid more in the UK, and it is feasible there.'

I did not want to move again. I was never keen on change, and each of the moves that Karen had led me on had been variably traumatic. Hayden, a colleague at work, told me how he had spent a winter in London.

'Grey weather, grey buildings and grey people,' was his judgement. I should have realised that a six-month winter in a climate with less sunshine than South Africa could not have resulted in a balanced opinion.

Karen employed her impressive negotiating skills with great effect. 'Let's take a holiday over there to see what it's like. Then we can decide if we want to go when we get back.'

I doubt that she had any intention of returning. We duly bought return tickets, but we also sold most of our possessions and leased our house to a tenant for six months.

The customs at Heathrow had apoplexy at the huge bags of pills that Karen insisted on carrying off the plane, but they let her keep all but two samples of each type. We never heard from them again, so no untoward contents could have been found.

My only impression of England had been from the 'Giles' cartoons and the wealth of literature that had originated from the country. Dickens and Shakespeare hardly made it sound attractive. *Bleak House* seemed an apt description of the rows of unpainted, grey suburban houses we drove past.

Fortunately we were put up by Karen's uncle and aunt near Gatwick and on the first day the kids had the delight of visiting the Hundred Acre Wood, alleged site where Winnie the Pooh had first been born in the imagination of his author.

On day two, I caught a train to London for a meeting at the only locum agency specialising in veterinary staff. I was met at the station by the owner of the agency, an ex-vet nurse, who told me to get back on the train and travel down to Emsworth to a desperate practice whose locum had failed to show for a three-week stint to cover the holiday of one of the vets.

I would have accepted the job regardless of what it entailed but Rick, the senior partner, insisted on showing me around the beautiful area, close to a colourful marina on which two dozen swans undulated slowly in the gentle waves.

The following day, the four of us were driven down to the town by Karen's uncle and we were installed in a spacious, recently refurbished flat above the practice. It seemed like a dream holiday to all of us, despite the noise from the traffic all day and the deafening dawn chorus of birdsong that started at four in the morning.

Karen seemed to thrive in the new environment, and she and the kids made daily forays down to the sea, only a few streets away. For the two little ones, their days were filled with endless delight as they experienced a new world of sights and experiences.

I relished the return to clinical work but was shattered to find just how much had changed in the eighteen months in which I had been employed at the laboratory. Two of the most widely used drugs in anaesthesia had been launched and the profession had been persuaded by the companies that marketed them that nothing else could compare in efficacy and safety. They were the 'gold standard' of anaesthesia. Everyone was familiar with them, except for me.

The medical insurance company sent us a letter to say that ME was now included in their list of conditions that were recognised by the profession and sufferers could claim for the time they were off work. We gladly re-submitted a claim and in turn a reply came to the effect that in the small print of the policy, only those working in South Africa were eligible to claim.

At the end of my three-week locum post, we bought an ancient campervan and had a glorious and totally unplanned trip around England and Scotland. The elderly man who sold us the van generously handed me a policy for the AA that he had taken out in our name, covering us for a year. We were forced to call on them three times during our trip, a fact that he had probably anticipated, but our gratitude for his gesture was immense.

Spending a night in Inverness, the kids delighted in the throng of wild ducks, geese and swans that patrolled the campsite. As I called them in for the night, they proudly showed me a nest they had constructed at the foot of the steps going up to the campervan door. Excitedly, they climbed into the bunk beds, animatedly speculating at what birds would lay their eggs in the nest that night.

As eyes drooped closed, I sneaked out and placed half a dozen hens' eggs in the nest, praying that no predator would come across the easy meal.

Morning was greeted far too early by two ecstatic kids who had discovered the nest and accepted unquestioningly that some mother could lay six eggs in one night and would choose a site in such an exposed position. I smiled at their joy and their obvious delight in the natural world around them.

We had bought return air tickets, a move designed to allay my suspicions, but I raised no objection when we used them to return to the land of our birth just long enough for me to pack up the household while Karen tried hard to cope with a resurgence in her ME symptoms, brought on by the stress of our move half-way across the world. The kids, in turn, revelled in their year without school.

Chapter 91

NO IN AT THE ROOM

We had landed at Heathrow in England with no job to go to and only an invitation to 'spend a few days' with a friend of a distant relative. I had no intention of staying beyond a few weeks' holiday, but life tends to ignore our wishes.

The following day I had found a position at a practice in Emsworth, on the coast. By the evening of the third day we were ensconced in a delightful studio flat above the practice.

I suddenly found myself having to face the reality of working in a strange country. Would the clients be the same? Would the pets be just like those at home? Would the animals speak the language I could understand? Tension began to build in my mind.

Late in the afternoon I ventured cautiously down the stairs to explore. The only door led into what proved to be the Prep room, nerve centre of most vet surgeries.

I watched the bustling staff, hoping to find some reassurance. After a few minutes a nurse brought through a ferret. I had never seen one of them. I knew exactly one disease of ferrets, and it was reportedly rare. Then an iguana arrived, and a few minutes later a huge boa constrictor was transported into the room in a pillowcase. I wondered how easy it would be for me to slip out and run away unnoticed. I could not handle these patients.

A friendly staff member laughed at my concerns, assuring me that only one of the vets on the team specialised in 'exotic' animals and I would only be expected to treat dogs and cats.

Given the chance, I had a quick look at the lay-out of the practice. The Prep room backed onto three consulting rooms. I walked though one of them and stuck my head out of the door at the far end. It opened onto the waiting room, with reception to one side. Simple.

The following morning, I made my way downstairs, again a full half hour before the front doors would open. Walking through to the waiting room, I was surprised to see a cluster of people in the corner with a large Labrador retriever.

'Just the person we need,' said a voice behind me. 'You must be the new vet.' I turned to find a plump receptionist with a friendly face. 'Jason here has cut his paw and Mrs Jones rushed him in as an emergency. I've put you in consulting room 1.'

More than a little flustered, I turned to welcome my first patient, who came over with wagging tail, leaving a bloody paw print with each step. Behind him came not only Mrs Jones, but Mister J as well, plus three children and an elderly lady of unknown status.

I turned back to the consulting room doors and was perplexed to find not three but four doors. Somehow, they had multiplied in the night. With a feeling of disbelief, I opened the first door and ushered the bevy of people in.

Jason and his parents walked in confidently and then stopped abruptly. The three children tripped over each other at the unexpected halt, and the elderly lady placed her cane on my foot and leant her whole weight on it.

Ignoring the pain, I stretched as tall as I could to try and work out the reason for the sudden stop and was aghast to see a toilet and basin at the far end of the room. Mrs Jones was half-doubled over the bowl from the pressure of the crowd behind her, and Jason was excitedly planting kisses on every face within reach.

I heard a muffled whimper behind me and turned to see the plump receptionist holding on to the back of her chair, her face turning a bright red as she struggled to control herself. The English have a strange sense of humour.

'Next door along,' she managed to say in a strangled whisper before hastily retiring to an unknown room behind reception.

I ushered the family out and into the next room, trying hard to salvage some self-confidence amidst the ruins of my dignity.

Chapter 92

CHESTER AND HAWKINS ESQ.

'Don't go anywhere near them.'
I was surprised by the vehemence with which Rick delivered the advice. I had finished the three-week locum that had been handed to me on a plate on our arrival in England and was looking for another place of employment. A practice in Hampshire was offering almost double the going rate for an assistant veterinarian.

'The reason they have to pay above average is because they are a nightmare to work for,' he continued. 'I have heard some pretty rough things about that practice.'

Whenever faced with a high-risk investment that promises better than believable returns, I invariably am attracted to it, often with disastrous results. I called the number given in the advert and was answered by a very attractive young female voice that somehow seemed a little familiar.

'Stuart? You're not the Stuart Phillips that graduated from Onderstepoort in 1984, are you?'

I agreed cautiously and the dam burst. Belinda had been in the same year at university as I was, only a lot younger and a lot more popular among the men.

'Don't believe a word they say about this place,' she enthusiastically counselled. 'The two partners are a nightmare. They will not talk to each other, but that means that I can manipulate them at will. I just play the one off the other.'

Belinda went on to describe how she had been angling to buy the practice from the two ageing partners but had made the mistake of marrying a recently graduated viticulturalist. My mind had not quite managed to remember what a viticulturalist did before she supplied the answer: 'He is an expert in making wine. We went to the wine district in the Cape for our honeymoon, and now he is determined to go back and make his career there.' Belinda was from the Cape Province in South Africa and knew her way around the country and the culture.

'I have got them to refurbish the entire practice and to purchase a load of new equipment.' She let me into her abandoned plans. 'The way to do it is to tell Mr Chesney that Mr Hawkins does not want to buy an ultrasound machine. Then I tell Mr Hawkins that Mr Chesney is not keen on it. They both then insist that we get one and they both feel that they have got the upper hand when it arrives. I just smile and enjoy using it.'

Accepting the job, it took me a while to find that the two older men did not respond to my winsome smile and coy tilt of the head as they had responded to my attractive predecessor. The partners had fallen out many years before and relied on a third party to manage the practice for them, while working as far away from each other as they could.

Mr Hawkins was old school and frequently expressed his displeasure at the younger generation. Mr Chester did all the equine and farm work and was known to be an eccentric character.

We were given the use of a small semi-detached house that had been described in the advert as fully furnished but contained only one double bed, which we quickly discovered had a broken frame that was propped up on tins of dog food.

'You should be able to get all the furniture you need at Boot Sales,' was the advice Mrs Hawkins gave us. We duly visited every Car Boot Sale we could but quickly realised that although it would be possible to find an old accordion and an antique pocket watch, household furniture rarely surfaces at these gatherings.

In desperation, we resorted to poring through the local newspapers and visiting private sellers in the evenings. One item we did not compromise on was a decent bed, although we did manage to find a double bunk for the two kids. Mrs Hawkins was scathing in her accusation of our self-indulgence.

'We used that bed for 45 years and it was good enough for us,' she said pointedly. 'Why did you throw it out?'

The nurses shook their heads and once they got to know us better, they let us know why the house had been so devoid of furnishings. The practice had been built fifty years before our time and a comfortable nurse's quarters had been included in the design. They soon found out that having a single nurse living on site was not ideal since she could not be on duty every night.

The living room of the nurse's section was then changed into a second bedroom and another young girl was taken on.

Ten years later, a third nurse applied for a position. She was a diminutive, shy creature and made no protest when the partners turned the built-in wardrobe into her room.

'They never replace anything that breaks. We just have to do without until the vet assistant leaves, and then we go and raid the vet's house. The keys are always in the office and the partners never go near the place.'

The longest-serving nurse had her finger on the pulse in every respect and ran the practice with precision, which I soon came to realise was not appreciated by the partners at all.

'There are plenty of other fish in the sea if she leaves,' I was told. 'We get an application for a job at least two or three times a week.' They had no idea of the bond the nurses, who acted as receptionists as well, had with the clients. Many owners came in asking for their favourite nurse and the tea-room walls were plastered with thank you cards addressed mainly to these young, dedicated girls.

Mr Chester took no notice of any regulations or management decisions relayed to him. Each morning he would arrive in a rush and tear through the practice like a tornado, collecting bottles of drugs and bits of equipment as he moved through the building. As he drove off, the head nurse would sigh and try to remember just what drugs he had taken, with the aim of filling out her daily order from the wholesalers.

One busy morning, Mr Chester had been gone for several hours when the client second on his list called to ask where he was, since he had not yet turned up. The nurses promised to find out and call back. They placed a call to his first visit and the response was both disturbing and typical of the man.

Mr Chester had arrived at the farm to put an elderly horse down, a procedure he had done many times in the past. Decrying the 'captive bolt' that most vets use, he produced a handgun, for which he had a licence, and aimed it at the exact spot between the eyes and ears of the ageing horse. Just as he pulled the trigger, the tired old mare had stumbled and fallen to her knees. The bullet missed her completely and nicked the gardener, who was obligingly holding her lead, in the leg.

The unfortunate man was led up to the house prior to being taken off to hospital and Mr Chester decided not to take any more chances, but to get up really close. The second shot did its job, and the horse was instantly free of pain. It was also free of any structures that were keeping it upright and it fell onto Mr Chester, knocking him into the grave and then falling on top of him.

The ambulance that called to take the gardener to hospital instead took two patients, one of whom had a broken rib and serious bruising over most of his body.

Mr Chester was a notorious speedster as he did his calls. Time spent in the car was not productive time and he just wanted to get to the next patient as quickly as he could. A new and enthusiastic police officer managed to record him exceeding the limit three times in one day, two of them just outside a large stable, firstly as he arrived in the morning and then as he left two hours later.

He was not given the option of a fine and points on his licence but was summonsed to appear in court. He did so without much concern; he'd had fines before, and he had also managed to get off a few by pleading clemency in that he was racing to an emergency. He was quietly confident of escaping any real censure and was duly shocked when the magistrate suspended him from driving for three months.

Mr Chester let the magistrate know his opinion of the bench and for his efforts he was suspended for a further three months—a total of six months in which he would have to get his wife to drive him to his calls.

Angrily he strode out of the court and climbed into his car. As he turned into the first public road, a strategically placed office flagged him down and informed him that he was driving while suspended and would be facing an even longer sentence.

I was let into the secret of his extreme ire by the head nurse, who knew all the gossip in the practice:

> 'Mr Chester is well known to have a string of young women at various places around the practice. His wife knows it as well and having her tag along to every call is going to cramp his style a little. It's no wonder he is upset.'

Chapter 93

ALTON AANS TOURS

Our first year in England proved to be enlightening, although we were exposed to factors that were unique to the strange environment we found ourselves in.

Karen had brief bouts of increased energy, but whenever she attempted to do anything, the insidious weakness returned and as a result she spent most of the year bedridden.

I was desperately worried for her, but the extra demands made by having to care for two little children on my own, plus provide for the four of us, meant I had little time to think about it. I was, after all, with the three most cherished beings that existed.

We had been given the use of a semi-detached house in a cul-de-sac, across the valley from the practice. It was nothing much, but the neighbours all proved to be extremely friendly and caring.

On the first day, I found Leigh leaning as far out of the window closest to the adjoining house and I pulled her back in alarm.

'I was just trying to spit on that man's head, Daddy. He is just next to our garden wall.' I was horrified. Having never been in such close proximity to neighbours, she was having to adapt to the non-confrontational society of a crowded neighbourhood.

Mike from next door became a good friend, though I never plucked up the courage to tell him of his close escape from an anointing from above.

A soft flurry of snow fell the second week that we were there and all four of us delighted in the white lace blanket that covered everything, although it was only a few millimetres thick. The kids wanted a snowman, which proved a challenge in that the supply of snow from our driveway never amounted to much. I fetched a broom and swept the drives of several neighbouring houses, wondering if the occupants would regard it as theft. Molly from next door came out with a plateful of warm mince pies to thank us for sweeping the concrete strip in front of her house, and we realised that the white powder we cherished was not as welcomed by everyone.

Having grown up in wide open spaces, it amused me to see how several of the driveways had manhole covers that partially spanned two neighbours' drives. A few of them had been painted, but only the half on the side of the house with the same colour had been done.

Each morning, Karen would valiantly attempt to make us all breakfast, but was forced to retire when it became too much for her to cope with. My heart went out to her, and before leaving we would make sure she had her basic needs beside her bed. Life for her held no joy during those first eighteen months.

I walked the kids across the open valley, past the duck pond and up the hill to the veterinary practice that was fortunately next to the school they attended. Leigh had never been to school, since in South Africa they only start at the age of six. Her teachers found that she had no concept of basic arithmetic or writing and just allowed her to float at the bottom of the class.

As I was collecting them one afternoon, Leigh's teacher stopped me at the gate and showed me a detailed drawing of the stone church across the road.

'I got all the kids to draw the church and after half an hour, everyone had produced the typical, lopsided rectangle with a trapezium-shaped roof. Leigh was the last one left drawing and I had to go over and tell her she had run out of time. I assumed she was not up to the task.'

Mrs Moran pointed to the sheet of paper Leigh had been working on. The delicate details of stone were etched into walls that could have been sketched by an accomplished artist.

'Your daughter has an amazing talent,' she said simply. I smiled. I alone knew just how many talents she had, I thought. I decided to try and encourage our littlest one to go as far as she could, a goal I later realised was shared by Karen and enthusiastically pursued by Leigh herself.

When the time came to move to a new county, and to take up the reins in a practice of our own, Karen experienced ever greater symptoms of fatigue, headaches and depression triggered by the stress. On her own decision, she and the kids left for an extended holiday back in South Africa, while muggins here was tasked with setting up the practice we had bought in Essex. Karen very wisely used the time in South Africa to coach both the kids, and in particular to try and channel the innate mischief in our youngest in a more productive path. Three months later they returned to the small island in the north and both kids had a far greater base to build on and excelled in later years.

Chapter 94

NEW YEAR GIFTS

Although Mr Chester attended to most of the horse calls, even he could not always be on duty. New Year's Eve provided me with a cherished memory of the English countryside.

A young gelding had managed to impale itself on a fence post and had a deep gash in his neck. I took down directions and drove to the area, expecting to find the stables fairly easily.

'Turn at the old pub,' the caller had instructed. I drove for miles without seeing a pub and eventually had to call in at a service station.

'Oh, yes,' the young girl at the counter informed me. 'The pub is five miles back.'

I duly retraced my steps but was still unable to find the elusive watering hole. Passing a house with a light on, I turned into the driveway and repeated my question.

'Oh yes. This is the pub. You are at the right place. It is no longer functioning as a pub, since we closed nine years ago.'

I was astounded. 'How is anyone supposed to know that this was once a pub?'

My congenial countryman shrugged. 'Everyone knows this as the Green Man Pub.'

The stables proved to be at the end of a long, steep descent into a wide basin. As I turned into the road, I caught site of a fox trotting across the valley, a crisp line of prints embedded in the pristine expanse of snow behind it. He paused and turned to watch me as I drove down, unconcerned by my intrusion.

The cold was intense but the setting so picturesque that I tended to forget the temperature, until I tried to draw up some local anaesthetic and found it had frozen in the bottle. I was forced to thaw it in my pocket, all the time wondering if the product would be affected by the freezing. Perhaps the icy cold would help numb the surgical site.

The gelding proved to be a star patient and hardly protested at all as I laid a neat row of sutures in his delicate, velvety skin.

Eyeing the steep slope covered in snow that I had managed to drive down but now needed to negotiate going uphill, in a small car totally unsuited to the countryside, I turned to ask for local knowledge.

'Just keep to the tracks. You should be fine,' the young groom commented.

'What car do you drive?' I asked, keen to learn more about the locals.

'Oh, I canna drive at all. Never been up that road either. Still, if you keep to the tracks it will all be fine.'

The little car slithered and slid as I tried to negotiate the road, aiming to keep the tyres in the deep grooves cut into the hard mud. It proved to be extremely difficult. Thinking about the lack of experience professed by the groom, I pulled hard on the wheel and the car bounced out of the tracks onto the ridge running next to them, and the jolting ceased immediately.

I laughed and thought back to my first day in England, when I travelled to London looking for a locum agency. Lost in the concrete jungle, I stopped to ask a local for directions.

'Well, you go left there, right. Then you go right, right. And then right again and then left, right. You'll be right for sure if you keep left then. Right?'

I had thanked him and walked around the corner to ask someone else. I wondered if he was chuckling to himself, but stealing a glance backwards, I could see him begging a cigarette from a friend unaware of the yokel he had sent on a fool's errand.

A visit that amazed me was handed to me after I had been working in the practice for six months. Mr Chester was unwell, and Mr Hawkins passed me a sheet of paper with an address that was over eighty miles away.

'Surely this can't be economically viable?' I protested.

'Oh yes, it is,' he assured me, and instructed me to load up the car with a long list of medications.

The horse stud proved to be near Stonehenge and it took most of two hours to find. I drove down a long, oak-lined drive to a rambling house in once-manicured gardens. Easing out the kinks in my spine, I hesitantly walked up to the front door and rang the bell. An elderly man in a dark suit opened the door and asked what I wanted.

'I'm here to see Mr, er … Mr Wikes?' I informed him. 'I'm the vet. From Alton.'

'Could you go around to the tradesman's entrance, please,' he replied. 'It's that way.' The door closed firmly in front of me.

For the first time I realised how my black countrymen must feel when treated as second class. Even when done in a kind and friendly manner, it still rankled. I wondered how often I had shown contempt to those I worked with, without ever meaning to. I walked around, feeling a mixture of both irritation and humility.

The patient I had been called to, a highly pedigreed Suffolk Punch stallion, had eaten a hearty meal of Yew tree and was suffering from the toxic effects of the greenery.

As sometimes happened, the client knew more about the condition than I did. His horses seemed to have a habit of indulging in this less than nutritious greenery and from experience he had learned a lot about the condition. I in turn knew the textbook learning but had never seen a case.

After dealing with the stallion, we drove to a dairy unit and then a piggery, both owned by the family. On the way, Mr Wikes explained the history of his family, who could trace their roots back to William the Conqueror.

Finally we ended our trip at the door to his dispensary, which he unlocked to proudly display a small room with shelves on three sides, all loaded with trays of bottles and bags of powders. The volume of medicines on this unit was at least twice the amount we kept at the surgery.

Mr Wikes picked up several bottles, one after the other, and quizzed me on the contents and what they could be used for. It amazed me that he should have such a stock of them when he clearly lacked any knowledge about them.

Locking up, he accompanied me to the car and when I opened the door, he eyed the drugs that had been loaded into the vehicle and asked longingly, 'What have you got for me today?'

Feeling uncomfortable, I professed ignorance of any consignments for him but promised that when one of the partners visited next, he could take it up with them. A little deflated, he allowed me to drive off and then turned to respond to his valet, who had arrived to summon him to lunch.

Chapter 95

A Heart on His Sleeve and a Breast on His Thigh

Timmy was a cat blessed with bravado. His blessing unfortunately turned out to be a disaster in disguise. One evening Timmy tried to outrun a speeding car and was hit on his hip and sent flying into a hedge. Despite his extensive injuries, he managed to make his way home over a half mile of garden walls and broken paving.

It was clear when his frantic owners brought Timmy in that he was in severe shock and pain. Our first concern was to stabilise him, before worrying about broken bones and torn muscles. The team was well versed in dealing with a trauma patient and within a very short time, he was on a drip and feeling the relief of powerful painkillers and drugs to get his circulation back to normal. The danger of vital organs being starved of blood and oxygen was averted. It was more difficult to help his owners.

A middle-aged couple with two children, all of whom were devoted to their feline family member, they suffered the agonising wait to find out if he would make it.

The night staff monitored Timmy through the dark hours and in the morning, we took a series of X-rays. He had a shattered pelvis and the skin covering the left leg was extensively damaged. We were able to call the worried family and give them the news.

Cats have a remarkable ability to recover from extensive damage to the pelvic girdle and provided the bones are not badly displaced, cage rest for an extended period is often an effective treatment.

The problem was that the left hip would never again be able to bear his weight due to multiple fractures of this ball and socket joint.

We decided to remove the top of the femur, so that his bones would not grate together. Once recovered, the muscles of the leg would be more than up to coping without the bones. It is a commonly performed procedure. More worrying was the condition of the skin over this leg.

Timmy had his wounds dressed and the bandages changed twice a day, but the embedded gravel chips and the deep infection won in the end. Even after the bones had begun to knit, his leg was devoid of skin from above the knee down to the hock joint. The area was too large for the remaining skin to grow over it.

Cats have the advantage in that their back legs can easily lie against their abdomen. Operating partly from hard-won memories of lectures but mostly by following the detailed descriptions in our library of textbooks, I loosened a tunnel of skin on Timmy's tummy and pushed his hairless leg through it. The hairy little paw protruded just behind his armpit. The abdominal skin was sutured to his leg and the whole bandaged up for a month. Timmy bravely learned to hop around and rub his head against anyone close enough for a cuddle.

In the days before patented medical pet shirts, Timmy's family made several tight-fitting suits from the sleeves of knitted jumpers to go over his body and keep the bandages firm. The two young girls decorated the sleeves with little hearts and other designs.

Once the skin had attached to the muscles of the leg, we made parallel cuts along the abdomen to free the limb, together with its attached tummy skin, and sutured the edges of the skin to each other around the leg. The final result was that his hind leg was now covered in skin that had once been on his abdomen.

Timmy seemed contented with his re-organised outer covering, despite the fact that the fur on his leg now faced upwards. His owners were thrilled, but no-one was as pleased as I was. The chance of being allowed to participate in an operation like this is very rare and very precious.

'We have one concern,' admitted Timmy's humans. 'He does not like the other cats to see his leg and often lies down on it when they approach.'

I was surprised and wondered why.

'He seems embarrassed,' they explained, 'by the fact that one of his nipples is now on his thigh.'

There's no pleasing some cats.

Chapter 96

LOST FOR WORDS

Although we had no speciality in treating birds and exotic animals, there are not many vets who will take on an avian patient and even fewer who will spend the considerable time required to nurse a wild bird to health. All vets, however, will make arrangements to get them treated by referring them on.

Since we had an interest in all species, we occasionally found ourselves asked to deal with an unusual patient. Karen shared my enthusiasm and I had from the beginning respected her skills and her empathy for all living things. She was on duty when the Red-tailed Hawk was brought in.

I was a little envious at first but watched with interest as the radiographs showed a fracture of the largest bone in the wing. It was going to be a difficult operation.

Many texts describe strapping a broken wing to the body of the bird, but in practice I found they never did well. The bulky bandage seems to immobilise them, restricts their breathing, and often overbalances them, no matter how carefully it is applied.

Karen left the traumatised bird in an oxygen cage to maximise the amount of the life-giving gas in its bloodstream and after four hours, she gave a combination of sedatives and pre-meds and finally an intravenous anaesthetic. The hawk was kept stabilised with a tube inserted into the windpipe to supply oxygen and a gas anaesthetic.

A sterilised knitting needle was used to align the bones by inserting it into the hollow centre of each section in turn. Newer techniques nowadays use a thinner pin that runs up the shaft of the bone and is then bent to penetrate the hard cortex and runs on the outside of the limb as well. In the past we used knitting needles to keep the weight down.

The bird recovered remarkably well and was ready to be released after a month.

We drove to a wide-open space and pulled off near a recently ploughed field. Soggy, grey weather had persisted for a week but cleared up just briefly for us that morning.

Karen opened the door of the carrying cage and ever so gently lifted the magnificent bird out. Sharp beak and bright, intelligent eyes on a head that moved swiftly from side to side, taking in its surroundings rapidly.

With a gentle sway, Karen tossed the hawk into the air and the wings immediately opened wide to catch the wind and allow it to soar a hundred yards and land in the centre of the muddy, ploughed field.

We waited for what seemed like hours, but our patient showed no signs of rising from the ground again. Left out in the cold, it would not survive the night. We had no choice but to go and retrieve it.

Neither of us had any protective boots and we just had to plunge in, sinking up to our ankles in the grey-brown ooze, and plod towards the hawk with thick clods covering our shoes.

We were only ten feet away from it when it suddenly stretched out its wings and launched itself into the air, soaring away towards a distant line of trees.

Peter calls this 'type-two funny': You laugh about it later but not at the time. We had nevertheless the deep satisfaction of seeing a broken wild animal put together again and released to live a life free of interference from people.

We barely had time to rush home and change before I had to leave to get to the new branch clinic I had opened in the next town. We had a full afternoon of appointments and I had seen Mrs Fincham on the list. She always took up twice as much time as anyone else.

Laura-lee Fincham lived life at full throttle, and someone had removed the silencer from her exhaust. She announced herself by the volume of sound even before she entered the practice, and she never failed to leave me smiling when she left. Smiling at her effervescent ebullience and her undying optimism, and smiling at the fact that after an hour in her presence I needed to sneak off and hide somewhere in silence.

As carer for her seriously disabled daughter, Laura-lee had to rely on short periods away from home while friends gave her a chance to get out and attend to life. She was always in a rush and her observations were so overwhelmingly off-beat.

The small branch practice was housed in a unit that formed part of a parade of shops, bordering two sides of a carpark. Ivy, the nurse-cum-receptionist, and I watched as Laura-lee's small car raced into the parking area and reversed smartly into a space at the farthest corner from the surgery. She got out, opened the rear door, and bent down several times as if picking up items from the car, before turning and using her shoulder to close the door.

Appearing around the front of the car, we were intrigued to see that she carried a handbag and several parcels on one arm while the other hand held a dog-lead which hung down, with a dog collar swinging from the end. We watched in silence as she made her way across the tarmac and between the cars.

As she neared the front door, I stepped over and held it open for her. Laura-lee walked over to the reception desk and dumped her bag and parcels on the counter. Turning to the dog lead she announced, 'Chaz has got a sore ear and …where's my dog?!' The last sentence came out as a shriek.

Ivy and I watched in amazement as Laura-lee flung open the door and raced back towards her car, calling for Chaz as she ran.

We were still wide-eyed when she appeared in the road on the far side, with the repentant Chaz now firmly attached by his collar and lead. Ivy caught my eye and then dissolved into tears of laughter.

Dog and owner returned to the practice and once again made their way to the reception desk, only by now Ivy had found it necessary to retire to the lady's restroom, leaving me to deal with the eccentric client on my own.

The ear infection was easy to resolve but as the pair left, I wondered whether the correct patient would be given the prescribed treatment.

The daughter was extremely blessed to have a mother capable of coping with the challenges that life tossed her way and carrying on regardless, even if the vet she consulted seemed to have bright shining eyes, a tic that made his mouth twitch and had to retire repeatedly to check something at the back of the practice.

Chapter 97

GOLIATH AND THE SURGEON

There is an illusion that plagues many of us that we should be able to do complex tasks that we have no experience of, just because we have achieved a certain level of skill in a different field.

I blame my father, actually; he just did everything that life threw at him. Whenever I pay a tradesman for some work, I have this guilty feeling that if it had been Dad, he would have just done the job himself.

A few years ago, I learned that I had a skill I had never even considered; I can run a hundred metres in under five seconds, while wearing Kevlar protective trousers and steel-capped boots.

I had asked a tree surgeon over to quote for the felling of five large fir trees at the bottom of our garden. He looked at the first one I pointed to, then walked ten paces away, looked up again and then walked fifty paces farther, before once again checking on our foe. Finally, he mentioned a figure that had me gasping.

'That's a big 'un. I don't think you'll get a better price from anyone else,' he said.

The second chap gave an even higher figure and the third mentioned a sum that amounted to several months of my salary. I decided that it was time for a bit of D.I.Y., which nearly turned out to be D.I.E. instead.

After all, I reasoned to myself, cutting a tree trunk cannot be all that difficult. I had seen logging companies in the area, and they seemed to drop the giants with ease. All you needed is a big enough scalpel.

There are numerous websites offering chainsaws for sale, even one that gives a free bottle of blood clotting agent with each saw, but their prices are just as off-putting. On an impulse I visited a local company that sold agricultural machinery and was immediately captivated by another of Dad's weaknesses – a bargain. I left with a very big chainsaw, plus helmet, face guard, earmuffs, Kevlar gloves, steel-capped boots and seatless Kevlar trousers. The salesman could not explain why the trousers were seatless, but I would soon find out.

I must admit to a sneaky suspicion that my actions were motivated by a late onset midlife crisis – my third. Beware the man who does not buy a Ferrari but goes out and returns with a chainsaw and a maniacal grin.

I read up all I could about tree felling but it was a little above me. One text talked about 'standing on the left of the tree'; I went out and looked at our trees, but they all seemed ambidextrous, and I could not tell which side was left and which was right. Eventually I just took a deep breath and began to work. The idea was to cut a deep notch a third of the depth of the trunk in the side to which you want the tree to fall, which was easy. Then you cut a few inches higher on the other side and the tree falls happily just where you want it.

The plot next to the house was agricultural land, and I planned to get the tree to lie down gently in the field, leaving our property unscathed.

I cut the notch and then moved to the opposite side. My saw was a third of the way in when a gust of wind sprang up and the tree gave a few sharp popping sounds and then, with a sigh, leaned over the wrong way, trapping my saw and instantly stopping it from running.

After half an hour of cursing and sweating, I fetched my secret weapon – a wedge that was meant to be inserted in the cut and tapped in with an axe to force the tree to fall. My wedge unfortunately was totally ignored by the tree, and I ended up with bruised palms from whacking it with the axe until the entire piece of metal was embedded deep within the tree trunk.

Eventually I had to leave the tree overnight but warned the neighbour not to go near it. He smiled and informed me that he knew about felling trees since he had been a green keeper for many years. He trotted off and then came back a little ashen faced and shook his head before asking, 'You aren't really trying to fell that monster, are you?' He should have said something before the tree ate my saw.

After a sleepless night, I had no option but to attack the tree with a handsaw and the axe, and since the chainsaw was on the other side, I had to chip out the wood from the notch on the side to which the tree should fall. Every few minutes the wood would give a few loud cracks and I would dash away. I told myself that it was not out of fear but because it was important to keep on my toes.

I noticed that my heart was racing at twice the normal rate, but that was purely due to the heat and the strain of wearing the heavy seatless trousers and steel-capped boots and had nothing to do with being afraid.

I decided to discard the helmet since if the tree fell on me, it would not raise a bump on my scalp, but rather break my neck. The muffs came off since they prevented me from hearing when the tree was going to fall. The boots would have taken too long to remove so they remained on. As for the seatless trousers, I nearly dispensed with all trousers for the sake of speed but the thought of attracting a crowd and being responsible for their safety prevented it.

After what seemed like hours, the tree let out a crack like a rifle shot and started to scream as it fell. I was all prepared to dash towards the house while the tree fell into the neighbour's field when I realised that it was falling the opposite way and was coming down on top of me.

That was when I found that I could run faster than Usain Bolt. The top of the tree only had fifty metres to reach the ground, but I had passed the hundred metre mark before it landed.

I did not stop before I was inside the house, and then the true value of the seatless trousers became evident as I dashed into the smallest room in the house since I urgently needed to relieve myself.

I did truly intend to fell the other four trees. Goliath had been no match for me, even if my bottom lip trembled whenever I thought of the mad sprint up the garden. I told myself that it was not my fault that we sold the house a few years later, before I had a chance to tackle them.

The new owner later let me know that he had taken the more sensible action of keeping his trousers on and paying the king's ransom to a company that came out with a team of experienced men and an impressive array of machinery.

Chapter 98

EARNING THEIR STRIPES

I never know what stand I should take regarding corporal punishment (although there were a few non-commissioned officers in the army that I would dearly have liked to give a few lashes to).

The need for physical punishment somehow never occurred when the kids were young. Peter responded to a serious talking to, and Leigh kept me amused with her entertaining and often ingenious mischief.

My first introduction to the concept of Dickensian beating had been sharp and unexpected. It occurred in the second week of senior school.

The music department for some reason split the boys and girls and tutored them separately, and we soon got to learn the fearsome reputation of the boy's music teacher. He arrived at our first lesson looking decidedly flustered and angry. Pushing a bunch of keys into my hands, he ordered me, 'Go to room 82 and bring the blue-covered books from the cupboard in the corner.'

I trotted off in severe anxiety, having no idea where room 82 was and wondering if I would ever find the required books. The master, meanwhile, left to collect some other items from the staff room. On his return ten minutes later, he found the chaos anyone would expect when leaving thirty teenage boys without an armed guard or at least someone in authority. He decided without hesitation to use his cane of each of them.

I returned with the books just as he was giving his vicious, insulation-tape covered cane a few practice cracks against his desktop.

'Get in the queue,' he commanded.

I protested that I had not been present when the rest of them started the uproar, but he replied with heat, 'You are part of the class. Get in line. Since you have the cheek to talk back, you can go first.' He grabbed me by the collar and forced me to bend over and then laid down two streaks of Napalm on my tender young cheeks.

I could not believe the agony. This could not be happening. I was sure that he had cut through the muscle and laid the bone bare. I swallowed my scream and the urge to do a version of Irish line dancing with overtones of a Cossack Kalinka. The only thing I could do was sit down as quickly as possible in the hope of smothering the flames.

The next boy in line was roughly bent double, with his face only a few feet from mine. His eyes were screwed tight, and his face contorted in apprehension. As the first blow landed, his eyes widened dramatically in disbelief and alarm and the second blow unhinged his jaw, which opened wide in horror as his feet shot forward, leaving the rest of his body to catch up.

Each of my classmates showed identical reactions and by the tenth boy, I was beginning to be first intrigued, followed by fascination, and finally great amusement as one by one they suffered the same fate, while I observed them at close hand.

As the last in the line skittered away in flames, a hand jerked me to my feet and bent me double once more.

'Since you enjoyed that so much, you can have a second dose,' he said and once again the fiery agony descended on my unprotected rear.

I so often endured the ministrations of the schoolmasters, since I found it impossible to remember to bring the grammar book on Mondays, a swimming costume on Tuesdays and a long list of things that my brain just did not have the ability to hold onto. Pain and humiliation never helped my cerebral cortex to improve.

It never occurred to me to ever use the same techniques on Peter or Leigh. More often than not, I found myself highly amused by their misdemeanours.

Called on to adjudicate in an argument between the two, both of whom were partially guilty, my imperfect memory recalled the wise sayings of one of my parents, which I duly imparted to the next generation.

'Two rights don't make a wrong!' I announced pompously.

The two squabbling siblings paused to consider my sage words and then burst into mischievous laughter.

'You got it wrong,' they crowed. 'It should be two wrongs don't make a right.' The laughing duo changed allegiance and joined forces in glee against the older generation. I smiled, happy to pretend I had intentionally made the mistake.

Karen had started a system of counting slowly and menacingly from one to three, with an implied threat of dire consequences should she ever exceed the magic number. We never seemed to get to three, and I had no idea what to do if we ever did.

I returned to the clinic one afternoon after doing the rounds on the farms to be met by our staff, most of whom were female, in great distress. A local bully that I had got to know had wandered in and was searching for loot in the rear of the practice. I marched in and grabbed him by the collar and directed him towards the waiting room.

'Out,' I commanded. 'Out, now. That's one.' He took a few hurried steps and raced past the crowd in the waiting room as I shouted after him 'That's two.'

I turned in embarrassment to see the bemused grins of all the parents in the room and the bewilderment of those still unencumbered by small offspring.

When the kids were a little older, I came home to find that they had left a trail of destruction as they moved through the house. Repeated demands that they clear it up failed and so I decided to use psychology. Vets are good at psychology. Sadly, getting a dog to sit by offering a liver treat does not qualify one as a parent.

I fetched a back garbage bag and began indiscriminately throwing everything in it: rubbish, toys, CDs, books, wrappers, clothes...

'What are you doing? That's my Lego.' The shout came from the far corner.

'And those are my sweets,' echoed the other corner.

I carried on relentlessly, explaining as I cleared up that someone had to take responsibility for tidying and if they did not help, then it was no fault of mine that I did not know what was rubbish and what was good.

The two of them retrieved the bag from the bin in the kitchen and began sorting out their possessions. I retired to a comfortable chair in triumph to read the new Dick Francis and enjoy a hot drink.

A short while later I noticed with appreciation that the lesson had been taken to heart. Out of the corner of my eye I saw little Leigh dragging a bulging black bag that was by now larger than she was, while Peter was throwing objects inside.

With a shock I noticed my reading glasses tossed in carelessly followed by a plateful of chocolate cake that I was saving for the time when my hunger and my overfull stomach reached a compromise.

'Hey,' I protested, but Peter turned to face me, hands akimbo on his waist.

'This place is a dump,' he announced. 'Someone has to clean it up.'

Chapter 99

AFRICAN THREADBARE PARROT

A beady eye watched me with apprehension from the safe depths of a cardboard box.

A caricature of comedy with elegantly plumed head and a skinny bald body. A small vulturine creature covered in moth-eaten grey down, the only undamaged feathers on the areas above the neck, where the sharply curved beak could not reach them.

Alfie could have been handsome in grey livery with bright red tail feathers, if only he could resist plucking each shaft out as it emerged through his fragile, chicken-thin skin.

'Why does he do it?' his perplexed owner wanted to know.

'There are many reasons for feather plucking in African Grey parrots,' I explained, 'Mites, infections, hormonal imbalances, pain, frustration, incorrect diet, boredom, and stress, to name a few. Most of these patients do not know they are birds since they have been brought up in isolation and have never seen another parrot. A lot of them identify with people and can feel love, jealousy, and possessiveness towards one person. Some of them even display to their owners as they would to their mates in the wild.'

Mrs Fotheringham blushed slightly and ducked her head. Her

husband nodded a little more vigorously. 'Stupid bird bites me if I go near him but can't get enough of Carol,' he admitted.

'What can we do to correct it?' she asked.

'Each case is different. Sometimes we can identify a single problem such as a bone infection which causes them to chew the feathers in the region, possibly due to pain. If there is a dietary problem or a hormonal imbalance, we can sometimes correct it with supplementation.'

'How much will it cost?' The ever-present spectre of money that rose to claim so many victims among our patients.

'That depends on the results we get,' I explained. 'We can start with some simple blood tests to detect damage or dysfunction of internal organs. We will include hormonal levels. If we find something, then we will treat it and see the result. If not, we will go on to the next step, which will be radiographs and analysis of his droppings for parasites. If we cannot find anything, then we will suggest a hormone implant and behavioural training to try and normalise his behaviour towards you and hopefully stop his destructive habit.'

'We don't have much money,' Carol admitted glumly. 'We couldn't pay for all those tests.'

'I could do just the very basics and treat for the most common causes in the hope that we are successful, if you like,' I offered.

The couple looked at each other and then at the floor. I looked at the bright, intelligent eye in the dark shadows and dreaded the answer I knew was coming.

'We had decided to have him put to sleep,' the husband commented. 'We don't want to see him suffer any more and we just cannot afford to treat him.'

I gave it one more try. 'What if we treat him with the very basic drugs and see what happens? I could give them to you at the minimum price so that we just cover our costs.'

The husband shook his head sadly. Carol turned abruptly and left the room, tears glistening in her eyes. I waited a few minutes and then silently printed out the consent form for euthanasia. He signed it without comment.

As he left the room, a wave of rebellion rose like gorge in my throat.

'Would you give him to me if I promised to pay for all the tests and treatment?'

He turned and contemplated me silently for a few minutes and then nodded his head. Without saying much more, he signed a second sheet of paper on which I had hastily scrawled an agreement whereby the couple relinquished all rights to Alfie, and I became his new owner. As they left, I carried my new charge through to the hospital ward and placed him in his cardboard carrier in a large, glass-fronted cage. The waiting room was filling up with impatient clients and I had already spent too much time on this bald parrot.

Vets tend to work unsociable hours. Most employers will allow their workers time off to visit a doctor; few will allow them time off to take Fido to the vet. As a result, everyone wants to come before or after work. Our days tend to finish long after most other professions.

Tiredly, I locked up the surgery and then picked up the cardboard box and my briefcase filled with paperwork that had not been completed during the day. I seldom managed the energy required to do it all at home, and most of it would make the return journey back to the surgery the next day, unfinished and demanding urgent attention.

After a long drive home, I coaxed a very wary, featherless bird into a large parrot cage that I had manhandled from the shed into the corner of the living room. Filling three bowls with water, pelleted food, and fruit for the parrot, I fed myself a sketchy meal of whatever I could find in the fridge and then stumbled up to bed. Karen and the kids were in South Africa, visiting her parents. I had the house to myself, and it seemed to echo hollowly with every step.

Why it had become impossible to sleep at three in the morning and then equally as impossible to wake up when the alarm went off at seven, I failed to understand. Bleary-eyed, I swept a hand over the bedside cabinet to fumble with the annoying electronic chirp and then lay back to allow my mind and body to reconnect.

Sleepily I made my way to the bathroom and then remembered that I had left my clothes on the stairway as I climbed it the previous night. I grimaced in mild appreciation at the thought that there was no-one around to disapprove of such sloppy behaviour. If I wanted to drop my clothes on the floor, then drop they would. In fact, I could go downstairs in the nude, and no-one would ever know. No-one was at home. With sneaky pleasure I waltzed down the stairs in naturistic freedom, enjoying the cool chill on my skin.

I was halfway across the living room a voice from behind said, 'Good morning.'

In frantic panic I leapt behind an easy chair and grabbed at a tea towel on the coffee table, desperately wrapping its inadequacy around my loins.

There was no-one in the room.

I peered behind the sofa and then lifted a corner of a curtain to see if anyone was watching from outside. My heart raced furiously while mixed emotions of fear and shame raced through my mind.

The second greeting came from the corner in which the parrot cage stood.

'Good morning.'

I peered closer and then chuckled with delight. Alfie surveyed me solemnly from a perch at the far side. I let the tea-towel drop and then hastily picked it up again as he cocked his head to one side in critical contemplation of my undress.

Feeling more than a little ridiculous at being embarrassed to be nude in the presence of a parrot, I backed out of the room and made my way upstairs to security and decency.

Behind me Alfie started whistling the first few bars of 'Greensleeves'. He never made it beyond the third line, at which point he would stop and then start from the beginning again, like a schoolboy learning his chords. His previous owners could have warned me of his vocabulary, I thought to myself. It might just have saved me from cardiac arrest.

Chapter 100

BACK FROM AFRICA

Taking Alfie home had been a spur-of-the-moment decision, one I was feeling increasingly apprehensive about as the hours passed. The family were due to return from South Africa the following afternoon and I was aware of a frisson of anxiety that was growing by the minute.

In our early careers, it had been difficult not to adopt a menagerie of injured and abandoned waifs. As a result, we ended up with an aviary of mostly one-winged birds, a black cat that visited our neighbour for ice-cream each day, a Siamese kitten we had seen running behind a local man in the middle of the African veld near Peddie in the Eastern Cape, and at least two dogs at any one stage in time.

All of this had to change after the diagnosis of our son Peter's extreme allergy to animal dander at the age of two years. At first, we had tried to be scrupulous in using the vacuum cleaner daily, progressing to replacing all carpets with ceramic tiles, plastic curtains, plastic-covered mattress and pillows and then eventually moving house to a higher altitude, away from other people and infections.

Each measure rewarded us with some mild success, the move being the most successful, but nevertheless, Peter spent many days in hospital on oxygen and very powerful drugs. At home, he became used to the daily routine of using a nebuliser and inhalers. And he loved his animals.

He would lie on his back on the floor with his bottle of milk and Paddy, the black cat, draped over his midriff. The severity of his allergy became obvious when he decided to emulate what his parents did and cut most of the fur off the ever-patient Siamese. We found him hugging the bald cat with the whites of his eyes protruding out of the sockets in bulging scleral oedema.

When we left South Africa, we left the animals in the care of loving friends, the poignancy of leaving a motherland made all the harder as we said goodbye to the four-legged members of our family. We knew we could never replace them for fear of triggering off respiratory failure.

Despite our measures, Peter continued to have asthma attacks, the worst being one Christmas day shared with a family who had three parrots. Peter ended up in hospital for the next two days.

I should not have taken Alfie home. I knew it and I felt more than a little guilty. I considered housing him in the outside aviary we had built, but as a fellow African, I knew how bitter he would find the English winter.

I told myself I did not have to worry. I was, after all, the man of the house. The decision maker. The one who wore the trousers. When allowed to. I began to feel even more nervous as the moment of their arrival at Heathrow neared.

When the three of them walked through the 'Arrivals' door, pushing an overloaded trolley in front of them, my heart leapt with joy and pride. Watching the handsome triplet tiredly make their way toward me, the feeling of love was almost tangible.

I had always felt like an ugly duckling in comparison to my family, and fortunately the kids had not inherited my looks. The implications of my self-image could have kept both Freud and Dr Seuss entertained for decades, but that is another story.

The drive home was almost in silence as the three sleepy passengers dozed on and off. We drew up at the front door and I carried the bags through and then stood beside the cage uncertainly.

Apart from the formal 'Good morning' and 'Goodnight' that he bestowed on me at either end of each day, Alfie had not uttered much else. I wondered if he would greet the newcomers or keep silent. I turned to face them, ready to defend my actions with a bravado I did not feel.

'Oh, look at him. Where are all his feathers?'

'He looks like he's wearing grey pyjamas.'

'Hullo Alfie. Hullo boy. How's my little man, then?'

Alfie perked up and marched to the front of the cage, his chest puffing out, head thrown back as he replied in equal tone and volume. He let out a joyous litany of little whistles and shouts, snatches of garbled song and unintelligible sounds as he stamped up and down on his perch. Leigh bobbed her head in unison, mimicking his display, a broad smile on her face.

So much for the apprehension. Alfie had become an accepted member of the family in the time it took for four hearts to beat in synchronicity. I stood back and admired the joy and rapture on their faces with interest. I had done good, without even trying. I wish more of life could be the same.

A sneaky, unwelcome little thought entered my mind: I had not been given the same welcome at the airport that Alfie, a member of the family for only a few hours, had received with spontaneous sincerity. The natural hierarchy in our little group was becoming all too apparent.

Chapter 101

TOO GOOD TO BE TRUE

Working in the hardware stores, Dad had learned how to open a padlock with two hammers, and I took great delight in showing Peter, although I was not always as successful as Dad had been. Peter watched attentively and then went off to explore the world of lock picking. I should have known better than to introduce him to a questionable skill.

I had yet to get my head around the new technology that was the Internet, but the young teenagers had accepted it as if it had always been with us. A neat little package arrived in the post and Peter proudly unwrapped a little kit of picks and levers. Within a very short time, no lock was safe from the growing dexterity and the intrigued mind that rose to all challenges.

One evening I arrived home to find that he was a little flustered. The double-glazed French doors of the back of the house had proved a challenge too great and instead of opening it with a flourish, Peter had succeeded in seizing the lock, which would now not open even with the key. He had spent the entire afternoon trying to manipulate the stubborn, unresponsive mechanism.

Eventually we resorted to summoning the services of a locksmith from the neighbouring town. The kindly man was impressed with his young protégé and spent an hour coaching him in the nefarious art of burglary. The lock that had defeated Peter proved to be broken, and both man and boy stressed the fact that it had been faulty before the attentions of a young trainee. The locksmith left after only charging us half his normal fee, offering to give any advice Peter should need in the future. I began to worry whether we would end up with a genius or a felon for a son.

Computers continue to be a source of bewilderment to me. With the onset of Wi-Fi routers, we got the help of a local whiz-kid who went by the name of Dr Bod. I never learned the origin of his title. Dr Bod would arrive unannounced and the first I would know was when I turned to use a computer, only to find that he was busy, tapping away at the keyboard. He left just as surreptitiously, and we were all at a loss as to what he had done.

Dr Bod used passwords and codes of his own choosing and often failed to let us know them. I could not decide whether it was a way of forcing the illiterate to call him out again when things went wrong, but I suspect that he just never thought to involve us in the maintenance of our systems.

The Wi-Fi was a complete failure. It stopped working the second day. Dr Bod arrived and began playing his concerto on the keyboard, and then suddenly he stopped abruptly.

'Someone has broken the password I set up to safeguard this,' he announced.

'No one here could have done that,' we assured him. He was not convinced.

'Someone must have known the password to get into the program and use your Wi-Fi. In doing so, they upset the connection to your computers.'

The difference of opinion seemed set to cause a lot of ill-will, until I became aware of Leigh listening to every word of the argument and looking increasingly uncomfortable.

'Do you know anything about this?' I asked.

She hesitated uncomfortably, making it obvious that she did know more than she was letting on. 'I could not get my phone to connect so I played around until I worked out the password, and now I can use it.'

'You couldn't.' Dr Bod was adamant. 'No one can crack a fifteen-character random password.'

Leigh did not agree. 'I knew that Mom and Dad would not be able to make up a clever password, so it had to be something that you just randomly chose. The easiest option is just to type the top row of keys on the keyboard.' She had our rapt attention. 'I tried it but there are not enough keys on one row, so I started a second time from the beginning to add in another four characters.'

We were all listening in amazement, Dr Bod still unable to accept it.

'It worked after I made a few changes. I'm sorry. I didn't know I had done anything that would affect the whole system.'

As always, I found it impossible to chastise her and had to force myself not to laud her ingenuity. As mischievous as ever, it looked as if my safe-breaker son might have an accomplice in an equally adept code-breaker sibling.

A little while later, Peter uncharacteristically took on a paper route, distributing a local free weekly magazine. Since he avoided anything resembling physical work, I was more than a little impressed. He was not lazy but could just not see the purpose of exerting himself for anything that could be done with a little thinking.

A month later, I noticed a small slip of paper that had fallen out of one of the magazines, and the reason for Peter's enthusiasm for the job became clear.

'DO YOU NEED AN SD CARD FOR YOUR COMPUTER OR CAMERA?' it read in bold print. 'HALF-PRICE SD CARDS delivered to your door. Just fill in this form and leave it outside your front door on the day your magazine is delivered.'

Peter showed no embarrassment when questioned. He had not thought it important enough to let us know of his little business venture and after a little thought, I realised that even though he was still in his teens, I could not find any fault with it. He had ordered an SD card for himself from a Chinese supplier and ended up paying a fraction of the cost. He was quick to see the opportunity and began collecting orders from his customers and sourcing the merchandise from the Far East.

'How many have you sold?' I was curious to find out if I would be supported in my old age, or if it would come to nothing.

'Fifty cards so far. I haven't had the last ten arrive from the suppliers yet.'

My second mistake was to allow him to detect that I was impressed with his entrepreneurial spirit. A little while later he asked for a thousand pounds.

'SD cards are fine, but the profit is not much. I believe I could sell whole computers and buy them from the same supplier.'

I was less than enthusiastic. It took a lot of hard bargaining on his behalf before I gave in and allowed him to place an order for one of the latest PCs from his contact in China. I wondered if they knew that they were dealing with a young boy.

Sadly, the computer never arrived and all attempts to contact the company failed to elicit a response. Peter had experienced his first brush with the shady world of online deceit.

His response was typical of his character. 'Give me another thousand and I will earn enough profit after a few deals to pay you back.'

I had been foolish once and was not to be drawn. Instead, Peter was given several menial tasks in the house and garden and to his credit, he worked off his debt with good grace.

The boy had learned an important lesson that hopefully would be remembered for the rest of his life. The man was harder to teach.

Some years later, I enthusiastically paid for a large tool chest on castors that was advertised at a fraction of the price asked for by local hardware stores. What arrived was a tiny plastic box of tools. All attempts to retrieve my money failed as the seller manipulated the selling platform and the well-known bank that deals in online transactions. I did not even have the opportunity to work off my losses to pay the bank back what I had lost.

Chapter 102

SCHOOL FOR PARROTS

Miss Moran greeted me enthusiastically in the foyer of the junior school. 'I see you've brought some props with you. That's excellent. The children love seeing things as well as listening. It makes it easier to hold their attention.'

I nodded and smiled, trying to balance the cardboard boxes in one hand while holding a sheaf of paper and my car keys in the other. From behind the grey-haired Miss Moran, the school secretary peered over her shoulder, eyeing my 'props' with interest.

'Mrs Fothergill will show you through to the hall, while I tell the teachers that you have arrived.' She beckoned to me to follow the younger woman through the far door while she strode off purposefully through a third door and down a distant corridor.

I was at the school with the intention of letting the neighbourhood know there was a new veterinary practice in town. With a bit of luck, my audience would be enthralled enough to relate to their parents what they had learnt that morning. The handouts in my hand unashamedly proclaimed our services and hopefully little fists would deliver them to parents in an at least partially readable state.

The hall proved to be a large room without any form of stage. I was directed to the one end, where I gratefully set the boxes on the floor. Kneading my aching arms, I carefully opened the larger of the boxes and lifted out Fred, a large, magnificently coloured leopard tortoise, and set him on the ground, where he remained immobile, legs and head tucked in under his shell. In order not to give the game away too soon, I upended the empty cardboard box over him, effectively hiding him from view.

The other box contained my newest acquisition, Alfie, the nearly featherless African Moth-Eaten Parrot. An ominous scratching sound came from the box and when I peered through one of the holes I had punched to allow free movement of air, my gaze was returned by a beady eye as Alfie marched around the interior, greatly put out by the enforced imprisonment.

The double doors at the far end of the hall burst open to allow a twin chain of small people to enter noisily, shepherded by four women, whose chief task seemed to be keeping their charges from erupting into chaos. Four little boys immediately broke rank and gathered around me.

'What's in the boxes?'

'Why are you here?'

'Did you bring the boxes?'

'Where is Miss Parsons?'

The questions came effortlessly, like insects lifting off the surface of a pond, seeming to need no answer before the next one was let free to soar upwards. Behind them, one of the shepherdesses noticed the boys and widened her attention to sweep them back into line. Eventually all the children had been coerced into tiny little chairs placed in concentric rows facing me and were concentrating for seconds at a time on the boxes.

'Good morning, boys and girls. Mr Phillips is going to talk to us about his work as a vet. Now if you will all be quiet for a moment, I'm sure Mr Phillips will have a lot of stories to tell you about his work.'

'What's in the box?' queried a little girl at the end of the front row.

'It's a skirrel,' announced a little red-haired boy behind her.

'Er, no. It's not a squirrel,' I offered.

'What is it then?'
'Well, who wants to guess what it is?'
'Is it sweets?' asked a tall, pale lad with thick glasses in the back row.
'Nope. It's not sweets. It can't be eaten but it does have a shell.'
'It's a skirrel,' repeated the little red-head.
'Skirrels don't have shells,' admonished the girl next to him.
'Skirrels have nuts, which have shells,' he retorted.
'It's not a skirrel.'

Two of the smallest girls in the front row suddenly screamed and jumped to their feet, pointing past me to the cardboard box. I turned in surprise to find the box moving erratically about the room.

Several other children joined in with shrieks that could have been delight or fear.

'It's all right, children. No need to worry. Mr Philips knows how to handle animals. Let's all keep quiet now and let him control whatever is in that box.' Miss Moran held out her arms as if to protect her flock while watching me anxiously in anticipation.

In answer, I bent over and lifted the box off Fred, who paused and blinked in the light. His handsome geometrically patterned shell in black and yellow glistened with polished perfection. He lifted his head cautiously and then resumed his staccato progress forward, diagonally opposing legs moving in unison.

'It IS a skirrel. I told you it was a skirrel,' cried the little red-head in triumph.

'This is Fred,' I announced. 'Fred is a Leopard Tortoise from Africa.'
'Why is he a leopard?' they wanted to know.
'They call them leopard tortoises because of the colour of their shells that are similar to the markings on a leopard.'

The smallest girls in the front row edged farther away until they were behind Miss Moran, each peering around her legs. Four of the boys moved forward and crouched over Fred, who rapidly disappeared into the safety of his shell.

'Come back to your seats, boys,' instructed Miss Moran. The four remained unmoved, fascination overcoming obedience. Two of them placed their hands on Fred's shell while a third tapped it enquiringly. Fred remained resolutely inside. The fourth boy stood up abruptly, with a squawk of surprise, before rapidly backing away to the relative safety of the other children. I turned to see what had caught his attention.

Alfie had chewed his way through the second cardboard box and was now hesitantly peering out at the assembled crowd. His bald grey body looked grotesquely vulturine, with a mop of perfect grey feathers adorning his head.

'What is that?' asked one of the younger students.

'It looks like a gremlin,' announced another.

'This is Alfie,' I announced, taking two strides over to the box and kneeling with hand outstretched to stop the escapee from fleeing.

As my hand closed around Alfie's chest, he bent his head sharply and sank a razor-sharp beak into my thumb. Blood dripped from my injury onto the floor, while curses reached my lips but thankfully exited silently.

'He's bleeding,' announced the little red-head. 'Poor thing. He must be hurt.'

Not as much as he was going to hurt if I ever got him off my thumb. I winced, trying to stop myself from beating him senseless on the floor.

Behind me the crescendo of noise erupted once again. Peering over my shoulder, I could just see Fred's rear end as he disappeared through the open door at the far end of the hall. From long experience I knew just how deceptively fast tortoises could move.

I turned and dashed after the errant reptile, still holding on to the parrot and leaving a row of blood spatters on the floor behind me. Fred fortunately had found a pot plant next to the front door and was munching on the leaves. I managed to wedge him between my free arm and a hip and carry him back into the room while an indignant Mrs Fothergill rescued her bedraggled pot plant.

Although I had managed to get my thumb and index finger on either side of Alfie's head and prevent him from sinking his beak into me hand again, his razor-sharp claws were deeply embedded in my wrist.

With relief I dumped Fred back in the box that Alfie had escaped from and turned my attention to the angry bird intent on shredding my arm with his claws and writhing in an attempt to free himself from the headlock. I upended the second box and pushed him into it. Things were finally returning to normal when I made the mistake of bringing my free hand close enough to incite a desperate lunge from my captive, who managed to pierce the end of my little finger with his beak.

I yelped in pain, trying to rid myself of this malevolent imp hanging from the end of my fingertips as I pushed him deeper into the box and shook him off.

Straightening up, I was met by five shocked adult faces and fifty curious little ones.

'What's a bludibastidbird?' asked the little red-head boy.

'That's enough then, children,' interrupted Ms Moran. 'Everyone line up and walk back to your classrooms quietly. Thank you Mr Philips, for a very er… interesting talk. Don't push, Johnny. Emma, you need to keep up with the rest of your class. There we go. No talking now.'

The little people exited the room in a noisy flock, together with their shepherds. Mrs Fothergill beckoned me to follow her and, once again burdened with two increasingly heavy cardboard boxes and a sheaf of blood-smeared paper, I meekly obliged.

As I walked out of the ornate from doors, she commented stiffly, 'We shall call you if we require a demonstration from you again.' I nodded glumly and headed for the car. The cardboard box shouted out suddenly, 'Bye. See you later.'

Mrs Fothergill bent down to pick up one of the papers I had dropped, and Alfie let rip with a wolf whistle that had her straightening up as if a rod had suddenly been forced down her spine. She glared at me.

Sheepishly I stowed my 'props' in the car while behind me Mrs Fothergill eyed me accusingly.

Chapter 103

PIGS IN BLANKETS

Hedgehog hoglets born late in the season often do not have enough time to grow to the required weight to sustain them through hibernation. Sick, weak, or starving little hedgehogs are often brought to us in autumn. Three little spikey balls were handed in just before Winter and I made them comfortable in a cardboard box filled with hay and placed in a cage in the hospital ward for security. We would have to look after them until someone could take them to the rescue centre two towns away.

In the cramped flat above the practice, we had made a warm enclosure for another waif, Herbie the Spur-thigh tortoise. Herbie had been found speeding down the high street of the town and had fortunately been scooped up by a passer-by before he was flattened by a car. Since we were very sensitive about keeping animal fur and feathers out of the flat for reasons of allergies, Herbie was made welcome by the family and had his own heat mat and basking lamp. The kids said goodnight to Herbie and were tucked into bed. Shortly afterwards we did the same. Herbie was already dozing, so he never replied.

In the morning, I was surprised to find one of the little hedgehogs curled up in the tortoise enclosure, enjoying the warmth of the lamp. There was no way that the little creature could have got there himself and I suspected one of the kids was playing a joke, but they earnestly defended their innocence.

Since the rise of each step on the staircase was greater than their body length, I doubted that the escapee could have climbed them on his own. The mystery deepened when the cage proved to be empty and the other two hoglets were nowhere to be found. In my mind I had a vision of one little hoglet standing at the stair and allowing the other one to climb on top and then onto the next level.

It was only later in the day when a nurse began to fill the washing machine with soiled towels and bedding from the cages, that two little prickly balls rolled out of the pile as she pulled up a thick blanket. They were solemnly replaced in their temporary home where they immediately resumed their interrupted sleep after what had clearly been a busy night. For extra security, we found a box with taller sides, and we also placed a board inside the gate of the cage. No piglet would be able to escape now.

The next morning all three little hedgehogs had made it up the long staircase and had not only moved into the tortoise home as squatters, but Herbie bore a little scar on his head where they had nipped him. He had retired to the furthest reaches of his enclosure.

Clearly these three were smarter than any of us and we were relieved, if a little sad, to see them packed off to the hedgehog rehab centre. They clearly needed it. Dianne, who came to pick up the 'Prickle-pigs' as she called them, was clearly delighted by them. She was one of an army of rural protectors of these charming little indigenous animals.

Some months later, I chanced upon her while driving along a narrow road, notorious for speeding locals. Her car was pulled as far as possible into the bushes on one side, lights still blazing in the dusk. Dianne was standing in the middle of the road, directing cars from both sides as they squeezed past. Twenty yards ahead were a row of rounded shadows on the tarmac. As I drew near, she pointed them out and asked if I would take her place as traffic warden while she went to collect the family of hedgehogs. I agreed, hoping that I would not meet the fate that had threatened the piglets instead.

Dianne walked hurriedly over to the spikey family and then stopped, straightened up and gave the largest one a kick of disgust. I was so distracted that a speeding car narrowly missed me as the surprised driver swerved past.

Walking back to her car, Dianne muttered under her breath, 'They're Road Apples. Nothing but horse manure.'

I laughed and then turned towards my vehicle, hoping that no-one I knew had witnessed the part I had played in the shepherding of a row of horse manure across the road at night.

Chapter 104

AN EYE FOR COLOUR

Julie Dickson had two veiled chameleons, wonderful little creatures that reminded me of my childhood. Although the chameleons on the farm did not have the large crest on the top of the head, they did in all other aspects resemble these two patients.

In a climate so far removed from their natural one, it can prove to be very difficult to maintain these delicate reptiles. Julie had gone to great lengths to provide exactly what they needed. The pair were called Houdini and Queen Victoria.

I first met Queen Victoria when she developed a painful swelling of the eye. It was impossible to examine it with the ophthalmoscope because the eye never stayed still for more than a few seconds.

Trying to put ointment in proved equally difficult and the salve generally landed on a completely different part of the head.

In the end I lent Julie a nebuliser that created a very fine mist of saline laced with the drugs we wanted on the eye. The infection resolved and I like to think it was because of our efforts.

Alice had been with us for years as a nurse. She had the biggest heart imaginable and was captivated by every creature that came into the practice. The chameleons fascinated her.

Alice also had an endearing weakness for incapacitating mirth that rendered her speechless. The first evidence I saw of this was when a drug company provided us with a small digital screen to sit on the reception desk and play an endless advert for a pheromone that was released into the atmosphere, through a device that plugged into an electrical socket. The pheromone in the air helped reduce the fear in dogs frightened by fireworks.

Allice noticed a client avidly watching the little screen and approached her to add her support for the product.

'This is wonderful,' she announced. 'The dogs are much calmer when it is used.'

'Yes,' replied the client, 'but how do you get the dogs to watch the video?'

Sheer incredulity chased across Alice's features, followed by delight and then a trickle of humour that rapidly became a tumbling cascade as she began to shake with silent laughter until she sank helplessly to the floor and buried her head in her arms while she sobbed silently.

I rushed in to try and smooth over the damage done but the client was not to be mollified and stalked off in high dudgeon.

I should have known better than to entrust Alice with the little reptile when, three years after the eye infection, Julie brought the silent little body of Queen Victoria in after she passed away at home.

We arranged to send her off for a cremation and I sadly asked Alice to take her through to the back and arrange the paperwork, while I saw the next client. Half an hour later Julie returned to say that she had changed her mind and would like to take Queen Victoria home to bury. I asked the receptionist to get Alice to bring the small body back while I ushered another client into the room.

As I opened the door to say goodbye to the client, I noticed that Julie was still waiting. With more than a little irritation, I walked through to the prep room to find out why Alice had not complied with a simple instruction.

Alice sat on the floor on the far side of the room, crying uncontrollably while a second nurse, Rene, stood red-faced with concentration at the tub-table, the chameleon in front of her.

'Hurry it up girls,' I chivvied them on. 'Mrs Dickson has been waiting for fifteen minutes.'

Rene looked imploringly at Alice.

'What's wrong with her?' I asked.

Rene hesitated, her sense of loyalty to her colleague warring with her need to come clean. 'Alice wanted to see how long the tongue was, so she unrolled it. It is longer than the length of her body, but we cannot roll it up again.

I was aghast. How could I give Queen Victoria back in this state? For a brief second, I even considered an amputation, but it was exactly this type of guile that trapped others into ever-deepening deception.

Part of the mechanism to unleash the fascinating projectile of a chameleon's tongue is the hydrostatic pressure from fluid rapidly forced into the tissues and then sucked out again as it retracts. The unrolled tongue had become engorged with fluid, and nothing would make it return to normal.

I thought of making Alice explain herself to Julie but realised that it would come out as gibberish and sign language, so in the end I went through and apologised on her behalf. Julie was kindness itself.

'Your nurses have always been so helpful and prepared to do anything for the chameleons. I would also have been tempted to do exactly the same.'

I retrieved the little reptile with its tongue gently wound around a small roll of gauze and as I waved them off as they drove out of the car park, I made a mental note to keep a closer watch on Alice and her insatiable curiosity and debilitating sense of humour.

Chapter 105

REALITY CHECK

I employed Ruth expecting to have to mentor her as she adapted to private practice, but at times it seemed to be the reverse. A recent graduate, she was stuffed to the gills with the latest knowledge and techniques of cutting-edge science. I learned to listen and respect.

The public adored her, and she soon became a favourite, asked for by name when clients made an appointment. The only credit I felt justified in accepting was that I had made a brilliant decision in getting her to join our team.

It was a bolt out of the blue when the head nurse confidentially divulged that Ruth daily circled the whirlpool of suicide. I was numb with surprise and concern.

A so-called reality program on vets was showing on the TV and I had found it hard to watch. The star of the series reconstructed brains for endangered snow leopards from Lego bricks and then spent seven nights without sleep while he watched over them recovering. It smacked just a little of hyperbole and exaggeration. I am fortunate never to be tempted to indulge in either. I confess that I can only go without sleep for six nights.

Over thirty-five years I have managed to get just below the surface of the gloss we cover our lives with and understand a little of what drives us and what sends us hurtling into the abyss.

The entertainment world and digital media are nourished by good-time snapshots, while the murk and grit of reality beneath is ignored. No-one puts on posts about their last failure. No-one admits to the agonising losses of life or the sapping downward slope of the imposter syndrome that leaves us feeling that we just are not good enough.

In our field bright, dedicated minds leave the comfort of the academic nest and fly solo for an extended, downward swoop. Not everyone manages to pull out of the dive and rise to soar. Many hit the trees or plough into the mud and must plod on with severely cropped wings and dirty feet.

Emotional blackmail from clients who want these wealthy professionals to treat their pets for free, and the complete incomprehension of the public of the financial realities of veterinary, a profession on a par with teachers, although few readers will accept it, can be soul destroying.

I spent a long evening thinking, and praying, about Ruth. The next day I asked to have a chat with her and prepared my best grandfatherly voice.

'When you wrote your final exam at university,' I asked, 'what grade did you need to qualify?'

'Fifty percent,' she replied, mystified at the direction I was leading.

'I know that you probably got in the seventies, eighties, or even higher, but the day after you qualified, how much did your clients expect you to get right in treating their pets?'

'One hundred percent.'

'More importantly,' I continued, 'how much did you expect to get right?'

'One hundred percent,' she admitted.

There was a pause while she considered the implications.

'We all make mistakes. All the time. We can only do our best. And when we need to, we can ask others for help, but at times we will get it very, very wrong.' She nodded, acknowledging the truth she had experienced.

'Not every client is going to want the tests or treatment you know to be best for their animal. Not everyone is going to agree with your assessment, not everyone patient you treat is going to recover. You will remember the one that does not work out and forget the nineteen that do.'

Ruth listened attentively but said little. After a while I ran out of fatherly advice and she stood up to leave. At the door she turned and said simply, 'Thank you.'

Eight months later, I was in a deep, dark hole, struggling to find enough light to creep forward, but having to continue regardless. In a state of numbness, I was asked to deal with a client who was disputing the bill.

'Your vet told me it was going to cost £200. I agreed and then later she phoned to say she needed to do more tests and more treatment, and it was going to cost £400. Now you thieving vets tell me the bill is £587.'

I could see the problem but struggled to get past the vicious anger and denial. I tried to explain the situation. 'The original amount was just short of £200 and the second lot of work done was close to £400. Most of that was the fee we have to pay the laboratory and some of it is our cost of the drugs dispensed. Together they came to nearly £600, or £587 to be exact. The extra £400 was added to the original £200.'

There was no attempt to understand, to compromise, to work with the team that had spent the day caring for her patient, and I was not able to do more in my state of grey existence. The meeting came to an end with the client screaming in my face that I was a 'white collar criminal' and slamming the door behind her.

I sat looking at the wall for a long time until a soft sound behind me made me turn my head. Ruth stood in the doorway.

'Is it time for a grandfather talk again?' she asked.

I smiled. Sometimes it helps just to have someone else acknowledge that they know where you are.

Chapter 106

Yes, Ma'm

June had been a children's nanny for years before joining us as a trainee vet nurse. It amused me to see how she used her child handling skills to good effect on her new patients.

A little Spaniel confined to a cage awaiting surgery let us all know of his displeasure by yapping incessantly. I noticed June walking through to the hospital ward and heard her admonishing the surprised little pooch.

'We don't do that here,' she informed him primly. He sat down and thought about it for a while and then decided that no matter what others thought, he did do that here, and started his yapping again.

The local Badger Rescue at times brought in injured wildlife or asked for our help to put a mauled badger to sleep. We quickly learned to respect these powerful animals, who did not take kindly to being handled. All treatment was done with a protective barrier between patient and staff.

Leigh had been given a sweater with broad black and white stripes, earning several comments about being related to Mr Brock, although the stripes ran horizontally rather than vertically.

A large cardboard box was standing in the store, just asking to be used for mischief. I persuaded Leigh to crouch down inside the box and closed the top flaps over her.

'June, could you give me a hand?' I asked since she was the first person to happen to pass by. 'I need to treat this badger and I can't do it on my own.'

'You're not going to let it out of the box, are you?' she asked, concern written all over her face.

'Yes.' I nodded. 'Don't worry, I'll be closest to the box, and I can handle them. If you could just flip open the top lid, I'll grab him from behind.'

She looked at me nervously and then moved a bit closer. Leaning over, she managed to reach the edge of the top flap with one finger and lifted it cautiously. Leigh erupted from the depths with a roar.

Poor June tried desperately to escape through the closed door behind her, scrabbling at the wall as if to dig her way out. Ashen-faced, she turned to face her assailant and then a look of fury replaced the abject fear in her expression when she realised that everyone watching was laughing with glee.

Contrite apology had little effect and for days I was mentally confined to the naughty step. Chastised, I moved about her with trepidation, but it was hard not to smile at the memory each time she walked stiffly out of the room.

Little people who accompanied their mothers, and occasionally fathers, into the consulting room were often a delight with their comments and observations. Laura was first into the room, followed by her mom and Whiskas the cat in a plastic cat carrier. The sweet little three-year-old tried hard to peer over the edge of the table, until I suggested that her mother might like to lift the little girl up and let her sit on the table next to the pet carrier. I opened the door of the cage and let Whiskas out. He came out willingly and happily rubbed his head against Laura, clearly used to her affection.

'What's wrong with Whiskas?' I asked Mrs Wilkins.

Laura answered before anyone else could respond. 'He's very poorly,' she informed me solemnly. Her precise diction made me smile.

I turned to address her directly and got a succinct history of Whiskas' actions for the past few days. He was clearly not eating much and had developed a lump on the side of his head. A small wound had become visible and was oozing gently.

So intrigued with the precise diction and serious discussion from such a tiny person, I could not resist opening the door of the consulting room and inviting Karen to listen too. Within minutes we were all captivated.

I needed to open the large abscess on his face, tribute to a fight two days earlier.

'Let' put him back in the cage and I'll take him through for surgery,' I addressed both mother and daughter, placing the carrying cage on the table and opening the door.

'You can go back in your jail now,' Laura advised her cat, and he obligingly entered the confines of the box while everyone smiled with delight.

I carried the patient through to the back, while June and Karen could not resist continuing the conversation, June going down on one knee to have a serious chat with the little girl. I wondered if she missed her previous profession.

Katy was a diminutive copy of her mother, who in turn was a nurse of immense ability and a mischievous sense of humour. She occasionally visited the practice, accompanied by her mother, and never failed to delight me, although she was clearly not as enamoured with me as I was with her.

Mrs Tivet brought in Chilly, a Chinchilla with dental problems, the curse of these soft but active bundles of energy. I showed Katy my patient, about the size of a small rabbit, sitting in her carrying basket. Katy declined to go closer but watched with big eyes.

Later I heard her telling her mother, 'Stuart has got a big mouse.'

I think I would also be scared of a mouse as big as Chilly.

Chapter 107

AFRICAN THREADBARE DOCTOR

Alfie's vocabulary became more apparent with each day. He particularly liked to laugh, and his repertoire ranged from a deep chuckle to a raucous falsetto shriek.

Although he liked to practice his laughing whenever the opportunity arose, there were certain triggers that immediately invoked his mirthful response. Any sign of pain or surprise in one of his human carers would result in a less than sympathetic chuckle of delight.

Having adopted Alfie, we had a responsibility to try and diagnose the cause of his feather plucking and hopefully do something about it. I felt reasonably confident that we would be able to at least rescue him from total nudity, even if we never restored his plumage to perfection. I have never been so wrong and so inadequate in my quest.

In order to perform the diagnostic steps, it was necessary to anaesthetise him and so minimise the stress of being manhandled. My traumatised fingers had learnt to wait until he grabbed hold of the bars of his cage in order to climb out of reach and then firmly grab his head, with thumb and forefinger on each side of his skull. Then his claws had to be prised from the lower bars and the furiously wriggling little body needed to be carefully extracted from the cage, trying not to put too much pressure on his head but at the same time never allowing the sharply curved beak to find flesh and wreak havoc in revenge.

By placing his entire head and torso inside an anaesthetic mask, we managed to fill his lungs and air-sacs with Isoflurane, the anaesthetic gas, while he counted backwards from ten. He never made it past five before falling asleep.

The first sample was the shaft of a broken feather that had miraculously missed his attention and was still embedded in its follicle. The tip of the shaft had enough blood on it for the laboratory to extract DNA and confirm that Alfie was in fact a boy. It went some way towards explaining why he loved the women in the family while regarding me as a beak-sharpening post.

A week after posting off the sample, a certificate arrived stating his sex. I pondered where to keep it and finally filed it together with the family's birth certificates. A few years later it was joined by a birth certificate for 'Bear Necessities' who was born at the Colchester 'Build-a-Bear' shop.

We also took half a millilitre of his blood and had it tested for any indications of infections, organ malfunctions, hormonal imbalances and mineral deficiencies. It did show an increased number of inflammatory cells, which was probably due to the damage he had caused to his skin by chewing away anything resembling a feather, but the rest of the tests returned normal results. A blood smear showed only the unique avian red blood cells that had nuclei, unlike mammalian blood.

While Alfie slept, we took a series of X-rays. Birds have large air-sacs that communicate with their lungs and surrounding their organs, which occur in the centre of the body in an hour-glass silhouette. Alfie had no obvious abnormalities.

We took the opportunity to clip his claws and file the excessive growth on his beak with a dental drill. I tried to reduce the sharpness of the vicious curve, but it was obvious that it would not make much of a difference.

Exhaling the anaesthetic gas, Alfie slowly regained consciousness. One eye opened and gazed balefully at me. He had no idea what had happened while he slept and his only recollection would be of this brute manhandling him into a plastic mask, a short nap and then waking up with a slight pain where the fine needle had entered his jugular vein and an indefinable difference to his claws and beak. His glare made it clear he was not a forgiving bird.

The rest of the staff watched my efforts with jaundiced eyes. When I failed to find a justifiable cause for Alfie's self-mutilation, Karen decided that the answer was to put a little waistcoat on him.

'Even if he chews it to bits, at least it will keep him too busy to worry about his feathers,' she reasoned. I sniffed at the idea.

Knowing I would be less than enthusiastic, Kevin, one of the other vets in the practice, was enlisted. His response was predictable. 'I don't do birds,' he stated flatly.

'All I'm asking you to do is hold him once I've caught him, so that I can put this little jacket on him.'

'You're joking, aren't you?'

'No. I'm serious. If we can distract him and keep him busy getting this off, then he may have time to grow some feathers.'

Kevin nervously obliged, holding Alfie's head firmly with one hand and using the other to control the body as a bespoke garment of distinction was fitted while Alfie screamed and swore as if we were cutting his throat. Three veterinary nurses watched the scene with interest.

'There you are. Fits him perfectly.'

'Can I let go now?' asked Kevin nervously, but before anyone could say anything, Alfie took advantage of the slight lessening of pressure from Kevin's fingers on his head to lunge forward and bite an unprotected wrist. Kevin yelled and flung the bird away.

'Ow. He bit me. Ow, stupid bird bit me. Owwwwwww.'

Alfie regained his balance on the table in front of Kevin and began an evil chuckle, strutting around, bobbing his head up and down in glee.

'It's not funny. Look he drew blood. Ow, that hurts.'

'He-he-he,' replied Alfie. 'Hee-hee.'

The concern on the nurses' faces slowly dissolved into supressed smiles at the sight of the little bird parading about in triumph. A few titters of amusement escaped from among them. Alfie responded with delight, broadening his repertoire of chuckles, wheezes, raucous laughs and delighted sniggers.

One of the nurses' faces turned slowly red and then a deep puce until she could no longer control herself and roared with laughter, doubling over and nearly collapsing with mirth. The other two followed suit, while Kevin nursed his wrist, trying to maintain his dignity but allowing a wry smile to betray his amusement.

Alfie reached a new level of showmanship as he played to his audience. 'Heh-heh-heh-heh. Ha-ha. Oooh. Hahahahaha.'

The waistcoat lasted an hour. The wrist took a week to heal, and injured pride was rapidly replaced by amusement and the story relegated to nostalgic memories.

Alfie had triumphed once more.

Chapter 108

NELLIE THE ELEPHANT

The brindle boxer had an enormous mass under her neck. It filled the space between the two jawbones and made it difficult for her to open her mouth, let alone breathe.

'Another vet operated on her a few months ago,' Mr Williams explained. 'We thought she was cured, but it has grown back, and it is growing much faster now.'

'We really need to get the records from the other practice, so that we can build on their work,' I responded. It was always very frustrating to be presented with a case, not knowing what had been previously done and what diagnosis had been made. 'Did the other vet send the lump to the laboratory for analysis?'

'No,' he admitted. 'He suggested it, but everything had cost so much and it was going to be another hundred pounds. I could not see the value of doing it.'

If only the previous clinician had been more insistent, but then I had no knowledge of what exactly had been said at the time.

Sheba lay down on the floor and breathed heavily, while I continued discussing her future with Mr Williams. Suddenly she gasped and spluttered, trying to sit up and collapsing back on to the floor.

I grabbed her head and tried to open her mouth. Her gums had gone a deep purple hue. In desperation we lifted her onto the consulting table, and I yelled for help from the nursing team. They arrived within seconds, and we tried unsuccessfully to get some air down the dying dog's throat.

'Give me that ET tube,' I yelled and grabbed a scalpel blade from a drawer.

There was no time to clip the area or sterilise it before surgery. I plunged the blade into the under-surface of the neck, struggling for lack of a handle to the scalpel.

A small amount of blood spurted out, which we ignored as I enlarged the hole until I could find the trachea, or windpipe, a clear tube of cartilage with annular thickened rings encircling it every few millimetres.

In desperation I punctured the trachea with the blade and then pushed the rubber ET tube into the air passage. Sheba now had access to oxygen, but she was not yet breathing.

Rolling her onto her side, we began pumping her chest. One of the nurses stuck the diaphragm on her chest and tried to find a heartbeat. She shook her head.

'Adrenalin,' I yelled. 'Two millilitres. Squirt it down the ET tube and then try to find a vein in case we need more. Give her the same amount of Dopram.'

The nurses acted without any comment, trained and vigilant. In my mind I chanted the little song that the first aid instructor had sung as she taught us the procedure. *Nellie the elephant packed her trunk, and said goodbye to the circus. Off she went with a trumpety-trump, trump-trump-trump.*' After every five beats of the drum, we paused to blow a breath of air into the ET tube.

Nothing happened. We continued pumping the chest, pausing every fifth beat to blow down the ET tube.

After what seemed hours, Sheba began to breath on her own.

'I can hear her heart now. It's beating on its own.'

The team were ecstatic. The suddenness of Sheba's collapse had caught us unawares and the adrenalin flowing in our veins could probably have resuscitated our patient several times over if only we had a means to deliver it to her.

I suddenly realised that Mr Williams was still standing in the corner. We usually asked the public to leave, but this time no-one had the time to do anything apart from concentrate on our patient.

'Thank you,' he said simply.

We operated two days later, and I found not a distinct mass as I had expected, but multiple tracts leading in and among the myriad of blood vessels and nerves in the area. It was when a pocket of yellow ooze erupted that I had my suspicion confirmed. It was not a tumour, but an abscess.

The infection had followed the routes of least resistance, bypassing the thick walls of the blood vessels and instead pushing between the less densely packed muscles and fascia.

In the end we left a large opening and packed it with an absorbent dressing, aiming to suck out the infection as it drained away. Sheba was given a mammoth dose of antibiotics and anti-inflammatory drugs. Slowly she recovered and the enormous hard lump decreased in size.

Colchester Zoo uncharacteristically invited us to visit and have a look behind the scenes. We were among a lot of very successful business owners, and I suspect the object of the exercise was to drum up financial support. They had chosen the wrong calibre of income in selecting us, but the dedication we observed on that tour stood them in good stead whenever I got the chance to promote the zoo in conversation.

The climax of the tour was going behind the public façade in the elephant enclosure as these mighty mastodons walked sedately into their night quarters. I had experienced the might and majesty of the African elephants in several safari parks back in South Africa, and even ridden on the massive back of a young bull elephant, but regarded their Indian relatives as pale shadows of the king. As I stood on the bare concrete floor and looked up almost vertically into the eyes above an impossibly long trunk, I felt a deep awe and gentle apprehension at the enormity of these giants and a distinct vulnerability while a very wet trunk-end smeared goo over my front and on top of my head. I was not about to complain to the king of the beasts.

Fifteen years later, I was introduced to a small group of people. An elderly man stuck out his hand to greet me. Turning to the rest of them, he said, 'This man saved my dog Sheba's life.' I was taken aback, not recognising him and for a while not even remembering her name. As he continued with the tale, the rush of adrenalin came back to me.

I had suffered several hard knocks just recently and his praise was more than welcome. Silently I felt a huge debt of gratitude for this client who was so open in his appreciation for my past actions. I ducked my head in embarrassment, but I could have just as easily put my arm around him and thanked him from the depths of my soul.

Chapter 109

SEMI PRECIOUS YET PRICELESS

Vet nurses often like to comment that they prefer animals to people, but I have noticed just how empathetic they are to all species, including the two-legged ones. They just don't like to admit it.

Ruby would do anything for her thirty-two cats and two dogs, and at the same time she looked after her disabled neighbour's needs without expecting any reward and seemed to have many people in her life who demanded her generously given time. The only time I saw her put animals before humans was when the latter were negligent or abusive towards their pets.

One weakness that Ruby had was her mild dyslexia, that seemed to be confined to her verbal skills. Name such as 'Felimazole' were turned into 'Felizi-mole'.

When Mr Peters brought in his Boxer dog, Caesar, with several lumps on its skin, we took a sample and looked at it under the microscope. A host of little round cells with dark staining granules set the alarm bells ringing. This breed seems to be a magnet for tumours, and the pathologist's report confirmed our suspicions of a malignant cancer. I was putting off the onerous task of calling him when he saved me the task by ringing in himself. Ruby took the call and then came to seek my advice.

'Mr Johnson wants to know if the lump was benignant or malign?' she asked.

'Tell him it is malign… I mean belignant… No, benignant,' I tried. She had completely thrown me with her spoonerism. 'Never mind, I'll speak to him myself…' I took the receiver from her.

'Hello Mr Peters. I'm afraid the growth was not good.'

Ruby had a long-suffering husband, Paul, who put his foot down firmly (probably into a moist pile left 'by accident' by one of her cats) and made a ruling that she was not allowed to bring home any more felines. She in turn quickly realised that so long as the cat was black, she could get away with it, since he was unable to tell the difference between the twelve she already had.

This worked until Ruby brought home one that only had three legs and she was hauled onto the carpet to explain why one of her cats had been so careless as to lose a limb. He was a little less tolerant went she took another kitten she had christened 'Roo' back to live with them. Paul expressed his irritation until the little waif sat up on its hindquarters in front of him and cocked his head enquiringly, his forelegs mere stumps from a congenital deformity. Roo knew how to charm his way into his heart and home.

The couple had different interests, but it was warming to see how they tolerated each other's foibles with humour. Ruby would regularly get home to find an upturned saucepan somewhere on the floor, a measure Paul had adopted to deal with offending animals who left surprises in their wake, without having to clean it up or deal with the offensive smell if left unattended.

Paul worked free-lance as a contractor, laying down drains for large housing developments. He was currently connecting the bathrooms of forty new houses up to the main sewer. The workmen also needed change rooms, and the temporary ablutions were linked into the network as well. Occasionally Paul would stop by on his way home, and I would hear the most recent update to the progress of the housing in the new development.

When a young woman brought in Chicco, her cat that was behaving extremely erratically, and gave us a fairly garbled account, both Ruby and I were aware of a rising sense of alarm. Something did not ring true.

Pinpoint pupils, staggering gait and excessive salivation hinted at a toxin. As the owner was leaving, she made a reference about wanting to keep the cat away from her boyfriend since he was a 'user' and could not be trusted. We wondered what she meant by user, but she was not forthcoming and made a rapid departure. I had taken blood samples which showed severe liver damage, among other problems, and on a whim, I sent them to an outside lab to test for opioids. The following day I received an urgent call from the laboratory to say that they had identified very high levels of heroin in the blood.

Ruby was incensed and girded up her loins to confront the young woman when she returned. Together we set about giving our patient intravenous fluids and liver supportive treatment. I pondered why an addict would give heroin to a cat when they went to such great lengths and cost to buy it in the first place.

Instead of the owner returning, we were surprised by a visit from the drug monitoring section of the borough council. They were well aware of the couple who owned the cat and in fact supplied them with Methadone in an attempt to help wean them off the hard stuff. The officers looked at the report from our laboratory and immediately discounted it. For it to hold up in any investigation, they informed us, the sample had to be taken in their presence and strictly labelled and tracked to the laboratory and beyond. Unfortunately, the second sample we took was negative for the drug.

The most likely cause of the discrepancy was that Chicco had metabolised the heroin during the forty-eight hours since the first sample. The drug enforcement officers and the RSPCA were unable to act, in light of the negative second blood sample. The couple looked as if they would escape any consequence of their actions, whereas Ruby looked as if she was in danger of taking the law into her own hands.

Chicco gradually improved over the following week and looked fairly healthy, but we knew there was significant damage to various organs of the body. Ruby spent hours nursing him and making a fuss over him.

On Friday, the young woman called to ask if she could collect her cat and from the back of the surgery I heard Ruby say, 'I'm very sorry Miss Watkins, but Chicco died this morning.'

I wondered if she knew more than I did and had failed to let me know, but when I rushed through to check on our patient, he was licking his leg and purring contentedly.

Ruby came through a little while later and for once her face matched her name. She avoided my gaze and I kept silent. While I pondered the implications of the case and the possible repercussions, Ruby spirited her charge out of the building, and I later heard Paul grumbling that he knew she had brought home another cat because they had no other calico-coloured cats at home. I in turn knew he was good-natured enough to allow Ruby the occasional cheeky misdemeanour. At any rate, he had more pressing things on his mind.

The workmen at the housing development had complained that the Port-a-loo toilets were blocked, and Paul had been summoned to sort it out. He had just taken delivery of a very powerful industrial compressor, capable of clearing substantial blockages in large pipes, and he was keen to try it out. The Port-a-loo toilets had been plumbed into the same underground pipes as the new houses.

The machine was impressive in the ease with which it blew the offending material down the pipes.

An hour later, Paul was busy packing his van when a group of white collars came striding past, vociferous in their joint indignation at the affront they had suffered at the hands of vandals. He paused to ask one of them what the problem was and had a minor sense of panic at the reply:

'Someone has sprayed all the new bathroom walls and ceilings in the new houses with sewerage.'

Paul nodded silently and then, as one of the top brass looked at him suspiciously, quickly joined in the denouncement of the younger generation, who clearly had no respect for decent folk. As the managers moved on, he hurried to load up his compressor and departed, determined to find a place for it in the depths of his shed at home until the fuss died down.

Chicco lived for several years in Ruby and Paul's house, until he eventually passed away from the damage inflicted on his liver. Ruby tried not to talk about him to me, but I was kept up to date with his progress through the grapevine of chatter among the staff.

We never heard from his previous family and our bad debtor list grew by one. It was a small price to pay, knowing that Chicco would never again be subjected to such abuse, and in any case, I did not have the gumption to face down an irate Ruby.

Chapter 110

MUCH ADO ABOUT NOTHING IN BEE MINOR

The warm sun streamed through the French window, creating slanted rectangles on the sitting room carpet. Sounds from outside floated into the softly drowsing house. Alfie sat on his perch at the back of his cage, listening to the afternoon as it ticked away.

A little black bumblebee flew in an undulating motion from the outside green into the cool of the kitchen, buzzing like a miniature outboard motor. Alfie opened one eye and then cocked his head, all the better to allow the sound to enter his ears.

'*Buzzzzzzzzzzzzzzzzz buzzzzzzzzzzzz zzzzzzzzzzzzzzzzzz.*'

Alfie moved sideways along his perch until he reached the point where it nearly touched the perch in front and then stepped onto it. His interest was obviously piqued by this new sound. His brain picked up on its cadence, stimulating the little grey cells that processed each new harmony, and calculated the exact frequency with which to replicate it.

'*Buzzzzzzzzzzzzzzz Buzzzz Buzzzzz Buzzzzzzzzzzzzzz Buzzzzzzzzzzz.*'

Alfie tried a simple '*Bzzzzzzzz.*'

The little insect in the Velcro lined pants-suit came back in syncopation. '*Buzzzzzzzzzzzzzz Buzzzzzzzzzzzzz Buzzzzzzzzzzzzz.*'

'*Bizzzzz Wizzzz Buzzzzzzzzzzzzz,*' replied Alfie. He hopped even closer to the front of the cage, which was open.

We had removed the front to have easier access to the reclusive little avian and after a few days he had rewarded us by edging onto the foremost perch and accepting little titbits from wary hands, held with all free fingers curled protectively back towards the palm.

None of us had ever seen him venture lower than the perches in his cage, and he never made any attempt to leave the security of the bars on three sides. Alfie was the world's biggest wimp.

'*Buzzzzzzzzzzzzzz Buzzzzzzzzzzzzz Bzzzzzzzzzzzz,*' hummed the little bee.

'*Buzzzzzzzzzzzzz Buzzzzzzzzzzzzz Bzzzzzzzzzzzz,*' replied the maestro mimic.

Alfie began to enjoy the musical conversation, buzzing in deep contentment whenever his new, as-yet unseen, friend uttered its unique sound. He began to bob up and down on the perch in delight.

The bumblebee buzzed repeatedly against the glass of the kitchen window in seeming aimless navigation until it veered away and made haphazardly for the living room door.

Alfie was still happily buzzing when a furry little black ball came out of nowhere straight toward his head. He leaped into the air, beating his featherless wings in futile desperation, and plummeted to the ground.

The family heard the metallic crash from the room next door where the television all but drowned out the frenetic buzzing of the intruder. As one, all four rushed through to investigate.

The cage was empty.

Alfie was nowhere to be seen. The bumblebee made a few abortive attempts to break through the glass of the French window before it seemed by luck to slip out of the open door.

A scratching noise from the fireplace turned our attention back from the glare of the outside sun. A soot-covered grey head poked up above the rim of the coal scuttle and surveyed the arena, ready to duck at the first hint of a little buzzing ninja.

Four chuckles erupted from four less than sympathetic people as we bent to examine the forlorn little bird inside his copper bolthole. Gently we coaxed him onto a well-protected, sleeve-covered arm, and lifted him up toward the cage.

'Oopsy-daisy,' he commented in a feminine voice, producing further chuckles of delight. Back in the safety of his cage, he hastily retired to the furthermost perch to pluck out a few remaining downy feathers from his almost totally bald chest.

As we left the room he gave a tentative soft little '*Buzzzz Buzzzz,*' but then seemed to decide not to tempt fate again and lapsed into silence, hunkering down and allowing his eyes to slowly close in torpid but safe inactivity.

Chapter 111

HAMMING IT UP

Sometimes when you try and orchestrate things to help others profit from each other, it all comes apart and lands on your head.

A young vet, Rebecca had a heart of gold and pet owners adored her. She only worked two days a week but had let it be known that she was looking for more income. I promised to try and help her.

It was early one morning when a film production company called to say they were filming a surgical operation and had been let down at the last minute by the hospital who were going to let them use their operating theatre. Did we have one they could use, and did we have a surgeon who would be prepared to be filmed for a few minutes? A light bulb went on the depths of my sleepy early morning mind. One cash-strapped vet and one film company needing an actress: a match made in heaven.

Rebecca was free and was keen to earn the moderate sum they were offering. We had a quiet day when it came to operations and it would be interesting to watch them film her. All was agreed.

The vehicles of the film company filled our car park and a horde of young people descended with clipboards, electric cables, cameras, cables, sound equipment, cables and even more cables. Within minutes half the practice was draped in electric wires and nameless people were poking cameras and microphones in every corner.

Then Rebecca called to say she had a migraine and could not make it.

The other vets made themselves busy, but the staff unhelpfully freed up my rota so that I was left with no choice but to don a surgical gown and glove up.

The film company had brought a pig carcass with them, purchased that morning from an abattoir. It was repulsive until a green drape covered its bulk, leaving only a small pink square of bare skin in the centre of the table.

Under the instructions of the director, I was put through the motions of making an incision in the patient. The camera magnified everything so that the screen was filled by the scalpel and the tips of my fingers. If I was going to be recognized by the public, it would only be by my digits.

Try as I might, every attempt ended with the director's growing impatience.

'You moved again,' he said tiredly. 'Your hands are out of shot again. Go again everyone. Rolling back to first mark. Standby ... And rolling.'

Hours later, I was heartily sick of the stress of stardom and wishing I had never been lured by the glamour of the silver screen. Eventually the director announced that he was satisfied.

'We are going to shoot the scene now. Remember that it must be perfect. We only have one patient with us. I am going to stop you if things go wrong.'

I nodded and my aching fingers were poised over the site, ready for stardom.

'And ... action,' came the command.

I lowered fingers a few millimetres and the blade touched the skin.

'Cut!' shouted the director.

I cut.

There was a collective indrawing of breath and then silence. All bar one of us knew that a cardinal mistake had been made. It took me a few minutes to realise that I had been the one at fault and even then, I felt a little peeved. They should have spoken English and not Show-talk.

They were not impressed. The massed horde slowly tidied up the mess, winding endless cables and then stowing them in their vehicles, careful not to look at me.

As the last car pulled out, the director shook my hand and thanked me for the use of the theatre. There was no mention of a contract for future productions. My life as a film star was over.

The star of the show never saw a royalty cheque, but we did get reimbursed for the costs of cremation for the co-star. They would, however, not pay for the return of her ashes, or for a plaque with her name engraved on it.

Chapter 112

CABBAGE LEAVES AND CLOTHES PEGS

Tanya Seventer was particularly concerned about Missie, her cat, who had developed mastitis, with swollen, painful mammary glands. Missie had been spayed so she could not be pregnant, and although we could gently express a small amount of fluid from each teat, there was no obvious evidence of sepsis. She had no temperature and there was no heat association with them.

'Cats can develop a hormonally induced inflammation of the mammary glands that is peculiar to the species.' I prattled on with scientific waffle. Ms Seventer was not particularly impressed.

'Can you give her some antibiotics for it?'

Resistance to antibiotics has become a serious problem in medicine and we really needed due justification to use them if we were going to try and prevent further problems.

'I would really prefer not to in this case.' I hesitated. 'I would suggest giving her an anti-inflammatory to take away any pain and if there is no improvement, then we can consider antibiotics.'

My client was not impressed. I had long noticed that dispensing complex and detailed advice and doing all I could for a patient often elicited the question 'I don't owe anything, do I?' whereas pulling out a syringe had the effect of stimulating the client to pull out their wallet. It was tempting at times just to give an injection to avoid a confrontation.

As I typed up a few notes on the case and dispensed the painkiller, I continued the conversation, trying awkwardly to avoid a fight.

'I have been told that with women, a cabbage leaf tucked into their bra gives them a lot of relief. Something to do with the natural soothing properties of the brassica family.' I turned to give the bottle to Ms Seventer, who appeared to be totally unimpressed with my scintillating conversation. 'Of course, you would have to first train Missie to wear a bra, and then you would have to buy one small enough for her.' I smiled and was met with silence.

I sighed as I closed the door behind her.

The next patient to arrive was a little ball of fluff that was feeling very sorry for itself. Hamlet, a Russian Hamster, had escaped from his cage and Ben, the old tom cat, had decided to make a meal of him. His owner had managed to rescue the little chap just in time, but he had several nasty wounds.

To treat the wounds, we would need to give an anaesthetic, since hamsters can be as aggressive as some other Russians. Many a vet could show scars on their hands from being too familiar with them.

Hamlet was in no state to deal with an anaesthetic. He would probably not survive. His owner was also doubtful whether she would be able to give him any medication. Fortunately, Hamlet proved to be very like many of the other patients of his ilk. I held a syringe with a few drops of a liquid antibiotic close to his mouth and he obligingly grabbed it with his two forepaws and bit the open end. A gentle squirt, and the liquid was in his mouth.

It would not always be as easy, as he became wise to the procedure and with time, he would start to turn his head away, but with persistence, he would hopefully be irritated enough to finally give in and bite at the syringe.

As they left, I thought back to Hammy, Leigh's little hamster, who had also escaped and had chewed a hole through the wall in the downstairs bathroom. For months after his escape, anyone visiting the loo would suddenly see a little head sticking out of the hole as Hammy investigated who had dared enter his domain. We never did catch Hammy and I have no idea what he lived on.

Mrs Prior brought in patient number three, a spaniel with ears that reeked of infection.

'I think Wilson has ear mites,' she announced.

In thirty-five years of practice, I saw only a handful of dogs with ear mites, whereas almost every practitioner will see a few with a yeast or bacterial infection every week. My money was on the latter and not on mites.

Dog with ears that droop down are particularly prone to otitis, as the moisture that is trapped in the ear canal provides a perfect habitat for yeasts and bacteria. The micro-organisms in the mouth also tend to move into the grooves or lip-folds below and behind the mouth, further spreading infection that can contribute to ear infections.

Using an earbud, I managed to get a small sample of the contents of each ear and spread them on a microscope slide. A drop of alcohol fixed the sample to the glass and a second drop of stain coloured the micro-organisms. Under magnification, the *Malasezzia* yeasts have a snowshoe shape, whereas the bacteria are little round cocci in groups or elongated bacilli. There were thousands in the tiny pinhead-sized sample I had taken.

As I discussed Wilson's ears with his owner, I commented that I had often been tempted to pin up the long, floppy ears of spaniels and other dogs, to allow some air in and give them a chance to dry out. Mrs Prior was enthusiastic about the idea.

'Could you please punch a hole in each ear flap, under anaesthetic of course, so that I can lace them together over the top of his head? I could tie them up while he eats. They get so dirty when they go in the food, and the ear canals would get a chance to heal.'

I laughed and declined. Such a procedure would clearly be regarded as unethical, unless of course Wilson gave his consent, but he was as uncommunicative as my Russian patient earlier.

Mrs Seventer brought Missie back two days later and handed me the unopened bottle of anti-inflammatory drug.

'I never used it,' she announced. I steeled myself for the inevitable demand for antibiotics, but instead, she turned Missie over to show me her flattened under-belly.

'Your advice worked,' she stated. 'I wrapped a cabbage leaf around her with a bandage and all the swelling has gone down. She's back to normal.'

She was gracious enough to give me the credit, and I allowed her the victory of winning the battle on her terms. I oozed enthusiasm over the complete recovery and then gave her a refund for the bottle of drugs she had brought back. I could not bring myself to charge for the time set aside for her second visit and she left smiling, and I sighed at the vagaries of our profession. Unexpected victories should be grasped whenever they come along; too many unforeseen complications come howling down from the wings when least expected.

Hamlet too, arrived back looking much better. His wounds had not completely closed, but my intention of knocking him out to clean them up now appeared to be unnecessary, as he scuttled about the cage, cheeks packed with seeds, oblivious to his earlier brush with death.

Mrs Prior brought Wilson in two months later. He had a neat little square of tissue missing from the tip of each ear flap.

'I have been clipping his ears up with a clothes-peg whenever I feed him, and it has worked wonders. Then I forgot to take it off last week and the pressure from the peg killed off a tiny square of each ear. Do you think they need any treatment?'

I examined the almost perfect little missing squares and shrugged. 'There is not much that we can do about it now. It would require plastic surgery to repair. We do a lot of skin modifications, and we are fortunate that dogs and cats have very elastic skin that allows us to move it about, unlike the problems human plastic surgeons have. I don't think it is worth putting him through the pain and risks. That is,' I continued, 'as long as you don't mind having a dog with two slightly modified ear flaps?'

She shook her head and left without any further intervention.

Owners, I thought to myself, *can be both the guardian angels of their pets, and occasionally the biggest threat to their survival.* Usually, however, whatever is done is due to the love the human has for its animal companion. That vindicates their intentions in most cases.

Chapter 113

A Father Comes of Age

I collected the kids from school and drove back to the main practice. The three of us sat and watched 'The Simpsons', before Peter commented nonchalantly 'Gerrit, Trevor and I are going to go kayaking down the Ardeche River in France during the holidays.'

I rubbed my eyes and swallowed hard. Had I heard right? This fragile son of mine, who well knew the colour of hospital walls and had never been away from home apart from school trips, was planning to venture out into the land of dragons and evil goblins. I was too taken aback to mount an effective defence.

The following day Adrian, father to Gerrit, the instigator of the idea, called and asked if the boys had told me of their plans. I affirmed that they had, trying to sound mature and in control.

'I think that we should go along as well. Don't you? It will be a father-son bonding trip.' I agreed, fiercely relieved that someone with a bit more knowledge and ability than I had was taking control. After all, Adrian and his family had made the trip down the river the previous year.

Adrian advised that I buy a tent with inflatable mattress and sleeping bags from a well-known camping store. He also provided an exhaustive list of equipment that would be useful. It seemed a huge outlay, but I was determined not to be shown up for lack of preparation.

Two weeks later, we approached the fast-running waters of the river which I eyed in trepidation. The three boys showed no sign of waiting at the water's edge, but instead launched their craft and sped away down river. I panicked.

There was no way that I would be able to do anything if, in the next few minutes Peter succumbed to his weak chest and was sucked under the water. I waddled down to the river carrying my huge pile of gear intent on getting afloat as soon as possible. Adrian paused and held up a hand.

'I have a confession to make.' he said. 'Last year, my youngest daughter and I got trapped under a rock in a fast-flowing section of the river. I have come back to try and conquer my fears.'

What about mine? I thought. How could he have kept this from me. Our boys were no doubt already drowned since I could not see any sign of them. I threw everything into the barrel that was strapped on the back of the kayak and jumped in. Adrian was left to fend for himself.

Unused to the task of paddling, I was quickly exhausted, but my desperation kept me going. Eventually I spotted three little kayaks in the distance. They had found a tributary and explored it before heading back to the mainstream. I caught up with them just as they were about to speed away again.

With an enormous effort I manage to catch up with Peter and hold onto his kayak.

'Are you OK. son?' I asked quietly, not sure that he would want his friends to hear the concern in my voice.

'Yes. Why?' he replied.

'Oh nothing, I was just checking up.' He sped off again, eager to catch up with the younger generation.

The three days were a testing time. I found every rock lining the bottom of the river, while the boys floated effortlessly on the surface. No-one else had brought any kit apart from sleeping bags and a change of clothes. My kayak was a full three inches lower in the water than any of the others.

Adrian and I had bought food for the three days, carefully planning each meal. The boys ate two days-worth of rations in the first meal. By the last day, we were down to a couple of slices of salami each, piled high with raspberry jam; a meal that tasted better than any I have eaten since.

Every few hours we faced a new challenge, including a chute built into a dam wall to allow canoes and kayaks to shoot over the wall and land twenty feet downriver, allowing me to turn in the air and land head down while the boys flew over and skimmed past with ease.

The sections of portage were another trial, as I hauled my loaded kayak and heavy barrel through the undergrowth. I never quite managed to catch up with Peter but at least I could keep an eye on him most of the time. I would never have been able to save him from drowning, but at least I would have been able to tell his mother where he had last been seen.

I was not aware that one of the boys had picked up the map given to us by the company that leased us the kayaks and had kept it to himself. Vital information concerning hazards in the river were not shared, or at least not with the older generation.

Signs in French occasionally appeared on the bank of the river and in my ignorance, I took them to be place names. On the final day, there was a large board bearing the words *'Dent Noire'*. It meant nothing to me and even if it had, 'Black Teeth' would not have sparked off the alarm the words were intended to do.

The map, I found out later, warned paddlers to keep to the left as they rounded a sharp turn and faced a plunge down thirty feet with viciously jagged black rocks gaping wide and ready to devour the unwary.

I led the way into the abyss and flew straight at the teeth, my kayak riding over the first few and then tossing me over some pretty nasty ones into the swirling torrent. My only thought was that Peter was seconds behind me and heading for the same fate.

I struggled against the current, aware that I was powerless to fight the force of nature as it played with me. I made it to the bank and pulled myself up to turn around in desperation.

The little boy that I spent so many hours rocking to sleep, holding a nebuliser mask over his face, sitting beside his hospital bed, came hurtling through the air above the water and smashed into the same rock that I had just christened.

I plunged into the water, intent on saving him, but was beaten back by the current. Ahead of me, Peter rose to his feet and manfully caught his fleeing kayak and pushed his way to the riverbank. I sank back exhausted.

As we paddled along the last stretch of water, aware that our adventure was coming to an end, Peter sped away from the other two boys and caught hold of my kayak.

'You alright Dad?' he asked

'Yes. Why?'

'Just checking.' he said.

Chapter 114

STIFF UPPER LIP

Before our move to sunny England, I had been convinced that the locals would be very different to the colonial remnants from down South. After a few months I realised that all the superficial distinctions were in fact of no consequence. Two years later, the core dissimilarities became a lot more obvious.

Although we had British grandparents, the tiny, crowded island was understandably reluctant to allow the massed hordes of the world to descend upon them and as a result, those controlling immigration made it as difficult as possible to get a toe in the door. Repeated submissions of a thickening wad of documents to the British embassy in Johannesburg inevitably resulted in their return in a crisp white envelope, requesting ever more information.

In desperation, I moved to the city and made a daily visit to the embassy. Each day I would inch along the winding queue, eventually reaching the counter, behind which an official sat in a cubicle. Handing over the application for visas, I then passed a thick wad of birth and marriage certificates, covering every relative the embassy could think of, as well as qualifications and work references. It generally took the person in the cubicle a few minutes to come up with three or four documents that were missing and each day it was a different assortment.

After two weeks of patient queueing and frantic searching through files and cupboards, I greeted the inevitable rebuff with a little less stoicism than usual. Turned away from the counter yet again, I walked dismally past the still waiting, expectant line of supplicants. The guard at the door had his back turned to me and on an impulse, instead of walking out onto the street, I re-joined the end of the queue.

It was a few minutes before closing time when I finally reached the finish line at the front for the second time that day. The official failed to recognise me, since all her attention was focused on the clock on the wall. Accepting my proffered paperwork, she lifted the coveted official stamp and christened each sheet of paper before handing them back and then rushing out the back of the cubicle. We were official and on our way.

Two years later I experienced the flip side of this scene as I made the trip into London in order to renew my passport at the South African embassy. Several months of correspondence had failed to deliver and I was now forced to attend in person. The embassy had all the paperwork required but I needed to find out why nothing had been resolved. Applications had to be handed in before nine in the morning and the results could be collected at three the same day.

I inadvertently chose the hottest day of the century and suffered severely from claustrophobia on the underground. There seemed to be no air movement at all.

A disinterested young man at the embassy looked disdainfully at the forms and then asked for my identity number. It ended in 006 and I commented that I happened to work with 007, the secret agent. The young man looked startled and gave me a sharp look of suspicion. Then his gaze travelled up and down me, finally meeting my eyes. We both laughed and once again the magic of the rubber stamp was applied to the paperwork. All I needed to do was return in the afternoon.

I had intended to spend the day seeing the sights of London but instead found a bench in St James Park and fell asleep. I had no idea that the queen too had a sense of humour. I was full stride into a stressful dream about chasing trains that were on fire when suddenly Armageddon arrived in full volume.

I shot upright and fell off the bench in fright. The cacophony all around me was deafening and I found it impossible to even find my heart, let alone stuff it back into my wildly beating chest.

It was the start of the changing of the guard and the mounted band had formed up around my bench. A platoon of drums and brass instruments had suddenly erupted into full voice, forever destroying my sense of security. For years the sound of a brass band would raise the hairs on the back of my neck.

The officer in charge gave a command that sounded distinctly like 'Caught another one, lads. Forward. March.', before the horses obligingly trotted past. Moustaches twitched and I was subjected to several equine snorts of derision, but the riders ignored me completely. They'd had their fun for the afternoon.

Tiredly I made my way back to the embassy and then caught the train home, reflecting as I passed through the steaming jungle of the tube that I just was not born to deal with the heat of this country.

Chapter 115

DAD JOKES

Working impossibly long hours without reasonable time off was expected of vets in the last quarter of the twentieth century. By law we had to provide a service every hour around the clock. It was not legal for a non-vet to own a practice and no-one contracted out to emergency service providers.

I had accepted my future while still at university and embraced it as inevitable. The biggest regret was that I could not spend more time with the two little people that were more important than life to me. Peter and Leigh were my chief delight.

As tiny toddlers, I pulled them around the surgery in carboard boxes harnessed to dog leads. They locked themselves in the cages and growled ferociously while I played along as the frightened vet.

I invented games to entertain them and played alongside them. Fetching them from school was never an onerous task. In summer we sneaked down to Kidd's Beach on Sundays, hoping for an afternoon without the inevitable call back to the surgery. The soft, golden yellow sand and the cluster of rock pools were the ultimate delight for two little people from a very early age.

Both loved animals and I was able to involve them with the raising of a wide range of little waifs and strays. They grew to occupy a large chunk of my heart and my thoughts. They also suffered a great deal from awful Dad Jokes and pranks. Pranks that did not always go a planned.

Peter had been given a large watch for one birthday which he prized for its elaborate complexity. A serious little boy, he was intrigued by puzzles and mechanics.

I had made Peter a bed above a desk, converting a double bunk for the purpose. The sides of the bunk bed made it difficult to see into the bed from the ground. I decided to surprise Peter one night.

Just before he made his way upstairs for the evening, I crept into his room and sneaked up the ladder and into his bed. He was going to get a shock when he made the same journey himself.

I had not counted on the length of time it took for a seven-year-old boy to make it past the dozens of distractions on his way. My mind followed the sounds as he progressed towards his destination on the top mattress. He dragged a coat-hanger across the bars of the stairway, producing a staccato rhythm; the thumps as he swung the bathroom door open were followed by the almost silent whispering of the pages while he spent a few minutes reading from his favourite book. Eventually the bedroom door opened, and I heard the shuffling below as he got ready for bed.

I was just stealing myself to leap up as he reached the top of the ladder when suddenly a heavy object landed with a painful crack on my skull.

'Ow.' I yelped. The pain broke through my reserve of silence. I looked down to find Peter's heavy watch lying next to me on the bed.

A little face appeared over the edge of the bunk. 'What are you doing in my bed?' he demanded.

'I was going to give you a fright, but you threw your watch onto my head.'

His face broke into a grin. 'I always do that so that I can see the time in the night. The face glows in the dark. Look, I'll show you.'

I clambered down and left him chuckling with delight while I went off to nurse my bump.

Years later, Peter dropped into the small branch surgery I was running. The little boy caterpillar had become a butterfly with an engineering degree and a healthy disregard for lesser mortals.

I wanted to put a shelf on the wall of the clinic and with an engineer son watching it was not a time to admit that I had forgotten to bring a spirit level with me. Vets are at least as intelligent as engineers and a little demonstration would not go amiss.

A length of drip tubing, relic from a patient that had been discharged, half filled with a coloured liquid, and I had my own method of marking two points on the wall that would definitely be on the level.

I blame those responsible for my education. Someone forgot to tell me about capillary action in a thin tube and the resultant shelf was as skew as the house that Jack built. Peter roared with unreserved delight.

At least vets are more intelligent than to fall about laughing uncontrollably in a room full of medical equipment and sharp instruments. The resultant injuries should hopefully act as a reminder for months to come not to doubt the prowess of an animal doctor who has the telephone numbers of at least a couple of handymen on file.

Chapter 116

ALL IN THE MIND

There is a sports centre just a few houses away from the veterinary surgery that is not particularly well utilised. I made good use of it by taking the two little kids to play with a tennis ball and racquets on the squash courts. They were good fun and amazed me with the speed at which they picked up the game.

When they flew the nest, I looked around fruitlessly for someone to join me on the court. The manager of the centre brushed aside any queries about squash clubs, stating simply: 'There is only one group of elderly men who meet each Friday night.'

Eventually, in desperation, I decided to join them for an evening. It was a lesson in congeniality and drive that will remain with me for life. Five men and one woman in their seventies collected on the balcony behind the courts to compare their aches and injuries of the week, before hobbling onto the courts and thrashing not only the tiny little black sphere of rubber but also any younger player fool enough to venture into their world.

Fred made his uncertain entry onto the court with a tight bandage around one knee as we watched from our vantage point on the balcony.

'He's not as wobbly anymore, is he?' commented one of the spectators.

I assumed they were talking about his knee but was quickly put right. 'Oh no, Fred did his cruciate ligament in, but he refuses to have it operated on. He's tired of hospitals after having six brain ops last year. He has been a bit unsteady for a few months since the last operation.'

Fred moved about the squash court with such speed and agility that I wondered if they were having me on. Given the chance to play against him over the next few months, it took me twenty games just to win the serve for the first time and then only because he started hitting the ball straight back to me. Although I have managed a few wins against some of the other players, Fred remains invincible. The only reason I keep coming back for more humiliation each week is that he is just an incredibly nice guy.

One week, after another gruelling pounding in which he moved from corner to corner of the court in short, lighting strikes, each time getting the ball neatly back to me so that I could actually hit it, I noticed the firmly corded muscles of his arms and the torso that would make a 16-year-old look over the hill.

'How do you do it, Fred?' I asked. 'Most people would give up after such extensive surgery.'

'I don't know really,' he replied. 'The pills help a little I suppose.'

My raised eyebrows prompted him to continue. 'They took out my hypothalamus and my thyroid doesn't work anymore, so I take a thyroid pill each morning.'

'I guess that would help.' I agreed, unconvinced.

'The cortisone pills probably do as well.' He offered. 'And the growth hormone injections seem to keep me on the go as well. Not sure about the testosterone injections; would they also have an effect?'

I agreed that they just might.

I had to admit that even with the aid of the same pharmacy in Fred's home, I still would not be a match for him. You can only build on raw talent if it already exists. The knowledge of the arsenal of doping agents injected into my opponent made it a little easier to accept the weekly humiliation.

Trish, the lone woman in the group is 70 and has Congestive Obstructive Pulmonary Disease. She should be taking it easy on a padded couch but instead she has one inhaler she uses if she wins the serve and two if she loses the point and must face the serve. Trish has played havoc with my street cred. I wonder how much those little inhalers would cost me ....?

Chapter 117

THE SEEDS OF DISCONTENT

One surprising difference between veterinary work in South Africa and in England are the commonly encountered grass seed awns that cause so much pain and suffering in the UK. It is perhaps also due to the areas we worked in, but in South Africa, we never saw the sudden influx of dogs with seeds in their ears, or paws or elsewhere.

The awns have a shape that makes them move only in the direction that the tip points. The spines prevent them being dislodged by shaking a head or licking a paw.

When they penetrate the skin, usually between two toes, but also frequently in the armpit or groin, the pain and irritation causes the unfortunate victim to lick the site continually. If they manage to get the awn out, or if it had not yet penetrated very deep, it then often gets taken into the mouth of the dog and lodges it the soft tissue at the back of the jaw.

Monty was a gorgeous flat coated retriever with a dark shining brown coat. He loved coursing through the fields, following scents his owner had no perception of. On this day he returned feeling very sorry for himself, with a painful back paw and continually shaking his head due to an awn that had found its way into the ear canal and had pierced the eardrum.

We found six grass awns embedded in our patient while he lay blissfully unaware under the effect of the anaesthetic gas that filled his lungs. There were also another four awns lying loose in his dense coat. I hoped we had found all the awns but warned Mrs Trenshaw to report any suspicion of signs that could be due to one we had missed.

We had also noticed a swelling on his chest wall. When I aspirated the contents with a fine needle, a clear fluid came out that proved to have a lot of inflammatory cells when I looked at it under the microscope. The suspicion was that he had another awn in the muscle of the chest wall.

Try as we might, we could not find an awn or any other cause of the inflamed lump. I left a small drain in the cavity that I had opened to investigate and for a few days some of the fluid seeped out but after the drain was removed everything returned to normal. Monty was all set for a full recovery as he beat his tail on the floor and rubbed his muzzle against my hand.

Three months after his battle with the grass awns, Monty returned with a history of just being 'not himself'. He was a lot thinner and less buoyant than he had been previously and a very clear symptom was the irregular heartbeat and the obvious heart murmur. He was also reluctant to resume his long walks in the countryside. I had bought a used ECG machine from a retired cardiac specialist and developed an interest in interpreting the fine line it traced on a strip of paper when attached to a patient. Monty had a serious heart problem, with a lot of electrical impulses that were totally abnormal and resulted in the heart chambers contracting out of synchrony, often when there was no blood in them. He looked at me with eyes that drooped, the spark that had been in them absent for now. Monty needed help.

I always found it difficult to refer patients to specialists, but often it is in their best interests. Monty made the trip to The Queen Mother Hospital at the Royal College. He showed no appreciation of the dedicated attention they had given him when he returned a week later, sporting a long scar on his chest wall between two ribs.

The specialists had managed to trace the path of a grass seed that had migrated from the lump we had investigated and had eventually ended up on the surface of the heart, where it caused the irregular beats as a result from damage it inflicted on the heart muscle. They had not found an intact awn, but there were numerous little bits from it that had slowly being broken down by the body defences.

Monty required ongoing cardiac medication for a further eight months. The symptoms slowly improved towards the end of this period and then Monty came in with the third and final episode of the saga. He had developed a lump on the opposite side of his chest.

In disbelief, I made an incision through the skin and after a detailed search, managed to see the black tip of what looked to be a grass awn. With a pair of fine forceps, I grabbed hold of the tip and gently pulled and to our amazement, pulled out the longest grass seed I have ever encountered.

It no longer had a tuft of spines attached to the tip, but instead had one long, black tail of an inch and a half. Could this monster have travelled right across the dog's chest? It seemed implausible.

Monty did not have a miraculous recovery but over three months his symptoms improved, and I was able to wean him off the cardiac drugs. He was never the same ebullient free spirit of his youth, but he went on to live a long and relatively normal life. I saw him for his vaccinations and a few minor problems and each time he came in, he would walk sedately over to me and rest his head on my knee.

Chapter 118

COOL DAD

For over two years, the children endured the embarrassment of being dropped off at school in a Veterinary Ambulance. One of them sat in the back seat, without any windows and suffered in silence. The more fortunate sibling got to ride in the front seat. I was forced to set up a rota to prevent squabbling in the ranks.

The two of them took great delight in changing radio channels when I was not watching. I habitually listened to Radio 2, the station chosen by the more elderly listeners, while the younger taste was for Radio 1. Since I was the driver and owner of the vehicle and could stop and order them to walk to school, I generally won, even though it was a war that all secretly enjoyed

Forced to leave the kids in the car for a few minutes while I collected something, I got back into the vehicle, knowing that I would have to set things right after allowing them free rein to the radio. As expected, the obvious sound of youthful music greeted my ears as the key turned.

We had only just got underway when I pressed the button to change channels. Nothing happened. I tried a third button and then a fourth, but Radio 1 continued to play uninterrupted. It was only after I took a quick glance at Peter as he slumped in his seat, that I notice the look of glee on his face. Behind me a suppressed chuckle gave the game away.

It took a good twenty minutes to reset all the buttons that Peter had set to Radio 1 and since my days were busy rushing to collect kids and race back to work, it was only the next day that I managed to at least get one choice to play my choice. I threatened blue murder if it happened again, the glint if amusement in my eyes no doubt giving the lie to the threat.

Six months later, we took the daring move of buying a more acceptable car, but Peter shattered my self-esteem by informing me that his friends all felt that a Citreon Berlingo was not a car suitable for a man to drive.

'They still think you are cool though.'

'Why?' I wanted to know.

'I told them that when I said I felt sick after eating too much chocolate at Easter, you didn't tell me it was my own fault and not to do it again. You told me that you had learned as a boy that if you drank a glass of milk, it made you feel a lot better and then you could eat more chocolate.'

I was abashed. Why could I not be known as a daring knight in armour? A clown with no sense of remorse would just have to do. It was the best I could manage.

Chapter 119

Sorry Constable

In the eighteenth-century, John Constable painted scenes from the beautiful countryside around Flatford and the Dedham Vale in Suffolk. The landscape remains in the whole unspoilt; wide open pastures patrolled by cattle who mark the miles on the rambling pathways with cow pats, and water voles that tunnel burrows along the riverbank, keeping watch on the occasional rowing boat bumping from bank to bank as it makes its erratic passage up the waterway.

Mark was coming to visit for a rare weekend from across the pond in the land of the Pilgrims. I searched fruitlessly for something quintessentially British to show him. Mark had been fortunate to have emigrated to a country where they spoke English. I in turn, struggled with natives that preferred colloquial dialects that left me guessing a lot of the time.

A friend loaned me two canoes and I planned for the two of us to make the trip from Flatford to Dedham and back.

Early on Saturday morning, we drove up to start of the route and then found it impossible to park near the water due to the numbers of cars in the area. I eventually found a small carpark with only half a dozen spaces, far from the village and any conveniences.

Both of us felt a growing pressure in the region of our bladders and having come from the African veld, assumed we could find a thirsty bush behind which to relieve ourselves. We had not counted on the population of 80 million on one small island that meant that most bushes are in the direct gaze of a dozen people at any given time.

There was a party of thirty-something hikers converging on our departure point and privacy was even less than an illusion. We decided to paddle a little way up the river until we found an area unpeopled by camera-toting tourists.

I had not used the canoes before and very quickly found them totally unmanageable since they had a penchant for going around in circles. The absence of a rudder meant that it was impossible to steer the craft and as a result the two of us made painfully slow progress up the meandering river Stour. It was several hours later that we finally made it round a bend and decided that we just had to take the chance while we had it.

Clambering ungracefully out of the canoes, we raced up to a small clump of bushes and seconds later felt the intense relief from answering nature's call.

Straightening up, I heard a soft cough behind us and turned around, only to freeze with embarrassment at the sight of thirty-something walkers pausing to allow us to finish before pushing past.

Lifting my gaze, I was aghast to see our starting point only fifty yards away, the river having made an almost full circle in its lazy passage across the floor of the valley.

Fortunately, neither Constable nor any other officer was anywhere to be seen and our spectators were prepared to forgive our indiscretion.

If they gave badges out to tourists as they do for boy scouts, we may have earned one for paddling, but certainly not for orienteering. I do wonder if the great painter ever included two desperate figures hiding behind a bush in his scenes.

Chapter 120

I Don't Mind

The human brain has a masochistic streak that allows it to enter the sleep mode late at night only to jerk awake a few hours later in frantic panic.

'Did I give Mrs Brown the tablets for Chico? .... Was it enough to suture that wound with only two layers? .... I am just a sham – I should not be doing this; I just keep messing up.'

No-one seems to be immune. Recurring dreams of sitting down to an exam only to find that it is a subject you have not studied for, or even worse, that you are sitting there naked. The lack of control is overwhelming.

We had only been working for a few months when Karen sat bolt upright in bed at three on the morning.

'I think I took out the ureters in that little dog yesterday. They were much too thin to have been the womb.' Her voice was filled with despair and worry.

The tubes running from the kidneys to the bladder lie roughly in the same position as the womb, only closer to the backbone. They are protected by a membrane that holds them against the backbone, so normally are not in danger. If the ureters were removed by mistake instead of the womb, the dog would certainly die.

In most young female dogs, the womb is as thick as a pencil, but in small dogs, it can be a lot thinner. Occasionally, in an immature dog, they can be as thin as a thread and look remarkably like ureters.

Karen fretted away for hours, which meant that neither of us got any sleep. In the morning she called the owner, only to find that Millie was alive and well and sleeping off her operation at home. Despite this, it was a tense week waiting until Millie came in for her post op check. She had no idea of the panic she had caused as she licked Karen and wriggled in delight at the extra attention.

Seven years later, the phone shrilled panic in my ear and the voice on the other end was full of anxiety.

'It's Jenny. I've been thinking about that little Maltese poodle that I spayed today. I'm sure I took out the ureters and not the womb.'

'Calm down Jenny.' I replied sleepily. 'I don't think you have. It's very difficult to mistake the two organs.'

'But it was just a thin cord. Much too thin to be the uterus.'

'Did it have little ovaries on the end of it?'

'Yes. At least I thought they were ovaries at the time, but they could have been something else.' She was winding herself up even further.

'If they were ureters, they would end inside the kidneys. You could not make that mistake.'

'I suppose so.' she conceded. 'But they were far too thin. I am sure they were ureters.

'Did they both join together at the cervix caudally?'

'Yes. I guess that means they must be the womb.'

'They were, Jenny. I am sure that a surgeon as careful as you would not have made that mistake. Go to sleep and call the owner in the morning.

The little Maltese poodle was fine. Jenny had lost a few pounds from worry but rapidly put them on again as she fretted over the next potential mistake she could have made.

Three years later, the same scenario was played over again.

'Hello. Sorry to wake you. It's Fiona, the locum vet. I'm just desperately worried. I think I took the ureters out by mistake when I spayed that little Jack Russel this morning.'

'No! You did not, Fiona. Take it from me. I've been down this path before. Twice. You would not remove the womb unless you found the ovaries to prove that it was the womb. Ureters do not end on ovaries, they end on kidneys. Now go to sleep.'.

A word of warning. Never work with women, even if ninety percent of the profession are female. Never work with people who care desperately for their patients. For that matter, don't work with men either. They mess up just as often and are just as prone to self-doubt and panic. And finally, even if you give your clients your number for emergencies, never allow your colleagues access to it. Not if you like your sleep.

Chapter 121

In Good Faith

Life was proving to be more than just a little trying and I was struggling with a host of complex issues way above my paygrade. Depression was edging in and colouring each day with grey sadness.

Andrew, a pastor at the church suggested that I try singing and then, knowing my limitations, he quickly added 'Not in public, but when you are alone in your car.'

I duly bought a couple of DVDs and one of my favourites was by Keith Townend called 'Who Walk by Faith and Not by Sight'. I turned it up loud and belted out the words tunelessly as I drove.

Keith, the new tenant, had moved into the annexe while I was at work the previous day. I'd had an early Spring clean and created a huge pile of rubbish near the kitchen door, waiting to go in a skip. On the other side of the door was a pile of things that could withstand the weather but which I want to keep. Between the two piles was a clear pathway leading up to the kitchen door.

Keith decided to add his unwanted rubbish to my pile. Unfortunately for me, he put his discards in the gap between my two piles.

I arrived home in the dark, got out of the car still singing 'Who Walk by faith and not by Sight' and strode confidently towards the house, my eyes still night-blind after turning off the car headlights.

My left foot suddenly found itself trapped in an old bucket and when my right foot took a huge step forward, it ended up in the open drawer of an old broken sideboard.

Needless to say, my faith was not able to keep me upright and I ended up sprawled among the bits of wood and broken metal. I did not smile at the humour at the time, but in my imagination, I heard a soft chuckle from above. I wondered if someone up there had a sense of humour as they used the scene to teach me a little more about my profession of faith.

There was an apple tree that grew next to the annexe in which Keith lived. The blackbirds feasted off its fruits throughout winter and each day there are a dozen apples on the pathway. The soft pulp from the ripe ones denied the unwary foot any purchase on the ground, while the smaller ones acted as ball-bearings on the concrete pathway.

I had been carefully sweeping them off the path to help Keith, but it crossed my mind that I might just bless him by allowing him to experience some divine humour and sweep them onto the path the following day.

Chapter 122

Two Left Feet

Broken legs in tortoises are a challenge to deal with. Too short and twisted to apply a bandage or cast, they seem to be reluctant to learn to use a crutch or zimmer frame. Few owners are, understandably, prepared for the costs of surgical plates and implants.

Surgeons are often left with few options other than rest and possibly raising the shell off the ground by sticking a little wheel or a skid under the plastron. This means that the tortoise does not have to raise the whole weight of the body and shell with each step, but they still have to use the leg to push themselves forward.

Speedy had an obvious fracture in his left humerus. He tolerated a thick bandage for several weeks but then it began to chaffe and the leg showed signs of atrophying from disuse. There was no evidence of healing on the x-rays. As a last resort, we left the bandage off but prescribed confinement in a small area plus a painkiller and a high calcium diet.

Fleur, a border collie was the opposite in mobility. She covered the ground faster than a low flying jet and seemed never to keep still, until that is, this irresistable force ran into an immovable object and the result was a sharply fractured bone and a lot of pain.

The diagnosis was easy to make and we offered several options including metal implants. Her owner, Mrs De'Arcy, was undecided and wanted to consult the rest of her family. As a termporary measure, we decided to put a Robert-Jones bandage on. Thick layers of padding compressed by multiple layers of bandaging, put on tightly enough to render the leg immobile.

The team of nurses got the materials ready while I saw the next case and then discharged a third one, the clock relentlessly mocking my efforts to stay abreast of the work. Finally I rushed back to the Prep Room and we set about encasing the painful limb in a soothingly rigid structure.

With a flourish I carried Fleur back to the waiting room and gently placed her on her paws on the floor in front of her owner. The hapless dog crumpled to the ground.

'It's her other leg. You've bandaged the wrong one.' Mrs De'Arcy was incredulous.

My mind searched desperately for an excuse but there was no posSible outcome apart from a profuse apology and a hasty retreat with patient back to the helplessly giggling nurses hiding out of sight.

Fortunately my mistake had not caused any injury except to my pride and Mrs De'Arcy was forgiving and seemed to have forgotten my blunder when Fleur walked out gingerly three days later after the bone had been pinned.

With the incident still fresh in my mind, I called Speedy's owner to find out how he was doing.

'Oh, he's fine. Hardly any lameness now, but I've realised that he must be left-handed.' his owner reported. With visions of a little terrapin writing his journal crossed my mind, but Speedy's owner continued:

'He used to hold down the greenery in his food with his left leg when he ate, but now he cannot do that and when he tries to bite the leaves, they often just get pushed away. I have had to learn to hold them for him.'

Chapter 123

ON YOUR MARKS

Some days are more memorable than others. Most are filled with dogs and cats, but occasionally the 'exotic' patients outnumber the more routine domestic species.

Sheldon, the 14kg Sulcata Tortoise, came in with a tennis ball stuck in the shell aperture meant for his hind leg. It was 10cm deep in this narrow cavity and only a small square of the ball could be seen in the depths. It took three days to work out how to remove it.

Trying to pull his leg out straight proved impossible. Sheldon's thigh muscles were in a different league to those in our arms and we lost every contest. It looked as if a general anaesthetic would be necessary, which in tortoises is not a simple procedure. Since they do not possess a diaphragm, and their chest walls cannot move, they breathe by moving their legs, head, and tail in and out. Under anaesthesia, it is necessary to ventilate them mechanically and since they do everything slowly, recovery from anaesthesia can take many hours, during which the ventilation must continue.

Success came on the day a visiting laparoscopic surgeon arrived to train our staff in keyhole surgery. During a break in the training, he asked about Sheldon, who was scrabbling in his cage and thumping rhythmically on the fibreglass floor.

When I described the problem and upended Sheldon to show the surgeon the ball just visible in the depths of the shell aperture, he was captivated, and it soon became obvious that nothing was going to get him to resume his training of the staff until we had the ball out.

Eventually we administered a strong muscle relaxant and sedative and then a very competent nurse held a rope looped around the leg and anchored to a chair on which he sat. I pulled Sheldon in the opposite direction and the specialist probed into the depths of the shell with several large artery clamps, patiently pulling at the outer covering of the ball and then later dragging little chunks of the inner rubber out into the light. It took over an hour to get the whole ball.

Sheldon was discharged with strict instructions to keep him off the court. He clearly had a penchant for stuffing the second tennis ball into his knickers when he served.

Reggie, the dwarf rabbit, arrived with gut stasis, a rapidly fatal condition in rabbits. These deceptively strong animals have a unique pacemaker in the gut, just as other mammals have in the heart. If it stops for any reason, it has to be restarted or the digestive system closes down.

Reggie responded to a drug used in babies with gut stasis, plus another human drug commonly used for car sickness in humans, as well as a diet syringed into his mouth, together with a source of fibre and bacteria required in the digestion process. Reggie was pooping to everyone's satisfaction that afternoon.

Leon, the veiled chameleon, had two inches of his intestines prolapsed. It was successfully replaced but for a while we thought we were going to lose him.

Our biggest success was to get them all to pose for a split second on the countertop before Reggie decided that the mobile leaf next to him might be edible and Leon needed to be rescued.

I like to complain about how hard my job is and how ungrateful the world appears, but in truth, I get so much that money cannot buy from our patients.

Just don't tell anyone or they will not want to pay my salary.

Chapter 124

BRAIN STUTTER

From an early age I realised that there were a few loose connections between my little grey cells. They just cannot retain facts, at least not in an ordered fashion enabling them to be recalled at will. The ability for my diminished RAM to function is inversely proportional to the level of stress it is subjected to.

I was never able to remember telephone numbers reliably. I twice forgot my own birthday and on one memorable occasion struggled to recall my name. The data is not lost; it is just misfiled. University professors grilling me in exams often expressed a profound scepticism at my struggling memory, but seconds later, free from the stress of an examination room, the information would be tripping off my tongue.

A depressingly regular event occurs most days. I will want to prescribe a basic drug for a patient, such as Aspirin. In my head I can see the little white tablets, see the tub on the shelf. I know they contain Salicylic Acid, a non-steroidal anti-inflammatory with a tendency to cause gastric ulceration; the drug is excreted by the kidney; comes in 300mg and 75mg and its name starts with a 'P'.

Where the P comes from, I have no idea, but once this nano-bit of misinformation is inserted into the mix, I have no hope of recalling the name of the drug.

Like most people with disabilities, I have learned to compensate with behavioural crutches, callipers, and braces. Apologising to the client, I mention that I will just make certain we have the drug on the shelf and go through to the pharmacy to look at the name. The self-deprecation on recognising the name Aspirin, which everyone knows, is made worse by the fact that I know where it is stored in an alphabetically arranged dispensary. 'P' does not occur at the front of the alphabet. Idiot.

Strangely enough, in the same conversation blighted by my faulty noggin, I experience no difficulty in recalling far more complex information, such as the parasite affecting rabbits called *Encephalitozoon cuniculi*.

It would be nice to be able to blame other signs of senility that started at the age of five on this same disability, but I guess that would be stretching it a bit. I clearly have more than one area of the brain that functions below par.

One possible explanation could be the fact that I have had two bolts of lightning course through me and have been subjected to 240 Volts of electricity twice as well.

As a boy, I escaped from a deluge of rain by running into the house. To pass the time, I started to make tea, but when I used a metal jug to collect water from a tap to fill the kettle, lightning hit the water pipes and knocked me backwards, sending the jug flying and leaving me on my back on the floor. Rosemary found it immensely amusing and begged me for a repeat performance. I declined and kept a healthy distance from the water tap.

Eleven years later, as I crouched up against the taps in a tiny bathroom in a rented flat, the heavenly electricity chose to use me as a conduit to the ground once more. Karen laughed until she cried. At least I am able to amuse the weaker sex.

Intending to strip the plastic insulation from the end of a length of twin-flex, I forgot to turn the power off and to this day I have a neat little chip in both front teeth, caused by the electricity sparking in my mouth.

When Mark and I replaced an electric geyser in the house shared by ten students, we turned the electricity mains off, but failed to let everyone know. Russel expressed his annoyance that his hi-fi had gone silent by finding the main switch and turning it back on, just as the two of us raised the geyser up into place in the utility room. Both of us ended up laughing at the spectacle of the other with hair standing on end and a blue aura erupting all around them.

I may not burn the brightest, but I am clearly a good conductor of electricity. I wonder how many little grey cells have become even smaller black cells.

After a long day at work, we still had to attend a medical lecture in a nearby town. I clambered into the van, feeling decidedly damp from the English mid-winter weather, and turned on the windscreen demister. Using a chamois cloth, I wiped what I could of the fog from the glass in front of me, but it seemed to make little difference. Repeated attempts, coupled with a fan blowing at maximum, had no effect. Eventually I had no choice but to drive off, albeit at a much-reduced speed than normal. The windscreen just would not clear.

Arriving late at the venue, I joined the small crowd as they drifted into the auditorium. Steven, a colleague from a neighbouring practice, pointed at my face and let me in on the secret. 'There's one lens missing from your glasses,' he said. The cause of the blurring had nothing to do with moisture on the windscreen.

On another night, I returned home close to the time that carriages turn into pumpkins, feeling absolutely exhausted. As I walked along a street lined by tall streetlamps, I noticed that my shadow kept perfect step with me and then suddenly, out of the corner of my eye, I saw a shorter, darker shadow rushing up behind.

I whirled about to confront my assailant, only to realise that it was in fact also my own shadow, but from a light much closer to the path. To add insult to injury, the out-of-line lamppost cracked me on the head as I took another step, still facing the rear.

Stuttering is no longer recognised as an official diagnosis by speech therapists, but instead professionals refer to Childhood-Onset-Fluency-Disorder. I hope one day they will recognise my disability as Childhood-Onset-Dementia. The trouble is that I will never know when my memory begins to become a problem; it always has been.

Chapter 125

ALFIE AND THE X-MEN

Alfie seemed to be happy at home and even started to grow a new crop of feathers. Then one day I arrived home to find him once more almost naked and the floor of his cage covered in grey fluff and individual long shafts, many with bloody ends.

We never learned what caused him to self-mutilate. Nothing seemed to help, and all the tests proved negative. Correcting his diet made little difference, although he took to the carefully balanced, organic food and fresh vegetables with gusto. Medications lasted only seconds in his beak before they, together with the treat intended to conceal them, were dropped unceremoniously on the floor.

I started taking him to work, sitting on the passenger seat beside me in a wire cat carrier. After a few days, he learned the routine and obligingly climbed into the carrier to make the trip to work and again to return home. He seemed happier to be part of a busy surgery.

The presence of a bird with an attitude split the staff into two camps: those who adored him and those who admired his prowess but lacked any close bond with their new avian colleague. Alfie became a firm favourite with the clients, particularly the elderly women who were surprised by a wolf whistle from the storeroom behind reception.

Alfie began to mimic the world around him. From the start he repeatedly made the sound of a fax machine connecting to the outside world.

Our telephones had a different tone, and it was not long before he began to drive everyone around the bend by sending them dashing to the phone only to realise that it was in fact Alfie.

Back in South Africa, the Xhosa men had joked that I was always on the phone to Mr Shaw, since all they ever heard was 'Sure, sure. Sure.' Alfie made me realise that little had changed when he began ringing the phone and then saying clearly in my voice, 'Hello. Yes. Sure. Sure. Bye.'

The scenario that really seemed to set him off was whenever there was no-one in the same room as him, but he could hear them talking in the next one. A laugh would instantly be repeated and those who were embarrassed by his reaction became victims of his unwitting mockery as both parties laughed with increasing volume.

Moving Alfie's cage closer to the X-ray room resulted in an unexpected complication. In order to prevent any unwary member of staff walking near the X-ray generator, despite the thick walls and lead-lined door with warning signs, we had a routine of shouting 'X-ray' a few seconds before pressing the button to take the shot. As the X-ray machine released the beam of energy, it emitted a clear 'Beep'. Alfie began to mimic the machine whenever he heard the warning call.

Initially the staff would stop and look perplexed at the button in their hand. They had not yet pressed it and the machine had gone off. With time we began to expect the double 'Beep', one mischievously avian and one mechanical.

After enduring the added complication to our daily work for several months, Alec decided to see how astute our little avian instigator was. Setting up the X-ray machine, he held the button in his hand and yelled the usual warning, with an unusual twist:

'X…men!' he called. Alfie remained silent. Alec repeated the charade, trying to con our echo into making the 'Beep'. Alfie was not to be fooled.

Alec then decided on an alternative twist and once more stepped out of the X-ray room with the button and shouted 'Radiograph'. Alfie was unfazed. 'Beeeep,' he replied.

Chapter 126

BITS AND BOBS

Working in close proximity with staff for many months brings times of conflict and stress and brief snatches of humour.

Jeanette had picked up the reins as manager of the small branch clinic despite her young age. With strong compulsive tendencies, she and I did not always find things easy, but she stuck to the job for five years.

Despite her obsession with cleaning, Jeanette seemed to feel that an over-production of foam in the kitchen sink meant that the coffee mugs would not need more than a brief dip in the froth to render them spotless. I had twice accepted a cup of brew from her only to find extraneous bits stuck to the sides of the mug when I reached half-way. The worst proved to be dried remnants of vegetable soup that the previous user of the utensil had for lunch.

She had no official training as a nurse, but qualified staff had proved to be in very short supply. Jeanette coped amazingly well, although she did have several failings. Although she had a large dog of her own, the more aggressive ones tended to cause alarm to flare in her eyes and a wild look of panic to take hold.

Duke was an extremely aggressive Rottweiler, and I was almost as nervous as Jeanette. Although the owner held him while I put a muzzle over his sharp end, it was by no means secure and the deep growls that emanated from him threatened dire consequences if he ever got to carry out his threats. I injected a combination of sedative drugs aimed at taming the wolf in him and allowing us to treat his inner lamb, if he had one. As he began to sway from the effects of the drugs, he managed with a vicious swipe of a foreleg to rip the muzzle from his face, only to turn and grin in Jeanette's direction.

I froze for an instant, but my assistant was not subject to the same inhibitions as she lunged for the cloakroom door and slammed it behind her. Duke took a few hasty steps toward her before knuckling over, to come crashing down against the door. Jeanette yelped in fright.

I cautiously moved to the rear of the big dog and used my foot to prod him. He snored but remained immobile. Crouching down, I listened to his chest for a few minutes, until satisfied that he was in no danger.

Duke had a broken nail that was causing him great distress. The break extended down into the nail bed and every time the loose end touched anything, he yelped. I used a large pair of artery clamps to grip the offending fragment and pulled it off with almost no effort while he slept on. There was no bleeding, and the nail bed was clean. I decided not to dress it, since Duke would inevitably have the dressing off in seconds and putting any form of collar on him to prevent him doing so would result in mayhem as he charged about trying to dislodge it. A hefty painkiller would prevent him from feeling much. I then managed to half pull, half roll our patient into a cage and inject the antidote to the sedative.

Jeanette remained in the cloakroom for the entire procedure. I had just finished when she opened the door a tiny crack and asked if it was safe to come out. The adrenalin still pumping through my veins had other ideas. I crept up to the door and scratched against the bottom of it with my fingers. Jeanette screamed and slammed it closed.

The charade continued for a further twenty minutes with two attempts by her to escape her self-imposed exile, until she caught site of my reflection in the window behind me and stamped out in high dudgeon.

'It's not funny,' she announced. 'I could have been badly hurt.'

I kept my mouth shut, knowing better than to wake the dragon that was infinitely more dangerous than the dog had been.

'Funny,' I thought, *'is in the eye of the beholder.'*

Things did not always run smoothly at the small clinic and at one stage I decided that she needed a good talking to concerning tasks that I wanted done in a certain way, and she had other ideas. The discussion became decidedly heated.

A quarter of an hour later, I walked through to the prep room to find her slumped in obvious shock on the floor, with her shoulders against one wall.

'What's the matter?' I asked, deeply concerned by the look of desperation on her face. Jeanette remained unresponsive. Just then Nicky, the nurse who ran the second shift, arrived and I met her in the front of the practice.

'Could you see if you can help Jeanette?' I begged her, while I began to look up the number for the emergency services.

Nicky returned just as I was dialling and indicated that I should stop.

'She sent a text to her boyfriend, and it was about you.' Nicky hesitated, obviously a little embarrassed. 'Since she had just typed in your name in the text, she made the mistake of sending it to your phone instead.'

It suddenly all became clear.

I thought about the situation and realised that to make it any worse would not be productive. Instead, I fetched my phone from my jacket pocket, typed in the security code and handed it to Jeanette. She took it wordlessly and spent a few moments obliterating all signs of her indiscretion while I returned to the front of the practice. A few minutes later, Nicky silently handed me the instrument and all three of us went back to our work.

A month later, Jeanette came back from doing some grocery shopping during her lunch break and let me know what she thought of me in no uncertain terms. I was taken aback and bewildered. Half an hour earlier she had left the practice with a smile.

We all found it a bit daunting to visit the local supermarket, for fear of encountering one or more of our clients. They inevitably recognised us, while we found it a great deal harder to recall them without their pet in tow. The other source of embarrassment we all seemed to experience was to suddenly find that despite vigorous scrubbing, we had failed to remove the blood smeared to the under-surface of an arm or our tunic still had a smear of undefined detritus on the hem. It was not unheard of to pull a wallet out of your pocket and have a rabbit dropping roll out as well, deposited by lop-eared Peter when you carried him back to the cage in your arms.

'You castrated those two cats this morning,' she said accusingly.

'Yes, I did. So?'

'You always put the bits on the side of the surgical table.'

'I do. It's easier to keep them away from the instruments until they can be dropped into the anatomical waste bag.'

'Well,' she said, 'I got to the checkout at the supermarket when the man behind me pointed out that I had a cat's testicle stuck to my knee.'

I started to laugh but rapidly changed my mind and moved to the other side of the prep table before guffawing in delight. The dragon of fury began to spark fire in her eyes when suddenly the funny side of it hit her and she too began to laugh ruefully. 'Just you wait until you drink your next cup of tea,' she threatened.

Chapter 127

THE SHARP END OF FINANCE

The rapidly growing practice began to put demands on my time and exceeded my abilities. I tried employing staff to make the load easier, but unwittingly took on replicas of myself who had the same failings, because I identified with them. Instead of resolving issues, at times they seemed to increase them exponentially. I began to look for a business coach, trying several groups and individuals that appeared promising without getting any result.

Alan had a detailed grasp of figures, graphs and calculations and for a while at least, he helped get me on track. My biggest problem was that I could concentrate for short periods, but a lifetime of seeing a different case every fifteen minutes or having the days divided into half a dozen surgical cases meant that I found it very difficult to remain focused on the matter at hand for a whole morning. I think Alan found my lack of attention span frustrating.

After a gruelling session one day, we slowly descended from the first-floor offices down the staircase, Alan still spouting advice while I tried unsuccessfully to appear to be listening.

At the foot of the stairs, Alfie sat in his cage, watching the world go by. The one side of the cage had been removed since he showed no inclination to venture out of the safety of his domain.

'Does your parrot bite?' Alan asked.

I nodded vigorously and emphatically. The wounds on my hands throbbed at the thought of the many nips they had suffered. 'Yes, he does. He bites really hard.'

Alan nodded and before I could stop him, he patted the bird on its head. Alfie gave him a furious look and then sank his beak into the offending extremity.

'Ah…ah…ah…owwwooooo.' Alan shook his hand desperately, his face drawn taut in agony as blood began to spurt onto his shoes and trousers.

The vicious little beak was eventually dislodged, allowing Alfie to retire to the rear of his cage in victory, while Alan whipped out a handkerchief to staunch the flow.

'Here, let me see that,' I offered, holding out my hand to grab the wounded arm and provide first aid. Alan was not having any of it but rapidly made for the door and was out and in his car before I got any closer. Alfie strutted about on his perch, chuckling to himself in appreciation.

Brian, one of the newer vets, came past just as I was mopping up the copious pool of blood.

'That looks serious,' he commented. 'Has an injured patient just arrived?'

'No. We just had one leave,' I replied. 'One who is intelligent enough to have known better.'

Chapter 128

A ROSE BY ANY OTHER NAME

Patients can sometimes be mutually embarassing for owners and vets alike. We have had several of the parrot family who are fairly versatile in their 'French' vocabulary. Owners who find it amusing to teach their charges to swear find it impossible to prevent them from doing so when they visit the doctor.

Charlie, the African Grey Parrot, had a reputation within his family for giving the game away when the teenage daughter came home in the early hours of the morning. At the sight of her tip-toeing in through the back door, he would announce loudly, 'Becky. Why are you so late? Becky. Becky. Becky. Ha-ha-ha-ha-hee.' His diatribe always ended with a string of expletives, which we were not sure could be ascribed to Becky trying to shut him up or the father voicing his opinion.

The smaller cockatiels have a more limited vocabulary but occasionally can be heard to utter a few obscenities that could only have been taught by their adoptive family.

Rosie was not very talkative when she was brought to the practice late one night. She was looking decidly upset and regurgitating small amounts of fluid, while persistently preening her feathers.

Mr Cooper had just installed a 'hands-free' soap dispensor above the kitchen sink. Rosie had free range of the house and had flown onto the countertop to inspect the work. Strutting about with a proprietary air, the little bird had inadvertently walked under the dispensor and triggered the mechanism that deposited a dollop of thick hand soap on her head.

Incensed and distressed, the little bird had immediately set about removing the offending goo with her beak and in doing so had ingested a considerable amount.

Mr Cooper had reacted admirably and grabbed his besmeared charge and, ignoring the beak that sank itself into his hand, had turned the tap on and given Rosie a quick shower, washing off most of the soap. Even in her distress, little Rosie listened to the loudly expressed obscenities uttered by her owner, her little brain trying to remember them for later. The next course of action for Mr Cooper was to call us for help.

We managed to find the list of ingredients in the brand of soap online and called the Poisons Institute to find out just how toxic they were. The toxicologist wrote down the names of the chemicals and promised to call us back. All we could do was wait for the next ten to thirty minutes.

In the bad old days of the twentieth century, many of the white people in South Africa named their dogs after the old tribal chiefs. The most popular moniker was 'Shaka'. The wiley old Zulu king deserved far more respect. Unifying the many small tribes in the South-eastern areas of the land, he was also attributed with changing the long, unwieldy throwing spear into a much shorter, wickedly sharp stabbing '*assegai*'. Shaka was a Southern hemisphere Napoleon until his half-brother Dingaan assassinated him and took the crown.

I doubt many white owners ever considered the insult they were inadvertently guilty of. I have no idea how our Zulu brothers felt whenever a dog was called by its owner, using the name of their greatest ancestor.

What was very obvious is how many dogs are racist and will bark aggressively at black people while ignoring the whites. In the Ciskei, I was repeatedly subjected to the reverse as dogs in the villages became incensed by my presence, the only white person venturing onto their land.

An elderly Zulu man brought a vervet monkey into the SPCA clinic with a wound on its leg. The placid animal took one look at the few white staff among the indigenous people and erupted with an aggressive display of hatred.

'*Nzondmlungu. Hai Nzondmlungu. Tula mange.*' The owner was clearly embarassed but the monkey was not to be silenced. Eventually the examination was conducted largely by the owner holding the damaged leg out for the staff to see and then collecting some antibiotics and painkillers for his vociferous patient.

As he left, I could not resist expanding my very lmited vocabulary. 'What does his name mean?' I asked, 'What does *Nzondmlungu* mean?'

The old man ducked his head and seemed embarassed, until one of the nursing staff commented, 'It means "Hates White People". White people are Mlungus.'

I laughed and the elderly man seemed relieved.

'*Igama lami ngiyesaba. Ngiyesaba kakhulu,*' I told the monkey as they left. The old man laughed. 'My name,' I had informed him, 'is "Afraid". Very afraid.'

Years later, in the cold of an English winter, I noticed all the nurses and receptionists collecting in the waiting room expectantly. It was only when I looked at the diary and saw that one of our regulars was next on the list that I understood the mischief in their bland expressions. Douglas, a newly graduated vet, picked up the client's card and then stopped short.

'This cannot be right,' he hissed at the receptionists. 'You're having a laugh.'

They all solemnly assured him that it was all legit.

'He can't really have the surname of Lillycrapper?' He sounded incredulous.

'Oh, he is a regular,' they assured him. 'Just go out and call him into the consulting room.'

Doug took a deep breath and marched out bravely into the sea of expectant faces. The assembled staff held their collective breath, waiting to see the young vet's discomfort.

'Could you bring Milo in, please,' he said firmly. Turning around, he stared defiantly at the ring of disappointment and led the way into room, followed by Milo and Mr Lillycrapper.

The Poisons Insitute was as excellent as always and the toxicologist had patiently looked through their database and then called to let us know of all the information they had collected on the possible toxicity of the soap. Most of the ingredients were recorded as causing discomfort and diarrhoea, but none of them were severely toxic.

Despite a few days with decidedly bubbly and slimy droppings, Rosie recovered uneventfully. The Poisons Institute sent their usual request for follow-up information regading the outcome, to be able to pass it on to the next vet confronted by a bird smeared with soap.

I called Mr Cooper to enquire how his charge was and was happy to learn that Rosie was back to her normal self. Mr Cooper could not resist adding that her language had improved significantly after having her mouth washed out with soap.

Chapter 129

SERPENTINE LOGIC

Jeremy placed the pillowcase on the consulting table and I looked at it warily, noticing the ominous firm bulge of a body that was thicker than my forearm.

Snake owners like to transport their charges in cloth bags tied with a loose knot at the open end. They invariably contain a specimen with which they are very familiar, whereas I would be treating the patient for the first time. Most pet snakes are very amiable to handling, but a lot of reptile enthusiasts will relate incidents in which they have been bitten. Fortunately, very few hobbyists have venomous species.

If given the option, I would probably have declined to see some of the wide range of snakes that were brought in, but a misplaced pride and the fact that no-one else in town would accommodate them meant that I saw a small number of them each week.

My approach was to allow the owner to get the patient out of the bag. Their attitude spoke volumes; if they showed any fear or hesitation, then it was wise to emulate them. Most clients obligingly lifted their snake out for inspection, and it was fairly simple to take it from them and examine it.

The little hognose snakes occasionally had an attitude, and the large pythons and boas sometimes tried to escape.

Interactions with snakes were not unusual on the farm where we grew up. One of my earliest memories was of three men hunting for a large *'Rhinkals'*, or ring-necked spitting cobra, that had caused Jeptha to drop the full bucket of milk on the doorstep as he stepped up onto the step leading into the kitchen. They all held long poles or wooden handled rakes. In those days the attitude was 'the only good snake is a dead snake' and many were mercilessly dispatched on sight.

Jeptha and his two colleagues could not find the snake and the search came to an end when Mom tossed a short coil of hosepipe among them. Only two of us found it amusing.

Years later, I noticed a small, toy rubber snake on the patio and picked it up by the tail, only to have it wriggle violently and curl its head up towards my hand. I tossed it away and ran in panic. No-one else had seen the incident, so none of us found it funny.

In senior high school, I took to running the length of the farm each afternoon, timing each run and hoping to improve on my speed. Reaching the far fence one evening, I turned and came face to face with a cobra that had reared up to almost face height on its tail, with neck flared out and obvious ill-intent in its attitude. My time that day was a record that I never managed to equal again despite months of training.

'This ball python has a lump towards the end of its body, just above the vent.' Jeremy pointed to the obvious swelling on the otherwise sleek form. 'She has not eaten for three months, so it cannot be food. She has never laid eggs in her twelve years, so I doubt it can be a retained egg,' he said.

I ran my hand along the length of the snake but there was no obvious cause for the lump.

'There are a number of possibilities,' I admitted. 'It could be the equivalent of an abscess, although snakes do not form pus. It may be a foreign body, such as ingested food or an egg, and it could also be a tumour.'

Jeremy looked at me expectantly.

'I think we will get the most information by taking an X-ray to see if we can identify what it is.'

Jeremy nodded in agreement and later in the day I placed the snake, still in its bag, on the X-ray table and got a rather stunning picture of my patient's bones. The lump was merely a poorly defined, slightly more opaque mass.

A lateral, or side, view always proves more difficult, but the staff had kept a small collection of cardboard containers in the radiography suite, and we managed to coax the python into a long tube intended to keep large posters pristine. While an assistant held her thumb on the X-ray machine button, I rolled the tube a quarter of a turn and then dashed out of the room and behind a brick wall, allowing the assistant to take the X-ray before the snake righted itself. The lateral view was no more informative than the first picture.

Our second decision, after consulting with Jeremy, was to use an ultrasound machine to survey the mass and at the same time, insert a thin needle into it and aspirate a few drops of the contents of the lump for analysis.

The sample we got looked to the naked eye like a putrid mess. The laboratory report confirmed that the sample taken was filled with a wide range of bacteria.

'This is the worst infection we have ever seen in a snake,' they commented. 'It is amazing that it is still alive, given the bacteria that we cultured.'

I offered Jeremy several possible options, but he had, understandably, decided not to allow the python to suffer any further. I detected a gentle sniff and he sadly wiped at his eyes as he signed the consent form.

'We use an anaesthetic agent to put them to sleep,' I told him. 'Would you agree if I offered to give an anaesthetic, open her up to see if there is anything we can do, and if not, to give her a double dose?'

Jeremy nodded acquiescence but neither of us felt very positive about it.

The lump proved to be three little mice bodies, compressed in the intestine just a few inches from the vent. They could not be passed because of a firm mass pressing on the gut. My needle had taken a sample from a decaying dead mouse.

Revulsion was soon replaced by curiosity as I examined the lump. It did not seem to be connected to any organ in the elongated body of the snake, but appeared to be a separate tumour. On an impulse I dissected it loose and placed it in a sample bottle, ready for analysis. Suturing the wound closed, I wondered if I should tell Jeremy. I did not want to raise his hopes unfairly.

In the end I did let him know and he gratefully accepted the poor prognosis but took his pet home to watch over her.

'Those mice must have been inside her for over four months,' he commented in wonder. 'It's surprising that she is still alive.' I nodded. Everything in the lives of reptiles seems to take forever.

This proved true except for the report from the pathologist, who confirmed that we had, in fact, removed a non-malignant tumour that was unlikely to spread and rarely regrew. Jeremy did not return for another year, but in the next few weeks we had a minor rush of reptiles and other 'exotic' pets brought in by new clients.

'Jeremy Stanger recommended you,' one of the new clients commented. 'He owns the pet-shop in town,' he added. 'Everyone knows Jeremy. What he doesn't know about snakes is not worth knowing.'

As nice as the praise was, I could not help wishing that Jeremy was besotted with puppies or kittens. It's not as much fun being licked by a patient with a forked tongue that cannot wag its tail or bounce on you.

Chapter 130

STRONG – SMELLING

The huge Neapolitan mastiff was grossly overweight, with an abdomen that swung beneath it like a mango hanging from a branch. I knelt to try and palpate the huge tummy, whereupon my patient obligingly lay down, making it impossible to feel anything.

The owner was a middle-aged woman, but she had brought along her son, a strapping twenty-something youngster who looked perfectly capable of lifting at least one half of the obstinate animal. I asked if he would give me a hand and received a grunt, which I took to be assent.

With a massive heave, we managed to get Juno half onto her legs, but my assistant decided he'd had enough, and he simply let go. I heard a snap and a jolt of pain shot up my arm, triggering rictus in my jaws and allowing a moan of agony to escape my clenched teeth.

For two days I struggled on manfully, nursing my badly injured limb, wondering if I should tie it up in a sling, risk taking an X-ray or perhaps just shoot myself. I very bravely dismissed all three, as well as the thought of shooting the patient or the young man. I was tough enough to survive this. On this decision, I placed a call to a physiotherapist, whose board I had seen near the local gym.

John, one of the nurses, chose that time to walk past, holding a lead attached to a corgi, the patient's little legs hidden under a coat that reached down to the floor. The two of them disappeared into the prep room at the back and I followed to lend him a hand. When I reached the room, he was standing in the middle of the room, facing the elongated, height-restricted canine.

'Sit,' he commanded. 'Sit Boris.' Boris looked at him but did not move. John bent over and lifted the curtain of hair near his rear legs.

'Bless him. He is already sitting. There isn't much difference in his case.' John was delighted by our new patient. He had never come across an example of the breed and clearly was not a regular guest of Her Majesty.

'So many of your clients bring you nice things.' Fran sounded a little wistful as she placed the biscuits on the table. The nurses had once again showed their true colours as they took care of Mrs Johnson's elderly Labrador retriever, and she had brought in a token of her appreciation. Since everything was openly shared among all the staff, I profited from the gifts of chocolates, biscuits and wine that the rest of the team received just as much as they enjoyed the offerings that came to me. A growing waistline seemed impossible to control as the calories poured in, and since most of the female staff seemed to be permanently on diets, I was forced to help them out by consuming far more than was good for me.

Receptionists at veterinary practices are the face of the business and their role is critical in dealing with clients and their perceptions and expectations. Receptionists will never be called upon to perform surgery or to know the intricacies of conditions and diseases, but their role is critical as the interface between the profession and the public.

When one of our number retired, we spent some time searching for the right replacement. A deep sense of empathy and warmth of heart are required and after a prolonged period of interviews, we employed a well-spoken woman who had no need of a job since her husband was wealthy in his own right, but she was passionate about getting a post at the vets. She had no idea what she was letting herself in for.

Fran was well groomed, and an expensive perfume could be detected when she entered the room. She also had a good knowledge of cosmetics.

Clients with animals who have digestive problems often feel the need to bring in samples of what their patient deposits on their carpet. Not only do they need to bring it to show us, but they often feel the need to bring large amounts of it.

Mrs Beasley arrived with her Newfoundland dog, aptly named Bear. He was a decidedly sad bear, having spent the night disgorging fluids from both ends.

'Yesterday I noticed a lot of blood in his diarrhoea,' Mrs Beasley commented. 'I saved some and I have it here in this jar.'

She produced a smart white pot with gold lettering on the outside and made as if to open it. Rotting faeces, mixed with blood and kept for 24 hours in a sealed container, was not going to be very pleasant and I managed, by moving fast, to prevent her from unscrewing the lid and spirited the container out of the room. The row of consulting rooms backed onto a large open plan area in which staff from every department mingled. I left the pot on the counter running along one of the walls.

Bear tolerated my prodding of his tum and a general examination in which it became clear that he was dehydrated and very sore indeed. His owner had no objection to having him admitted for the day for us to run fluids into his vein and to provide a powerful solution for his pain. I promised to analyse his poo but did not add that a fresh sample would undoubtedly be produced at regular intervals according to her tale of the horrendous night she had endured.

As for the offering she had brought in, I would make cure that it was confined to the 'noxious waste' container as soon as she left.

Bear was admitted to the hospital and after a very short time he seemed to feel a lot better. His digestive problems rapidly improved and he was sent home on a corrective diet and an electrolyte solution.

I was tiredly packing away instruments and pharmaceuticals that had become dispersed during the afternoon when Fran came through to let me know she was leaving.

'Oooh,' I heard her say, 'has someone brought you something nice? I bet it smells divine.' I looked up just in time to see her lift the white jar to her nose and bend the edge of the lid open a tiny crack.

The thoughts that ran through my mind in the next few seconds were that people really could turn green, that I was possibly going to have to catch her to stop her collapsing to the floor and hitting her head and finally, that if I could not control my laughter, I was going to end up collapsing from mirth, if she did not kill me first.

Fran managed to close the lid forcefully and replaced it on the countertop while her eyes slowly uncrossed. Her upper lip was curled in distaste.

'That's nasty,' she observed, inducing a fresh wave of paralysis in my limbs.

She clearly had no desire to stay and discuss the matter but left while I was still clutching at anything that would offer support. I wondered if she was going to return the next day or whether I was going to need to start the selection process all over again.

The physiotherapist dismissed my explanation that 'the 50kg dog damaged my arm' and instead spent a good hour examining it and manipulating it. Finally, he turned to me and made his diagnosis: 'It was not the dog that damaged you; it was the mouse.'

I felt unreasonable outrage and pique at his assertion. I knew it was the dog; no mouse was heavy enough or strong enough to wreck my arm. The physio, though, was not finished.

'Do you spend most of your day at the computer?' he asked.

Enlightenment flooded over me as I confessed to being a slave of the digital masters that rule our lives. I did spend my days typing and manipulating the computer mouse.

'You have an RSI, a repetitive strain injury. You need to give your arm a rest from the computer for a while until it heals. The pain you felt on lifting the dog was a symptom of the damaged muscles in your arm that were not up to the strain.'

I silently muttered an apology to the young man and to the patient. Juno, the Neapolitan Mastiff, turned out to have Cushings Disease, an over-production of cortisone from the adrenal gland, and was progressing well on a drug that blocked this hormone plus a weight reduction diet. His physician, in turn, slowly healed on a program of rest, daily exercise, and a silent humility at the acknowledgement of lack of physical fitness.

Chapter 131

ONE EGG OR TWO

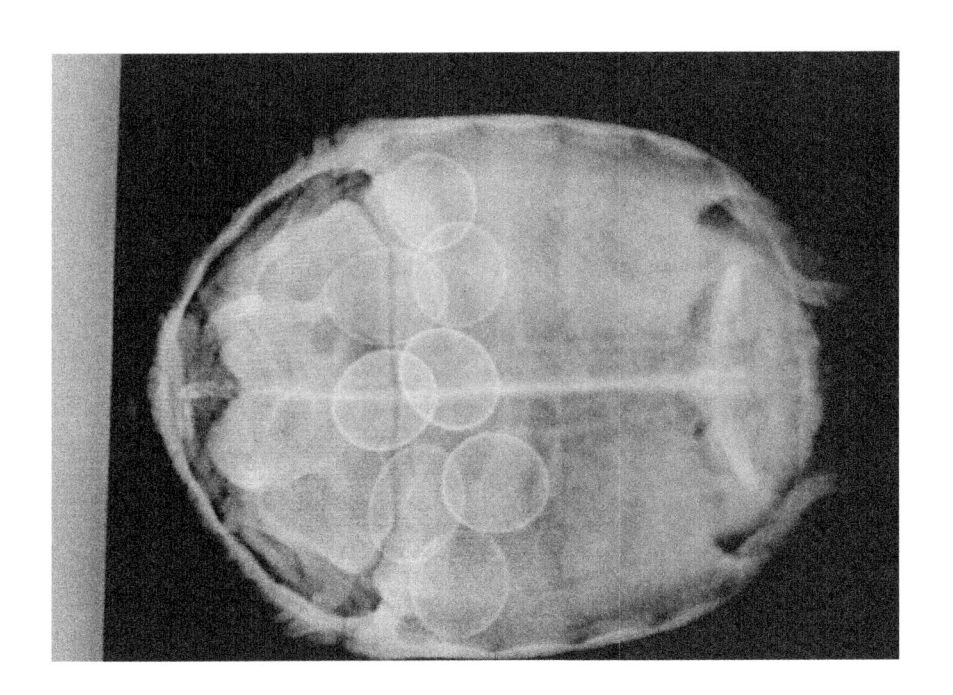

$\mathcal{M}$rs Johnson dipped her hand into the small box she had carried into the consulting room and then held it out, palm upwards, for me to inspect. It took a moment to realise that the tiny little half walnut in her palm was in fact a miniature tortoise. I felt a rush of motherly affection and then told myself to be more professional. Social inhibitions can be very restrictive for males of our species.

Baby tortoises must be one of the most endearing animals. Clients are often beguiled into buying these little replicas of walnut shells when they are only a little bigger than a thumbnail and as they grow, the tedium of regular upkeep often loses its attraction, and rescue centres are overloaded with orphans looking for a new home.

Very few new owners consider the exacting husbandry required by their new pets and few, if any, are prepared for the complications in keeping a female tortoise that needs to lay eggs on a regular basis.

Each year, a new crop of follicles develops on one or both ovaries and is shed into the coelomic (abdominal) cavity, in preparation for travelling down the oviduct, in which they are fertilised and then out into a freshly prepared nest in the soil, dug by the prospective mother.

Many captive tortoises are incapable of enabling the egg development to succeed, often due to inadequate calcium in the diet, incorrect temperature control, overlong hibernation periods and the absence of other tortoises to interact with them. The eggs often only develop into the follicle stage and then remain in the coelom of the tortoise, slowly filling her with heavy, inactive structures that compress the organs and prevent normal functioning.

Other tortoises do develop full-sized eggs that have a firm shell, but the process of giving birth does not go well, often for the same reasons that cause retained follicles. The mother may just be very uncomfortable, or she can show signs of prolonged inappetence and sluggishness and even signs of straining to pass the eggs.

The tiny animal in Mrs Johnson's hand was too young to suffer from any inability to lay eggs; instead it had a problem that would prove far harder to resolve.

On close inspection, it was obvious that the little creature had two heads and six legs. Two developing embryos in the same egg had fused during the miracle of new life and the resultant combination was a little disturbing.

'Can you do anything to help it?' Her request struck a chord and I wished for the millionth time that I had more knowledge, more ability, more of every attribute required to attend to the vast array of challenges the animal kingdom presented us with. I considered the unfortunate little being and shook my head, perplexed as to what to do.

'Do both heads act the same?' I asked. 'Do both eat?'

'No. We have only ever seen the one on the left eating. The other head seems just as healthy, but it must get its nutrition from the body and the food that the left head takes in. We have never seen either head drinking.'

The absence of drinking was of no concern; many reptiles get all their water requirements from their food, provided it contains adequate moisture content. I spent a long ten minutes considering and then asked if I could think about it overnight. Mrs Johnson left in a more cheerful mood, apparently reassured that I would present her with a solution the next day. For my part, I had no illusions. This was way beyond my limited skills. Possibly even beyond anyone's skills.

Mr Milligan arrived with a more elderly tortoise called Tommy that had not eaten for two weeks. There were very few clinical signs at all, and the husbandry seemed reasonable. Any mammal would have been gaunt, with protruding ribs. The shell of the tortoise is in fact made up by the animals' ribs that have been adapted, and instead of shrinking from the outside as thin mammals do, tortoises lose body mass internally, remaining the same shape on the outside.

Over the years I had developed a 'Tortoise Protocol' which involved stepwise procedures designed to give us the most information. The steps started with the tests most likely to make a diagnosis. Mr Milligan agreed and fortunately our first procedure produced results. An X-ray showed the clear presence of fully formed eggs. Tommy had finally shown his owner that 'he' was in fact a 'she' and was expecting as well. His owner was speechless.

Tommy enjoyed a warm bath, described in the textbooks as aiding them to start the laying process. I have never seen any effect but most of them enjoy the pampering experience. Our second procedure was to provide the correct temperature and a bank of lightly compacted soil on one side of the vivarium. The third step was to administer one injection of calcium and another of the hormone Oxytocin. Since reptiles have a hormone slightly different to Oxytocin, using the mammal drug does not always work, but the correct version is only available in very select research centres. This time it worked.

Tommy produced eight perfect eggs. To make sure all of them had come out, I took another X-ray and was gratified to see that she had no more.

A sneaky imp of mischief landed on my shoulder and whispered in my ear. I tried to resist and act responsibly but he was more persuasive than I and in the end, I took a final X-ray of Tommy, but placed three eggs underneath her. The result made it look as if they were still inside.

Two tired nurses came to check on the patients and sighed when I showed the X-ray and asked them to prepare for surgery. Removing eggs from the depths of a tortoise can be a very long procedure since the plastron, or underneath shell, must be cut in the form of a trapdoor and eventually glued back afterwards. Only one of us found it amusing when I let them in on the secret. The other two just shook their heads and went off to finish the other tasks for the day.

Little Rumpelstiltskin returned two days after his first visit, bringing along his owner with him. I had no hard and fast plan but gave her the options of leaving him as he was in the hope that he could survive, trying to refer him to a specialist, or I could try and see if I could operate on him. Mrs Johnson chose the third choice, despite my warnings of a very guarded prognosis.

I had never operated on a walnut before, let alone one with two heads. I was unable to safely administer an anaesthetic and instead gave the smallest dose of a strong sedative, which was also a very effective painkiller. Then we injected minute amounts of local anaesthetic into the tissues and slowly dissected away the extraneous body parts.

It was easier than expected, largely because the bones had not yet hardened and were still more cartilage than calcified bone. I finished, nevertheless, feeling far from confident in the result. Perhaps we should have just let him be.

Mrs Johnson came back for the routine post-op examination two days later but then never returned again. I assumed that our little patient had died.

Two years later a patient was paced on the consultation table for me to examine. I did not recognise the owner and the hand-sized tortoise did not ring any bells. Mrs Johnson allowed me a few minutes to examine him before she said simply, 'It's Rumpelstiltskin, the one you operated on.'

I was taken aback and examined the little tortoise again. He was smaller than the others that had hatched from the same clutch and on close examination, he walked with an odd gait, but he had survived and he seemed happy. I was overjoyed.

Tommy survived for a further eighteen months and I like to think that we gave him a chance at a happy life, but the doubts still come in the dark hours of the morning. Perhaps he could have lived without the procedure. Tortoises are more tolerant than humans and the chances of being made fun of at school are less likely for them.

Chapter 132

BITTER SWEET SUGAR

I had never seen a sugar glider before Tiffin and Marley arrived in a small plastic carrier. I had taken the time to read up on the little creatures and was familiar with most of their needs and ailments. Handling them proved to be a greater challenge.

Bright eyed and agile, with soft tan-grey fur and a white tummy and a darker stripe down the back, these little marsupials had a habit of launching themselves off heights and gliding for considerable distances. I had joined a society for veterinarians who treated sugar gliders, an excellent resource with a huge amount of advice.

Tiffany stayed in her little cocoon of bedding and after a little while, two smaller little faces popped out. Tiffany had given birth to twins only a week previously. All three of them made a loud chittering noise and when they felt threatened, it became louder and more intense.

Marley was a lot more sociable, but even he was very wary. He allowed his owners to gently pick him up, but I noticed that they took the precaution of first donning a pair of thick gloves.

'We called at least half a dozen vets before someone suggested we try this practice. The owner of the pet shop gave us your name.'

I shrugged resignedly. A year earlier I had made the mistake of treating a batch of snakes for a client, only to find that he was proprietor of a local pet shop, and in gratitude, he had sent several patients to me. I enjoyed the diversity of the 'exotic' patients, but it was difficult work and not particularly financially rewarding. No vet could make a living treating only the 'small furries' and the budgies and canaries that came in with high expectations and hopeless prognoses. Very few owners feel they should actually pay for a professional's time if their pet is not worth more than a few pounds.

I was, nevertheless, glad to finally get acquainted with a family of sugar gliders and silently thanked the pet shop owner.

'Marley needs to be neutered,' the owners informed me. 'We had no intention of breeding from them, but we forgot to tell them, and we had no idea how quickly they grow into puberty.' Marley sat watching his family with an air of pride and virility.

I agreed to do the operation, hoping it would be as simple as described in the textbooks. I had a sneaky suspicion that I might not be wise in not following the example of the half-dozen vets who had declined before me.

Briony peered into the plastic temporary home of the gliders and announced rapturously, 'Oh, I love them. They look so sweet.' She was halfway through her training as a veterinary nurse and full of enthusiasm for all the patients.

I left her with the task of placing the unopened carrier into a large, secure cage and attaching the paperwork to the clipboard on the front. Hopefully their chances of escaping would be minimal if they had a double barrier. I had not taken into account the curiosity of a young nurse.

I returned to the long list of clients that would continue to arrive for several hours more. Behind me I could hear Briony cooing in delight. 'I just love them,' she repeated.

A year earlier I'd had another 'exotic' animal that gave me more than a little concern.

Desmond Farley spent the first ten minutes relating his personal history at the local zoo. He no longer worked for them but had a wide range of wild animals at home. He seemed to know a fair bit about their care. When I got the chance, I asked about the occupant of the cat carrier he had placed on the chair behind him.

'It's a meerkat,' he stated simply. 'He is losing weight and not eating very well.'

The hairs on the back of my neck stood up in apprehension. Far from being the cuddly pets portrayed by some of the media, these predators pack a lot of punch. They are a major source of rabies in parts of Africa.

'Are you able to handle him?' I asked. When faced with an aggressive species or a venomous snake, I abandoned all pretence at superior knowledge and allowed the handler to show me how. If they were unable to, it brought into question whether they should be keeping the animal at all.

A small number of clients are under the impression that because a professional has spent years studying diseases and surgical techniques, they should be adept at manhandling their pet Rottweiler that savaged Aunt Mabel when she sat on it. We, in turn, are always very grateful to be given the heads-up that 'Fluffy does not like to be touched.' It gives us a chance to gird our loins or make for the door, or at least to have time to make the choice.

Desmond assured me that he knew how to master his meerkat and proceeded to open the door to the carrying cage, from which an ominous growling was coming.

Fearlessly, he stuck his hand in to grab the animal and the growling erupted into a high-pitched electric buzz-saw.

The hand was withdrawn rapidly and this time it was covered in blood. The man attached to it grabbed the wrist with the other hand and did a little pirouette about the room, grimacing in agony.

I slammed the door closed and made sure both that it was securely locked, and that my fingers did not come within reach of the millions of sharp teeth that were whirling about the interior.

The next client in the waiting room was left in her chair for a further half hour while I patched up my client, until he finally left, swathed in bandages and given strict instructions to make his way to the local hospital. He stiffly declined to be driven there and insisted on carrying his meerkat in its cage with him. Short of forcing him into a car, we had no option but to watch as he left, climbing into the passenger seat of a car driven by a woman who had shown remarkable intelligence by not coming into the practice with him at all.

As for the little sugar glider admitted that morning, I was reminded to hurry up and finish with the consultations and to get a move on with the growing list of operations when Briony came into the consulting room and gingerly stuck her hand under the tap. A bright flare of red blood covered the basin and she, too, was holding her wrist and grimacing in pain.

'I hate those sugar gliders. Look what she did to me.'

I cringed at the sight of her fingers, two of which had deep puncture wounds.

Having never performed a castration on a sugar glider, I was more than a little apprehensive when his turn in the theatre arrived. The texts described the little testicles suspended by a long, thin scrotal stalk. They spent a long time describing the delicate separation of the various blood and other vessels in the neck of this stalk and using a very thin suture material to tie them off.

The anaesthetic proved to be more of a challenge. Marley had first to be coaxed into a Perspex anaesthetic chamber, which involved me chasing him about a small room for ten minutes while the nurses cheered from the other side of the door.

Once inside, he slowly succumbed to the aerosol anaesthetic agent, at least immobilizing him long enough for me to push his face into a little mask attached to a machine by means of a thick tube.

Over the years, we had been forced to try innovative methods for handling a diverse range of little patients and the cardboard inner tube of a toilet roll was used to cover the rest of the little body, preventing him from using his legs should he wake prematurely.

Injecting local anaesthetic into the minute little structures was another challenge but we finally succeeded.

I had been fortunate enough a few years earlier to have been given a trip to the veterinary congress in Florida, USA and had returned with a hefty bill and the promise of the delivery of an entire system for keyhole surgery.

We had never been warned that the long, thin cauterising and cutting clamps tend to break very easily. A small collection of damaged instruments accumulated in the storeroom. Although they were no longer suitable for endoscopic surgery, some of them could still clamp and cauterise. One of them did the job, and the tiny little scrotal stalk was neatly separated in seconds.

Marley woke up uneventfully and went home. A few days later, he returned for a post-operative check-up, but I could not get any of the staff to hold him and our judgement was based solely on his unreduced agility and the brief glimpses of the surgical site as he flashed past in his cage.

The operation had been a success and although we spilt a fair amount of blood, none of it had come from our patient. The definition of success would probably differ depending on whether I was asked or if Briony and, indeed, Marley were consulted.

Chapter 133

A Dozen Worms for Sixpence

Mrs Harris had two cats, named Brandy and Whiskey. It made things interesting when she went out late at night calling for them; the neighbours all thought she had a serious addiction.

'One of my cats is wetting on the carpet and I don't know which one it is,' she complained. The aroma left by a cat is one of the less pleasant smells of nature. We decided that if she brought one in and left it with us for the day, we could collect urine at the surgery and she could collect urine from the other one when it used a litter tray, filled with a non-absorbent litter at home.

We soon had a little bottle of liquid with a label stating 'Brandy' on it. Later in the day it was joined by a second bottle labelled 'Whiskey'. Whiskey clearly had a urinary tract problem and was sent home with medication.

The next day I noticed several clients looking a little disconcerted and only afterwards I realised that I still had the two little bottles on the shelf behind me. Clearly my scrub top had no pocket for a hip flask.

The reaction from the clients became even more pronounced when a third little bottle joined them, bearing a label that clearly read 'Worms 4 Sixpence'.

Sixpence had arrived at the surgery a week earlier, a little blackbird fledgling brought in by a concerned member of the public. As these little birds come of age, they hop out of the nest and are cared for by their parents for a further week or so, while they make short little flights and hide under the shrubbery. When Mom or Dad blackbird arrive on the scene, the juveniles dart out and start to flap one wing, keeping the other immobile. The parents respond to the prompting and shove a worm down the gaping orange beak. We get a lot of them brought to us by concerned humans, worried that the little bird has a damaged wing.

Sixpence had thrived on a mixture of manufactured foods, but it was time to teach him to fend for himself. I spent a long time digging up worms, and some of the staff would help by bringing in little bottles with a few of them from their own gardens.

Leigh proved to be the best at raising little waifs and strays, and in her hands the survival rate was far higher than in mine. She soon became delegated as chief surrogate mum, until we realised that she was spending many hours each day caring for the orphans in her care and I had to hold back in enlisting her.

Years later, I was reminded of the little bottles on the shelf when I was given the task of clearing out the house we had sold. Sleep did not feature prominently on my agenda at the time, and I spent many nights emptying cupboards and packing the contents into boxes by way of a distraction.

It was a painful task. The gouge in the plaster that had brought a frown to the buyers represented the many hours that the rocking chair had scraped the wall as I rocked little Scott, my new grandson to sleep. The stain on the floor brought back memories of good times with kids who slopped things as they moved from room to room. Together with Sixpence, they had long since flown the nest.

A cupboard had a dozen bottles lurking in the depths. Most of them were filled with greengages in syrup, a disastrous attempt of mine in the summer to preserve the bounty in the garden that ended up with a range of bottles containing what looked decidedly like green balls of horse poop. They were edible, but no-one else was convinced of the fact.

One bottle proved to contain peaches. I was perplexed. How did a bottle of peaches escape unscathed in one of our cupboards? I loved peaches, a legacy from the many winter nights when Mom would open a large bottle of the yellow fruit that she had preserved the previous summer. There was a sticky rectangle on the side of the bottle, testimony to an old label that had since fallen off, but nothing else to identify the origin of the bottled fruit.

I could not resist the temptation and soon was savouring the soft, rich peaches. They tasted just a little off, but I put that down to the obvious age of the bottle. Besides, I had been a student for many years and students would eat anything, even if it floated over their heads in a green mist when they opened the fridge door. As I worked, I returned several times to the open jar and with each mouthful the flavour improved. I told myself that it must have been the top layer that was not perfect. After a few hours, I was disappointed to realise that I had finished the entire litre of peaches. I had even drunk the syrup.

The next morning, I woke on the sofa, immediately aware of two things: One was that for the first time in months I had slept a full eight hours. The second was that the horses that produced the bottled greengages had clearly all kicked me in the head. It was aching as if a whole herd had trampled on it while I slept.

Stumbling to the kitchen I fumbled in a drawer for some painkillers and flicked the switch on the kettle. I lay flat on the bench next to the kitchen table and then my eye caught sight of an old label lying on the ground. I could just make out a date that was twenty years previous and the words 'Peaches in Brandy.'

Chapter 134

THE PETER PRINCIPLE

Achieving a level of modest ability in one field often leads us to be promoted or to move into a higher position which requires skills totally unrelated to those which resulted in our elevation in the first place.

The Peter Principle states that we will continue to rise until we reach our level of incompetence.

Veterinarians are typically driven, motivated individuals with a deep empathy for their patients. It is a caring profession. Most of us lack business skills and many are incapable of managing people. Nevertheless, unless we choose to specialise and thereby restrict our involvement to one discipline within the broad spectrum of the profession, promotion invariably means leading a team of vets, an activity much like herding cats into a swimming pool.

I was different, or so I thought. I had managed to achieve the ability to get a group of diverse people to work as one. I had spent years attending management courses and reading tomes of business practice. I knew my way around the labyrinth of financial acumen and the vagaries of purchasing from a host of suppliers, who regularly ate vets for breakfast.

Even in the early years, I had adapted to employing people with exceptional skills from an increasingly female pool of graduates and a growing tendency to part-time work. I had learned that employees needed recognition and encouragement, plus the feeling that their role was contributing to the welfare of their environment, both in terms of society and dealing with nature. I had it organised.

Rachel was a bubbly, enthusiastic young women oozing with talent and motivation. She was outgoing and confident, in contrast to my introverted hesitation. Rachel knew what she wanted. I had bottled my innate reserve and employed her, even though we were in many ways opposites. I knew the clients would like her.

For a week, Rachel assisted and learned how things worked and where to find the essentials. She was due to fly solo the following Monday, but I intended to be on hand in case things went wrong.

The start of the week can be extremely busy, as clients bring in patients that have been ill for two days, while the owners have been reluctant to pay the surcharge for emergency treatment, but we nevertheless had managed to limit the cases to eight.

Opening time arrived but Rachel did not. When the second client arrived a little early, I was unable to wait any longer and decided to see the first patient.

Timmy had come for his first vaccination against the two most common viral diseases prevalent in the UK. He crinkled his little bunny nose as he sniffed my hands but allowed me to check him over. There was nothing wrong with him and his owner answered all the questions concerning his care correctly. I applied pressure to a fold of his skin with one hand while inserting the needle with the other. All he felt was the first hand gently squeezing the scruff of his neck, and he showed no reaction.

Job done, I took a little time telling Timmy's owner about *E cuniculi*, the parasite that could lodge in his brain, among other organs, causing severe complications. Most rabbits pick up the parasite but very few develop the extreme symptoms. It can be prevented by treating with a very basic wormer. Timmy's owner declined the treatment, but I recorded our discussion. We'd had one owner threaten to sue us when their rabbit died from the parasite, but we had been able to point to the warning in the patient's history. I made a mental note to tell Rachel to inform every owner about the potential risk.

The second patient proved to have an ear infection. Smearing a small amount of the muck in the ear on a glass slide, I was able to identify both a yeast infection in one ear and a yeast plus bacteria in the other. I made another decision to coach our new employee on the method of making smears. Few new graduates seemed to have been trained in this aspect. Rachel was still nowhere to be seen.

Sooty, a cat of the colour described by his name, demurely allowed me to vaccinate him and when his owner asked if I would pop a pill in his mouth, I showed how easy it was if his head was tilted back and the pill was simply dropped on the back of his tongue. I felt very buoyed up by my ability to do this simple procedure, although I knew we had the upper hand when cats were in our territory. I would not find it as easy in his house. *I must make sure Rachel learns the trick*, I thought. Nothing impresses more than the simple art of dosing an animal.

I felt even more pleased with myself after giving Jake, the German shepherd, a vaccination for Kennel Cough that had to be administered in the nose. After many years, I had learned the trick of giving it without him even knowing and certainly without any reaction apart from sneezing a few times. I made another mental note to show Rachel how to do it. Speaking of Rachel, where could she have got to?

I was doing well but Rachel was still absent. I began to feel a rising anger and resentment.

Rachel walked in just as the second-last patient left. There was no apology, no grovelling for forgiveness. She had merely stopped at the other branch to chat to Karen before driving on to her place of work. With a growing disbelief, I beckoned her into the consulting room to deal with our final client.

She took forty-five minutes, when I had drummed it into her the previous week that each patient had only a quarter of an hour. When she came out to ask my opinion, I was more than just a little surprised.

'Major has a broken dewclaw on his left foreleg. It is hanging off and very painful,' she let me know. 'I have arranged to him to come back tomorrow for an anaesthetic, since he has already eaten today, and we will put a dressing on it and give him antibiotics. I have already prescribed a painkiller for today.'

Major's owner, Mr White, looked impressed at the thoroughness of our new vet. Major, the Dalmatian, was not so sure.

'I have worked out an estimate,' Rachel continued. 'It will come to several hundred pounds, but Major should feel a lot better once it is all sorted.'

The sheer audacious confidence of her words, plus the respectful attitude shown by Mr White, somehow seemed too much for me to take.

I picked up a pair of artery forceps and, while holding his leg very firmly above the offending joint, I grabbed the wobbly dewclaw and pulled it off with minimal effort. Major pulled his leg away in surprise, but the deed was done. He licked the base of the dewclaw and then licked my hand. Without the loose end of the nail to cause pain each time it moved, there was now just a broken stump. It must have been a little sensitive but the acute pain each time the claw moved was gone.

Major bounded out of the room happily. Mr White paid his relatively modest bill and left as well, not looking at Rachel and making no comment.

With one act of unthinking crassness, I had belittled the person I had taken such pains to employ. Her credibility was in tatters and her professional ability in question. She resigned a month later and left amicably enough but clearly relieved at the chance to move.

Years of training, scores of professional development courses, and I had broken every rule I had been taught.

I had reached my level of incompetence.

Chapter 135

SANTA COES TO DINNER

Mom passed away in South Africa, nine thousand kilometres away, on the opposite side of the world to where we lived. Dad followed her fourteen months later. Between the two events, five of the events on the most stressful life incidents list in popular psychology occurred. I became a hollow shell that would have collapsed like a lace handkerchief dropped from an uncaring hand, had I not spent a lifetime treating sick animals and from habit my limbs kept moving even though brain and heart no longer functioned.

After doing more than ten thousand surgical procedures in the past, I found myself staring at a patient on the operating table that had a neat scar just below its navel. I had no idea how it or I had got there and no concept as to what had been done to it.

The list of procedures on the surgery wall had one patient listed as 'Milly – Labrador – spay'. The dog in front of me was a Labrador. Had I operated on her? Or perhaps I had just incised the skin and sutured her up again.

I noted that the Isoflurane percentage was on 5. A level of 2 percent of this potent anaesthetic agent was usually used to keep patients fully anaesthetised. She should have died from the extreme level. I quickly turned it down and watched her breathing closely.

When Judie, the assisting nurse, turned her back for a second, I desperately scanned the contents of the 'Clinical Waste' bin. There were two blobs that each had a portion of an ovary visible even from a distance. Someone had separated Millie from them.

'Don't forget the staff Christmas meal on Friday,' Judie admonished. I nodded but had in fact totally dismissed it from my mind. 'Have you got your Secret Santa gift yet?'

'I have,' I lied. I did remember that I had drawn Hilary's name from the empty tub labelled 'Norodine Tablets'. I had better buy her something that afternoon.

The prospect of sitting down to a meal with thirty other members of staff, all of whom I knew well, and making polite conversation filled me with abject fear. How was I going to survive?

Most of them were polite and pleasant towards me, but a large group had called me to task in the middle of my year from hell and told me bluntly that I was not up to scratch, and they were all thinking of leaving if I did not change. None had left but facing them had become an ordeal for me.

I visited the closest large town that afternoon and bought a delicate and aromatic keepsake that cost twice the limit set by the rules of the mutual secret trade in gifts. I hoped Hilary would like it.

As I left the shop, I noticed a Santa suit at half-price. The retailers had wisely realised that if it was not sold in the next few days, it would languish in the cellars for another year before having any chance of being disposed of. On an impulse, I bought the suit and spent that evening manufacturing a luxurious beard from a roll of cotton wool, with a small pair of glasses and black gumboots that had traipsed behind many a reluctant farm animal in the past.

On the night, a bevy of glamorous women filled the venue and to my shock, I realised that they were the same people who filled my days in green tunics and scrub tops, wrestling with large dogs and comforting crying kittens. They certainly scrubbed up well. As so often happened, I felt decidedly scruffy and awkward among them.

No-one noticed when I slipped outside and made my way to the van in the snow. With a lot of difficulty, I managed to put the suit on and attached the cotton wool to my face. A large black 'body bag' from work had been filled with the gifts bought by all the staff for each other. Turning, I headed for the door of the restaurant.

The bitterly cold night air rapidly frosted up my glasses and my warm breath trapped by the cotton wool made it impossible to see anything. A sudden cry alerted me that someone else was nearby.

'Oh… oh… Oh… Sint Nicholas. Oh… You make me scared. I thought you were the real Sint Nicholas. I got such a big scare.'

I tilted my head down to see the young waitress in front of me. She had popped out into the cold to get more drinks from a porta-cabin and come face to face with a stumbling old man in a red suit. This foreign lass kindly took me by the arm and led me to the door, allowing me to enter alone.

Our party of thirty had been seated near the end of a large hall in which several hundred other revellers were also dining. I had not counted on anyone but those I knew being present. The hall erupted into cheers and clapping from all five hundred diners as Santa stumbled into their midst, carrying a large bag filled with parcels. Far from achieving my aim of camouflage, I had suddenly exposed myself to public scrutiny. Only the fact that I was in disguise kept me from faltering.

Fortunately, I made it to our table and sat down among the astonished staff, who only recognised me when I began to dish out the gifts from the bag. I could still not see, so I had to be helped by two of them to read out the labels.

I survived the ordeal. Not so easy to cope with were the multiple issues that I had left at home. I wondered how I was going to make it through the next year and whether Santa would be able to make a repeat entrance in twelve months' time.

I wondered, too, if our clients would be happy to be seen by a vet hiding inside a Santa suit when they came to call. It had proved so much easier to function when masquerading as a fictitious character.

I made a note to ask all the staff to be extra vigilant and to warn me if Santa did something stupid such as keep a patient on 5% Isoflurane again.

Printed in Great Britain
by Amazon